The Isle of Wight Rifles at Gallipoli

By

Graeme Brookes

Copyright © 2024 Graeme Brookes

ISBN: 978-1-917425-47-6

All rights reserved, including the right to reproduce this book, or portions thereof in any form. No part of this text may be reproduced, transmitted, downloaded, decompiled, reverse engineered, or stored, in any form or introduced into any information storage and retrieval system, in any form or by any means, whether electronic or mechanical without the express written permission of the author.

CONTENTS

Recruitment and Training
- The First Months of War
- Bury St. Edmonds
- Watford

Deployment to Gallipoli
- Travelling to the Dardanelles
- The August Offensive
- Landing at Suvla Bay, Gallipoli, 10th August 1915
- Settling In, 11th August 1915
- Officers of the Isle of Wight Rifles on 10th August 1915

Anafarta Ridge
- Anafarta Ridge, 12th August 1915
- Holding the Gains, 13th – 14th August 1915
- Aftermath of the Isle of Wight Rifles' First Offensive
- Was the Operation on Anafarta Ridge a Success or a Failure?
- Known Casualties for 12th-14th August 1915
- Prisoners of War
- Officers of the Isle of Wight Rifles as of 15th August 1915
- Their Baptism

Continuation at Suvla Bay
- Dissent in the Ranks
- Kiretch Tepe Sirt
- Notes on the Period of 15th August 1915 - 20th August 1915
- 21st August 1915 – Battle of Scimitar Hill
- News Reaches Home
- The Remainder of August at Gallipoli

ANZAC
- September 1915
- October 1915
- November 1915

Redeployment
- The Great Storm
- Evacuation
- Where Next?

Roll of Officers, Warrant Officers, Non-Commissioned Officers and Riflemen Proceeding Overseas
- Officers Serving with the Isle of Wight Rifles
- 'A' Company
- 'B' Company
- 'C' Company
- 'D' Company
- Company Unknown
- RAMC Attached
- Other Attached Personnel
- Known Re-Enforcements from the Second Battalion of the Isle of Wight Rifles
- Other Officers of the Isle of Wight Rifles

Miscellaneous Information
- Gallipoli Roll of Honour
- Men from Buckinghamshire
- Photos
- Acknowledgements

References

FOREWORD

I dedicate this book to my grandfather, Reginald James Brooks Butt, who at the age of 16 joined the Isle of Wight Rifles with his cousins and went on to serve with the Isle of Wight Rifles at Gallipoli as one of the embedded Royal Army Medical Corps soldiers. My grandfather died several years before I was born but his wartime recollections have been passed down to me by my father and have inspired me to write this book. I am very proud of my grandfather and despite the detailed research on the Gallipoli campaign, I still struggle to comprehend what he and his fellow soldiers had to endure.

I would also like to pay my respects to all those brave men who served with the Isle of Wight Rifles at Gallipoli, many of whom did not make it home and many whom suffered long lasting physical and mental trauma. They fought with distinction and have left a lasting legacy on the Isle of Wight.

This book details the Isle of Wight Rifle's involvement in the Gallipoli campaign The research included the battalion's War Diary, personal accounts and the wealth of information printed in the Isle of Wight County Press during the campaign, such as, letters home, poems and updates on soldiers. In addition, I have undertaken research on every soldier that was listed as having deployed to Gallipoli with the Isle of Wight Rifles as I strongly believe that every one of these men deserve to be remembered. This research is presented in annexes at the end of the book and is drawn from army records as well as the above mentioned sources.

The official name of the Isle of Wight Rifles is the '1/8th (Isle of Wight Rifles, Princess Beatrice's) Battalion, The Hampshire Regiment' but various names have been used. In army documentation the battalion has also been referred to as the '8th Hants' and the '$1/8^{th}$ Hants' while the Isle of Wight County Press during the Great War used the names; 'Imperial Service Battalion' and 'Island Rifles'. For ease, I have used the name 'Isle of Wight Rifles.'

I hope you enjoy the book and learn a great deal about the men of the Isle of Wight Rifles and their Gallipoli campaign.

Graeme Brookes

Recruitment & Training

The First Months of the War

After Britain's declaration of war on Germany on 4th August 1914, the men of the Isle of Wight Rifles, a Territorial battalion of the Hampshire Regiment, were embodied on 5th August 1914. The battalion was ordered to take over the manning of strategic forts on the Isle of Wight, such as Bembridge Fort, which formed part of a layered defence of the Royal Naval base at Portsmouth.

Although Britain had the might of the Royal Navy, the world's largest navy, it had a small Army that also had the duty of policing the British Empire. In contrast the German Army was a formidable size and on 3rd August had begun its invasion of Belgium. The fall of the Belgian ports to the Germans would have been a major blow and threat to Britain and so the British Army had to be deployed to France and Belgium with the utmost expediency and furthermore, the British Army needed to rapidly expand. A huge recruitment campaign began and with the promise of a swift victory by Christmas, the chance of a foreign adventure and a duty to serve the King and Country, men flocked to join the British Army.

The Isle of Wight Rifles were a Territorial Force battalion which formed part of the Hampshire Regiment and had detachments across the Isle of Wight including at Cowes, Newport, Ryde, Sandown and Ventnor. On mobilisation on 4th August 1914, the battalion numbered 25 Officers and 540 Other Ranks and the Commanding Officer was Lieutenant Colonel Rhodes. He had taken command of the battalion in 1913 and had previously served in the Regular Army, *'but never saw active service.'*[1]

On the 10th August 1914, Newport's Drill Hall was designated as the battalion's depot with Major AE Mayes commanding it.

---

[1] Report attached to the Isle of Wight Rifles War Diary (WO95/4325), August 1915

Major Mayes had the support of a permanent staff instructor and 4 Other Ranks.²

A recruitment drive was quickly launched by the Isle of Wight Rifles and one such recruitment event took place on 4th September 1914 at Sandown. It was attended by a group of cousins; Reginald James Brooks Butt, George Henry Cooper, William Charles Cooper, Frank Henry Butcher and the two Whites, one of whom was likely to be Charlie White. Reginald James Brooks Butt was 16 years old and was due to leave Sandown to go back to school at Portsmouth Grammar. His elder cousins George and William Cooper lived close by in Avenue Road and further along Avenue Road lived Charles White. Frank Butcher however, came from Newport. All took the pledge to join the Isle of Wight Rifles on 4th September 1914 and that night they spent the first of many nights at Sandown Barracks. Reginald James Brooks Butt recollected that on the first evening he was made to polish brass which '*he found to be an imposition.* '³

During the first few months of the war the Isle of Wight Rifles continued to man the coastal forts on the Isle of Wight. These included Bembridge Fort, Culver Down, Nodes Point Battery, Puckpool Battery, Sandown Barracks Battery, the Cable Landing at Gurnard Bay and Yaverland Battery. The battalion had taken over this role from the 4th Royal Fusiliers who had deployed to France on 13th August 1914.⁴

In November 1914 the company based at Ventnor was moved to Chichester to hold the coastal forts there and Captain P V P Stone, the battalion's adjutant, was posted back to the Norfolk Regiment with whom he preceded to France. This meant that the battalion had lost an experienced officer and in the report

---

² From research undertaken by Ian Meadows based on records held at Carisbrooke Castle.
³ Recollection from Private Reginald James Brooks Butt's son.
⁴ From research undertaken by Ian Meadows based on records held at Carisbrooke Castle.

attached to the Isle of Wight Rifles' War Diary for August 1915 it stated that with the departure of Captain Stone there was *'no one capable of laying down a syllabus of work for producing an efficient fighting unit.'*[5]

A typical day for trainee riflemen would consist of a wake-up call at 5am followed by a drill session at 7.30am. Breakfast would be served between 8am and 9.30am and lunch would be served between 1pm and 2pm with the riflemen being allowed half an hour for their lunch. The afternoon would include an hour of drill and Tea would be served at 5pm. The riflemen would be given their own time at 9pm and 'lights out' was at 10pm. Route marches and runs would be used to improve the recruits' fitness. Church parades were held on Sunday mornings.

Accommodation for the riflemen varied depending on where they were based. Those based at Newport Drill Hall had their accommodation upstairs in the Drill Hall. At Sandown Barracks some of the men had to sleep under canvas until huts became available for them. If sleeping under canvas, they were issued with waterproofs as well as blankets. There was a concerted effort across the island to get more blankets for the men.

After pressing to be accepted for overseas service, the Isle of Wight Rifles were accepted in December 1914. The battalion consisted of men who had expressly volunteered for overseas service. Due to the success of the recruitment campaign, a reserve battalion – the 2/8th Hampshire Regiment had also been formed by December 1914. Recruitment continued into 1915 and more men put themselves forward for overseas service. A rifleman wanting to be accepted to the 1st Battalion of the Isle of Wight Rifles would have to pass a rifle firing test.

Although the majority of the Isle of Wight Rifles consisted of men from the Island, over forty men of the battalion came from

---

[5] Report attached to the Isle of Wight Rifles War Diary (WO95/4325), August 1915.

Buckinghamshire and there were also a few men from other areas in England such as London, Chichester and Portsmouth. The men from Buckinghamshire had been recruited with the help of Lieutenant Colonel Rhodes who had previously worked on a country estate in Buckinghamshire as a bailiff. They came from High Wycombe and the surrounding area and were given a *'£1 signing-on bonus that was being offered by the recruiting officer who knew the area well.'*[6]

Rifleman William Buckett wrote the following about some of the recruits from Buckinghamshire in a letter to his sweetheart, Emmie Tutton, on 21st April 1915 whilst based at Newport Drill Hall with the reserve battalion of the Isle of Wight Rifles:

> We had ten more recruits come this morning from Bucks and they are a rough lot but they do not sleep up stairs with us. The Sergeant made them sleep downstairs in the drill hall so it is alright.'[7]

It is likely that one of these men was Rifleman Frederick Cecil Adby from West Wycombe. He enlisted on 20th April 1915, presumably in his home area and on being accepted was sent to Newport, arriving on 21st April 1915. Rifleman Adby was then posted on to 'D' Company of the Isle of Wight Rifles. The majority of the men from Buckinghamshire were either placed in 'C' or 'D' Companies.

---

[6] http://www.marlowsociety.org.uk/MRWW1/userfiles/file/Rifleman-John-Brooks.pdf
[7] https://sites.google.com/site/iowrifles/where-emmie-and-will-lived/letters-from-will

Bury St. Edmunds

With the 1/4th Suffolks being sent to France, the 163rd Brigade of the 54th Division (East Anglian) required an additional battalion and the Isle of Wight Rifles were selected. The Isle of Wight Rifles joined the 1/5th Suffolks, 1/4th Norfolks and the 1/5th Norfolks in the 163rd Brigade under the overall command of Brigadier General Brunker DSO. The 54th Division was commanded by Major General F S Inglefield CMG DSO.

On the 26th April 1915 the Isle of Wight Rifles arrived at Bury St. Edmunds, joining the 1/5th Suffolks who were already based there. The Officers were billeted in the Suffolk Hotel and the men were billeted with families in residential streets. Four riflemen typically shared a bedroom with two men per bed.

Shortly in to their stay at Bury St. Edmunds, the Isle of Wight Rifles experienced the beginnings of modern warfare. On 30th April 1915 German Zeppelin LZ.38 commanded by Hauptman Erich Linnarz bombed Ipswich followed by Bury St. Edmonds just after midnight. Residents had not adhered to the orders of keeping lighting to a minimum and consequently Bury St. Edmunds was visible in the night sky. A high explosive bomb was dropped near the train station and then incendiary bombs were dropped whilst the zeppelin flew over the town centre. In the area of Butter Market and the Suffolk Hotel, four shops were burnt down resulting in the death of a collie dog belonging to one of the shopkeepers.[8]

The Zeppelin's next target was the barracks. A high explosive bomb was dropped but it missed the barracks and further incendiary bombs were then dropped along the Newmarket Road. Another high explosive bomb was released over Westley

---

[8] https://www.eadt.co.uk/news/remembering-bury-st-edmunds-first-zeppelin-raid-100-years-on-1-4054830

but caused no damage and finally, the Zeppelin targeted Woolpit Warren with a high explosive bomb.[9]

Daylight showed the extent of the damage and despite no casualties occurring it must have been quite a shock to both the civilians of the area and the soldiers based at Bury St. Edmunds. Further raids occurred and after one raid a rumour quickly surfaced that the owner of the Griffen Hotel who was German had been using a light to guide the Zeppelin in to drop bombs. This led to a mob descending on the hotel to enact their revenge. Rifleman William Buckett 2370 of 'B' Company sent a letter to his sweetheart on 15th May 1915 describing what happened:

> We had a raid here on the Griffen Hotel and we were called out about 9.30pm just as I had sit down to supper. The man was a German, he said he would wash his hands in English blood so they soon set about him. I had to stand outside the Hotel for an hour and a half with fixed swords and it was not a very nice job with stones flying about my head but I got over it alright.[10]

A General Musketry Field Fire Course was held on 4th May 1915 on a range with eight targets. This appears to have been the only opportunity for many of the riflemen to have fired live ammunition since leaving the Isle of Wight as in the Officer's Report attached to the Isle of Wight Rifles' War Diary for August 1915, the Officer wrote, *'the only ball ammunition fired before active service was a short rapid course lasting one day.'*[11]

The Isle of Wight Rifles were equipped with the Lee-Enfield long barrel rifle rather than the up-to-date Short Magazine Lee-Enfield rifle which the regulars were issued with. Not only would the Isle

---

[9] http://www.stedmundsburychronicle.com/Chronicle/C20pics/zepp1915.jpg
[10] https://sites.google.com/site/iowrifles/where-emmie-and-will-lived/letters-from-will
[11] Officer's Report attached to the Isle of Wight Rifles' War Diary August 1915 (WO95/4325).

of Wight Rifles embark for Gallipoli with a distinct lack of live-firing practice, they were also issued with an older version of the British Army's issue rifle.

WATFORD

Following a period at Bury St. Edmunds, the Isle of Wight Rifles were sent to Watford. An advance party left for Watford on Tuesday 18th May 1915 and the remainder of the battalion arrived at Watford on 20th May 1915 after five hours of travelling. Just a week later, the battalion was inspected by Princess Beatrice at Cassiobury Park in Watford.

Watford in 1915 was bustling with troops and space for training was limited. There were no available halls for the Isle of Wight Rifles to use as barrack rooms and due to this no training would be undertaken on wet days. Callowland Recreation Ground was used as a barrack square and the men were billeted in family homes in residential streets just as they were in Bury St. Edmunds.

Training primarily consisted of route marches and the occasional night exercise. For example, a route march to St. Albans and back took place on 1st June 1915 and bivouac training took place at Hemel Hempstead between the 16th and 18th June 1915.[12] With the arrival of a number of mules from South Africa, the transport section was able to begin their training with the mules. The Isle of Wight Rifles' Officer who wrote the accompanying report to the battalion's War Diary for August stated that *'from the purely military side, the training was worse than useless.'* He went on to write that *'the weapons and methods of warfare introduced by the War were untaught and no one had so much as seen a bomb until arriving at Gallipoli.'*[13]

During their time at Watford, there were two recorded incidents involving Captain Ellery. The first incident was mentioned in a letter from Rifleman W H Buckett to his sweetheart on 4th June

---

[12] https://sites.google.com/site/iowrifles/where-emmie-and-will-lived/letters-from-will
[13] Officer's Report attached to the Isle of Wight Rifles' War Diary August 1915 (WO95/4325).

1915. Rifleman W H Buckett stated that one of the men was given 4 days of imprisonment at St. Albans for swearing at Captain Ellery on a night exercise. This man was later confirmed to be Dallimore.[14]

The second incident was recorded in the report attached to the Isle of Wight Rifles War Diary for August 1915:

> About a fortnight before going on active service, a Company Commander had occasion to tell his Company before dismissing them that he was dissatisfied with their work and unless they showed more keenness he would have extra parades. The parade ground was the street in which they were billeted and the officer's lecture was listened to by the inhabitants, who sent a deputation to the Brigadier. The Brigadier listened to the deputation, and without waiting for explanation or investigation, reprimanded the Company Commander in their presence. The Officer asked to be relieved of his Company, but his request was refused, and as a result of the loss of discipline the Company declined to follow its Commander into action on the 15th August, in spite of the threats and entreaty of the Brigadier himself, who was present.[15]

It transpired that the company mentioned above was 'C' Company and the officer was therefore Captain Ellery.

In their free time, the men were able to go to the theatre and visit the fun fair when it was in town. On Sundays, after Church Parade, the men would try to visit London. This involved requesting a pass to London. Leave was much harder to come by but some of the men were able to get some time off. The promise

---

[14] https://sites.google.com/site/iowrifles/where-emmie-and-will-lived/letters-from-will
[15] Officer's Report attached to the Isle of Wight Rifles' War Diary August 1915 (WO95/4325).

of leave would tend to be broken and delayed. Many of the men were allowed 48 hours of leave prior to deploying to Gallipoli.

One of the riflemen used his enterprising nature combined with his civilian trade to make extra money in his free time. Rifleman Sid Porter of 'D' Company was billeted in a home in Parker Street that belonged to Mrs Holland and when he was off duty he ran *'a barbers in Mrs Holland's garden shed where all the soldiers came for haircuts at 1 ½ d a time.'*[16]

Whilst at Watford, the men received inoculations which included one for Enteric Fever. Some men experienced bad reactions including a very painful arm and feeling unwell. Those with the bad reactions were given time off to rest.

Rumours of where and when the battalion would be sent abroad were rife. News of their deployment to Gallipoli was given to them to by Lieutenant Colonel Rhodes on a parade at Moor Park and on 20th July 1915 the men were issued with their new khaki drill uniform and pith helmets for their service in the hotter climate of Turkey.

The Isle of Wight Rifles left Watford by train at 2.30pm on 29th July 1915. Their destination was Liverpool to embark on the Aquitania for Gallipoli.

---

[16] JUBILEE GREETINGS, Watford Observer, Friday August 18th 1972.

Travelling to the Dardanelles

The Isle of Wight Rifles arrived at Liverpool Alexandria Dock at 9.30pm on 29th July 1915. They spent the night aboard the Aquitania, a luxury Cunard Liner which had been requisitioned for war service and was now their transport to the Dardanelles. As well as the Isle of Wight Rifles, the rest of the 163rd Infantry Brigade, the London battalions of the 162nd Infantry Brigade and the 54th Division's Head Quarters embarked on the Aquitania. This amounted to a fighting force in the region of 7,000 to 8,000 men.

At 1pm on 30th July 1915 the Aquitania left Liverpool Alexandria Dock leaving behind Lieutenant Curtis along with the Isle of Wight Rifles' Transport Section and their South African Mules who had been scheduled to travel to Gallipoli at a later time. For the majority of the men of the Isle of Wight Rifles it was their first time travelling abroad, net alone going to war. Only a few of the men had actually been to war before.

After a period at anchor the Aquitania along with two destroyers finally set sail at 11pm and were met by a further three destroyers in the Irish Sea. The destroyers were tasked with protecting the Aquitania from enemy U-Boats that lurked in the Irish Sea. Whilst traversing the high-risk areas in the Irish Sea, the Aquitania had to constantly change direction to avoid enemy U-Boats.

On 31st July 1915 a storm began to develop and the winds rose to gale force. Private Reginald James Brooks Butt recalled seeing the destroyers vanish beneath the waves and then re-emerging thirty feet above the Aquitania on the crests of giant waves. Many of the men became sea sick and the decks became awash with vomit.[17] Another soldier, Sergeant Joe Guthrie of 1/11th London Regiment (Finsbury Rifles) recollected in an interview with Nigel Steel which was later added to the Imperial War Museum

---

[17] Recollection from Private Reginald James Brooks Butt's son.

Collections, that a machine gun belonging to the 10th Londons was washed away whilst the Aquitania was rolling in the storm.[18]

An Officer of the Isle of Wight Rifles kept a diary and sent it back to the Isle of Wight County Press who then preceded to publish the diary – the first publication being in the Isle of Wight County Press on 21st August 1915. It is probable that the officer was Captain Marsh and the entries for 31st July 1915 and 1st August 1915 were as follows:

> Saturday July 31 – Wind blew a gale as we got outside, and about noon the destroyers left us apparently unable to keep up. Passed Lizard about 1pm. In the afternoon we passed through a storm and a few men started sea-sickness, but I had a big lunch and felt fit.
>
> Sunday August 1 – Just beginning to feel the Bay, several men sick; boat rolling pretty heavily all day, but no pitching noticeable. Heard that the liner Iberian had been torpedoed outside Liverpool four hours after we left; lucky escape. Expect to pass Gibraltar in early morning.[19]

SS Iberian was sunk by a torpedo from U-Boat 28 approximately 9 miles to the south west of Fastnet Rock on 30th July 1915. Fastnet Rock lies off the coast of South East Ireland.[20]

To defend the Aquitania from hostile surface vessels, U-Boats and aircraft, machine guns were placed around the ship. Rifleman Fred Rayner in his memoir, wrote that one of the battalion's machine guns was mounted on the Aquitania's bridge and as he

---

[18] IWM Collections:
https://www.iwm.org.uk/collections/item/object/80012762
[19] Isle of Wight County Press, 21st August 1915
[20] https://www.naval-history.net/WW1NavyBritishBVLSMN1507.htm

was in the machine gun section, he undertook duties manning the machine gun.[21]

The Aquitania was a fast luxury liner with 10 decks and powered by coal. Conditions on board were generally good. The men were allocated cabins but those on the lower decks who found it too hot at night chose to sleep on the upper decks. Water and food were plentiful. Lance Corporal Beverton wrote in a letter to his parents dated 1st August 1915 that the Aquitania was *'fitted up like a first class hotel,'* and in a further letter to his parents dated 5th August 1915 he described his time on the ship as being *'more like a holiday than anything else.'*[22]

During their time on the Aquitania, the Isle of Wight Rifles would have a session of physical drill every morning. There were also parades and duties for them to undertake. Those men who wished to earn extra money volunteered as stokers. Working as a stoker meant that they worked *'four hours on and eight hours off for 5s or 6s a day.'*[23]

Gibraltar was passed around 4.30pm on Monday 2nd August 1915 and the next evening, the Aquitania sailed past the Tripoli coast. Both Sicily and Crete were passed in the following days and about 8am on Friday 6th August 1915, the Aquitania docked at Mudros Bay, Lemnos. The voyage had taken six and a half days. The men remained on the Aquitania until 9th August 1915 and on Sunday 8th August 1915 a Church Parade was held. It was the *'last time the band played on the Aquitania.'*[24]

---

[21] Fred Rayner's memoirs: http://fightingthroughpodcast.co.uk/16-gallipoli-ww1-memoir/4593981882

[22] Extracts of Lance Corporal Beverton's letters to his parents printed in the Isle of Wight County Press, 21st August 1915

[23] Extract of Lance Corporal Beverton's letter to his parents dated 1st August 1915 and printed in the Isle of Wight County Press on 21st August 1915.

[24] Rifleman Albert Mills' Diary Transcript: https://sites.google.com/site/iowrifles/rifleman-mills-diary/the-diary-transcript

An order came through at Mudros that each battalion on the Aquitania should hold back 5 officers and 200 other ranks as a reserve. It was decided that Captain Fardell, Lieutenant Read, Second Lieutenant Brannon and Second Lieutenant Ratsey and 183 NCO's and riflemen would be left behind. The officer's report attached to the Isle of Wight Rifles War Diary for August 1915 stated that Company Commanders '*chose their least promising soldiers,*' and that the officers and men were '*disgusted at being singled out to stay behind at the last minute.*'[25]

For those who remained at Mudros, roughly half of them were based at the rest camp. Here the men had to get used to basic Army food such as bully beef and the intense heat. Consequently, many men fell ill with diarrhoea. The other half of the men stayed on the Aquitania helping to convert the ship into a Hospital Ship. In a letter home to his mother which was published in the Isle of Wight County Press on 6th November 1915, Rifleman Osman wrote:

> I was not in the charge which our regiment made, as about a hundred of us were left on the ship for another week to get the ship ready to take the wounded.[26]

The Isle of Wight Rifle's War Diary for 9th August 1915 stated that 25 Officers and 750 Other Ranks '*disembarked on to SS Osmanieh, Fauvette and Carron at 2.45pm.*'[27] Private Reginald James Brooks Butt recalled climbing down a rope ladder that was attached to the large hull of the Aquitania with full kit on and embarking onto a smaller ship whilst the Aquitania was rolling. He mentioned witnessing some men fall into the sea but these

---

[25] Officer's Report attached to the Isle of Wight Rifles War Diary August 1915(WO95/4325).
[26] Isle of Wight County Press, 6th November 1915, p5
[27] Isle of Wight Rifles War Diary August 1915 (WO95/4325).

men presumably survived as there were no recorded casualties for the 9th August 1915.[28]

SS Osmanieh, Fauvette and Carron arrived at Imbros around 9pm on 9th August 1915 and that night the men slept on board the ships awaiting their landing at Suvla Bay.

---

[28] Recollection from Private Reginald James Brooks Butt to his son.

The August Offensive

With the ongoing stalemate at Gallipoli, a major breakthrough was sought and an initial agreement to commit extra forces was made at the Dardanelles Committee on 7th June 1915 with Lord Kitchener agreeing to commit 3 'New Army' Divisions; 10th (Irish), 11th (Northern) and 13th (Western). Later in June 1915, 2 Territorial Divisions; 53rd (Welsh) and 54th (East Anglian) as well as the 2nd Mounted Division were added to the force forming IX Corps. Command of IX Corps was given to Lt. General Stopford whose experience was mostly in staff and administrative positions.

General Sir Ian Hamilton stated that the objectives for the August campaign were as follows:

1. To break out with a rush from Anzac and cut off the bulk of the Turkish Army from land communication with Constantinople.
2. To gain such command for my artillery as to cut off the bulk of the Turkish Army from sea traffic with Constantinople or with Asia.
3. Incidentally, to secure Suvla Bay as a winter base for Anzac and all the troops operating in the Northern theatre.[29]

Suvla Bay was chosen to land the majority of IX Corps as it was relatively undefended and it was deemed that it would be a suitable location for a major base. Beyond Suvla Bay, lies a broad plain and a Salt Lake, which incidentally was dry in 1915. Beyond the plain is high ground. Kiretch Tepe Ridge is at the Northern boundary and the Sari Bair Range is on the Southern boundary. To the East lies Anafarta Ridge.

The first troops of IX Corp, the 13th Division, successfully landed at Anzac Cove in the days leading up to 6th August 1915 – the

---

[29] Battle Story – Gallipoli 1915, Peter Doyle, The History Press, p121

beginning of the August Offensive. The remaining divisions began to land at Suvla Bay from the 6th August 1915 tasked with breaking out of Suvla Bay in conjunction with a break out from ANZAC Cove and thus dealing a fatal blow to the Turks. The Isle of Wight Rifles as part of the 54th (East Anglian) Division was designated as reserve troops for this offensive and landed on 10th August 1915, a few days after the first British troops landed at Suvla Bay.

Any initial advantage gained by the Allies at Suvla was quickly squandered. A lack of impetus from commanders and worn-out men suffering from thirst and heat exhaustion meant that the high ground surrounding Suvla Bay was not captured and held. The Turks were able to bring in reinforcements and deploy to the high ground, thus dominating Suvla Bay. By the time of the landings of the 54th Division, the Turks were firmly in position and a breakthrough at Suvla was beginning to look increasingly difficult and unlikely.

Landing at Suvla Bay, Gallipoli, 10th August 1915

At 1pm on Tuesday 10th August 1915 the Isle of Wight Rifles aboard SS Osmanieh, Fauvette and Carron began to arrive at Suvla Bay. One Company of the Isle of Wight Rifles along with the 163rd Brigade's headquarters and the 5th Suffolks travelled to Suvla Bay on SS Fauvette whilst the majority of the Isle of Wight Rifles were aboard SS Osmanieh in the company of 4th and 5th Norfolks and 54th Division's headquarters.

Headquarters of the 54th Division along with the 163rd Brigade and its headquarters, three battalions of the 162nd Brigade and its headquarters and one battalion of the 161st Brigade including the 161st brigade's headquarters all landed at Suvla Bay throughout the 10th August 1915. The 163rd Brigade began their landing at 'A' Beach, Suvla Bay, at 3.30pm. The men boarded punts and were towed to the beach by small steamers. One of the boats used to transport the Isle of Wight Rifles was an old tug boat called the Water Witch.[30]

Although the Isle of Wight Rifles' War Diary for August 1915 stated that the battalion landed at 9.10pm, accounts from the ranks suggest that the battalion's landing was staggered. Rifleman Aylward of 'A' Company wrote in a letter published by the Isle of Wight County Press on 18th September 1915 that he *'landed at about 4pm.'*[31] Sergeant Albert Bishop of 'B' Company wrote in his diary that he landed at 5pm[32] and Rifleman Sidney Downer of 'C' Company wrote in a letter home, *'we arrived at the fighting base on Tuesday August 10th at about 8.30pm.'*[33] The latter part of the Isle of Wight Rifles' landing occurred at dusk and into the evening and the clear starry sky led to a rapid drop in temperature.

---

[30] The Isle of Wight Rifles, D J Quigley, Saunders
[31] Isle of Wight County Press, 18th September 1915, p6
[32] https://sites.google.com/site/iowrifles/sgt-bishop-diary
[33] Isle of Wight County Press, 4th September 1915, p4

Covering fire for the landing was provided by warships of the Royal Navy, including HMS Swiftsure. Sergeant Harry Green of 'D' Company, Isle of Wight Rifles, wrote the following in a letter to his old work colleagues:

> The sight in going from Imbros to Suvla was grand. As soon as we got within range of the forts the Fleet started shelling them for all they were worth, and that gave us a clear run so we all landed safely.[34]

Both the Isle of Wight Rifles' War Diary entry for 10th August 1915 and the Officer's Report, stated that there were no fatalities or woundings during the landing. However, Rifleman Albert Saunders of 'B' Company is recorded as having died on 10th August 1915 and he is commemorated on the Helles Memorial. Further research indicates that he did not die on the 10th August 1915. According to Rifleman Saunders 1914/15 Star Medal record he 'Died on or since 12/8/1915' and likewise his record in UK, Army Registers of Soldiers' Effects, 1901-1929 also suggests that he died on or since 12th August 1915.[35] In addition, the Isle of Wight County Press on 18th September 1915 reported that Rifleman Saunders was missing. It therefore seems more likely that Rifleman Saunders was killed during the advance on Anafarta Ridge.

Private Reginald James Brooks Butt recalled that the battalion came under fire during the landings and Bandsman George Langdon of 'D' Company said that *'before their landing shells dropped dangerously near them.'*[36] Sergeant Albert Bishop wrote

---

[34] Isle of Wight County Press, 25th September 1915, p6
[35] www.ancestry.co.uk: British Army 1914/15 Star records and UK, Army Registers of Soldiers' Effects, 1901-1929.
[36] Interview with Bandsman Langdon, Isle of Wight County Press, 30th October 1915, p5

in his diary that it was *'very hot fighting,'* and there was an *'aeroplane duel at 7.30pm, both lost in clouds.'*[37]

There is one known casualty on 10th August 1915 - Rifleman Charles Ash of 'A' Company was shot in the shoulder by a Turkish sniper.[38]

A fascinating account of the landings was published in the Isle of Wight County Press in September 1915. It came from letters written by Sergeant Alfred Gywnne Jones of 'D' Company to his mother which he began writing on 9th August 1915 and continued writing on 10th August 1915:

> *I am writing this on my way towards the firing line. Am only about three miles off, and can, of course, both see and hear our ships firing and the shells bursting on the hills. They aren't half giving it to them. Expect I shall soon have to stuff my ears up with something. Goodness knows how many they are firing a minute. We moved from our first stop to an island a bit nearer, stopped last night and am now nearing a landing – the first. Just seen the Liberty (Lord Tredogar's hospital yacht, belonging to Cowes) again bringing back wounded. Our troops have affected a new landing. We have to reinforce. Have now received my baptism of fire. Talk about the Narrows being forced! By what I can see we have a lot to do yet. It is very hot; I am nearly roasted and feel very dirty. The land in front of us appears to be all on fire and is smoking everywhere. I am just about to land. Some on our boat have done so. Can now hear rifle fire. There is what looks like a town ahead. Don't think it will be long, as shells are dropping on it.* The writer conveyed good wishes from Sergeant Leftwich.

---

[37] https://sites.google.com/site/iowrifles/sgt-bishop-diary
[38] https://livesofthefirstworldwar.iwm.org.uk/lifestory/74803

Writing later the same day Sergeant Jones states:

We have not yet landed, but expect to shortly. The town I referred to is now on fire; smoke is rising in clouds. Our landing place was only effected four days ago, but now enemy's batteries have been blown off the top of the hills, and our troops have occupied the place. They tell me that it only took eight of our battleships to blow them to pieces. A German aeroplane is overhead and anti-aircraft guns are firing at it, but it is too high for them. One shot went near. Some of our aeroplanes are chasing it. I believe we are at the nearest point to ____. We have landed safely. As I did not come in the same boat here, but came with head-quarters staff, 50 of us have been detained as guard to divisional head-quarters, just behind the firing line. Expect it will only be for a day or two. There were 100 of us at first, but only 50 needed, so the officers tossed up. We lost; hence the result.[39]

From the letter it appears that Sergeant Jones sailed on the Osmanieh and that the men on their way to Suvla Bay believed that the British held the high ground. The reality was that a lot of the high ground was in fact held by the Turks, such as Teke Tepe Ridge and Anafarta Ridge.

After landing, the men began to unpack the boats but this was cut short at 9.30pm as the 163rd Brigade with the exception of the 4th Norfolks were ordered to move a mile in land to the second line that was situated up the hill from the beach. The 10th and 11th Londons of the 162nd Brigade and the 5th Essex of 161st Brigade were also ordered forward to support the 163rd Brigade. For the men who landed later in the day, there was little time to unpack anything. Kit was piled up and left on the beach near to where

---

[39] Isle of Wight County Press, 4th September 1915, p6.

they had landed. Half of 'C' Company was given the task of staying behind to unload the boats along with the 4th Norfolks.[40]

Fifty men from 'D' Company including Sergeant Alfred Gwynne Jones and Rifleman Harry Baker remained behind the front line to guard the 54th Division's headquarters which was in *'Bivouac to the right of Punar,'*[41] and roughly a *'mile from the shore.'*[42]

It was a clear night with a starry sky and the temperature rapidly dropped. As the men advanced they saw the aftermath of previous fighting. Lance Corporal Albert Watson of 'C' Company described his first evening at Gallipoli in a letter home:

> The first night was a very trying one for we landed and went straight and took up a position....There had been a big fight all day and you can imagine our feelings as we advanced over the ground in semi-darkness amongst the dead, sometimes falling against equipment or clothes abandoned by the Turks in their hurry to get away from the cold steel.[43]

In a similar account, Sergeant John Rayner of 'C' Company wrote in a letter to his old school, Barton Council Boys' School, that they passed *'abandoned Turk trenches,'* and they could *'smell dead Turks in bushes.'*[44] Sergeant Rayner in the same letter also described an incident during the initial advance inland where a soldier in a regiment in front them, accidentally shot his rifle whilst they were moving forward wounding three soldiers in front. The horrors of war and the accidents that can happen were quickly becoming apparent to the men.

---

[40] 163rd Brigade's War Diary for August 1915
[41] 54th Division's War Diary – August 1915
[42] Rifleman Harry Baker's letter published in the Isle of Wight County Press on 18th September 1915, p6
[43] Isle of Wight County Press, 5th September 1915
[44] Sergeant John Rayner's letter to his old school, dated 27th August 1915 and published in the Isle of Wight County Press on 18th September 1915, p6.

According to the Officers' Report attached to the Isle of Wight Rifles' War Diary for August 1915, *'the whole brigade [163ʳᵈ] was concentrated in a fold in the ground about a quarter of a mile inland between Hill 10 and Karakol Dagh.'*[45] Testimonies from the men suggest that the distance inland was actually a little further but nonetheless, the 163rd Brigade was located between Hill 10 and Karakol Dagh with the 10th Division located on the brigade's left flank and the 53rd Division on the right flank, in the vicinity of the Salt Lake.

The men referred to the area in and around Suvla Bay as the '*Sporting Ground.*'[46]

Further units of the 54th Division were scheduled to land on 11th August 1915 onwards. The Division had landed without its Signal Section Headquarters and with limited Field Ambulance support. As such, the Signal Section of the 53rd Division and the 3rd (Welsh) Field Ambulance were loaned to the 54th Division.[47]

---

[45] Officers' Report attached to the Isle of Wight Rifles' War Diary of August 1915
[46] Rifleman Barton's letter published in the Isle of Wight County Press on 4th September 1915 in page 8.
[47] 9th Corps – General Staff War Diary and 54th Division ADMS War Diary

Settling In, 11th August 1915

There is no information available from the battalion's War Diary on what happened on the 11th August 1915 but the Officers' Report attached to the War Diary stated the following:

> Nothing was done on the 11th except a little bathing and watching the wounded of other battalions being removed to the beach. At night the battalion slept with piled arms under sentries, but with picquets thrown out. There was certain amount of rifle fire in the neighbourhood of Karkol Dagh and at Chocolate Hill, and occasional shrapnel and common shell which did no harm. To those under shell fire for the first time, the common shell (it could not be called High Explosive) seemed the most dangerous. The shrapnel at that time was being burst very high in the air.' [48]

Although the Officers' Report mentioned that there was a little bathing on the 11th, the bulk of the battalion were holding a newly formed line looking out onto Suvla Plain and Anafarta Ridge after having received orders to consolidate the line. This line was in a Northerly direction. The Report on Operations from 10th August to night 17/18th August attached to the 54th Division's War Diary for August 1915 stated:

> On 11th August this line was consolidated, the 163rd Brigade remaining in the first line trenches and the 161st Brigade (less one battalion, not yet disembarked) being in the second line. The 162nd Brigade less one battalion remaining in bivouac in reserve.[49]

The 1/5th Suffolks were located on the left flank, with the 10th Division to their left. The Isle of Wight Rifles were in the centre

---

[48] Officers' Report attached to the Isle of Wight Rifles' War Diary of August 1915
[49] Report on Operations from 10th August to night 17/18th August, 54th Division War Diary for August 1915

and to the right of them, were the 1/5th Norfolks. At this time the 1/4th Norfolks were unloading stores at the beach and the 5th Essex were placed in support of the three battalions of the 163rd Brigade that were in the front-line trenches.

Accounts from Sergeant Bishop, Rifleman Aylward and Sergeant John Rayner all stated that the battalion moved forward in the early morning of the 11th. It was here that the battalion began to dig in and subsequently came under shell fire and some rifle fire:

> Next day (11th August 1915), directly it was light, we moved further in land without opposition and dug ourselves in, in very rocky soil. Here we came under shrapnel fire, which hastened us on with the digging. Every time we heard the screech of the shells we crouched in our dug-outs as a partridge sits close to the ground when in danger.
>
> Extract from Sergeant Rayner's letter to Barton Council Boys' School [50]

In addition to Sergeant Rayner's description of the soil being very rocky, Rifleman Edward James Watts of 'C' Company gave a good impression of what the land was like where the Isle of Wight Rifles were holding the line on the on 11th August 1915 and into the morning of 12th August 1915. In a letter to his wife on the morning of 12th August 1915, Rifleman Watts wrote:

> This is a very desolate part – all holes, rocks, sand, thorn branches and scrub. Looks like a night-mare of desolation.[51]

Turkish artillery had the range to target Suvla Bay and 'A' Beach came under shell fire on 11th August 1915. A number of mules were killed along with their Indian drivers and kit belonging to

---

[50] Isle of Wight County Press, 18th September 1915, p6
[51] Portsmouth Evening News, Wednesday 01 September 1915

the Isle of Wight Rifles was also destroyed. This was confirmed in a letter by Rifleman Leonard Eldridge of 'B' Company where he stated that '*the Turks blew our packs to pieces whilst they were stacked on the beach.*'[52]

During the day the temperatures soared and the limited food and lack of water made conditions even more uncomfortable for the men. Rifleman Aylward wrote:

> We began to find out what water was worth; it was getting scarce, and there was not a chance of getting any until the Indians with mules brought enough to fill all our water bottles.[53]

And, Rifleman Edward James Watts' letter to his wife on the morning of the 12th August 1915 included the following:

> Water is very scarce. It is brought up by large tank lighters from down the coast. It is a bit brackish, but we are glad to drink almost anything liquid. Our rations are not very varied at present – bully beef, biscuits, and jam, also half a pint of tea morning and evening per man (when we can get it).[54]

Private Reginald James Brooks Butt spoke about only having half a bottle of water a day at times at Gallipoli for drinking, washing and shaving. Consequently, the men quickly gave up shaving. He also mentioned how the extreme heat at Gallipoli would liquefy the jam and corned beef and by the time he had raised the food to his mouth to eat it, it would be black with flies.

As the sun set on 11th August 1915 the temperature dropped sharply and the men spent a cold night holding the line in their summer uniform. Sergeant John Rayner was one of the men who

---

[52] Isle of Wight County Press, 4th September 1915, p6
[53] Isle of Wight County Press, 18th September 1915, p6
[54] Portsmouth Evening News, Wednesday 01 September 1915

was in charge of the outpost that night and *'nothing untoward happened.'*[55]

Sergeant Bishop's Diary reported that there were no casualties on the 11th August 1915 and the Officer's Report attached to the War Diary does not mention any casualties being taken. However, Rifleman Arthur Rann of 'B' Company is recorded by the Commonwealth War Graves Commission as having died on 11th August 1915. Further research indicated that Rifleman Arthur Rann was actually killed in action a day later. Both the Army's 1914/15 Star record and the UK, Soldiers Died in the Great War, 1914-1919 record stated that Rifleman Arthur Rann 'died on or after 12th August 1915.'[56] In addition, the Isle of Wight County Press initially published that Rifleman Arthur Rann had been taken prisoner. Therefore, it is more likely that Rifleman Arthur Rann was killed on 12th August 1915 during the advance on Anafarta Ridge and in the ensuing chaos, there was uncertainty regarding his fate.

---

[55] Sergeant John Rayner's letter to Barton Council Boys' School, Isle of Wight County Press, 18th September 1915, p6
[56] www.ancestry.co.uk: British Army 1914/15 Star records and UK, Soldiers Died in the Great War, 1914-1919.

Officers of the Isle of Wight Rifles on 10th August 1915

10th August 1915	Company
Lt. Col Rhodes	
Major Lewis	
Major Veasey	
Capt Ellery	C
Capt Holmes-Gore	
Capt Loader	
Capt Marsh	
Capt C Ratsey	C
Capt D Ratsey	D
Lt Giddens	QM
Lt Ledward	
Lt Pittis	MG Officer
Lt Seely	
Lt Young James	
2nd. Lt Bartlett	C
2nd. Lt Fox	
2nd. Lt Kingdon	
2nd. Lt Latham	
2nd. Lt Murphy	
2nd. Lt Raymond	
2nd. Lt Shelton	
2nd. Lt Sutton	
2nd. Lt Watson	
2nd. Lt Weeding	B
Capt Raymond	RAMC

Mudros
Capt Fardell   D
Lt Read
2nd. Lt Brannon   D
2nd. Lt S Ratsey

UK
Lt Curtis   Transport Officer

Anafarta Ridge

Let us tell how the Island Rifles,
Eight Hundred of the best,
Crossed Anafarta Valley
To Anafarta Crest.
And how with their Trusty leader,
Colonel Rhodes the brave,
Dashed through the Turkish valley
To Victory or the grave.[57]

---

[57] An extract from an unknown soldier of the Isle of Wight Rifles poem that was sent home and published in the Isle of Wight County Press. It was later reproduced in the book, 'The Isle of Wight Rifles' by DJ Quigley.

Anafarta Ridge, 12th August 1915

Thursday 12th August 1915 is one of the most important and bloodiest days in the Isle of Wight Rifles' history. Their attack on Kuchuk Anafarta Ova was very costly and became known to the men of the battalion as the advance on Anafarta Ridge.

At 7am the 5th Essex were relieved from the support trenches by the 1/4th Norfolks and the four battalions of the 163rd Brigade were now together holding the line. Orders were given to the Commanding Officer of the 1/5th Norfolks, Colonel Sir Horace Proctor-Beauchamp, *'to assume local command of the Brigade in the trenches.'*[58]

During the morning, the Isle of Wight Rifles spent their time improving the trenches that the battalion had begun to dig the previous day. Supplies were also brought up to the front line. Lance Sergeant Harold Rayner of 'A' Company was given the task of guiding the water supplies to the front line and during this time he came under sniper fire:

> On the morning of the 12th August [1915] I was told to make my way back to the base to act as a guide for the water mules, a distance of about 2 miles, consisting of rocky, sandy and open ground, but I had no sooner started than I became a mark for a Turkish sniper, who kept potting at me for about half an hour, but fortunately missed each time; some of the shots were too close to be comfortable.[59]

---

[58] 163rd Brigade's War Diary for August 1915
[59] Isle of Wight County Press, 18th September 1915, p6

Interestingly, Rifleman Edward James Watts felt that the snipers were generally not great shots but that there were enough of them in good positions to cause trouble for the men.[60]

At Corps Headquarters, a morning conference was held to plan the next offensive and subsequently orders were given. The Report on Operations from 10th August to night 17/18th August in 54th Division's War Diary for August 1915 recorded:

> On morning of August 12th at a conference at Corps Headquarters Instructions were received the Division to advance on the following morning and occupy the line Pt. 278 South of 119 O.7. – Teke Tepe – Kavak Tepe - As a preliminary to this operation it was decided that it was necessary to clear during the afternoon of the 12th KUCHUK ANAFARTA OVA of any parties of the enemy found in that neighbourhood. Instructions were received for 1 Brigade of the Division to advance at 4pm to the Eastern edge of the village.
>
> These verbal instructions were not received till about 12 noon and the G.O.C. 163rd Inf Bde who was at Divisional Headquarters was instructed to carry out the task assigned for that afternoon – Artillery support being arranged for by the Navy.'[61]

Whilst the Corps conference was being held, maps of the ANZAC area had mistakenly been issued to the Isle of Wight Rifles and the replacement maps which were subsequently given to the battalion were noted to have *'obvious errors on them.'*[62]

---

[60] Rifleman Edward James Watts' letter to his wife written on the morning of 12th August 1915 and printed in the Portsmouth Evening News on Wednesday 01 September 1915.
[61] Report on Operations from 10th August to night 17/18th August, 54th Division War Diary for August 1915
[62] Officers' Report attached to the Isle of Wight Rifles' War Diary of August 1915

Later in the day, the 1/5th Suffolks received maps of the Helles area.

The 163rd Brigade's War Diary stated that the orders for the afternoon's advance at 4pm were received at 1.15pm and *'instructions were telephoned to Colonel Beauchamp to order the Brigade to be ready to advance at 1600.'*[63] However, there was a breakdown in communication and when the 163rd Brigade Headquarters established itself by the frontline at 3.25pm it became clear that the Isle of Wight Rifles had not received the orders and later still, it was found out that the 1/5th Suffolks had also not received notification of the planned advance.

From the Isle of Wight Rifles' War Diary, it appears that the battalion's Commanding Officer, Lieutenant Colonel Rhodes, first received the battalion's orders for the advance at 3.30pm and the Officer's Report attached to the Isle of Wight Rifles' War Diary stated:

> At about 3.45pm, on the 12th August, Company Commanders were sent for by Battalion Headquarters and informed that an advance was to be made immediately towards the hills marked on the map under the name of Kavak, Tepe and Tekke Tepe. The advance was to be pushed at all costs, but it was not expected that there would be any opposition but snipers would cause a certain amount of trouble.
>
> When asked what the objective was to be, the C.O. said that Brigade were unable to tell him. He was also uncertain as to whether there were to be any troops on the flanks of the Brigade. The C.O. said that he had

---

[63] 163rd Brigade's War Diary for August 1915

> protested strongly to the Brigadier at the vagueness of the orders, but without success.⁶⁴

Captain Clayton Ratsey had missed the briefing by Lieutenant Colonel Rhodes to the Officers regarding the battalion's orders and on finding out that the battalion was to shortly advance, he is reported to have said, *'My God we'll all be killed.'*⁶⁵

The 1/5th Suffolks did not find out about the planned advance until after 4pm:

> It was not until well after 4pm that the 1/5th Suffolks knew anything of even a contemplated advance and then only because the Brigade Major of 163rd Brigade arrived in Battalion HQ and wanted to know Why the !! What the !! etc. etc. hadn't the battalion moved off.
>
> This was easily explained to him, as nothing was known of a move anywhere. It was then ascertained the orders had been sent to one of the other battalions on a memo form to be noted etc and passed on and returned by last named. The 1/5th Suffolks was the unfortunate battalion to be the last named and had never received these orders.⁶⁶
>
> Report attached to the 1/5th Suffolks War Diary for August 1915

According to the report attached to the 1/4th Norfolks' War Diary, the reason for the delay in the advance was due to *'having no runners to issue the orders,'* and, *'Colonel Sir Horace Beauchamp himself brought the orders to the 4th Battalion on foot before the operations started.'*⁶⁷

---

⁶⁴ Officers' Report attached to the Isle of Wight Rifles' War Diary of August 1915
⁶⁵ The Isle of Wight Rifles, D J Quigley, Saunders
⁶⁶ Report attached to the 1/5th Suffolks War Diary for August 1915
⁶⁷ Report attached to the 1/4th Norfolks War Diary for August 1915

Accounts from officers within the 163rd brigade suggest that their understanding of the advance's objective was to clear the surrounding area of snipers. For example, the report attached to the 1/5th Suffolks War Diary stated that the advance '*was purely a sniper drive*' and in a letter from an unnamed officer of the Isle of Wight Rifles dated 17th August 1915 and published in the Isle of Wight County Press on 4th September 1915, the officer wrote that the orders were to '*advance across the front and beat the scrub for snipers, of whom dozens abound.*'[68]

Due to the breakdown in communication of the orders, the planning and preparation time for the advance was very limited. Sergeant Ernest Barnes' letter that was published in the Isle of Wight County Press on 4th September 1915 confirmed the rush into battle:

> On Thursday 12th we advanced about 4 o'clock just as tea was being carried up and we had to leave the tea and get to business.'[69]

The men did not have enough time to eat and replenish their water bottles and as such they went into battle without sufficient water and food to sustain them over a period of time.

As planned, HMS Talbot of the Royal Navy began bombarding the Turkish positions at 4pm. However, according to the 163rd Brigade's War Diary, the advance did not start until 4.40pm. The Brigade's positions meant that the Isle of Wight Rifles were in the centre with the 1/5th Suffolks to their left, the 1/5th Norfolks to their right and the 1/4th Norfolks were in support. The Isle of Wight Rifles were organised such that 'C' Company was in the centre with 'A' Company to the left and 'D' Company to the right. 'B' Company were in support and were ordered to carry

---

[68] Isle of Wight County Press, 4th September 1915, p6
[69] Isle of Wight County Press, 4th September 1915, p6

entrenching tools. One platoon of 'C' Company was given the task of carrying the machine gun ammunition.

With bayonets fixed, the Brigade advanced on the sound of bugles and moved in extended order at a brisk pace without support on either flank. Bugler Reginald Peachey of 'B' Company was immediately wounded in the leg by a sniper as he played his bugle to start the Isle of Wight Rifles advance. The reflecting sunlight having drawn attention to him from a waiting and prepared sniper.[70]

Despite the wounding of Bugler Peachey, the initial part of the advance did not come under significant enemy fire and to a limited extent it was supported by naval gunfire and artillery. Men from the New Zealand Army who were onlooking from the high ground near Saribair said at a later date that the Brigade's advance on 12th August *'looked more like a drill movement than an attack.'*[71]

Once the Isle of Wight Rifles reached the first small ridge that lay in front of them, the Turkish Army opened up on them. Shell fire came from the right flank and both machine gun fire and rifle fire were experienced on the left flank from the high ground. Rifle fire was also experienced in the centre and in addition to this, camouflaged snipers were concealed in the scrub and trees that lay in the plain. The battalion, advancing uphill, was out in the open and exposed. Rifleman Sidney Downer of 'C' Company said that *'it was like going through a hailstorm with the bullets flying around.'*[72]

The initial advance of the 163rd Brigade on Anafarta Ridge was as follows:

---

[70] The Isle of Wight Rifles, D J Quigley, Saunders, p8
[71] Officers' Report attached to the Isle of Wight Rifles' War Diary of August 1915
[72] Rifleman Sidney Downer's letter published in the Isle of Wight County Press, 4th September 1915, p6

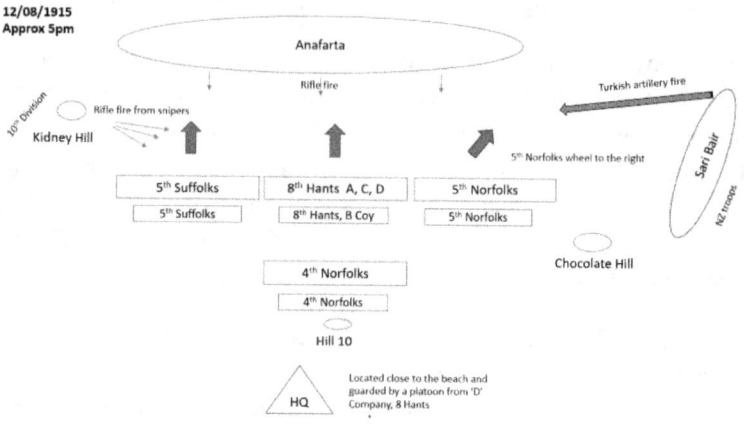

Casualties began to mount up but some of the men had very lucky escapes. Sergeant Harry Green of 'D' Company saw a dud shell land 10 yards in front of him as he reached the first ridge, Rifleman Leonard Hamilton of 'B' Company was saved by his cigarette tin in his coat taking the full impact of a bullet and Rifleman Leonard Eldridge of 'B' Company was shot in his left eye but lived to tell the tale:

> It was lucky for me that it was a spent bullet that I stopped, as it did not go in very far; in fact I pulled it out almost as soon as it was in there, bound up the wound, had a smoke, and walked back to the RAMC camp.[73]

It would appear that Rifleman Eldridge embellished what happened in his letter home as the bullet that struck his eye is on display at Carisbrooke Castle and the accompanying note states that the bullet was removed at a dressing station and was given

---

[73] Isle of Wight County Press, 4th September 1915 p6

to Rifleman Eldridge to keep as a souvenir. He later framed the bullet and called it, *'the Bullet that saved my life.'*[74]

Chaos quickly ensued and there was an intermingling of companies and even battalions. 'B' Company found themselves in the front line of the attack even though they were the support company. This was due to the faltering of the forward companies and the rate at which parts of 'B' Company advanced. According to Lance Corporal Thorn of the RAMC who was attached to 'C' Company, *'Comic Urry's platoon ['B' Company] went charging at the Turks singing "We are the Hants boys" and they haven't been seen or heard since.'*[75]

The three Urry brothers; Edward, Frederick and William, all died on the 12th August 1915. All three served in 'B' Company but it is not known if they served in the same platoon together.

Rifleman Pullen of 'C' Company found himself separated from the Isle of Wight Rifles. In a letter home dated 19th August 1915 he wrote:

> Just after we started into action I got lost, and in company with a few of our fellows found ourselves mixed with the Norfolks. When our regiment was relieved we were left behind, but I cannot speak too highly of the way Lieut. Beck, of the Norfolks, treated us.[76]

Lieutenant Albert Edward Alexander Beck was an officer with the 1/5th Norfolks and the nephew of Captain Frank Reginald Beck from Sandringham Estate. They both died during the advance on 12th August 1915 and for his actions on the 12th, Lieutenant Albert Beck was awarded the Military Cross. During the advance, the 1/5th Norfolks veered right and became ahead of the Isle of Wight Rifles. The company of the 1/5th Norfolks led

---

[74] Carisbrooke Castle Museum
[75] Lance Corporal Thorn's letter to his mother dated 18th August 1915 and printed in the Isle of Wight County Press.
[76] Isle of Wight County Press, 4th September 1915, p6

by Captain Frank Beck advanced further than the remainder of the 1/5th Norfolks and seemingly disappeared. However, they had not vanished, they had fought their way to a farm and became surrounded by Turks where they were then captured and executed by the Turks.

On the left flank of the Isle of Wight Rifles, the 1/5th Suffolks were exposed to the rifle fire and machine gun fire coming from Kidney Hill on the left flank. The supporting company of the 1/5th Suffolks broke off to the left to deal with the threat and as a result the forward three companies of the 1/5th Suffolks were unsupported in taking the ground in front of them and subsequently trying to hold the ground. However, elements of the supporting company were able to make contact with the 10th Division.[77]

Snipers began to become a significant problem for the Isle of Wight Rifles. They were well camouflaged with their faces painted green and used both ordinary bullets and explosive bullets. The Isle of Wight Rifles used covering fire to deal with the snipers and some were captured, including females - *'one Turkish girl was found with 74 identification discs in her possession.'*[78] Rifleman Alfred Morgan of 'C' Company wrote, *'I am glad to say I brought three down out of a tree.'*[79]

At one point in the advance the ferocity of the Turkish response caused the battalion to come to a standstill. Sergeant Rayner of 'C' Company gave the following account:

> We reached open ground with trees dotted about. Here we met a perfect hail of rifle fire and we came to a temporary stop taking what cover we could. We pushed

---

[77] 1/5th Suffolks War Diary
[78] Rifleman Barton's letter published in the Isle of Wight County Press on 4th September 1915 on page 8.
[79] Rifleman Alfred Morgan's letter published in the Isle of Wight County Press on 9th October 1915 on page 8.

forward again. I had no thought whatever but to keep going, and I passed on my way many wounded who at other times would have put one off for some time.

The fire by now was murderous and we had some of the more advanced parties fall back on us. I was near our Colonel [Lieutenant Colonel Rhodes] and when he called for all the line to charge we went like one man.[80]

One of the men wounded in the latter part of the advance was Sergeant Albert Bishop of 'B' Company. He was shot through the neck at about 6.30pm and despite of this was able to crawl back to a field dressing tent and receive treatment. He was subsequently invalided off Gallipoli and recovered from his wounding.[81]

During the advance, the Isle of Wight Rifles' Machine Gun Section, which was commanded by Lieutenant Pittis and included Sergeant Woodford, Lance Corporal Lamb and Rifleman Fred Reynar, were not able to use their two maxim machine guns due to the difficulty in carrying them and keeping up with the advance. Lieutenant Pittis resorted to requesting the use of stretchers to help carry them and Captain Raymond, the Isle of Wight Rifles' Medical Officer, duly obliged. Meanwhile, with the insufferable heat and in the face of enemy activity, the men decided to discard equipment that was not of use to them.[82]

The Turks resorted to setting some uncut cornfields alight in an attempt to stop the advance. Rifleman Leonard Eldridge later wrote:

---

[80] Sergeant John Rayner's letter to Barton Council Boys' School, Isle of Wight County Press, 18th September 1915, p6
[81] Sergeant Bishop's Diary: https://sites.google.com/site/iowrifles/sgt-bishop-diary/transcript
[82] Officers' Report attached to the Isle of Wight Rifles' War Diary of August 1915

> When a lot of our wounded were lying a corn field the Turks set fire to the corn, and they also shelled the stretcher-bearers as they were carrying the wounded off the battlefield.[83]

Sadly, those men who had been immobilised by their wounds were caught in the burning fields. The fire caused the Isle of Wight Rifles some difficulty and also caused the 1/5th Suffolks to fall back slightly. As the smoke began to clear, close by fortified Turkish positions came into view. Captain Ellery, the officer in charge of 'C' Company, felt that he had no option but to get the men in his company into the cover of a sunken lane that lay behind them. He and Sergeant Lewin Channing each led a group of men and as they retreated to the sunken lane they provided each other with covering fire.[84]

Some men of the Isle of Wight Rifles reached the Turkish trenches and took them. These were possibly the men of 'D' Company who were operating to the right of 'C' Company. Unfortunately, there were not enough men to make holding the trenches tenable. Sergeant Harry Green of 'D' Company gave the following account of the battle:

> The bullets came like hail. What with our Fleet and artillery and the Turkish guns and rifle fire it was a perfect hell. But on we went, men falling in all direction and the Turks flying in front of our bayonets, and we took the trenches but then our supports were not strong enough to hold them, so we had orders to retire. I shall never forget it. I got stranded once and everybody round me was either put out or wounded. It was in a cornfield with the corn tied in bundles and I crawled under one of these, but very soon shifted as the snipers had me in line.

---

[83] Rifleman Leonard Eldridge's letter published in the Isle of Wight County Press 4th September 1915, p6
[84] The Isle of Wight Rifles, D J Quigley, Saunders, p10

I got back into a ditch and then crawled through a bit of a copse. The bullets were sticking in the ground all round me, and how I got as far as I did God only knows. But I got into a bit of open ground and was just congratulating myself, when bang! In the back of the left shoulder and the bullet came out under my ear. I still pottered on, when I got another right through the left foot, and that finished it. I worked my way into a trench, where we were going to make the final stand – when I heard that our troops were going to retire again. I thought my number was up, but another order came, "Hang on at all costs." Of course I was finished, so I laid and watched the scrap. When it got dark they took me to the field dressing station and doctored me up a bit. I was hit at about 8.30pm and got there at midnight, so you can guess the plight I was in.[85]

From 6pm onwards, men from all battalions of the 163rd Brigade began to take up defensive positions along the sunken lane and a bank. Riflemen Harold and Clarence Hayden of 'C' Company wrote in a letter to their parents that the Isle of Wight Rifles had *'gained nearly 2 miles and held the place with about 300 men till the others came up,'* and Rifleman Aylward of 'A' Company who was acting as his Captain's observer wrote, *'7pm gained over a mile of ground including a well. We formed a line of defence, Norfolks, Suffolks and Hants mixed together.'* Company Sergeant Major Minns of 'C' Company was instrumental in gathering the men that were falling back and bringing them to the sunken lane.[86]

Further along the sunken lane, to the righthand side, lay four wells which were in the hands of men from the Isle of Wight Rifles. This overall position was roughly two miles from the starting point of the advance and is likely to be the location of the

---

[85] Sergeant Harry Green's letter published in the Isle of Wight County Press on 26th September 1915
[86] Letters published in the Isle of Wight County Press, September 1915

trenches that Sergeant Harry Green made his way back to and the position where the order, *"Hang on at all costs,"* was referring to. Here the men began to dig in and by 8pm a defensive line had been established with approximately 800 men. This included the Isle of Wight Rifles' two machine guns and machine guns from the other battalions in the brigade. Lieutenant Hubert Wolton of the 1/5th Suffolks after the war said that the *'men cheered and waved their helmets when two machine guns came up – entirely manhandled.'*[87]

In addition to the newly formed forward line, a supporting line was established by two companies of the 1/4th Norfolks on a spur behind the sunken lane.

The digging of trenches was impeded by the loss of suitable equipment during the advance and sandbags were not available to bolster defensives. As such, a lot of work was undertaken during the evening to establish deeper trenches and better defences. Due to the hard nature of the ground and a lack of spades, the men had to scrape at the ground using their entrenching tools. A rudimentary Regimental Aid Post was also setup and run by Captain Raymond.

The 3rd (Welsh) Field Ambulance had been designated as one of the Field Ambulances to support the 54th Division. By 4.40pm the 3rd (Welsh) Field Ambulance had set up a dressing station near Point 28 in preparation of the attack and at 4.45pm the first case arrived - the casualty may have been Bugler Peachey who had received a gunshot wound to the leg whilst sounding the advance. According to the 3rd (Welsh) Field Ambulance's War Diary, eight cases had been sent to the Clearing Hospital by 6.15pm and by 8.30pm, another thirty-two cases had been treated and sent on to the Clearing Hospital.[88]

---

[87] Gallipoli, Peter Hart, Profile Books, p360
[88] 3rd (Welsh) Field Ambulance War Diary August 1915

With the onset of darkness, an effort was made to try and get wounded back to the dressing stations. One of the men involved was Sergeant Ernest Barnes of 'B' Company:

> After dark Perkins (Lance Corporal H. Perkins of Newport) asked to be carried back, as he was wounded in three places, but we had to leave him under a tree until a stretcher came, as he was suffering much pain. Then I helped carry Bertie Wray back, but he died soon after.[89]

Lance Corporal Perkins later made it back to the medical facilities provided by the Royal Army Medical Corps and was invalided off Gallipoli. Rifleman Bertie Wray passed away in the early hours of the 13th August 1915.

An attempt to follow up the 54th Division's advance was made by one and a half battalions of the 159th Brigade and half a battalion of the Herefords from the 53rd (Welsh) Division, however, *'they lost track with it in the bush in the darkness and were withdrawn.'*[90] This meant that the 163rd Brigades' right flank was roughly 800 yards in front of the 159th Brigade's line and as a result of the gap, Turkish snipers were able to move in and harass the 163rd Brigade.[91]

Nearing the end of the day, at 11pm, two battalions of the 161st Brigade moved forward to occupy the trenches that the 163rd Brigade had previously held. No additional manpower for the 163rd Brigade was made available but there were attempts to get supplies up to the firing line. This however proved very difficult due to the response of the Turkish Artillery in the area.[92]

---

[89] Sergeant Barnes' letter published in the Isle of Wight County Press, 4th September 1915, p6.
[90] 53rd (Welsh) Division General Staff War Diary August 1915
[91] The Isle of Wight Rifles, D J Quigley, Saunders, p10
[92] 163rd Infantry Brigade War Diary August 1915

Below shows the positions held by the 163rd Brigade around 7pm on 12th August 1915:

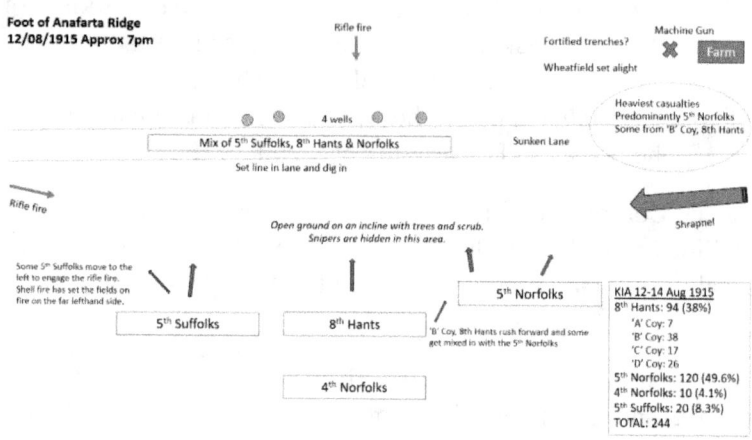

Holding the Gains, 13th – 14th August 1915

Friday 13th August 1915

At midnight, the Turkish Army launched a counterattack. Several accounts from the men stated that when the Turks were either attacked or launching an attack they would call out, '*Allah.*' With the aid of the Isle of Wight Rifles' two machine guns the attack was repelled. Corporal Lamb later praised Lieutenant Pittis for his bravery throughout the fighting.

During the early hours of the 13th August 1915, the 163rd Brigade continued to consolidate the defensive line that had been established and by 5am, at Point 28, the Brigade Headquarters had been setup.[93] Point 28 lay roughly 300 yards from the firing line. Meanwhile, the Turkish Army brought in reinforcements.

Command of the 163rd Brigade in the frontline was passed to the Isle of Wight Rifles' Commanding Officer, Lieutenant Colonel Rhodes at 6am.[94] However, Lieutenant Colonel Rhodes' command was short lived as later in the day he had to return to base due to being '*worn out.*'[95]

Snipers were still causing the Isle of Wight Rifles' difficulties. Men would be sniped at as they attempted to get water from the captured wells and the line as a whole was under the threat of sniper fire. One of the victims to a sniper was Sergeant Woodford:

> Am sorry to say we have lost one of the Old Boys' in poor George Woodford. He had been doing splendid

---

[93] 163rd Infantry Brigade War Diary August 1915
[94] 1/5th Suffolks War Diary August 1915
[95] An Officer's Diary published in the Isle of Wight County Press, September 1915

work with his machine gun in the front trench, and was shot by a sniper clean in the forehead. Fortunately the shot killed him instantaneously.[96]

Another casualty to the snipers was Hubert 'Dink' Watson of 'B' Company. He was killed *'whilst giving a wounded man a drink.*[97] Other acts of compassion and bravery occurred such as the act of Corporal George James of 'B' Company which was recollected by Lance Corporal Thomas Alexander of 'B' Company in a letter home:

> We drove the Turks back about 1½ miles, but lost rather heavily. I must not forget to tell you about Cpl. George James of Newport. He crawled out of the trenches under a hail of bullets and rescued a wounded man who was helpless. I don't expect you will hear much about it as there was only myself and a few others who saw him do it, but still he deserves as much praise as if he did it in the sight of the whole battalion.[98]

For the men in the frontline, on top of the constant sniping they endured the scorching heat of the sun with little in the way of shade. The men were now able to source water from the captured wells but at the risk of falling victim to snipers and their food was limited to biscuits. The wounded who had made it back to the dressing stations were now on their respective treatment journeys. Sergeant Albert Bishop of 'B' Company who had been shot in the neck the previous day wrote the following diary entry on Friday 13th August 1915:

---

[96] Letter written by a member of the RAMC attached to Isle of Wight Rifles, published in the Isle of Wight County Press, 4th September 1915, p8
[97] Letter written by Rifleman Frederick Reynard on 18th August 1915 and published in the Isle of Wight County Press on 4th September 1915, p6.
[98] Letter by Lance Corporal Alexander written on 16th August 1915 and published in the Isle of Wight County Press in September 1915.

Wounded in the neck at 6.30pm yesterday. A sad day for the Island, I'm afraid many have dropped. I was hit while advancing. It was hell. The boys were grand - they went forward like heroes. I crawled back to a field dressing tent and was bound up. Stayed there the night. Was carried down to the sea this morning. Am writing this sitting on a stretcher waiting for a boat to take me off to a hospital ship. Have no news yet. Heavy firing all night. A lot of Hants are in wounded. Besides the one through the neck, I had one through my helmet and one through my haversack. Thank God I am here. I never expected to get out of it. Went off to ship at 2pm. 400 of us there. Had some Bovril and pudding. What a God-send.[99]

Medical services came under significant pressure from the vast numbers of wounded men and cases of diseases such as dysentery. The 3rd Welsh Field Ambulance reported the following:

> Great difficulty was found in coping with transport, no wagons being available and distance great to Collecting Station also shortage of stretchers.[100]

To make matters worse for the 3rd Welsh Field Ambulance's medical staff and the wounded, they came under shell fire at approximately 6pm. No casualties were reported from this shelling.

An attempt to collect the wounded was made by twenty-five men from the Essex Brigade. They went out onto the battlefield unarmed flying the Red Cross flag [101] and later in the evening the 3rd Welsh Field Ambulance moved their dressing station to Point 28.

---

[99] https://sites.google.com/site/iowrifles/sgt-bishop-diary/transcript
[100] 3rd Field Ambulance War Diary August 1915
[101] Report attached to the 1/5th Essex's War Diary

General Sir Ian Hamilton's Diary entry for 13th August 1915 provides an enlightening insight into the events and decision making at the strategic level. General Sir Ian Hamilton stated that *'The Brigade of the LIVth sent on to Kuchuk Anafarta Ova made good its point'* and he felt that the planned attack on Kavak Tepe on the 13th August should have been implemented. His diary entry for the 13th August highlights his frustration with his commanders' unwillingness to push forward and their negative views of the Territorials. He wrote with respect to the Kavak Tepe attack being cancelled:

> But no; Stopford and Reed count the LIIIrd Division as finished: the LIVth incapable of attack; the rest of the IXth Corps immovable.[102]

General Sir Ian Hamilton had a more positive view of the Territorials and in his diary entry of the 13th August 1915 he stated that he thought the Isle of Wight Rifles were, *'good.'* Of note, he wrote that the Territorials would *'fight right enough and keen enough if they were set fair and square at their fence'* and *'We might still do something with a change of commanders.'*[103]

Although General Sir Ian Hamilton was alluding to the situation at Suvla being turned around, the opportunity to deal a fatal blow to the Turks had pretty much been lost prior to the landing of the 54th Division when the Turkish Army beat the British Army in the race to claim the high ground around Suvla. With the attack on Kavak Tepe cancelled and the 163rd Brigade being left unsupported to hold the ground they had taken, the chances of making a success of the Suvla Bay landings further slipped away.

---

[102] Gallipoli Diary, Volume I by Ian Standish Monteith Hamilton
[103] Gallipoli Diary, Volume I by Ian Standish Monteith Hamilton

Saturday 14th August 1915

The Essex Brigade (161st Brigade) were tasked with relieving the 163rd Brigade and began to move forward during the morning. However, they mistakenly opened fire on the 163rd Brigade. This was documented in the report attached to the 1/4th Norfolks War Diary and in the report attached to the Isle of Wight Rifles War Diary as follows:

> At about 5 o'clock in the early morning of the 14h August, the Essex Brigade appeared advancing from the rear, and on sighting the 163rd Brigade immediately opened fire with machine guns.
>
> A signaller of the Norfolks, a boy of 18 saved the situation by standing up and signalling to the Essex, who immediately ceased fire. This signaller received no recognition for his having done this, and was killed a few days later.[104]

On ceasing fire, the Essex stopped their advanced and remained where they were until the late afternoon when they attempted to relieve the 163rd Brigade for the second time. None of the Essex Battalion's War Diaries from the Essex Brigade mention advancing in the early morning on the 14th August 1915 to relieve the 163rd Brigade but the 1/5th Essex's War Diary mentioned that a small patrol had undertaken a reconnaissance of the area prior to their advance.

At 10am a stretcher bearer party went out to collect the wounded, some of whom had been wounded on the 12th August. Bandsman Jim Westmore of 'C' Company and Lance Corporal Thorn, RAMC attached to the Isle of Wight Rifles took part in retrieving

---

[104] Officer's report attached to the Isle of Wight Rifles' War Diary August 1915.

the wounded. Below is an extract from a letter written by Lance Corporal Thorn on 16th August 1915:

> On Saturday we had a busy time. Some men had been wounded, and laid under fire. Men were asked to go and get them, and we Hants fellows went. Before starting the Church of England chaplain, who went with us, said a prayer, and then we left, Capt. Raymond accompanying us. We had about six miles to go there and back under fire all the time.[105]

Lance Corporal Harry Cull of 'A' Company was one of the men who was rescued on Saturday 14th August. He had a flesh wound to his right thigh caused by a bullet on the 12th. Below is an extract from a letter he wrote to his mother from a hospital in Malta:

> I was wounded on Thursday evening and lay about under fire until Saturday afternoon, when our clergyman found me, fetched a stretcher party and had me taken away.

These accounts are a testament to the bravery of the stretcher bearers, medics and clergymen who put their lives at risk, unarmed, to help their fellow men.

Throughout the morning successful efforts were made to establish a telephone line connecting the firing line with Brigade Headquarters and to also connect the new frontline trenches with the trenches held by the 53rd Division on the right flank. There was however, still a gap between the left flank of the 163rd Brigade and the position of the 10th Division.

A counterattack was launched by the Turks at 1.15pm but was defeated:

---

[105] Lance Corporal Thorn's letter dated 16th August 1915 and published in the Isle of Wight County Press in September 1915.

At 1.15pm the enemy counter attacked on the left but was driven off by the fire of our two Battalion machine-guns. In the event of the attack being successful we should have been completely surrounded and the only course open to us would have been to fight ourselves out with the bayonet which would have resulted in very heavy casualties.[106]

Orders were issued by the 54th Division Headquarters to the 161st (Essex) Brigade to relieve the 163rd Brigade. The 1/5th Essex's War Diary provides a thorough description of the battalion's experience during the operation:

Advanced to relief of 163rd Brigade. Advance commenced at 4pm. The distance to be covered was about 1 mile over open country. Advance was made in lines of platoons in single file, practically the only formation which could be used in the thick scrub through which the first part of the advance was made. Enemy opened shrapnel fire the moment the advance commenced. We were also under a fairly heavy rifle fire from the left flank, probably from irregular bodies of snipers who were known to be in the vicinity. A machine gun opened fire behind us and caused casualties amongst our battalion and the 5th Norfolks and the 8th Hants whom we were relieving.

We were under orders not to fire and all water cans, machine guns and various impediments had to be carried in the advance. The men were very steady under fire. Direction was not well kept, partly owing to indefinite information as to exact objective and partly being obliged to change direction twice to get round the crest of a hill.[107]

---

[106] The Isle of Wight Rifles' War Diary August 1915
[107] 1/5th Essex's War Diary August 1915

An extract from the report attached to the Isle of Wight Rifles' War Diary indicated that a battalion of the Essex Regiment was unaware that they were undertaking a relief operation. They were of the understanding that they were going into an attack and assumed that the line held by the 163rd Brigade were Turkish positions. It is not clear which battalion of the Essex Regiment fired their machine gun at the 1/5th Essex and the 163rd Brigade but the likely battalion was the 1/6th Essex as they also relieved the Isle of Wight Rifles.

It was not possible to identify who may have been wounded during the friendly fire incident. During the advance, according to the 1/5th Essex's War Diary, 14 NCOs and Other Ranks were killed, around 60 were wounded and a few men were reported as missing. With regard to known casualties for the Isle of Wight Rifles on the 14th August [but not necessarily from the friendly fire incident] Rifleman James Devereuax of 'A' Company and Rifleman Thomas Newman of 'C' Company died of wounds and Corporal Harold Rayner and Rifleman Albert Coombes both of 'A' Company were wounded. Rifleman Coombes subsequently died of his wounds on 24th August 1915. Both Lance Corporal Frank Le Brun of 'D' Company and Rifleman Charles Stark of 'C' Company who had been wounded on the 12th August passed away and Lance Serjeant William Silvester of 'C' Company died from heart failure.

According to the Isle of Wight Rifles War Diary, their relief began at 6.30pm. The 1/5th Essex War Diary relieved both the 5th Norfolks and the Isle of Wight Rifles and the 1/6th Essex also relieved the Isle of Wight Rifles, completing their relief at 10.30pm.

At 11pm, the Isle of Wight Rifles were able to begin their trek back to the original trenches that they had held prior to their advance on the 12th August. The men were unable to take any wounded back with them or to tend to those who had been wounded on the route to their relief. One of those left behind was

Corporal Harold Rayner of 'A' Company. He had received a gunshot wound a couple of hours before the Essex Brigade arrived at the firing line and was taken back to base the next morning by a couple of the Essex Brigade's RAMC personnel.[108]

The 1/7th Essex took up positions next to the 53rd Division but half of their battalion mistakenly entered the trenches held by the 159th Brigade of the 53rd Division. The remaining battalion of the Essex Brigade, the 1/4th Essex, relieved the companies of the 4th Norfolks that were holding the high ground known as Norfolk Hill, which lay behind the firing line, on the 15th August.

By 3am on 15th August the planned relief of the 163rd Brigade had been completed. The Isle of Wight Rifles, heavily depleted and back in their original trenches prior to their attack on 12th, were reunited with the fifty men of 'D' Company that had been guarding the 54th Division's Headquarters.

---

[108] Corporal Rayner's letter published in the Isle of Wight County Press in September 1915.

Aftermath of the Isle of Wight Rifles' First Offensive

Sunday 15th August 1915

Finding themselves back in the reserve trenches, the Isle of Wight Rifles were able to take stock of their ordeal and the scale of the losses began to fully sink in. Sergeant Ernest Barnes of 'B' Company admitted that it brought him to tears:

> I was all right except being parched and starved till Sunday, when I had to call the roll of my platoon. I could not keep the tears from my eyes when I found how many killed, wounded and missing we had.[109]

A number of men could not be accounted for as is evidenced by a letter written by CQMS Bertie Clark of 'D' Company to his wife on 16th August 1915:

> Out of the four officers who went into action with our company only one returned. One is badly wounded and I have since heard that he is dead. Capt. Ratsey and Lieut. Young-James are missing, so is our Sergt-Major. I have not heard how many casualties there are in the battalion, but there must be a good few, as they say some companies lost more men than us. I forgot to tell you that Corpl. Arnold, whose people live in lower Sandown, is missing.[110]

Captain Donald Ratsey and Lieutenant Alexander Young-James had in fact been killed on the 12th August 1915. Major Lewis was also initially reported as missing but had been killed on 12th as well. Company Sergeant Major Frank Fielder was reported

---

[109] Sergeant Barnes' letter published in the Isle of Wight County Press on 4th September 1915, p6

[110] CQMS Clark's letter to his wife dated 16th August 1915 and published in the Isle of Wight County Press on 4th September 1915, p6

missing and was later presumed to have died on 12th August 1915. Corporal Walter Arnold received a gunshot wound to his right leg and was taken prisoner.

The advance on Anafarta Ridge and subsequently holding the new ground gained cost the Isle of Wight Rifles 8 Officers and 89 Other Ranks killed in action and a minimum of 48 Other Ranks wounded. Please note that the number of wounded is likely to have been substantially higher. The number cited accounts for those known to have been wounded between 12th August and 14th August. One officer, Lieutenant Colonel Rhodes, and four Other Ranks are known to have become ill during this period as well.

Comparing the casualty rates across the 163rd brigade from 12th August to 14th August 1915 in terms of those killed as per data from the Commonwealth War Graves Commission, it is clear to see that the highest casualties were taken on the right flank of the brigade. The 5th Norfolks who were operating on the right flank lost 120 men, the Isle of Wight Rifles who were in the centre of the brigade lost 97 men and the 1/5th Suffolks who were operating on the left flank lost 20 men and the rear battalion, the 1/4th Norfolks, lost 10 men. The 163rd Brigade lost a total of 247 men killed in action. The 1/5th Norfolks' casualties accounted for 49% of the 163rd Brigade's casualties and the Isle of Wight Rifles accounted for 38% of the number of men of the 163rd Brigade that were killed in action. Of those killed, the vast majority of them died on 12th August 1915.

Breaking down the number of Other Ranks killed in the Isle of Wight Rifles on 12th August 1915 by company shows that 5 men from 'A' Company died, 37 men from 'B' Company died, 15 men from 'C' Company died and 23 men from 'D' Company died. 'D' Company were operating on the right flank of the battalion and 'B' Company were in the rear. However, during the battle, 'B' Company found themselves at the front and took heavy casualties.

For a long time, mystery surrounded the 1/5th Norfolks losses on 12th August 1915. A platoon of the battalion went missing in a haze of smoke. It was later found out the 1/5th Norfolks had wheeled to the right during the attack and one platoon had advanced quicker than the other platoons. This platoon reached a farm and its surrounding areas which formed part of the Turkish frontline and became surrounded. It was here that they met their fate. After the war, the 1/5th Norfolks' Chaplain, Reverend Pierrepoint Edwards, went back in search of the missing 1/5th Norfolks in the vicinity of Kuchuk Anafarta Ova and found a large number of dead bodies, mainly from the 1/5th Norfolks but also from the Isle of Wight Rifles and the 1/5th Suffolks. Sadly, it was only possible to identify two of the soldiers from the 1/5th Norfolks – Private Cattor and Private Barnaby.[111]

Some of the Isle of Wight Rifles' missing men made it back to dressing stations and were invalided off Gallipoli whilst some of the other missing men that had not died, were taken prisoner. One of those taken prisoner was Rifleman Sydney Porter of 'D' Company. During captivity Rifleman Porter became an orderly and barber at the officers' camp at Afion Kara Hissar. Here he met and became good friends with Thomas White who went on to become Sir Thomas White, Governor of Australia. In Sir Thomas White's book, 'Guests of the Unspeakable,' Sir Thomas White described the atrocities inflicted on Rifleman Porter:

> Private S. A. Porter, 8th Hants Territorials, who during his captivity served as an orderly in No. 4 House in the officers' camp at Afion Kara Hissar, gave me the following facts regarding his capture. I have seen the various wounds that he received, and have reason to believe his story to be true in every detail. (He also had two brothers taken prisoner in Kut, one of whom died as a result of his treatment.) Pte. Porter was a signaller in

---

[111] https://www.historic-uk.com/HistoryUK/HistoryofBritain/5th-Battalion-Norfolk-Regiment-The-True-Story/

advance of the leading platoon on the day of the big advance on August 12th, 1915, at Suvla Bay. Portion of a shell struck him, carrying away a large portion of the right buttock. After freeing himself from a field telephone which he carried, he roughly bandaged the wound and commenced to crawl back to some cover, but before reaching it he lost consciousness through loss of blood. When he regained consciousness the attack was over, and he heard enemy voices close at hand. Soon afterwards a Turkish soldier approached and finding him still alive struck him many times on the head with the edge of a shovel, inflicting severe gashes that rendered him unconscious. (These blows left long depressions in Porter's skull.) Once more regaining his senses, he found himself lying on his face and heard a Turk approach, load his rifle, and while standing near his feet fire point blank at his head. The bullet struck him in the back of the neck, gouging out a wound at least four inches long and coming out below the left ear. He was again left for dead, but a party of Turkish soldiers on seeing him move bayonetted him no less than twelve times. One thrust went through his arm, another made a bad wound in the stomach, a third punctured his cheek, while the remainder were scattered over various other parts of his body. Fortunately for him the Turkish bayonets were of the old-fashioned pointed variety, or recovery would have been impossible. He again lost consciousness but woke to find a more humane party of Turks were taking him to a dressing station. Nevertheless, they made him walk with a rope tied around him, which they jerked whenever he stumbled. Though he was a diminutive little fellow he miraculously recovered and quickly, - his most painful memories being the dressing of his wounds without chloroform, while being held down by burly wardsman. Although his wounds when healed could be plainly seen he found them only a slight inconvenience, so much so that when we were allowed to play football he proved himself a dashing outside right!¹¹²

Due to his remarkable escape from death, Rifleman Porter became known as "The Man the Turks Could not Kill."

Whilst there has been evidence of brutality from the Turks, not all of them behaved in such a manner. Writing to his mother on 24th August, Rifleman William Wheeler of 'B' Company described his experience of the Turks:

> The Turk is a pretty fair fighter. We were forced to retire on one occasion, but retook the lost ground again later, and we found that they had dressed our wounded and left their water bottles for them. When I was taken to the first dressing station there was a Turk lying on the next stretcher to mine. He spoke very good English, and asked me if I wanted a cigarette. Of course, I did not refuse, for I was dying for a smoke.[113]

The excerpt above highlights that the Turks could also show acts of compassion and kindness.

Throughout the 15th August, the Isle of Wight Rifles were subjected to shellfire and Rifleman Harry Baker of 'D' Company was wounded in the leg by a piece of shrapnel. The Isle of Wight Rifles also welcomed those of the battalion who had been left behind at Mudros.

With regard to the rest of the 163rd Brigade, the companies of the 1/4th Norfolks that were left holding the small hill (Norfolk Hill) behind the front line were relieved by the 1/4th Essex. However, around 2pm the Turks began to attack the 1/6th Essex threatening to push them back. Meanwhile on the left flank, the 10th Division with the support of the 162nd Brigade of 54th Division were launching an attack on Kiritech Tepe Sirt with a secondary

---

[112] Guests of the Unspeakable, Sir Thomas White
[113] Isle of Wight County Press, 4th September 1915, p8

objective of taking Kidney Hill. As such, it was decided to send the 1/4th Norfolks back to Norfolk Hill to support the 1/4th Essex and for one company of the 1/5th Suffolks to move forward towards the boundary with the 10th Division. Gains were made along Kiritech Tepe Sirte up to Jephsons Post and Kidney Hill was taken but all at very high costs to the battalions involved.

Was the operation on Anafarta Ridge a success or failure?

Operational orders to the 54th Division as per Field Message R.15 from IX Corps were for the Division to, *'clear the ground to the front to the Eastern boundary of the village of ANAFARTA OVA'* and to, *'consolidate the line so as to include the village.'* [114] The 54th Division's Commander was given the discretion to decide on the size of force to employ and he chose to use the 163rd Brigade for the task.

The purpose of this operation was to pave the way for an attack on the line, 'CREST 119.5.4 – KAVAK TEPE' the following day. The 53rd Division were tasked with supporting the advance of the 54th Division's 163rd Brigade.[115]

Whilst the 163rd Brigade did make an advance of nearly 2 miles further inland and during so capture and kill many Turkish snipers, the Brigade fell short of taking Anafarta Ova village. The furthest part of the advance was made by a platoon of the 1/5th Norfolks who breached the Turkish line and made a final stand in the area of a farm held by the Turks. The support of the 163rd

---

[114] IX Corps General Staff War Diary
[115] IX Corps General Staff War Diary

61

Brigade by the 53rd Division failed to even make contact with the 163rd Brigade.

As a result of the advance having to halt, the high levels of casualties, the lack of support for the 163rd Brigade and General Stopford's lack of confidence in his forces, the following day's offensive on Kavak Tepe was cancelled. Strategically, this cancellation of a planned attack was another major blow to the chances of making a success of the Suvla Bay landings.

A number of factors caused the 163rd Brigade's advance to be checked. Firstly, the resistance put up by the Turkish Army in the form of snipers, shellfire and machine gunfire played a huge part in defeating the advance and a large number of casualties came from shell fire and enfilading fire from both flanks. However, the heat, distance covered and lack of water and food played their part in sapping the energy of the men and thus helping to stall the advance. The Isle of Wight Rifles' officer who wrote the report on the operation maintained that *'the attack came to a standstill, not because it came up against an enemy's defensive position, but because the men were too weary to go further, and on account of the complete disorganisation.'*[116]

Contrary to the Isle of Wight Rifles' Officer's report, elements of the battalion came up against Turkish defensive positions and the 1/5th Norfolks found themselves amongst Turkish forces. When an inquiry into the operation was made after the war in 1931, it was reported by the surviving officers of the Isle of Wight Rifles that *'there were no Turks in their immediate front,'* however, Captain Jewson of the 1/4th Norfolks, in response to the 1931 report, commented that he thought *'there were snipers all over the front,'* and that, *'opposite the 1/5th Norfolks on the right flank there were definite enemy positions held in moderate strength.'*[117]

---

[116] Officer's report attached to the Isle of Wight Rifles War Diary August 1915
[117] Report attached to the 1/4th Norfolks War Diary

Another critical aspect in halting the advance were the fires that took place. Lance Corporal William Halsey (later Sergeant) of 'C' Company, Isle of Wight Rifles, felt that this action by the Turks was the decisive factor:

> If they call it a failure at Suvla it was not because 8th Hants could not run, and I believe now that if the Turks had not set the bush on fire, we should have taken Anafarta Hill.[118]

There was a definite lack of support for the 163rd Brigade's advance. Although the Royal Navy and Royal Artillery provided support, there was no support on the flanks and the 53rd Division failed to link up with the 163rd Brigade. Likewise, there was no follow up from the 54th Division to reinforce the position. Captain Jewson of the 1/4th Norfolks not only believed that support on both flanks was necessary but also suggested that an evening operation under the cover of dark could have helped, as is evidenced by his response to the 1931 report:

> It is quite certain that, had the attack been postponed until dusk, the brigade could undoubtedly have advanced a considerable distance without difficulty, but there would, of course, have been the danger of losing direction, as it is difficult, scrubby country, and the advance could be of no possible service unless operations took place on either flank more or less at the same time, to clear the Turks off the high ground.

Major P. G. Wilson of 1/5th Suffolks also emphasised the lack of support in his response to the report dated 13th February 1931:

> I would like to stress the point that all orders from Brigade to Battalion were extraordinarily vague and the CO of 1/5th Suffolks gave me my orders for the advance

---

[118] Sergeant William Halsey's letter published in the Isle of Wight County Press on 16th March 1916

> on 12 Aug. (p.17) he had only been told we were to advance, no objective was mentioned, and all we knew was that our left flank would probably be in the air and subject to enfilade fire. Another brigade, the Essex, I believe was supposed to come up and reinforce us at midnight, but presumably as the original attack on the ridge was cancelled at the last moment (unbeknown to us) presumably that is the reason they never arrived. If only the original plan had been adhered to I am sure we should have captured the ridge and held it.[119]

Major Wilson not only discussed the lack of support as a reason for failure but also addresses a pertinent point in that the dissemination of the orders was very poor. The orders were distributed late to individual battalions and there was a lack of clarity on the objectives. This left the battalions of the Brigade with little time to prepare and confusion as to their ultimate purpose. In an ideal world they would have had time to have attempted a reconnaissance of the area and to plan their attack.

Considering the vagueness of orders to the battalions, the lack of preparation time, lack of support, a hostile climate and having to advance in the open in the face of shellfire and enfilading fire, the men of the Isle of Wight Rifles and the rest of the men of the 163rd Brigade made a valiant effort. They showed fortitude, bravery and determination in the face of heavy casualties and stood their ground for two days with little provisions and under constant sniping.

Rifleman Sidney Downer's letter to his mother nicely summarises the positives of the Brigade's action:

> The general in command of the operation congratulated our brigade on their wonderful work in capturing and hanging on to the position, for they could not get up anyone to relieve us, and if we had given way it would

---

[119] Report attached to the 1/5th Suffolks War Diary

have been a proper disaster, as we should have lost two of the only four wells anywhere round for miles.[120]

Although the 163rd Brigade did not take Anafarta Ridge they captured ground and vital supplies of water and as such should be commended for their efforts, resolve and bravery.

---

[120] Isle of Wight County Press, September 1915

Known Casualties for 12th-14th August 1915

12th August 1915

Officers

Killed
Major Ernest Hastings Lewis
Captain Arthur Holmes Gore
Captain Graham Loader
Captain Clayton Ratsey, 'C' Company
Captain Donald Ratsey, 'D' Company
Lieutenant James Alexander Young
Second Lieutenant Laurence Watson
Second Lieutenant Frederick Raymond
Total: 8

'A' Company

Killed
Lance Corporal Eric Raymond
Lance Corporal Edward Miles
Rifleman Walter Ballard
Rifleman George Hills
Rifleman William Langdon
Total: 5

Wounded
Lance Corporal Harry Cull
Rifleman George Barton
Rifleman George Houghton
Rifleman Stanley Jeffery
Rifleman Robert Rashley
Rifleman Frank Saunders
Rifleman Albert Trott
Rifleman Arthur Warne
Rifleman Reginald Warne
Total: 10

'B' Company

Killed
Company Sergeant Major Walter Purkis
Corporal John Barton
Corporal William Witham
Lance Serjeant Harry Leal

Wounded
Serjeant Albert Bishop
Serjeant Herbert Whittington *
Lance Corporal Harry Perkins

Rifleman John Baker
Rifleman Leonard Ball
Rifleman Frank Brett
Rifleman William Buckett
Rifleman William Finch
Rifleman Edward Foster
Rifleman Frank Green
Rifleman George Guy
Rifleman Arthur Hale
Rifleman Bertram Hamilton
Rifleman Herbert Harvey
Rifleman Lawrence Hatcher
Rifleman Jack Hurry
Rifleman John Knight
Rifleman Ernest Parsons
Rifleman James Pocock
Rifleman James Punch
Rifleman Arthur Rann
Rifleman Edwin Read
Rifleman Richard Read
Rifleman Charles Rolf
Rifleman Albert Saunders
Rifleman Reginald Sibbick
Rifleman Arthur Simmonds
Rifleman Harry Smart
Rifleman George Toogood
Rifleman Harry Trowbridge
Rifleman Edward Urry
Rifleman Frederick Urry
Rifleman William Urry
Rifleman Walter Vincent
Rifleman Alfred Ward
Rifleman Francis Yeates
Total: 37
* Taken prisoner

Bugler Reginald Peachey
Rifleman Frank Cass *
Rifleman Arthur Downer *
Rifleman Leonard Eldridge
Rifleman Robert Hayles *
Rifleman Albert Humber
Rifleman Leslie James
Rifleman Vernon Jolliffe
Rifleman George Prince
Rifleman Sidney Sheath
Rifleman Albert Wilton
Total: 14

'C' Company

Killed
Corporal Thomas Boyce
Lance Corporal Alfred Whittington
Rifleman Joseph Stark
Rifleman Herbert Baker
Rifleman Adolphus Ballard
Rifleman George Holbrook
Rifleman William Mayo
Rifleman George Meecham
Rifleman Herbert Peach
Rifleman Bernard Rolfe
Rifleman Harold Searle
Rifleman Raymond Trinder
Rifleman Edgar Tyzack
Rifleman Charles Watkins
Rifleman Gilbert Whittington
Total: 15

* *Taken prisoner*
+ *Died later*

Wounded
Corporal Joseph Mabb *
Lance Corporal Albert Watson
Rifleman William Colenutt
Rifleman Charles Orchard
Rifleman George Reeves *
Rifleman Albert Sheath *
Rifleman Charles Spragg
Rifleman Charles Stark +
Rifleman Edward Watts
Total: 9

'D' Company

Killed
Company Serjeant Major Frank Fielder
Serjeant Reginald Groves
Serjeant Frederick Leftwich
Corporal Douglas Sparks
Lance Corporal Salmon
Rifleman William Abbott
Rifleman Thomas Arnold
Rifleman Robert Bilk
Rifleman Henry Burton
Rifleman Andrew Cheesman
Rifleman Henry Cole

Wounded
Serjeant Harry Green
Corporal Walter Arnold *
Corporal Thomas Oliver *
Lance Corporal Frank Le Brun +
Lance Corporal Edwin Woodnutt
Rifleman Reginald Downer
Rifleman Cecil Manning
Rifleman Sydney Porter *
Rifleman Joseph Stallard *+

Rifleman Philip Gilbert
Rifleman Percy King
Rifleman Frank Lee
Rifleman Frederick Miller
Rifleman Percy Paine
Rifleman Frederick Read
Rifleman Arthur Russell
Rifleman Albert Sarney
Rifleman Ralph Sawyer
Rifleman Albert Sinnicks
Rifleman Albert Tyzack
Rifleman Arthur Watson
Total: 23

Rifleman Alfred Thomas *
Rifleman Wilfred Weeks
Total: 11

* *Taken prisoner*
+ *Died later*

13th August 1915

Killed
Serjeant George Woodford, 'A' Coy
Rifleman Clifford King, 'B' Coy
Rifleman Hubert Watson, 'B' Coy

Wounded
Serjeant Ernest Elliott, 'C' Coy
Serjeant Hugh Love, 'C' Coy
Rifleman Percy Knight, 'B' Coy
Rifleman Joseph Ince, 'D' Coy

Died of Wounds
Rifleman Bertie Wray, 'B' Coy

Sick
Lieutenant Colonel Rhodes
Rifleman George Wheeler, 'B' Coy

14th August 1915

Died of Wounds
Lance Corporal Frank Le Brun, 'D' Coy
Rifleman James Devereuax, 'A' Coy
Rifleman Thomas Newman, 'C' Coy
Rifleman Charles Stark, 'C' Coy

Wounded
Corporal Harold Rayner, 'A' Coy
Rifleman Arthur Coombes, 'A' Coy

Sick
Rifleman R Aylward, 'A' Coy
Rifleman Albert Barton, 'A' Coy
Rifleman William Hinks, 'A' Coy

Died
Lance Serjeant William Silvester, 'C' Coy

N.b. A large number of men have been recorded as wounded but it was not possible ascertain the date that they were wounded, merely a rough timeline of when they would have been wounded.

On 29th July 1916, the Isle of Wight County Press published a list of men who had been reported as missing and confirming that they were officially presumed to have died on 12th August 1915.

Prisoners of War

Below is a list of the men who were taken prisoner during the advance on Anafarta Ridge[121]:

Sergeant Herbert Whittington, 'B' Company *

Corporal Joseph Mabb, 'C' Company *

Corporal Thomas Oliver, 'D' Company *

Rifleman Frank Cass, 'B' Company *

Rifleman Frederick Cox, 'D' Company *

Rifleman Arthur Downer, 'B' Company *

Rifleman Robert Hayles, 'B' Company *

Rifleman Sydney Porter, 'D' Company *

Rifleman George Reeves, 'C' Company *

Rifleman Albert Sheath, 'C' Company *

Rifleman Joseph Stallard, 'D' Company *+

Rifleman Alfred Thomas, 'D' Company *

*wounded, +died later

---

[121] Research undertaken by Ian Meadows

Officers of the Isle of Wight Rifles as of 15th August 1915

Name	Company	Comments
Lt. Col Rhodes		*Sick - at base camp*
Major Veasey		
Capt Ellery	C	
Capt Fardell	D	*Joined from Mudros*
Capt Marsh		
Lt Giddens	QM	
Lt Ledward		
Lt Pittis		MG Officer
Lt Read		*Joined from Mudros*
Lt Seely		
2nd. Lt Bartlett	C	
2nd. Lt Brannon	D	*Joined from Mudros*
2nd. Lt Fox		
2nd. Lt Kingdon		
2nd. Lt Latham		
2nd. Lt Murphy		
2nd. Lt S Ratsey		*Joined from Mudros*
2nd. Lt Shelton		
2nd. Lt Weeding	B	
Capt Raymond	RAMC	

Their Baptism

Only the boys from Sandown,
With head-quarters close to the sea;
Some thought of home service merely,
And treated the thing as a spree.

We were proud, in the main, when selected,
And brigaded to go to the Front,
To the heat of the Turkish "Babas,"
From Vectis, to share in the brunt.

But the story I'm trying to tell you –
At home, out of sound, shot, or shell –
Is how our boys went from their dug-outs
To the mouth of a veritable hell.

You've all heard the popular notion
Of a soldier's baptism of fire;
How, of course, at the start there's a quaking,
Though his nerves may be stronger than wire.

But I honestly think our baptism,
As our loss only too plainly shows –
Mown down by the shrapnel and rifle –
Was stern enough, heaven only knows!

I could tell you a lot, but the Censor
His far-reaching pencil might wield –
How a few of "B" charged the Turk's trenches,
Far advanced from the rest of the field.

One of two returned safe, but others,
Sore wounded, crawled back to the line,
Which supporting troops were entrenching,

Looking round for lost pals all the time.

The Rifles and three more battalions
Remained of the starting brigade;
Hung on for three days in position,
For which they so dearly had paid.

I'll an officer mention 'ere closing
These doggerel lines I have made,
His uncle in pluck close resembling.
His grit from our minds will ne'er fade.

His bravery and dash adds lustre
To a far-famed Island name,
Though risen in rank he has no swank,
But heartens us all just the same.

Though I've mentioned this one, in justice,
The others should not be passed by;
I could not say enough-they're the true British stuff
Which suffices-enlarge I'll not try.

Gallipoli Dug-outs, August 31st
Corpl. G. H. James
I.W. Rifles[122]

N.b. the Officer referred to is Second Lieutenant Weeding

---

[122] Isle of Wight County Press, 25th September 1915, p6.

Continuation at Suvla Bay

Dissent in the Ranks

Monday 16th August 1915

Throughout the day there was heavy fighting at Kiretch Tepe Sirt in the vicinity of Jephsons Post and Kidney Hill. The battalions of the 30th and 31st Brigades of the 10th Division and the 162nd Brigade of the 54th Division were under severe strain. A decision was made to send the Isle of Wight Rifles and the 1/5th Suffolks to take over the support trenches held by the 10th Division on the northern slope of Kiretch Tepe Sirt. Orders were received by the Isle of Wight Rifles at 3.10pm and they were instructed to lead the manoeuvre:

> The call for assistance from Jephsons Post was urgent, and the Brigade Commander was forced to send his Brigade across exposed country in full view of the Turks and parallel to the firing line. From the shelter around Hill 10 to the foot of Karakol Dagh lay open flat ground of nearly a mile in length without any cover.
>
> The Brigade Commander himself was present and supervised the movement of the Brigade. The Companies were ordered to move across the open ground in lines of eight men in extended order with their flank to the enemy, being about 100 yards between lines. This singular order made the advance unnecessarily slow, resulting in the tail of the Brigade arriving at Jephsons Post hours after the fight had ceased. It also had a bad effect on the men waiting their turn to advance, and watching the advance of their comrades in front. On this occasion it was that one of the Companies of the 8th Hants refused to move and were eventually sent to the beach.

The Turks who had a clear view of the movement of the Brigade, immediately opened with a well placed shrapnel fire, and caused a number of casualties. There were very few, if any, casualties from rifle fire, owing to the distance from the firing line. On reaching the slope of the hills, the men came under cover in the ridges, but on reaching the summit were met by a heavy shrapnel fire.

The shells were bursting at a height of only a few feet above the ground and an unfortunate rifleman of the 8th Hants had an arm carried away by a shell which did not explode until it had gone on another fifty yards.

As the Battalion moved along the ridge, they could see the fight still going on in front of them but before the leading files would join in, the Turks retired about 100 yards into a strong point and the action ceased. No effort was made to follow them, as no one realised the importance of occupying further ground along the ridge. The men of the 10th Division were probably at that time too exhausted to make another advance. There was also a scare that ammunition was running short.[123]

Officer's Report attached to the Isle of Wight Rifles War Diary for August 1915

It was 'C' Company that refused to move and they were commanded by Captain Ellery. The Officer who wrote the report that is quoted above also felt that one of the reasons 'C' Company disobeyed orders was because Captain Ellery had lost favour with the men over an incident during the battalion's training at Watford.

---

[123] Officer's Report attached to the Isle of Wight Rifles War Diary for August 1915

Part of 'A' Company and 'B' and 'D' Companies made the move towards Jephsons Post and they took up the trenches that had been designated as support trenches. However, these trenches had no trenches in front of them so were in effect front line trenches. To the right of the battalion were the 6th Inniskillings.[124]

Brigade Headquarters began establishing itself at Kiretch Tepe Sirt at 8pm and by 10pm the 4th and 5th Norfolks had also arrived in the area.[125]

Rifleman Frederick Miller of 'C' Company was killed during the 16th August 1915 and CSM Walter Minns of 'C' Company was wounded in his left shoulder by a piece of shrapnel whilst traversing a ravine. Despite the wounding he remained with his men for two days before finally seeking more advanced medical attention.[126]

Both Sergeant Barnes and Sergeant Newman from 'B' Company were wounded by shrapnel. A piece of shrapnel caused damage to Sergeant Newman's leg and Sergeant Barnes was hit twice during the day:

> The next day [Monday] I was lying in the when a spent shrapnel ball hit me on the helmet just hard enough to bring up a bump on my head. I think that was a very lucky escape, as it would certainly have killed me had it struck me with full force. Later in the day one went through my left boot, smashing my big toe but not doing much harm besides, and I was carried off on the stretcher to the boat, where I was looked after all right.[127]

---

[124] The Isle of Wight Rifles War Diary August 1915 & Officer's Diary published in the Isle of Wight County Press September 1915
[125] 163rd Brigade Headquarters War Diary August 1915
[126] Rifleman Deness' letter to his wife published in the Isle of Wight County Press, 6th November 1915, p6.
[127] Sergeant Barnes' letter published in the Isle of Wight County Press on 4th September 1915, p6.

It was not possible to identify the rifleman that lost his arm. It is also likely that there were more casualties taken on 16th August 1915 other than of those mentioned. A number of soldiers have been identified as having been wounded between August 1915 and early September 1915 but it was not possible to ascertain the exact dates that they were wounded.

Kiretch Tepe Sirt

Tuesday 17th August 1915

Those of the Isle of Wight Rifles at Kiretch Tepe Sirt continued to hold the support trenches and were joined by the rest of 'A' Company. 'C' Company were *'left at Brigade Head-quarters to provide fatigue party to bring up rations etc.'*[128] The men once again found themselves with very little water and the attempts made by mule companies to bring water supplies from the base up to them were met with shellfire.[129] At one point, such was the desperation for water, men tried to drink seawater to quench their thirst.[130]

At 3pm the 163rd Brigade received orders to relieve the battalions of the 10th Division that were occupying the trenches on the saddle ridge next to Jephson's Post.[131] Initially, the 1/4th Norfolks were supposed to be taking over the line that the Isle of Wight Rifles were holding but the new orders required the 1/4th Norfolks, and the number of men from the 1/5th Norfolks who were with the 1/4th Norfolks, to relieve the 6th Munster Fusiliers and the 6th Inniskilling Regiment of the 30th Brigade, 10th Division. The 1/4th Norfolks left their positions at 7pm to climb the hill to Kiretch Tepe Sirt and arrived at Brigade Headquarters at 12pm. From there, they proceeded to take over the trenches held by the 30th Brigade in the vicinity of Jephson's Post.[132]

---

[128] An Isle of Wight Rifles' Officer's Diary published in the Isle of Wight County Press, September 1915
[129] 163rd Brigade Headquarters War Diary August 1915
[130] The Officer's Report attached to the Isle of Wight Rifles' War Diary, August 1915.
[131] 163rd Brigade Headquarters War Diary August 1915
[132] Diary of Captain Montgomerie of the 1/4th Norfolks, F. LORAINE PETRE, THE HISTORY OF THE NORFOLK REGIMENT 1685-1918, Vol.II. (Norwich: Jarrold & Sons, Limited, 1953), https://www.gallipoli-association.org/on-this-day/august/17/

The Isle of Wight Rifles held the line which ran from the sea shore up to within a couple of hundred yards of the crest of the ridge. Jephson's Post was not only defended by the 4th and 5th Norfolks but also by a machine gun crew from HMS Beagle who were located in the trenches at Jephson's Post. HMS Beagle herself was operating close to the shore line and was available for support:

> The destroyer was able to render effectual help on several occasions; for if there was any movement in the Turkish lines, she at once opened fire with her guns. At night also her searchlight was directed on the Turkish line as it stretched up the hill, rendering the enemy's trenches clearly visible to our troops while our own were in darkness.
>
> Captain M. B. Buxton, 1/5th Norfolks[133]

However, there was a drawback to the search light. The Officer's Report in the Isle of Wight Rifles War Diary for August 1915 stated that *'it was most comforting to have this beam of light in front of the position, but although it prevented the Turks from moving, yet it effectually stopped the sending out of patrols on our part.'* [134]

Due to the ground consisting of hard rocks, the Isle of Wight Rifles were unable to dig trenches and instead resorted to constructing sangers similar to those that had been used on the Indian Frontier.[135] The Turks did not have a system of trenches

---

[133] Diary of Captain M. B. Buxton, 1/5th Norfolks, F. LORAINE PETRE, THE HISTORY OF THE NORFOLK REGIMENT 1685-1918, Vol.II. (Norwich: Jarrold & Sons, Limited, 1953), https://www.gallipoli-association.org/on-this-day/august/17/

[134] The Officer's report attached to the Isle of Wight Rifles' War Diary, August 1915.

[135] The Officer's report attached to the Isle of Wight Rifles' War Diary, August 1915.

but utilised the lay of the ground to hide snipers and machine gun nests.

There are two known casualties for the 17th August 1915. Rifleman Lawrence Searle of 'A' Company was killed in action and Rifleman Ivan Grinham of 'A' Company was wounded by a piece of shrapnel in his right wrist. He was subsequently admitted to the 3rd Welsh Field Ambulance for initial treatment of his wound.

Wednesday 18th August 1915

On the 18th August 1915 the Isle of Wight Rifles maintained their positions at Kiretch Tepe Sirt and a number of casualties were taken. Second Lieutenant William Bartlett was killed by a sniper whilst bringing rations up to the line, Rifleman William Dunstan of 'B' Company died of wounds and Rifleman Hubert Haward of 'C' Company and Rifleman Harry Sheppard of 'A' Company were killed. Rifleman Edgar Fleming of 'B' Company, one of the battalion's stretcher bearers, was shot in the right hand by a sniper whilst collecting water, Lance Corporal James Rackett of 'A' Company was wounded and Captain Raymond, RAMC, reported sick. Captain Raymond was suffering from shell shock and exhaustion and had lost the hearing in one of his ears. He was subsequently invalided back to England.[136]

Thursday 19th August 1915

Brigadier General Brunker DSO, the commander of the 163rd Brigade, reported ill and was replaced by Major Evans DSO,

---

[136] Lance Corporal Thorn's letter to his mother dated 19th August 1915 and published in the Isle of Wight County Press in September 1915

DAA & QMG, a Staff Officer from the 54th Division Headquarters.[137]

By 19th August 1915, Lieutenant Colonel Rhodes was on his way back to England. He had hurt his leg which necessitated him being invalided off Gallipoli and this meant that command of the battalion was officially passed to Major Veasey. According to the letter written by Lance Corporal Thorn to his mother on 19th August 1915 the Isle of Wight Rifles were down to *'about ten officers'* and he also included in his letter that *'several of the battalion were suffering from sunstroke and dysentery.'*[138]

During the evening, the 5th Norfolks relieved the Isle of Wight Rifles and the Isle of Wight Rifles took up positions on the ridge behind.[139]

Friday 20th August 1915

Following their move, the evening before, the Isle of Wight Rifles stood their ground at their new home. Writing from 'Sea View Dug-Out,' Company Sergeant Major Arthur Charles Early of 'C' Company (he was promoted following Anafarta Ridge) wrote the following to his wife which was subsequently published in the Isle of Wight County Press:

> Here we are again and still smiling, though at times we don't feel much like it. We have been bombarded once more this morning, but we are getting wise now, and as soon as they begin we strike work and get under cover till they have finished. We got a message from the trench

---

[137] 54th Division Adjutant & Quarter-Master General's & 163rd Brigade's War Diaries.
[138] Lance Corporal Thorn's letter to his mother dated 19th August 1915 and published in the Isle of Wight County Press in September 1915
[139] 5th Norfolks War Diary and the Officer's War Diary published in the Isle of Wight County Press in September 1915

just now that they wanted water, so a party went off with some and the corporal got hit in the arm. Lieut. Bartlett was killed on the same job on Wednesday, so it is evidently risky to move in the daytime. We have made a fine dug-out with empty ration boxes filled with earth and are fairly comfortable under the circumstances. I shan't be at all sorry to get back again, for this life is all very well to stay at home and talk about. Clean shirts would be very nice, to say nothing of 'a good blow out' of something you really fancied. I shall have plenty of fancies when I get back. But we must not bemoan, for there are many poor chaps worse off than we. I have had one shave, and a fine job it was getting off a week's growth with cold water![140]

Due to the shortage of available water, the men rarely shaved. At times the men had to rely on just half a bottle of water to quench their thirst and for washing and as a result they remained in their dirty clothes. The only chance to wash properly was when the men were back at the beach and were given an allotted time to bathe.

Danger was ever present and Private Reginald James Brooks Butt said that no-where was safe at Gallipoli as even at the beach they could be shelled by the Turks. Bringing rations and water up to the front line ran the risk of shell fire and being hit by a sniper as is evidenced by the death of Lieutenant Bartlett on Wednesday 18th August 1915 and the wounding of the Corporal (name unknown) on Friday 20th August 1915.

According to the Officer's diary that was published in the Isle of Wight County Press in September 1915, the men witnessed a battle between Royal Navy destroyers and a shore battery and the destroyers came out of the encounter unscathed.

---

[140] Isle of Wight County Press, 18th September 1915, p6

At IX Corps Headquarters, planning was undertaken for an operation the following day. Originally the 54th Division were designated as one of the divisions to be used for the attack but the plans were changed so that the 54th Division would be held *'in a state of instant readiness'* so that they could be used to deal with any Turkish forces that broke away during the attack.[141] These orders were received by the Isle of Wight Rifles at 3pm.[142]

In addition to the death of Second Lieutenant Latham, Rifleman Henry Horscroft of 'B' Company died of wounds.

Notes on the Period of 15th August 1915 – 20th August 1915

There are discrepancies in the dates given by the Isle of Wight Rifles' Officer's report that was written for the Aspinall-Oglander review. Firstly, the report mentions that the Isle of Wight Rifles moved to Kiretch Tepe Sirt on the 15th August 1915. This move in fact occurred on the 16th August 1915 as is evidenced by the Isle of Wight Rifles War Diary for August 1915, The Isle of Wight Rifles' Officer's Diary that was published in the Isle of Wight County Press in September 1915 and the 163rd Brigade Headquarters War Diary August 1915.

The Isle of Wight Rifles' Officer's report states that Brigade Major Swan was wounded at Kiretch Tepe Sirt on the 16th:

> On the 16th in the morning at about 8 a.m. the Brigade Major (Major Swan) who apparently had no idea where the firing line was, was seen walking along the hillside, trying to find the Brigade. The Turks allowed him to get within 200 yards of the position and then fired at him with machine guns, wounding, but fortunately not killing him. In spite of this mishap, Brigade Headquarters, the

---

[141] 54th Division General Staff War Diary August 1915
[142] Officer's Diary of the Isle of Wight Rifles, Isle of Wight County Press, September 1915

following morning at about the same time, sent up a ration party, and although frantic efforts to stop them were made, they also met the same fate, a valuable officer being killed.[143]

However, this incident could not have occurred on the 16th August 1915 as the Isle of Wight Rifles were not at Kiretch Tepe Sirt on the morning of the 16th instant. On the evening of the 16th August 1915, Brigade Headquarters established itself near to the front line at Kiretch Tepe Sirte and so it is plausible that this incident happened on the 17th August 1915. It also fits with an officer being killed whilst bringing up rations the following morning as Second Lieutenant Bartlett was killed performing this role on the 18th August 1915.

The Officer's Diary that was published in the Isle of Wight County Press in September 1915 also has at least one date discrepancy. It gives the date of Second Lieutenant Bartlett's death as the 19th August 1915 but this is contrary to the date of 18th August 1915 given by the Commonwealth War Graves Commission and Army records. Also, on the 19th August 1915 the Officer's Diary notes that Brigade Major Swan was wounded that day but the diary provides no further information on the incident. The next day, Second Lieutenant Latham was killed but the circumstances of his death was not documented and so it cannot be confirmed that Second Lieutenant Latham was the officer killed bringing up rations that the Officer's Report in the War Diary was referring to. It is possible that Brigade Major Swan was indeed wounded on 19th August 1915 but given the context of Brigade Major Swan's wounding in that he was searching for the front line and an officer was killed bringing up rations the following day, the 17th August 1915 seems to be a likelier date for his wounding.

---

[143] The Officer's Report attached to the Isle of Wight Rifles' War Diary August 1915

21st August 1915 – Battle of Scimitar Hill and News Reaches Home

'We spent a miserable afternoon listening to the assault of the 29th Division'[144]

Combat casualties and sickness had reduced the Isle of Wight Rifles to just 263 men on 21st August 1915. Dysentery was causing significant problems and roughly fifty people per day were reporting sick.[145] Private Reginald James Brooks Butt said that at one point, such was the shortage of manpower, the men had to remain in the line suffering with diarrhoea and dysentery with holes cut in the bottoms of their trousers. With such low numbers, the battalion was defending the line with just one man every 200 yards.

A large-scale assault on the Turkish line was planned on 21st August 1915 with the aim of linking Suvla Bay and Anzac Cove. The objectives were Scimitar Hill (Hill 70), 'W' Hills and Hill 60 and the Isle of Wight Rifles were placed in reserve as part of the operations on Scimitar Hill and 'W' Hills:

> At 11am received orders that 10th, 11th and 29th Divisions were going to operate on our right and that we were to be prepared to advance and take and consolidate any ground we could in front.
>
> Officer of the Isle of Wight Rifles' Diary [146]

---

[144] Officer's Report attached to the Isle of Wight Rifles' War Diary, August 1915
[145] Officer's Diary of the Isle of Wight Rifles, Isle of Wight County Press, September 1915
[146] Officer's Diary of the Isle of Wight Rifles, Isle of Wight County Press, September 1915

The 29th Division were tasked with taking Scimitar Hill, the 11th Division 'W' Hills and the ANZAC forces along with the British Army's 29th Brigade were tasked with capturing Hill 60. The 2nd Mounted Division, located at Lala Baba, were held in reserve.[147]

Prior to the offensive on Scimatar Hill and 'W' Hills, an artillery bombardment undertaken by land-based artillery and ships of the Royal Navy commenced at 2.30pm. Thirty minutes later, the attacks on Scimitar Hill and 'W' Hills began and at 3.30pm the advance on Hill 60 was launched.

Whilst the fighting was taking place the Isle of Wight Rifles were waiting to be called into action:

> On the 21st August, the Brigade received orders to make a general attack, and spent a miserable afternoon listening to the assault of the 29th Division on the other side of Jephsons Post. The order to go over the top never came, as the 29th Division had failed to advance.
>
> Officer's Report attached to the Isle of Wight Rifles' War Diary, August 1915 [148]

The attack by the 29th Division failed to dislodge the Turkish Army but at times was close to doing so. Around 3.40pm, the 1st Battalion of the Royal Inniskillings came within 150 yards of the Turkish trenches at Scimitar Hill. Here they were subjected to enfilading fire from Anafarta Spur and the artillery fire set the scrub alight. Despite coming under heavy fire, the 29th Division secured a position at the foot of the hill. [149] In contrast, the assault on 'W' Hills faltered and the decision was made to order the 2nd Mounted Division into the battle. Meanwhile, the Anzac Corps

---

[147] Gallipoli, Peter Hart, Profile Books
[148] Officer's Report attached to the Isle of Wight Rifles' War Diary, August 1915
[149] https://www.royal-irish.com/events/battle-of-scimitar-hill-suvla

whilst subjected to enfilading fire from Hill 100 made some progress in taking and holding some ground at Hill 60.

At 4pm the 2nd Mounted Division were ordered to advance from their positions at the rear of Lala Baba. Led by the 1st County of London Yeomanry, the 2nd Mounted Division marched across the Salt Lake towards Chocolate Hill. After half an hour, Turkish artillery shells and shrapnel began to fall among the advancing troops but the men steadily continued despite the dreadful casualties and on nearing Chocolate Hill, the remaining men advanced at the double. From Chocolate Hill, they were to support the attacks at both Scimitar Hill and 'W' Hills.

An attempt was made at 7pm by the 29th Division to dislodge the Turks at Scimitar Hill and the first line trenches were reached. However, the Turks managed to force the 29th Division back. Later in the evening, the 2nd Mounted Division had to retire to Green Hill. The sought after decisive breakthrough had been defeated. Approximately 5,300 men were killed, wounded and missing from the action that day.[150]

In the area that the Isle of Wight Rifles were holding the line, Turkish forces began to form on the ridge at 2350 hours but naval gunfire from a Royal Navy destroyer forced the Turks to retreat.[151]

Corporal Ridgway is the only known casualty for the Isle of Wight Rifles on 21st August 1915. He was wounded in his left arm.

Meanwhile, back on the Isle of Wight, news of the Isle of Wight Rifles' action at Gallipoli together with the death of Rifleman Bertie Wray was printed in the Isle of Wight County Press:

---

[150] Gallipoli, Peter Hart, Profile Books, p378
[151] Officer's Diary of the Isle of Wight Rifles, Isle of Wight County Press, September 1915

ISLE OF WIGHT RIFLES IN ACTION

NEWPORT MAN THE FIRST CASUALTY

The first intimation received in the Island that the Imperial Service Battalion of the I.W. Rifles may have been in the fighting line at the Dardanelles came on Wednesday evening in the melancholy form of an official announcement from the War Office to Mr. E.J. Wray, of High Street, Newport, stating that his second son, Rfn. B.H. Wray, had died on August 13th "from the effects of wounds." The news came as a great surprise to Islanders generally, as it was thought that they would barely arrive by that date, but it has since come to light that they were conveyed on a very fast liner, which completed the voyage in 6½ days. Very profound, sincere, and general sympathy is felt with Mr. and Mrs. Wray and the members of their family in their heavy bereavement. Rfn. B.H. Wray, of "Bertie" as he was more popularly known amongst his many friends, was held in the highest esteem as a good sportsman and an all-round fine fellow. By his death the Newport Rowing Club loses one of its most capable oarsmen and keenest members. He has stroked many crews to victory on the Medina, installing those behind him with that grim determination to do the utmost, which was so characteristic of his nature, and which very probably led him into the very forefront of the fight in which he nobly died doing his duty to King and country. He was also a very popular member of the Literary Society and the Conservative Club, and had figured in the Literary Society's billiard team on many occasions, always playing a sound game. He had been in the I.W. Rifles for over four years. He resigned just before the war, but soon after the commencement of hostilities he was one of the many members of the Newport Rowing Club who responded to the appeal made by their popular captain

(Sergt-Major Walter Purkis) to fill up the ranks of the regiment. He celebrated his 29th birthday the day after leaving England. He was, an old Grammar-school boy, and during his school days showed much promise as a cricketer, although he had since forsaken the "pitch" for the river. Since the receipt of the sad news the flag at the Rowing Club Boat-house has been flying at half-mast. [152]

The Remainder of August at Gallipoli

22nd August 1915

Fighting at Hill 60 continued into the 22nd August 1915. At 0600 hours the 18th Battalion of 5th Australian Brigade launched a further attack on the hill and were able to capture a couple of Turkish trenches. However, despite the progress, the Turks still held ground at Hill 60. [153]

There is no entry in the Isle of Wight Rifles' War Diary for the 22nd August 1915. The only information available is that of the diary entry of one of the battalions Officer's which was later published in the Isle of Wight County Press:

> Aug. 22nd – A few shrapnel came over in the early morning, but did no damage. The Padre (the Rev. P. Edwards) came up and had a short service immediately behind our lines, which practically all the battalion attended. The mail came with letters and papers of August 4th.[154]

Despite the extract from the officer's diary mentioning no damage inflicted by the shrapnel or in fact any activity which

---

[152] Isle of Wight County Press, 21st August 1915, p8
[153] Gallipoli, Peter Hart, Profile Books, p381
[154] Isle of Wight County Press, September 1915

would cause casualties, official records have seven deaths recorded for the battalion on the 22nd August 1915. These were:

- Corporal Sidney Bunce – initially recorded as 'missing';
- Rifleman Isaac Foss – initially recorded as 'missing';
- Rifleman Lancelot Halliday – recorded as 'presumed dead';
- Rifleman Ernest Kerley – recorded as 'presumed dead';
- Rifleman Ernest Symes – recorded as 'KIA';
- Rifleman George Toogood – initially recorded as 'missing'; and
- Rifleman Charles Wapshott – initially recorded as 'missing.'

All these men have no known graves and are commemorated on the Helles Memorial. It is possible these men were killed during the advance on Anafarta Ridge on 12th August 1915 and an administrative error led to their deaths being recorded on 22nd August 1915 instead.

Rifleman Cyril Crook was reported as being 'sick' and was invalided off Gallipoli. He was admitted into Nasrieh School Military Hospital in Cairo suffering with consumption.

23rd August 1915

A reconnaissance patrol consisting of Second Lieutenants George Fox and Stephen Ratsey, Lance Corporal John Woollings and Rifleman Bertie Young was sent out to find the location of enemy snipers who had been active. The patrol found the enemy *'entrenching in two lines facing South area 125 P 2 and 3 (The Boot)'* and, *'reported that there were three lines of trenches in terrace fashion on the spur directly in front of JEFFERSONS*

POST on the reverse slope.'[155] The snipers were believed to be '*located in caves at the bottom of KIRETCH TEPE SIRT.*'[156]

Machine gun fire was used in an attempt to suppress the snipers but proved to be counter-productive as the sniping only increased in retaliation. As a result, it was deemed that anti-sniping parties would be a better solution. However, the Isle of Wight Rifles' War Diary intimated that the battalion had not been trained for such endeavours.

For their efforts, the patrol received congratulations from the Commanding Officer of the 54th Division and Lance Corporal Woollings and Rifleman Young were both promoted.[157]

Two men of the battalion passed away. Rifleman Sidney Downer died from a gunshot wound to the chest and Rifleman Oliver Harding, who had been wounded, died on a hospital ship and was buried at sea. Both men are commemorated on the Helles Memorial.

24th August 1915

During the day, a few high-explosive shells landed in the Isle of Wight Rifles' position but thankfully caused no casualties.

In the evening, at 7.30pm, 'A' Company began digging defences in front of the headquarters on the knoll. Cover for this was provided by a party from 'D' Company.[158]

Rifleman Arthur Coombes, who had been wounded on 14th August 1915, succumbed to his wounds. He is commemorated on the Helles Memorial.

---

[155] 163rd Brigade War Diary, August 1915
[156] Isle of Wight Rifles War Diary, August 1915
[157] Officer's Diary published in the Isle of Wight County Press, September 1915
[158] Officer's Diary published in the Isle of Wight County Press, September 1915

25th August 1915

In preparation for a planned take-over by the 5th Bedfords later that day, Captain Hills visited the Isle of Wight Rifles' position at 6am. However, the decision was made to not proceed with the relief and the battalion was informed of this at 6pm. Throughout the day the men were subjected to sniping.[159]

Several casualties were reported for the day:

- Sergeant Raymond Sibley died of wounds overnight at the Field Ambulance. He was buried by Captain Ellery but his grave was unable to be located at the end of the war and so he is commemorated on the Helles Memorial.
- Rifleman Charles Barton died of wounds on a hospital ship bound for Malta and was buried at sea. He is commemorated on the Helles Memorial.
- Rifleman Joseph Stallard who had been wounded and taken prisoner during the attack on Anafarta Ridge, died of his wounds in a hospital in Constantinople. He is buried at Haidar Pasha Cemetery.
- Rifleman Frank Morgan was shot in the leg by a sniper. He recovered from his wounds and returned to active service.
- Rifleman Sidney Morey dislocated his right shoulder and was invalided off Gallipoli.

26th August 1915

The Isle of Wight Rifles were informed in the morning that the 11th Division would relieve them at 8pm so that the battalion could go to the Divisional rest camp.

---

[159] Isle of Wight Rifles' War Diary, August 1915

During the morning, Corporal George James wrote the following letter which was later published in the Isle of Wight County Press on 18th September 1915:

> August 26th – Still kicking you see. I am writing as we are lying in our dug-outs, where we go during the heat of the day, returning to the fire trenches from dusk to dawn. As we are now in reserve, we are able to do this and we also get better food.
>
> Excuse the rather shaky writing – it is not due to nerves, but to the fact that there are four of us squeezed together, viz…, Bill Early, Arch Chandler, Trickett (a pal of Early's) and myself. The only trouble we have now is the scarcity of water.
>
> We have a cupful served out to us twice a day, which we at once convert into a quite drinkable cup of tea, as we find that that stands by us much better than water alone. Matches are very scarce. Yesterday we had one box served out to every six men, and we manage to get a light for our pipes by just keeping the fires going with embers.
>
> We can see the Turkish trenches about 700 yards from us, and our guns on sea and land give them a good shaking up each day, especially the large destroyers, which stand off our flanks and fire 20 or 30 high explosives and then dodge the returning shells. We get practically no shell fire where we are now. It is only the snipers who trouble us, and our machine-guns are constantly playing on the scrub in front, as it is impossible to spot them with direct rifle fire; they are so cunningly concealed and seem to fire ammunition which, even at night, shows no sign by flame or smoke.
>
> Frank Morgan, the Ironmonger's son, was shot through the leg on Tuesday (25th August), but I hear he is progressing favourably, although owing to the explosive

bullets which the snipers use the wounds caused are bad. I have since heard that Wheeler is safe in hospital, for which I am very glad, as he suffered greatly while waiting for the stretcher bearers, whose work is rendered very difficult, as the Turks give them rifle fire when in a small party and shrapnel when they get to the Red Cross vans. They also shell our ambulances and dressing-stations. This is an absolute fact, as we were in trenches for a day where I could plainly see this going on.

Being now situated on the flank and only about a quarter-mile from the sea, we have now been allowed to have a bathe in batches daily for the last four days. Owing to some unknown reason this pleasure was debarred us yesterday, but we have hopes of one to-day. I should like a real good wash with soap and water, though. I have had one shave since arriving 17 days ago. Some of our older men have a respectable beard and look more like Boer farmers.

If water was as plentiful as bully beef we should be drowned. We get plenty of tobacco issued, and this morning we had a splendid breakfast of good bacon and tea, which we cooked individually. Those mess tins which we had to keep so beautifully clean and polished for kit inspections at home show sad signs of wear and tear.

We expect to be relieved tonight and go to base for a day or two, when we shall take the opportunity of having a change of shirt at any rate and of replenishing our stock of necessary articles from our valises, which were stacked at the landing place on our arrival.

Our daily menu for the last three days has been: Breakfast – cup of water (made into tea), bacon (jolly soon fried), and biscuits; dinner – bully beef (if you feel like it): tea – cup of water (converted into tea), biscuits, and jam; supper (voluntary) – remains of bully eaten in the fire trenches with a mouthful of water if you can save or scheme a drop from the QMS. If you can manage to do the latter you are looked upon either as a hero or a rogue according to the nature and outlook of the rest of the chaps.

Char. Early (Sergt A C Early) has been promoted to Company Sergeant-Major in place of C.S.M. Purkis, who is missing.

As I am writing we are having a good morning shower from the snipers, who have no doubt spotted our resting place by the blankets slung up to keep the sun off, also to dry them, for the nights are cold with heavy dews.[160]

At 10pm, the West Lancs and Yorks Regiments arrived and began to take over the fire trenches.[161]

Rifleman Philip Chapman was wounded during the day and subsequently died of his wounds on 5th September 1915 at a hospital in Malta. He is buried at Pieta Military Cemetery.

27th August 1915

Orders were given at 4am for the Isle of Wight Rifles to head to Karakol Dagh. The battalion reached there at 6am and were then granted four hours of rest. At 10am the men went to 'A' Beach and collected their packs which they had left there on 10th August when they landed.

During the day Lance Sergeant Alfred Jones wrote the following letter to his parents:

---

[160] Isle of Wight County Press, 18th September 1915, p6
[161] Isle of Wight Rifles' War Diary, August 1915

Here we are again, feeling quite 'OK.' I am writing this in a dug-out, which I share with my platoon-commander (2nd-Lieut. Stephen Ratsey). I must say he is a fine fellow, like the Captain. I have just heard that Fred (meaning Sergt. F .G. Leftwich since reported missing) is all right, wounded, but safe at Alexandria. I am so glad. It is astonishing how one gets hardened to the terrible sight here, but the hardest is losing friends. As I told you, I had a violent attack of 'something,' but soon recovered. It must have been the 'shrapnel cure' that did it, as we were shelled out of the base. We are now in the second line trenches. We keep losing two's and three's owing to the snipers, but we have got rid of a lot of them. One of the prettiest things I have seen was a torpedo-boat shelling the Turks the other night by searchlight. Of course, I have had some narrow escapes, from snipers mostly and shells. One burst too close to be comfortable the other day, otherwise I have been lucky. We are going back to the base for a few days rest, the first time we have been out of the trenches since landing. I have managed to bathe once or twice, but it was rather risky. The weather here is trying: hot all day and very cold at night, thunderstorms occasionally, and when it rains it rains – and that is the only time we get a really good supply of water. Water is worth more than gold, so are matches and cigarettes etc. Money doesn't count here. I have the same amount of money in my pocket that I had when we landed so if I stay here long I shall get rich! Shall be glad of papers and books. How is the war progressing? Haven't heard anything since leaving England. From what we see here I should say that the Turks fight more fairly than the rotten Germans.[162]

---

[162] Isle of Wight County Press, 18th September 1915, p6

The rest at base was to be short lived as at 3pm the General Officer Commanding of the 54th Division informed the battalion commanders of the 163rd Brigade that they would be moving to Lala Baba over-night.

Another attack on Hill 60 was undertaken by the Australians, New Zealanders and the 5th Connaught Rangers at 4pm with limited success - the Turkish line was pushed back to the southern slope.[163]

Rifleman William Lunnon was the only known casualty for the day. He sprained his back and was admitted to a hospital on Mudros.

28th August 1915

Following the completion of the relief by the Essex Brigade, the Isle of Wight Rifles left at 1am for Lala Baba and arrived there at approximately 4.30am. Here, the battalion took over dug-outs on the cliff overlooking the beach and had a period of rest. During the day, the Isle of Wight Rifles were visited by Colonel Evans whom advised that the battalion would be transferred to the ANZAC sector on 2nd September[164] and in the evening, a company of the Isle of Wight Rifles was sent to hold the reserve trenches.[165]

There were no known casualties for the 28th August 1915.

29th August 1915

One company of the Isle of Wight Rifles remained holding the reserve trenches and a casualty was taken. Rifleman Harold Hayden was shot in the head whilst on Guard duty:

---

[163] Gallipoli, Peter Hart, Profile Books, p382
[164] Officer's Diary published in the Isle of Wight County Press, September 1915
[165] Isle of Wight Rifles War Diary

> He was hit in the head in the morning and died at sunset. He died quite peacefully, and never regained consciousness. Poor chap, he had only just gone in the trench and taken over guard when he was struck. I saw him just as he was going in and he said to me 'I have put my blanket in your dug-out, Happy; look after it for me.' He was just handing a periscope to the captain and said I can see three of four working over there (meaning Turks) when a bullet came through the loop-hole and struck him; he fell back, and never spoke again.
>
> Extract from Rifleman Denness' letter to his wife which was written the following week[166]

Rifleman Hayden was taken to the 7th Field Ambulance but succumbed to his wound in the early evening. He was buried the next day.

The remainder of the battalion were kept in their dug-outs at Lala Baba by the Turkish artillery. This gave the men time to write letters home and below are two of the letters which were published in the Isle of Wight County Press on 18th September 1915:

> August 29 – We are now in dug-outs at a base, where some of the naval men landed, marching here on Friday night from where we originally landed. We are having a rest and feeding splendidly. We are situated right on the cliffs and have only to walk down a path to be into the sea, but the hours of bathing are before 8am and after 5pm, owing to attracting shell fire. We had a couple of Taubes over this morning, and soon after had a treat of Turkish delight in the shape of shrapnel and about two

---

[166] Rifleman Denness' letter to his wife, Isle of Wight County Press, 6th November 1915, p5

high explosives, which pitched amongst the mules, finishing off about 50 and wounding a few Indians. We are moving tonight to some reserve trenches. We saw some 3rd Warwicks who landed this morning, a draft from Parkhurst, and presently we are going to find out the 13th Hants, there being several Newport fellows with them. I had a sea wash and a shave this morning, and you can realise how welcome and refreshing it was. We are well established here now in every way, and there is every hope of an ending at any time. There was a big scrap here last night, commencing at about dusk and lasting until after 6 this morning, and I understand our troops have advanced a couple of miles in two days. But, as I said before, the country is very difficult, as there are so many natural fortresses in the shape of hills. Somebody played "My little grey home in the West" on a violin last night, and I guess most of our minds wandered.

Corporal George James

Arrived in these rest trenches after travelling nearly all Saturday night. I believe we stop here a day or two. Anyway, we ought to, as it will be the first rest we have had. Last night was my first sleep all night for a week. There are rumours of our moving to another part of the Peninsula with the Australians, but things get altered every day so one never knows anything. The food here has been good. The last day or two we have had bacon for breakfast again, and we had bread today. Just think of it! Of course, we have to cook our own. It is marvellous, when you consider the number of troops here, how the arrangements are carried out. I draw the rations for my platoon in bulk and then issue them to my section commanders.

> The battalion has had to be rearranged. We have only three companies, instead of four now. Have just heard that we have to go up to the reserve trenches again tonight and then on to the firing line, so they are not going to give us much rest. I don't believe our fellows will stand it, as half of them are sick. All seem to be suffering with dysentery. It makes you so weak. These rest trenches are not by any means safe as shells keep coming over here. One killed some mules just now, but no men. One hears of rumours here of a peace conference going on, but I expect it is a yarn. You hear nothing else but them. I wish it was true. It seems as though I have been here years already. At times you can scarcely imagine there is a war on here; it is so quiet. They you get a rude awakening. Last night there was firing going on all night. To-day does not seem like Sunday. I suppose the casualty list of our regiment has been published by this time. I wish we could find out where the missing are. It is bad enough to lose men, but 'missing' might mean anything.

Lance Sergeant Alfred Jones to his parents

As mentioned by Lance Sergeant Alfred Jones, the Isle of Wight Rifles were reorganised into three companies. The report attached to the Isle of Wight Rifles War Diary for August 1915 wrote the following:

> At this time the C.O. decided to re-organise the Battalion into three Companies instead of four. Two of the old Companies were to remain in their original formation, but the remaining two were to be organised as one and

placed under an Officer who had never served with either. The result was complete confusion.[167]

At the time of the battalion's re-organisation, the Isle of Wight Rifles had lost a significant number of Officers and Other Ranks through both combat and sickness and so the idea of re-forming into three companies is understandable but as far as the Officer who wrote the report was concerned, the re-structuring made matters worse.

The fighting that both Corporal James and Lance Sergeant Jones referred to in their letter was the further allied offensive on Hill 60 which began at 1am and was launched by the 10th Light Horse of the Australian Army. Some trenches were taken by the 10th Light Horse and they created a defensive barricade using sandbags. However, the Turks fought back fiercely. They launched three counterattacks in the vicinity and pushed the 5th Connaught Rangers out of the trench that they were holding but were unable to make more progress as the 18th Battalion of the 5th Australian Brigade reinforced the position. The end result of the combat was that despite more ground having been taken by the Allies, the Turks had not been fully dislodged from Hill 60.[168]

Around 8pm, the Isle of Wight Rifles were on the move again. This time to relieve the 10th Londons from their positions at the side of Salt Lake.[169]

30th August 1915

The Isle of Wight Rifles continued to man the trenches by Salt Lake and were joined by Captain T Flynn, a doctor from the 31st

---

[167] The Officer's Report attached to the Isle of Wight Rifles' War Diary August 1915
[168] Gallipoli, Peter Hart, Profile Books, p383/4
[169] Officer's Diary published in the Isle of Wight County Press, September 1915 and Isle of Wight Rifles War Diary

Field Ambulance, RAMC. He filled the void that had been left by Captain Raymond.

At 5.45pm four officers undertook bomb throwing training on the beach and at 7.45pm Sergeant John Rayner and 14 men left for a course on bomb-throwing at Hill 60[170]:

> I was detailed with a party of men to go to the trenches recently captured by the Australians, there to go through a course of bomb-throwing. At dusk we fell in and, with the Australian guide, proceeded to our destination, about four miles in advance, and to the right of the trenches we already occupied. We often had to call a halt whilst the guide made sure we were on the right track, as there had been instances of men losing their way and walking almost in the Turkish lines. Many a Turkish bullet sang by us or hit the earth with a dull plop, and we felt more comfortable when we entered a dry water-course, where we had a good rest. We reached the Australian rendezvous behind the firing line without a mishap, and were shown where we could rest for the night – a small ravine with dug-outs cut in the side as a precaution against stray bullets. Here in the open we saw several Australians who had been killed during the day and in the pale moonlight they looked more like sleeping than dead men. Three old school mates were with me, William Woodford, Walter Mew, and Charles Courtney. We were not far from the first-line trenches, and could plainly hear the explosion of the bombs, while the rifle fire from the snipers was continuous.[171]

Sgt Rayner's letter from Intermediate Base, E Med. to the Headmaster of Barton Council Boys' School on 3rd

---

[170] Officer's Diary published in the Isle of Wight County Press, September 1915 and Isle of Wight Rifles War Diary

[171] Sgt John Rayner's letter from Intermediate Base, E Med. to the Headmaster of Barton Council Boys' School on 3rd November 1915 and published in the Isle of Wight County press, 27th November 1915, p5

November 1915 and published in the Isle of Wight County press, 27th November 1915, p5

During the evening, the 5th and 7th Essex began their move to ANZAC.

Rifleman Stanley Small is the only known casualty for the 30th August 1915. He had injured his knee.

31st August 1915

August 31st was the birthday of the Officer who wrote the diary which was published in the Isle of Wight County Press. This Officer is possibly Captain Marsh. Unsurprisingly, he wrote, *'My birthday, and I don't want to spend another in a place like the Gallipoli Peninsula.'*[172]

Sergeant Rayner along with 14 men of the Isle of Wight Rifles began their training with the Australians:

> ….we went into the trenches, these being approached by a deep winding sap. I can tell you we did not want any warning to keep our heads down. These trenches, which had been captured from the Turks three days before, were of grand formation, being in three lines and connected with communication trenches, making it a real maze. Our men were placed at intervals along these trenches, and they soon fraternised with the Australians, who proved fine comrades. I had a position near where the communication trench which ran into the Turkish line was cut off. This will tell you how near we were to the Turks, for all that parted us was a rough barricade of dead bodies and sand-bags. We would slip up to the barricade, throw a bomb over, and pop back round the corner again. This had to be done constantly, for as soon

---

[172] Officer's Diary published in the Isle of Wight County Press, September 1915

as there was a lull over would come the bombs from the Turks, and they did a little damage at times....We were sometimes able to smother them with a sandbag, or overcoat, and sometimes to return them with compliments....it was a most difficult thing to get the wounded out, as the trenches were too narrow to allow the passage of a stretcher, so they had to be carried on a waterproof sheet or blanket. Things went on pretty well, as the trenches were well made, and very protective, but there were incidents that will want some forgetting. ....Whilst doing this work were shelled by the Turks from a range of hills which dominated our position.....It was a most dangerous policy to look over the parapet, as the snipers were not very far off, and so periscopes were used. In front and to the left was low ground, over which nothing could move without being detected. This was covered with low prickly bushes and trees at intervals, with a profusion of vegetation – no unlike our thistles. Nothing could be seen on the right except the parapet of the Turkish trench. At this point the opposing forces were only 20 yards apart, and the distance gradually widened until in places it was 500 yards. At one point the Turkish trench ran at right angles, and it was a favourite spot for our snipers. This same piece of trench afterwards came under the fire of our howitzer batteries, which soon altered its shape, the high explosive shells converting it into a heap of sandhills, and practically filling in the original trench. Many dead Turks lay between our lines. Whilst observing for one of the Australian snipers I had the glass of the periscope shot away, this being a favourite target practice of the Turkish snipers. We often had to go to the rear to get water from a well about a mile and a half behind, and then over would come the shrapnel from the Turks. We soon learnt to go in as small parties as possible and dubbed the place 'shrapnel gully.'[173]

Sgt Rayner's letter from Intermediate Base, E Med. to the Headmaster of Barton Council Boys' School on 3rd November 1915 and published in the Isle of Wight County press, 27th November 1915, p5

In the afternoon a French aeroplane, a Maurice Farman, flown by Sergeant Louis Garsonnin along with Sous-Lieutenant Jean Allier as the observer, ran out of fuel and performed an emergency landing between Lala Baba and the position of the Isle of Wight Rifles. The aircraft was immediately fired upon and it was estimated that the Turks fired 175 shells at it. Despite this, only one shell managed to hit the aircraft, damaging its tail, and a piece of shrapnel wounded the pilot. The observer avoided being hurt. Both Corporal James and the Officer who wrote the Diary that was published in the Isle of Wight County Press, mentioned the incident and intimated their surprise that the Turks could fire that many shells as the men were under the impression that the Turks had a shortage of ammunition.[174] [175]

At 10.30pm the Isle of Wight Rifles were relieved by the 9th Warwicks and returned to Lala Baba.

The Isle of Wight Rifles' War Diary reported the following losses for August 1915:

- 2 Officers killed, 14 OR killed.
- 2 Officers wounded, 139 OR wounded

---

[173] Sgt Rayner's letter from Intermediate Base, E Med. to the Headmaster of Barton Council Boys' School on 3rd November 1915 and published in the Isle of Wight County press, 27th November 1915, p5

[174] Officer's Diary published in the Isle of Wight County Press, September 1915 and Letter by Corporal G James dated 1st September 1915 and published in the Isle of Wight County Press on 25th September 1915, p6

[175] https://aegeanairwar.com/articles/came-down-suvla

- 9 Officers Missing, 135 OR missing.
- About 100 in Hospital suffering with dysentery and debility.

The actual death toll for the battalion was 10 Officers and 118 men. In addition to those wounded and sick, 12 men had been taken prisoner of which one later died of his wounds.

There were no known casualties for the 31st August 1915.

During the latter part of August, Captain Ellery was taken sick and spent a period of time recuperating. He returned to the battalion in early September.

ANZAC

SEPTEMBER 1915

1st September 1915

A period of rest was granted to the Isle of Wight Rifles back at Lala Baba. During the day they received orders to prepare to move to Kaiajak Aghala (also known as Hill 60) in the ANZAC sector at 8pm. However, this move was delayed as the Turks launched an attack at Kiretch Tepe Sirte and as a result the Isle of Wight Rifles had to be held back as a reserve.

There was one known casualty for the 1st September 1915 – Corporal Angus Lennox (previously Lance Corporal). He later wrote about his experience:

> At present I can only walk about for about 10 minutes at a time, and then only with difficulty. On the 1st September I was lying in my dug-out when a high explosive shell dropped a bit too close to be pleasant, and when it burst it took me, the dug-out and a lot more earth with it, and put me down about 50yds away. It was a miracle how I escaped, but only my face was damaged, except, of course, that I was a mess of bruises and sprains. Then concussion set in, and when I came round at the hospital I could remember nothing; my memory was gone. It is nearly well now, although there are blanks still. Of course, it has shattered my nerves – that was inevitable – but I was lucky, as this is not the only narrow shave I have had.[176]

Corporal Lennox was treated at a hospital in Malta and returned to active service.

---

[176] Cpl Lennox's letter, published in the Isle of Wight County Press, October 1915

2nd September 1915

At approximately 1.30am, the Isle of Wight Rifles left for ANZAC. They arrived in the area of the South Wales Borderers Gully around 3.30am and immediately had to dig. This area was subjected to shell fire from the Turks, including from a captured French 75mm gun, so work including fatigues had to be undertaken in the dark. The Isle of Wight Rifles would from this point onwards spend periods of time in the trenches at Hill 60.

In conflict with the battalion's war Diary, which has no mention of the battalion entering the trenches, the Officer of the Isle of Wight Rifles' diary entry states, *'at 7.30pm, relieved New Zealanders in trenches'* [177] For his entry on the 3rd September 1915, the Officer writes that 'A' Company replaced 'C' Company in the trenches. This suggests that 'C' Company were sent to the trenches on 2nd September 1915. In addition, the party under Sergeant Rayner were still in the trenches with the Australians on their bomb throwing course.

Rifleman Arthur Victor Salmon of 'C' Company was wounded in the head, chest and arms by a Turkish bomb. He was invalided to Malta and despite his wounding was able to return to active service. The Officers' Diary said that the Turks held a communication trench which was approximately 25 yards from the trenches held by the Isle of Wight Rifles and it was *'the centre of the bomb-throwing industry.'*[178] This is presumably where Rifleman Arthur Salmon was wounded.

---

[177] Officer's Diary published in the Isle of Wight County Press, September 1915
[178] Officer's Diary published in the Isle of Wight County Press, September 1915

3rd September 1915

'C' Company were relieved by 'A' Company in the trenches at Hill 60 during the evening and 150 men of the Isle of Wight Rifles joined the New Zealand Light Horse in the trenches at Cheshire Ridge. The battalion's machine guns at Hill 60 were put to use against small groups of advancing Turks.[179]

Shrapnel from one enemy shell wounded Bandsman Percy Purnell, Rifleman George James Langdon and Lance Corporal Norman Lansdowne Russell at Stafford Gully.[180] The shrapnel entered Lance Corporal Russell's right shoulder, smashed his right collar bone and passed across his chest. Lance Corporal Russell had the shrapnel extricated from his left breast and spent time at the 19th General Military Hospital in Alexandria. He was discharged from the Army on 4th October 1916 owing to illness.

Private Reginald James Brooks Butt treated Bandsman Purnell's wound. He recollected to his son that the shrapnel had entered 'Perce' Purnell's abdomen and ricocheted off his pelvis in a downward trajectory. Bandsman Purnell was invalided off Gallipoli. He was discharged from 2/8th Hants on 18th August 1916.

Rifleman Langdon was hit in his knee by the shrapnel and had it removed at a *'clearing hospital on the beach.'*[181] He was invalided off Gallipoli to Lemnos on a NZ hospital ship and had further treatment at the St. Elino hospital in Malta followed by Northwood Red Cross Hospital. He returned to serve with the Isle of Wight Rifles and survived the war.

Three men were also killed on the 3rd September 1915. Corporal John Cook was killed by a sniper whilst in the trenches and is

---

[179] Isle of Wight Rifles War Diary and Officer's Diary published in the Isle of Wight County Press, September 1915
[180] Isle of Wight County Press, 30th October 1915, p5
[181] Isle of Wight County Press, 30th October 1915, p5

buried at the 7th Field Ambulance Cemetery, Rifleman Frederick Hollis was killed and is commemorated on the Helles Memorial and Rifleman Owen Trevett was killed by a stray bullet whilst carrying water. Rifleman Trevett's parents received news of his death by a letter from Chaplain-Captain the Reverend J C L Blamires (NZ Armed Forces). The letter was subsequently published in the Isle of Wight County Press on 25th September 1915. Chaplain-Captain the Reverend J C L Blamires stated that 'Rifleman Trevett was carrying water and a stray bullet shot him through the chest' about 8.30pm on Friday 3rd September.[182] Chaplain-Captain the Reverend J C L Blamires grabbed his surgical bag and rushed up the hill to attend to Rifleman Trevett. On reaching Rifleman Trevett, he found a couple of New Zealand soldiers were already with Rifleman Trevett. Just two minutes later, Rifleman Trevett passed away.

Rifleman Arthur William Karley was admitted to a hospital on Mudros suffering with dysentery. He returned to active service and survived the war.

4th September 1915

Another day was spent in the trenches. The Isle of Wight Rifles' War Diary stated that the *'smell from dead bodies was very disagreeable and lack of disinfectant very apparent.'*[183] Private Reginald James Brooks Butt said that the dead bodies would blacken and swell until the stomachs would burst open. Invariably, the decaying bodies attracted swarms of flies:

> The flies are troubling us more than the Turks at present. We are now with the Australian and Indian troops. …..I think this out here will soon be over. ….We have a nice old job with the flies. We have a little jam at times; we

---

[182] Isle of Wight County Press, 25th September 1915.
[183] Isle of Wight Rifles War Diary, September 1915

> put it on our biscuits, eat with one hand, and keep the flies off with the other.[184]
>
> Rifleman Charlie White, September 1915

The heat would cause the jam to liquefy and as soon as it was poured onto the rock-hard biscuit a swarm of flies would try to land on the biscuit. The mixture of intense heat, flies and numerous dead rotting bodies helped disease to spread quickly and dysentery was rife. Shortly after writing the above letter to his friend, Rifleman Charlie White fell ill with dysentery. He subsequently died on 23rd September 1915.

Rifleman Trevett was buried in the morning by Chaplain-Captain the Reverend J C L Blamires. However, despite having been buried, Rifleman Trevett has no known grave and as a result he is commemorated on the Helles Memorial.

On the 4th September 1915, Corporal George James wrote the following letter to Mr Scott:

> We have been having a good rest cure lately in the reserve dug-outs, and are now with some Colonials. We are having good weather, but if we could only ex-communicate the flies! To remedy this evil somewhat I made a mosquito net out of an old respirator, and it appears to be answering the purpose very well. We are getting plenty to eat now. For breakfast this morning we had a good thick rasher of bacon, with jam, biscuits, and a cup of tea. We have been from left to right of the line since our arrival, commencing in the centre, then going to the left, and then working across in stages. I see by a War Office report that 42,000 Welsh miners are out on strike. We have no details of course, but we think it pretty 'rotten' of them. The report states that at a conference they were given nearly all they asked for, so

---

[184] Isle of Wight County Press, 2nd October 1915, p8

I hope it is settled now. They ought to come out here on a 'bob' a day. We have had few casualties since the big advance, and all are merry and bright again. We are engaged in trench warfare now as the country is so difficult to advance over. The Turkish position is about 150 yards away from us, across a gully. I guess the old rug sellers have had about enough of it, for they are almost entirely on the defensive, and it is only the German influence which keeps them going. Every advance we make is going to be costly, but it is the only way, and the bayonet plays a more important part than the bullet.[185]

The gully mentioned could be Stafford Gully. With the Isle of Wight Rifles in close proximity to the Turks, casualties were inevitable. Rifleman Ronald Weaver was killed instantaneously by a shell and is buried at 7th Field Ambulance Cemetery. Bugler Sydney John Smees was wounded by a piece of shrapnel in the head. He was invalided off Gallipoli and admitted to the Bombay Hospital in Alexandria. As a result of the wounding, Bugler Smees was discharged from the Army on 10th December 1915. Rifleman George White 2304 was wounded by shrapnel in his left shoulder. He was discharged from the Army due to 'sickness' on 11th August 1916.

Further news from Gallipoli was printed in the Isle of Wight County Press on 4th September 1915. This included a casualty list, letters from the front and known information about some of the soldiers. The newspaper also reported that Sergeant Herbert Whittington and Rifleman Arthur Downer were being held prisoners in Constantinople.

News from the prisoners of war gradually reached home. Rifleman Robert Hayles' letter of 4th September 1915 to his

---

[185] Isle of Wight County Press, 2nd October 1915, p8

mother was published in the Isle of Wight County Press on 9th October 1915:

> I am quite well now and out of hospital, but we have not got to the English prisoners' camp yet. There are about 50 of us in this prison, all in one room, and I shall be glad to get moved, for we have nothing to do except sit about all day. It will be better when we get to the camp, and we shall get better food, so one of the officers told us. …..I should like a few Woodbines and some money, as we can spend it in camp, I understand.[186]

5th September 1915

At 7.30am the battalion was relieved from the trenches and at 8am a Communion service was held by Reverend Pierrepont Edwards MC. The men were kept occupied during the day and night by providing trench working parties.

The War Diary states that *'a large number of men were suffering from dysentery.'*[187] One of those men who fell ill with dysentery was Sergeant John Rayner. He had to be invalided off Gallipoli.

Rifleman Philip Evershed Chapman died due to the wounds he had sustained on 26th August 1915. He is buried at Pieta Military Cemetery in Malta.

6th September 1915

Captain John Fardell led a group of 150 men who went for trench warfare training with the Australians. The remainder of the men provided working parties for the trenches.[188]

---

[186] Isle of Wight County Press, 9th October 1915, p8
[187] Isle of Wight Rifles War Diary, September 1915
[188] Officer's Diary published in the Isle of Wight County Press, September 1915

Rifleman Alfred Thomas Morgan was wounded in the foot by shrapnel. He was invalided off Gallipoli and taken to Cairo for hospital treatment. He later returned to active service with the Isle of Wight Rifles.

7th September 1915

The Isle of Wight Rifles returned to the trenches at Hill 60 at 7am. Trench activity included sniping which was undertaken with the use of a periscope. The Turks would leave biscuit tins on their parados which would reflect the sun. If the biscuit tin went dark, it meant that a Turkish soldier's head was in the way and thus a target for the sniper. However, the Turks caught on and began to use a helmet on a stick to place between the tin and the sun, whilst using one of their own snipers to focus on the movement of the periscope.

Major Veasey made time to write a letter to the Editor of the Isle of Wight County Press:

> Sir,
>
> Doubtless by this time the casualties suffered by the battalion at present under my command have been made public. Much as I should like to do so, it is obviously impossible for me to write individually to the relations of our gallant comrades who have laid down their lives for their country. May I therefore be permitted to crave the indulgence of your columns to express our deepest sympathy for the relations and friends of the fallen in their great sorrow. I can only assure them that they worthily upheld the traditions of the Isle of Wight under conditions which might well have unnerved even the most hardened Regular troops. And if their glorious example has the effect of making others join, and thus provide us with reinforcements, which are sadly needed, they will not have fallen in vain.

>Yours faithfully
>
>A.C.T Veasey, Major
>
>O.C. 1/8th Hampshire Regiment
>
>("Princess Beatrice's" Isle of Wight Rifles)[189]

Given the large number of casualties sustained on the 12th August 1915 it is understandable that Major Veasey could not write to each individual's parents.

Another letter of interest was penned by one of the Isle of Wight Rifles' officers:

> Since my last letter we have been on the trek several times, and are now about eight miles from where we landed. We are occupying trenches with some Australians and New Zealanders who are putting us up to all the tips of trench warfare, for we are now in about a similar position out here to that in France, with the Turks' trenches about 50yds in front of us, so it is fairly exciting. I had to take the guns up into the fire-trench, and they have been there ever since. I was up with them for 72 hours on end. During that time I did not get a wink of sleep, as we had to be continually on the look-out for an attack, especially at night, whilst in the day-time, when you might get off for an hour or two, there are the flies – millions of them – and they seem to increase daily. They swarm over your food and into your tea, and give you no peace. I am afraid an anti-fly campaign, such as is conducted in England, would not be of much use. The bombs and trench mortars are a feature of this warfare, and they are being thrown from both sides day and night. The trench I was in was about 35yds from the Turks. Our mortars have been doing very good work, and the last

---

[189] Isle of Wight County Press, 25th September 1915, p6

night I was up there they blew up one of their bomb-proof shelters. I was relieved on Sunday by S_____, and have had two jolly good nights' rest. I shall be going up there again tonight for 48 hours. We are living like fighting cocks. We are having an issue of bread almost every day now, and are expecting some eggs in tomorrow. The Colonials are fine fellows and very hospitable. They cook some wonderful dishes, and seem to have a lot of food sent them privately from home. The Australians and New Zealanders took three trenches about a week ago, after a very severe fight, and when I was up in the fire-trench there were hundreds of dead Turks and our Colonials lying about, as, of course, nobody could get out to bury them.......The regiment has had several casualties since I last wrote, although all the officers are all right.[190]

This letter was probably written by Lieutenant Pittis as he was in charge of the Machine Gun Section.

The officer was clearly impressed with the Australians and New Zealanders. As a contrast, Private Reginald James Brooks Butt was not so keen on the Australians. He said that they would always try to sell alcohol and they would whinge. The selling of alcohol maybe did not go down too well with him as he had taken a pledge to not drink alcohol under the Temperance Movement. Private Reginald James Brooks Butt also stated that the Australians were not as disciplined as British troops and the Australians could be too gung-ho which sometimes got them into difficulty. However, despite his views, a number of men in their letters appeared to both like and respect the Australians.

During the night, the Turks threw approximately ten bombs into the centre section of the Isle of Wight Rifles' positions. Thankfully there was no serious damage as the bombs had a long

---

[190] Isle of Wight County Press, 2nd October 1915 p8

fuse which allowed the men to throw overcoats over the bombs and thus dampen the explosions.[191]

There were no known casualties for the battalion on 7th September 1915.

8th September 1915

After 24 hours in the trenches at Hill 60, the Isle of Wight Rifles were relieved at 7am. The officer's diary notes that they had little chance to rest as sleeping at night in the trenches was not allowed and during the day the battalion had to provide working parties.

Whilst in the trenches, Sergeant Percy Hobbs was wounded in the leg by shrapnel. He was invalided off Gallipoli and spent time at a hospital in Malta before returning to active service.

Rifleman John Beaumont was admitted onto Her Majesty's Hospital Ship Assaye suffering with a *'disordered action of the heart.'*[192] As a result of this, he was discharged from the Army on 11th July 1916.

9th September 1915

Once again, working parties for the trenches were provided by the Battalion.

Lance Corporal Percy Stay was invalided off Gallipoli suffering from dysentery and an enlarged Thyroid Gland.

10th September 1915

Major Veasey was invalided off Gallipoli to Mudros suffering with dysentery. He was subsequently admitted to a hospital in Malta for further treatment. Command of the battalion was

---

[191] Isle of Wight Rifles War Diary, September 1915 and Officer's Diary published in the Isle of Wight County Press, September 1915
[192] www.forces-war-records.co.uk: Military Hospitals Admissions and Discharge Registers WW1

passed to Captain Ellery who had just recently returned to the frontline after a bout of illness.

The battalion provided working parties for the trenches and Rifleman William Sharpe was killed in action. He is buried at the 7th Field Ambulance Cemetery.

11th September 1915

At 7am the Isle of Wight Rifles relieved the 5th Suffolks in the trenches at Hill 60. They remained in these trenches until 5.30pm when they were relieved by the 1/4th Northants. The planned bombardment of Hill 60 at 6pm was cancelled.[193]

Rifleman Alfred Victor George Woodford died of wounds. He has no known grave and is commemorated on the Helles Memorial.

Sunday 12th September 1915

A Communion service was held at 8am and the rest of the day was spent preparing for a planned move to temporarily join the 161st Brigade, 54th Division. The Isle of Wight Rifles set off at dusk and arrived at 10pm in the gully to the side of Australia Valley. One of the battalion's companies took over the reserve trenches that were being held by the 7th Essex.

Corporal Frederick Blow had a lucky escape from a bursting shell:

> I am keeping fit and well. Things are much quieter with us now, except a few shells which burst amongst us occasionally. I had my rifle smashed on Sunday, and the fellow I was talking to was wounded rather badly, so you see we have to look out a bit sometimes.

---

[193] Isle of Wight Rifles War Diary, September 1915

Corporal Blow's letter to his mother dated 14th September 1915[194]

The only known wounding for the day was Lance Corporal Percy Boxall. He was wounded by shrapnel so he may have been the man that Corporal Blow referred to in his letter. Lance Corporal Boxall was invalided off Gallipoli and received further treatment at a hospital in Malta. He later returned to active service with the Isle of Wight Rifles.

In addition to the wounding of Lance Corporal Boxall, Rifleman Percy Reed was given medical treatment for heat stroke.

13th September 1915

The Isle of Wight Rifles were employed as reserve for the 161st Brigade and provided working parties. They also prepared further dug-outs in the gully that they were occupying. The battalion's war diary estimated the battalion's strength to be 450 men and commented that each day roughly 100 men were reporting sick. Despite a shortage of medical supplies, the majority of the men received some form of treatment for the illnesses (mainly dysentery and diarrhoea) that they were suffering with.[195]

One of the battalion's companies held *'a short line of reserve trenches at the head of the gully,'* during the evening and continued to do so on a rotation basis over the subsequent evenings of occupying the gully.[196] Sergeant Harry Hall, in a letter to his wife on 13th September 1915 described the gully as *'a very pretty spot.'* He also wrote, *'Fellows out here who have been to France say that the Western Front is a picnic compared*

---

[194] Isle of Wight County Press, 2nd October 1915, p8
[195] Isle of Wight Rifles War Diary, September 1915
[196] Officer's Diary published in the Isle of Wight County Press, September 1915

to here,'*¹⁹⁷* which is a testament to how tough it must have been at Gallipoli.

Sergeant Arthur Marlow was no longer with the Isle of Wight Rifles. He had been transferred to act as a chef for Brigade Headquarters, and in his words, *'to practice his culinary knowledge on bully beef and biscuits.'*¹⁹⁸

Rifleman Arthur Eldridge is the known casualty for the day. He was wounded in his right wrist which resulted in him being discharged from the Army on 24th April 1916.

14th September 1915

Between the 14th and the 17th September 1915 the Isle of Wight Rifles remained at the same location and provided working parties for the 161st Brigade. Development of the gully was being made by various units and as part of the development a road was being built.

According to the Officers' diary, the battalion's Officers were as follows:

- Commanding Officer: Captain Ellery
- Adjutant: Lieutenant Seely
- Quarter-Master: Lieutenant Giddens
- Machine Gun Officer: Lieutenant Pittis
- 'A' Company: Captain Marsh, Second Lieutenant Shelton and Second Lieutenant Weeding
- 'B' Company: Captain Fardell, Second Lieutenant S Ratsey and Second Lieutenant Kingdom
- 'C' Company: Second Lieutenant Murphy.

---

[197] Sergeant Hall's letter to his wife dated 13th September and published on page 8 of the Isle of Wight County Press, 9th October 1915.
[198] Sergeant Marlow's letter of 13th September published on page 8 of the Isle of Wight County Press, 16th October 1915

Second Lieutenant Fox was not with the battalion as he had been appointed as a bombing officer.[199]

Lieutenant Walter Felix Read passed away in a hospital in Alexandria, Egypt. He had been invalided off Gallipoli suffering with dysentery but subsequently fell ill with appendicitis at Alexandria which resulted in his death. He is buried at Alexandria (Chatby) Military and War Memorial Cemetery, Egypt.

15th September 1915

There were no known casualties on 15th September 1915.

16th September 1915

Rifleman Albert Newnham reported ill with myalgia. He recovered and returned to active service.

17th September 1915

Rifleman Albert Victor Salter was wounded and unfortunately passed away on the 20th September 1915 as a result of the wounding. He was 17 years old and is buried at Embarkation Pier Cemetery, Gallipoli.

Rifleman Sydney Pierce was admitted to hospital with dysentery. He was discharged from the Army due to 'sickness' on 29th July 1916.

18th September 1915

Captain John Fardell reported sick with Enteric Fever. He was initially invalided to Mudros and subsequently to Alexandria, Egypt. On returning to England, Captain Fardell was transferred to the 2/8th Hants.

---

[199] Officer's Diary published in the Isle of Wight County Press, September 1915

An attack by the Turks began at 4.30pm. During the assault, two of the battalion's companies held the reserve trenches whilst the remaining company was kept as a reserve. With the aid of naval gun fire, the Turks were successfully defeated and at 5.45pm the battalion was told to stand down.[200]

Rifleman Arthur George Silsbury was killed in action and Rifleman George Chick died of wounds on 18th September 1915. Both are buried at the 7th Field Ambulance Cemetery.

19th September 1915

The Isle of Wight Rifles were granted a day of rest. During the day the men were informed that it was believed that thirteen of the brigade's officers were being held as prisoners at Constantinople.[201]

Corporal George James wrote the following letter to his Bible Class back on the Isle of Wight:

> Sunday September 19th – A few lines from a dug-out in Gallipoli. I am glad to say that I am fit and well at present, as are all the St. John's men, except Sid Porter, who was posted as missing after the advance.
>
> At present our battalion is having as much rest as the flies, fatigues, and occasional turns in the trenches will allow.
>
> I can assure you how very much we appreciate now the Sunday afternoon gatherings we had at home, and we wish, that we could just flit home to the Legh Richmond-hall for one brief hour each week.

---

[200] Isle of Wight Rifles War Diary, September 1915
[201] Rifleman Francis Damp's letter of 21st September 1915 and published in the Isle of Wight County Press, 16th October 1915, p8.

Our baptism of fire was certainly rather severe for fresh troops, but I can honestly say that our chaps acquitted themselves splendidly, and many deeds were done by them that day, unnoticed, which were worthy of the best traditions of the British arms.

Mr Ashmead Bartlett's description of the nature of the ground at Anzac, where we are now, is a very faithful one. Looking round it seems impregnable; every hill is a natural fortress. But we have made good progress, and are well established now.

To both sides it is a case of the invisible enemy, though our chaps get fed up with the 'trench crawl,' which consists of maintaining a stooping attitude when moving along a trench or sap, so as to prevent any part of the anatomy appearing over the top. When we were 'green' to the game we were very much troubled and worried by the snipers, but we soon found that the only antidote to this was anti-sniping. This sometimes entails an hour's careful watching through a periscope or loophole before the offender can be located and a full stop put to his career. Searching with machine-guns, though, is the most successful way of dealing with them.

I am now in the unfortunate positions of platoon-commander and sergeant combined, as we have lost our officer and platoon-sergeant, but I think I'll struggle through all right.

We get good food now, but the water is scanty.

With my best wishes for the Bible Class, gymnasium, and shooting club, and to your health to enable you to carry on until we come back and after.[202]

---

[202] Isle of Wight County Press, 16th October 1915, p6

Rifleman Arthur John Greenham passed away from dysentery at Imtarfa Hospital, Malta. He is buried at Pieta Military Cemetery.

20th September 1915

On the 20th September 1915 the Isle of Wight Rifles received welcome mail from home which included copies of the Isle of Wight County Press. In addition, news was received from Alexandria regarding a number of men who had been missing since the 12th August - eighteen men had been reported as in hospital with wounds and twelve as having died of their wounds. The Isle of Wight Rifles' War Diary noted that of those men invalided from Gallipoli either due to illness or wounding, none had returned to the battalion.[203]

According to a letter written by Signaller (Rifleman) Hubert Buckett on 21st September 1915, the Turks attempted another advance but *'were easily repulsed.'*[204] There is no mention of this event in the battalion's War Diary but the War Diary did mention that the battalion provided working parties again.

Corporal Percy Wills of the battalion's machine gun section began writing a letter to his mother which he completed on the 22nd September 1915. In it, he provides a good insight into some of the tasks the men were given whilst they were with the 161st Brigade:

> Here we are again! Still enjoying life and health in spite of all the Turks can do. Of course it is a dangerous life and a rough one, but it has its compensations. Look at the excitement and the experiences we get! They easily outweigh all the disadvantages, and give one a broader

---

[203] Isle of Wight Rifles' War Diary, September 1915.
[204] Rifleman Hubert Buckett's letter to his mother dated 21st September 1915 and published in the Isle of Wight County Press, 16th October 1915, p8.

view of the world. I don't think I would have missed it even if I had known of all the hardships to be gone through.

For the past few days we have been away from the firing line, but we get plenty to do to fill up the time. In the morning we have instruction on the machine guns to keep us in form. One can soon forget, there's so much of it. Then there is trenching to be done, supplies to be fetched from the base, roads to be made, and a hundred other jobs to be done. In one place our engineers are tunnelling through a hill, and several times the machine gunners have been told off to help in that, so you see the time does not hang much, and it is all very interesting.

Since we landed everything has improved wonderfully. What was once a barren spot is now getting quite civilised. At one place we have laid down a tramline for supplies. Of course the cars are only drawn by mules, but it makes the transport lots easier. There are thousands of mules about, and sometimes they cause lots of fun, especially when they have decided that they have done enough for one day. You know what a mule can be, but the Indians who are in charge of them soon make them alter their minds.

I've got some boiled rice and raisins for tea, so you can guess I shall be busy.

I must thank you for the County Press. It seems like old times to be able to read of how things are going on, and as you may imagine we don't miss much.

We get alarms now and again, and on Saturday, the 18th, we had to rush up to the trenches with our guns as the Turks were trying to attack us, but beyond their wasting a lot of ammunition nothing came of it and a few shells from our warships soon quieted them down.

> If anyone asks how I am tell them I'm in the best of health and quite enjoying myself, with plenty of 'big game' shooting to be had.[205]

Rifleman Albert Victor Salter died as the result of the wounds he received on 17th September. He was just 17 years old and is buried at Embarkation Pier Cemetery.

21st September 1915

The Isle of Wight Rifles continued to provide working parties and were informed that four officers and two hundred riflemen would be detached to the 1/5th Essex on 23rd September. They were scheduled to replace the 4th Essex in the frontline.[206]

Around this time, Rifleman Denness wrote a letter to his wife which was published in the Isle of Wight County Press on 6th November 1915. Some extracts from the letter are below:

> I cannot say I am in the best of health, as I have been pretty badly run down lately, and my nerves or something have gone wrong. All the chaps are like it. We have had enough of this. Our division has been out here longer than any other, and I think we are the only Territorials here now.
>
> The Turks are nearly starved; they come over to us every day saying they are all 'fed up.' One came into our line yesterday; he was wounded and in an awful state. He was so far gone that he could not eat anything at first. All he had on him was a piece of dry bread and some berries; he said they only get one meal a day and that was only

---

[205] Letters by Corporal Percy Wills (machine gun section) to his mother dated Sept 20th & 22nd and published in the Isle of Wight County Press, 16th October 1915, p8.
[206] Isle of Wight Rifles War Diary.

bread and cheese at 8 o'clock at night, and they are, like us, always at work. I see in one letter in the paper that the Turks fire on our hospitals. That is not right; they only did it once, and then they sent a man down to apologise. It was not their fault, as we had guns in front of it and ships behind, so you could not blame them for it. I am sure there are no cleaner fighters in the world than the Turks.

The only thing we do not like is that we cannot get our morning wash and shave, and a good bath now and again.[207]

Most of the letters written home were relatively upbeat considering the trials the men were enduring. The men presumably did not want to worry their loved ones and so put on a brave face. To find a letter with such honesty really makes the reality of the mental strain at Gallipoli hit home. It wasn't just the British and Allied soldiers facing severe strain. As evidenced by the letter, the Turks were suffering extreme hardships too.

There were no records of casualties on the 21st September 1915.

22nd September 1915

Once again, the Isle of Wight Rifles provided working parties.

There were no records of casualties on the 22nd September 1915.

23rd September 1915

The Isle of Wight Rifles detachment, which comprised 'A' and 'C' Companies, left to join the 1/5th Essex at 6.30pm. Below is the diary entry for the 1/5th Essex on 23 September 1915:

Place: Opposite Hill 100

---

[207] Rifleman Denness' letter to his wife published in the Isle of Wight County Press on 6th November 1915.

Summary of Events and Information: Took over the right subsection of the trenches held by the 161st Brigade from the 1/4th Essex. Two companies of the 1/8th Hants being attached to us to make up the necessary strength. Divided subsection into 2 parts. The right half to be garrisoned by 1/5th Essex, the left by 1/8th Hants. Relief completed by 2100 o'clock.[208]

Two deaths occurred and one man reported sick on the 23rd September 1915. Sergeant Cecil Hastings Wales died in a Maltese hospital of Typhoid and Rifleman Charlie White died of dysentery on a hospital ship headed to Malta. Both are buried at Pieta Military Cemetery, Malta. Rifleman Charles Owen Coulbert was invalided off Gallipoli suffering with dysentery and fever.

24th September 1915

Those of the Isle of Wight Rifles that were attached to the 1/5th Essex remained in the trenches and the rest of the battalion continued providing working parties.

Rifleman Reginald Harold Morey was wounded. On recovering from his wounding, he returned to active service.

25th September 1915

A demonstration was made by 'ANZAC' to the right of the trenches held by the 1/5th Essex and two companies of the Isle of Wight Rifles. This caused the Turks to respond and expend a lot of ammunition.[209]

There were no records of casualties on the 25th September 1915.

---

[208] 1/5th Essex War Diary, September 1915
[209] 1/5th Essex War Diary, September 1915

26th September 1915

During the evening, the trenches held by the Turks at Chunuk Bair were targeted with high explosive shells. There was also *'considerable fighting with bombs etc. on Hill 60'* reported on the 26th. [210]

The Isle of Wight Rifles War Diary recorded that 2 men were wounded (one of those being Rifleman Reginald Morey) and 44 men were sent to hospital during the week 20th September 1915 to 26th September 1915. It was also noted that 4 men had returned to the battalion from hospital. This left the battalion with 430 Other Ranks and with Lieutenant Weeding reporting ill, the battalion had 9 Officers.[211]

27th September 1915

Between the 27th September and the 30th September, the Isle of Wight Rifles continued providing working parties and two companies remained in the trenches with the 1/5th Essex.

Rifleman Frank Bax passed away from dysentery on a hospital ship and was buried at sea. He is commemorated on the Helles Memorial.

28th September 1915

Rifleman Oliver James Morgan was shot in his right foot. The wound appears to have not been too severe as Rifleman Morgan was promoted to the rank of acting Corporal on 12th December 1915.

29th September 1915

In the trenches, the 1/5th Essex and the two companies of the Isle of Wight Rifles were subjected to fire from the captured French 75 gun. The 1/5th Essex's War Diary states that there was *'some*

---

[210] 1/5th Essex War Diary, September 1915
[211] Isle of Wight Rifles' War Diary, September 1915

damage to the parapet etc. Own 6" Howitzer registered with 12 Rounds on trenches on "Hill 100" doing some damage.[212]

There are no recorded casualties for the 29th September 1915.

30th September 1915

Corporal Wills had a lucky escape on the 30th September. *'A shrapnel case, weighing about 6lb, came down about 3 inches from his foot'* but did no harm to him.[213]

Rifleman William North died of Enteric Fever on the Gallipoli peninsula. The location of his grave is unknown and as such he is commemorated on the Helles Memorial.

The Isle of Wight Rifles' War Diary recorded that the battalion had 9 Officers and 403 Other Ranks on its strength.

---

[212] 1/5th Essex War Diary, September 1915
[213] Corporal Wills' letter to parents on 1st October 1915 referring to the previous day, published in the Isle of Wight County Press, 30th October 1915, p5.

OCTOBER 1915

1st October 1915

The Isle of Wight Rifles continued to provide working parties and two of the battalion's companies remained with the 1/5th Essex in the trenches in the vicinity of Hill 100 and Sandbag Ridge.

Rifleman Sidney Charles Day was wounded in the left knee by shrapnel. The wounding resulted in him being discharged from the Army on 16th May 1916.

2nd October 1915

Plans to relieve the companies of the 1/6th Essex on 4th October with the remaining companies of both the 1/6th Essex and the Isle of Wight Rifles were communicated to the battalion.[214]

Rifleman George Henry Ash passed away from Enteric and Pneumonia at a hospital in Malta. He is buried at Pieta Military Cemetery.

3rd October 1915

Shell fire from the captured French 75 gun was noted by the 1/5th Essex's War Diary.

Rifleman Charles Henry Guy was reported as being ill with Enteric and Dysentery and Rifleman Ernest Saunders was admitted onto H.M. Hospital Ship Assaye suffering with diarrhoea. Both men returned to serve with the Isle of Wight Rifles.

---

[214] Isle of Wight Rifles' War Diary, October 1915

4th October 1915

At 5.45am the Isle of Wight Rifles relieved those of the 1/6th Essex who were holding the trenches that *'were situated about 800 yards to the right of Hill 60.'*[215] The battalion was joined by the remaining half of the 1/6th Essex.

Around 9am, after an artillery exchange, the Turks unleashed heavy rifle fire on the positions to the right of the Isle of Wight Rifles. Two accounts of this event are below:

> We had a bit of a flare up again this morning. It started by one of our shells knocking down some sandbags and exposing a lot of Turks, and of course, our chaps in the trenches opposite them started blazing away, and then they started all along the line; bullets must have come out in sheets, judging by the sound they made. That and the noise of the shells bursting everywhere was enough to make one deaf, and you had to shout to make yourself heard. However, it did not last more than an hour, and now it is quiet again.

Corporal Wills' letter to his parents dated 4th October 1915 [216]

> We are taking our turn in the trenches, having started yesterday, and I have just done 24 hours. We had just had breakfast dished out of bread, jam and tea, when the Turks started firing all along the line, and there was a scramble.
>
> ….It only lasted about half an hour, and then all was quiet again. I was near a loophole, and we could stand and watch the shells from our warships bursting in the Turks' trenches and them run like mad, and we would 'peck' at them.

---

[215] Isle of Wight Rifles' War Diary, October 1915
[216] Isle of Wight County Press, 30th October 1915, p5

Rifleman Ernest Walter Parsons' letter dated 5th October 1915 [217]

Despite the intensity of the shell fire and rifle fire it appears that no one from the Isle of Wight Rifles were wounded. There were however, three incidents of illness:

- Rifleman Joseph Johns was admitted onto H.M. Hospital Ship Assaye with Enteritis;
- Rifleman Albert Stone was admitted on to H.M. Hospital Ship Assaye with Pyrexia of unknown origin; and
- Rifleman Albert Charles Mills was admitted into a hospital on the Gallipoli peninsula with suspected Diphtheria.

All three men returned to active service.

5th October 1915

The main body of the battalion spent their time *'improving the trenches and making new fire positions.'*[218]

Lance Corporal James Rackett who had recently recovered from a wounding was admitted into the Canadian Hospital on Mudros suffering with dysentery.

6th October 1915

The Isle of Wight Rifles War Diary states that from the 6th October to the 8th October there was the *'usual sniping'* and the battalion *'occasionally had casualties.'*[219]

Lieutenant Pittis was invalided off Gallipoli with Enteric Fever on a hospital ship bound for Gibraltar. On recovering, he returned to serve with the battalion in Egypt and Palestine and was killed during the Second Battle of Gaza on 19th April 1917.

---

[217] Isle of Wight County Press 6th November 1915, p5
[218] Isle of Wight Rifles War Diary, October 1915
[219] Isle of Wight Rifles War Diary, October 1915

7th October 1915

Fourteen of the men (Other Ranks) who had been wounded during the advance on Anafarta Ridge rejoined the battalion. In addition, the battalion welcomed eight officers who had been posted to them from the 8th battalion of the Wiltshire Regiment.

There were no reported casualties on the 7th October 1915.

8th October 1915

During the evening there was a *'violent storm of wind and rain.'*[220]

Rifleman William George Young was killed in action. He is buried at the 7th Field Ambulance cemetery.

9th October 1915

The Isle of Wight Rifles' War Diary recorded the following:

> Day passed quietly but at 7.30pm we received information that the enemy had opened a gas cylinder on the Indian Brigade lines left of Hill 60; nothing was however noticed from our position. Received information that the remainder of the Battalion would join us on the 11th and relieve the two companies of the 1/6 Essex which are now attached. Whilse these two Companies have been away attached to another Unit it has been more difficult to keep the organisation and work of the Battalion in touch and it appears wherever possible it would be better to keep Units together.[221]

At some point during the day, in the trenches occupied by the 1/5th Essex and 'A' and 'C' Companies of the Isle of Wight

---

[220] 1/5th Essex War Diary, October 1915
[221] Isle of Wight Rifles' War Diary, October 1915

Rifles, an enemy aircraft flew low over their position. It was targeted by a machine gun but to no avail.[222]

Rifleman Sidney Charles Ginger and Rifleman George Frederick Walker were killed in action. Both are buried in the 7th Field Ambulance Cemetery.

Rifleman Thomas Twitchen was invalided off Gallipoli to Malta. He rejoined the Isle of Wight Rifles in Egypt on 29th December 1915.

10th October 1915

Another day was spent in the trenches by all the companies of the Isle of Wight Rifles in their respective positions.

Rifleman Albert Charles Mills was discharged from hospital and returned to the battalion.

There were no reported casualties on the 10th October 1915.

11th October 1915

Concerns were mounting over the ability to continue the Gallipoli campaign with the onset of winter, the overall poor health of the men and the degradation of vital equipment. This led Lord Kitchener to ask General Sir Ian Hamilton on his view on the number of possible casualties from an evacuation and in response General Sir Ian Hamilton made it clear that he opposed an evacuation.[223]

'A' and 'C' Companies rejoined the Isle of Wight Rifles, taking over the positions that 'A' and 'C' Companies of the 1/6th Essex had been holding. It was noted that the weather was turning – the

---

[222] 1/5th Essex War Diary, October 1915
[223] Gallipoli, Peter Hart, Profile Books, p395

nights were becoming very cold and there was a North Easterly wind.[224]

There were no reported casualties on 11th October 1915.

12th October 1915

Serge clothing and a *'part issue of winter underclothing'* was given to the men in the trenches. This must have been most welcome as the weather remained cold with a strong North Easterly wind.[225]

Rifleman Stanford Fisk fell ill and boarded a hospital ship at Anzac Cove. He was invalided to Cairo, Egypt. Rifleman Fisk returned to serve with the battalion and was killed in the Third Battle of Gaza on 2nd November 1917.

13th October 1915

General Birdwood visited the line held by the 163rd Brigade.[226]

There were no reported casualties for the 13th October 1915.

14th October 1915

On the 14th October 1915 the decision to replace General Sir Ian Hamilton with General Sir Charles Monro was made by the Dardanelles Committee.[227]

Back at Gallipoli, it remained cold due to the North Easterly wind and the Isle of Wight Rifles were involved in teaching five Officers and 120 men of the 1st Norfolk Yeomanry in trench duties.[228]

---

[224] Isle of Wight Rifles' War Diary, October 1915
[225] Isle of Wight Rifles' War Diary, October 1915
[226] 163rd Brigade War Diary, October 1915
[227] Gallipoli, Peter Hart, Profile Books, p396
[228] Isle of Wight Rifles' War Diary, October 1915

Captain Ellery was invalided off Gallipoli to Cairo, Egypt and as a result, command of the battalion was transferred to Captain Marsh.

15th October 1915

Another cold windy day was spent in the trenches.

There were no reported casualties on the 15th October 1915.

16th October 1915

It was Private Reginald James Brooks Butt's 18th birthday and it was not to be a quiet one in the trenches:

> A demonstration was carried out in conjunction with the ANZAC Army Corps at 4 'o'clock this morning but failed to draw fire from the enemy. Sgt Ellaway was wounded whilst on observation duty during the demonstration. Weather much milder again. Usual trench routine carried out and no movement of any importance were recorded by our Observers. The signallers of the 1/6 Essex were relieved by the signal section of the 1/5 Essex under Lt Womersley.[229]

Sergeant Percy Ellaway died of his wounds later in the day. He is buried at Embarkation Pier Cemetery.

17th October 1915

On the 17th October 1915, the headquarters at Imbros was vacated by General Sir Ian Hamilton and Field Marshall Birdwood was placed in temporary command.[230]

Lance Corporal Walter John Butcher passed away at the 21st General Hospital, Alexandria. He is buried at Alexandria (Chatby) Military and War Memorial Cemetery in Egypt.

---

[229] Isle of Wight Rifles' War Diary, October 1915
[230] Gallipoli, Peter Hart, Profile Books, p396

18th October 1915

Yet another day was spent in the trenches and it was reported that it was *'very quiet along the whole front.'*[231]

There are no known casualties for the 18th October 1915.

19th October 1915

Second Lieutenants William Gordon Harker, Alfred Olaf Hytten, Charles Arthur Pocock and Percy John Shelly joined the battalion in the trenches. They had previously been with the reserve battalion of the Isle of Wight Rifles.

Rifleman Robert Sothcott was wounded in the knee by a piece of shrapnel. He went on to serve with the 4th Hants and then the 17th Hants but was discharged on 2nd February 1917 due to issues with his knee.

20th October 1915

The battalion's new officers were examined by the Medical Officer and Lieutenant Seely was sent to ANZAC to collect cash from the Field Cashier.[232]

Rifleman George Dimmer was killed in action. He is buried at the 7th Field Ambulance Cemetery.

21st October 1915

The 1/5th Essex relieved the Isle of Wight Rifles from posts 1-5 and the battalion then *'took over posts 14-23 from the 1st Norfolk Yeomanry.'*[233]

Lieutenant Fox was wounded whilst throwing an enemy bomb back out of the trench that he was in. The bomb exploded when

---

[231] Isle of Wight Rifles' War Diary, October 1915
[232] Isle of Wight Rifles' War Diary, October 1915
[233] Isle of Wight Rifles' War Diary, October 1915

it reached the top of the parapet, severely injuring him and resulting in the loss of an eye.

22nd October 1915

It continued to be cold with some rainfall.

There are no known casualties for the 22nd October 1915.

23rd October 1915

Corporal Charles Whitticom was invalided off Gallipoli on Hospital Ship Glenart Castle suffering with jaundice. He later served with the RFC/RAF and survived the war but sadly passed away on 22nd November 1918.

24th October 1915

There are no known casualties for the 24th October 1915.

25th October 1915

Better weather was noted in the Isle of Wight Rifles' War Diary.

CSM Minns rejoined the battalion following recovering from his wounding.

26th October 1915

The battalion carried out its usual routine and the weather was noted as *'cold and dull.'*[234]

There are no known casualties for the 26th October 1915.

27th October 1915

Warmer weather returned to the Peninsula. At 11.45am the Turks launched a 10-minute artillery bombardment of shrapnel shells on the trenches and the gullies next to the position of the Isle of

---

[234] Isle of Wight Rifles' War Diary, October 1915

Wight Rifles. It was suspected that 10pounders were used. No casualties were recorded from this or for the day overall.[235]

28th October 1915

After a long period in the trenches, the 1/6th Essex relieved the Isle of Wight Rifles. The battalion moved to Inglewood Gully where they improved the dug-outs and provided fatigues.[236]

There are no known casualties for the 28th October 1915.

29th October 1915

Continuation of fatigues and improving dug-outs was undertaken by the Isle of Wight Rifles.[237]

Lance Corporal Thomas Alexander who had been admitted into a hospital in Malta with cellulitis in his hand and right foot passed away. He is buried at Pieta Military Cemetery, Malta.

30th October 1915

A swift visit of the Peninsula was undertaken by General Sir Charles Monro on 30th October. After visiting ANZAC, Helles and Suvla, General Sir Charles Monro concluded that the situation was untenable and a breakthrough at Gallipoli would not be possible. He therefore recommended an evacuation to Lord Kitchener by telegram.

Back on the Isle of Wight, an amusing article was posted in the Isle of Wight County Press which included sections of a letter by Corporal Walter Warren:

> OUR FIGHTING EIGHTH'S HUMOUR
>
> As indicating the irrepressibly good spirits of the I.W. Rifles, now styled the Fighting Eighth, "a letter to the

---

[235] Isle of Wight Rifles War Diary, October 1915
[236] Isle of Wight Rifles War Diary, October 1915
[237] Isle of Wight Rifles War Diary, October 1915

Sultan of Turkey," signed by Corpl. W. J. Warren, of Brading, has been sent to us. It acknowledges repeated messages in the form of whistling shells, humming bullets, and other kinds of "music," but comments on their delivery as being very bad, saying "we were watching a little of your firing the other day at an aeroplane, which was stationary behind our lines, and after sending over 157 shells (they must have been sea shells), the machine was only covered with dust. With a bit of luck, old chap, you ought to get the iron cross."

He encloses a suggested advertisement as follows: "Gallipoli House, well situated amongst undulated woods, and commanding lovely sea views, in extensive pleasure grounds, all on our own. Ten reception rooms, 14 bedrooms, four bathrooms (I don't think), with hot and cold supplies. Servants very polite and obliging. Rent for winter. Bullets, shrapnel, and high explosives are among the game to be found in the shooting grounds of Gallipoli. Absolutely freehold as long as you can hold it."[238]

The incident regarding the aeroplane occurred on 31st August 1915 and so this letter was most likely written during the first week of September.

There were no known casualties on 30th October 1915.

31st October 1915

Bishop Price held a communion service in Braans Gully and several of the battalion attended.

---

[238] Isle of Wight County Press, 30th October 1915, p5

Bugler Albert Downer was killed by a sniper whilst *'polishing his boots.'*[239] He is buried at the 7th Field Ambulance Cemetery, Gallipoli.

A shrapnel shell killed Rifleman Frederick Smith, wounded Corporal John Scott in the knee, wounded Rifleman Archibald Chandler in the ankle and wounded an artilleryman from the New Zealand Army. Both Corporal Scott and Rifleman Chandler recovered from their wounds and returned to active service.

Rifleman William Maybee was invalided off Gallipoli with dysentery. He spent time at hospitals in Gibraltar and then Devonport and was discharged from the Army on 18th August 1916.

---

[239] Isle of Wight in the Great War, M. J. Trow, Pen & Sword Military

NOVEMBER 1915

1st November 1915

Between the 1st and 5th November 1915, the Isle of Wight Rifles continued fatigues duty and improving dug-outs in Inglewood Gully.

2nd November 1915

On the 2nd November 1915, Captain Marsh wrote the following letter to Lieutenant Colonel Rhodes:

> I have opened your letter of the 6th ult, as Ellery left us on the 14th ult. He wrote a line from Alexandria on his arrival, but I have not heard from him or of him since. Other departures amongst the officers are: Pittis (invalided to England), Murphy, Ratsey, Pound (8th Wilts, attached to 8th Hants), Pocock, and Shelley. Our casualties for the month have been slight, with the average number of sick. We were relieved from our duty in the trenches on the 28th ult., and are at present in the rest gully. Things were quiet all the time we were up. I note what you say as to parcels from H.R.H. Princess Henry. They are not yet to hand, but when they arrive I will have the contents distributed. We have had one case of cigarettes and tobacco from the I.W. County Press. I acknowledged direct to the Editor. Inside each packet was a post-card, which the men filled in. These were ready addressed to the various donors. I omitted to include Fox in the casualty list. He was bombing officer for the 163rd Brigade, and got a piece of bomb in his eye – the left one. It is feared he will lose the use of it. The Brigadier had previously recommended him for consistent work, and we had an official message yesterday that he had been awarded the Military Cross. Major Veasey should be in England by now. He sailed

from Malta on the 9th ult. Deptford is all right also Q.M. Giddens, Cooney, and Seely. We have an exceedingly nice M.O. attached to us – a Canadian; he has only been on the Peninsula a fortnight. Nothing has been heard of the missing officers or men beyond what has already been officially reported. You will notice I have referred to some 8th Wilts officers attached to us. They belong to the New Army, and for some extraordinary reason were sent along to this battalion. Our own people – Duffield, Harrison, Phillips and Randall were sent to the 2nd Hants and Dublin Fusiliers.

We have had letters from Duffield and Harrison, and both say they are quite comfortable. The promised rainy season has now been postponed by the official prophets until January. November, we are told, is the finest month of the year, and so far the forecast has been correct. The past ten days have been perfect – bright sunshine, a gentle warm breeze, and warm nights. Prior to that we had a fortnight's rough weather – very cold, N.E. winds and rain on three or four days, but not in any quantity. The men are exceedingly well equipped now – serge clothing, flannel shirts, socks, pants, vests and soft winter caps. All the underwear is of excellent quality, the shirts from Canada, vests etc from Australia. There is also to be an issue of gloves or mittens, leather jerkins, and mufflers. There is now an E.F. canteen at Imbros. Purchases are made weekly. Things are sold to the men at cost price, and the money remitted with the next week's requisition. You can get tinned tomatoes, herrings, sardines, vinegar, chocolate, biscuits, salmon – in fact, almost anything usually sold in dry canteens. All the men have drawn one lot of pay, about 10s all round, so they have the money to buy what they want. Rations are very good now – bacon daily, fresh meat and bread every third day, onions, rice, jam, milk and bully ad lib. They now issue a boiled brand of bully, which is quite good – not in the least salt. It is difficult to suggest anything that the men are really in want of, but cigarettes are always welcome. The ration is irregular and small. What there is left of the battalion are pretty fit now. Till, the orderly-room sergeant, left us yesterday with a temperature, and feared influenza. Giddens heard from Raymond today, also from Ellery. The latter is in hospital, 'The Gizrah,' at Cairo, and says he is still in bed.[240]

Second Lieutenant Stephen Ratsey had fallen ill with dysentery and jaundice and was sent to Raz-El-Tin Military Hospital. The orderly-room sergeant with suspected influenza was not Lance Sergeant Stears (RAMC attached) as he had departed Gallipoli during October. Lance Corporal Thorn (RAMC attached) may have taken over the role of orderly-room sergeant. He was invalided off Gallipoli during November 1915.

As evidenced by the letter, the supplies to Gallipoli were improving. The food available was better but it still fell short of providing a well-balanced and sufficient diet to the men. Combined with the conditions at Gallipoli, it is not surprising that the rates of illness remained to be very high.

Rifleman Christopher Arnold died of pneumonia whilst recovering from his wounding that he had received in the early parts of the Isle of Wight Rifles' Gallipoli campaign. He is buried at Alexandria (Chatby) Military and War Memorial Cemetery.

Lance Corporal Oliver Lacey was invalided off Gallipoli on a hospital ship bound for Malta suffering with dysentery and rheumatism. During July 1916 he was transferred to the Royal Engineers.

3rd November 1915 – 5th November 1915

There are no known casualties for this period.

---

[240] Isle of Wight County Press, 4th December 1915, p5

6th November 1915

By 6.30am the Isle of Wight Rifles had completed the takeover of the trenches *'on the right of sector at Stand-to'* held by the 1/4th Essex.[241] The weather was reported to be warm and sunny.

Rifleman Harold Arnold was invalided off Gallipoli to Egypt suffering with dysentery.

7th November 1915

Over the night of the 6th/7th November 1915 a listening patrol consisting of Lieutenant Pavey, Rifleman Harry Read and an unknown rifleman came under fire and Lieutenant Pavey was wounded. The men made back into the trenches and for his efforts, Rifleman Harry Read was promoted to Lance Corporal.

In the evening, another patrol went out. Second Lieutenant Rowe was wounded and Lance Corporal Tosdevin was killed.

8th November 1915

On the 8th it became clear that Second Lieutenant Rowe had been wounded and Lance Corporal Tosdevin was reported as having been wounded and missing after participating in the patrol on the evening of 7th November 1915. Lance Corporal Tosdevin was later presumed to have died of his wounds on the 7th November 1915. His body was not found and so he is commemorated on the Helles Memorial. Lance Corporal Tosdevin had been wounded during the advance on Anafarta Ridge and had only recently returned to the battalion.

Newly promoted Lance Corporal Harry Read found time to write to his mother about his experience on the listening patrol:

> I am in the pink and going great guns. We continue to have dry weather – some days hot, others cold, with

---

[241] Isle of Wight Rifles' War Diary, November 1915

perhaps, but not very often, a shower to lay the dust. I am in a dug-out at the back of the trenches, and I want to tell you some of the excitement we have been having here lately. The other night I was told off with another rifleman to go on listening patrol at midnight with an officer, so you can bet when the time came we were there. After crawling along on our knees and wriggling on our stomachs for just on two hours we had to begin all over again, for we had got out of our course right on top of the enemy; so we made another start. This time, however, our luck was properly out, for the officer went a little bit too far, and the Turks opened fire, and he had the misfortune to stop two of the bullets – one in his leg and the other across his nose. All we could do then was to get back, which we did without further damage. The Turks were letting us have it hot all the time, so we had to be content with crawling and then taking a header into our trench, which we were jolly thankful to reach with a whole skin. Last night another patrol went out and shared the same ill luck, for the officer was hit and is still missing. He was wounded when we made our advance, and only came back from hospital about a fortnight ago. What awful luck!

You will have noticed that I am an NCO....

I suppose there is something in being promoted on the battlefield.

Lance Corporal Harry Read's letter to his mother dated 8th November 1915[242]

There is no record of the death of an officer or an officer missing, however, as mentioned above, Lance Corporal Tosdevin was reported as missing and wounded (subsequently believed to have been killed) and had also been wounded on 12th August 1915 so

---
[242] Isle of Wight County Press, 11th December 1915, p8.

Lance Corporal Read may have in fact been referring to Lance Corporal Tosdevin in his letter.

No casualties have been recorded for the 8th November 1915.

9th November 1915

The only information of note for the 9th November 1915 was that a catapult was brought up to the trenches.

There were no reported casualties for the 9th November 1915.

10th November 1915

It was reported in the battalion's War Diary that the catapult was used effectively against a working party and that the weather was warm with a southerly wind.[243]

There were no reported casualties for the 10th November 1915.

11th November 1915

The Isle of Wight Rifles remained in the trenches and there were no reported casualties.

12th November 1915

The battalion's War Diary stated that there was '*nothing of interest to report*' and the weather remained warm with a little rain during the night.[244]

No casualties were reported on 12th November 1915.

13th November 1915

Lord Kitchener began his visit to Gallipoli arriving in the ANZAC area in the afternoon. On completion of his visit, he recommended a full withdrawal from Gallipoli.

---

[243] Isle of Wight Rifles' War Diary, November 1915
[244] Isle of Wight Rifles War Diary, November 1915.

There are no known casualties for the 13th November 1915.

14th November 1915

Second Lieutenant Brannon along with 22 other ranks returned to the Isle of Wight Rifles from either having been sick and/or having recovered from wounding. One of the men returning was Rifleman George Wheeler.

No casualties have been recorded for 14th November 1915.

15th November 1915

At 1100 hours, the Isle of Wight Rifles came under fire from a light gun. Later in the day, at 1700 hours, a combined attack on Hill 60 was undertaken by both mines and artillery. Four men from the 1/4th Essex were wounded in the mining tunnel during this operation.[245]

The weather had taken a turn for the worse. During the day there were rain showers accompanied by a southerly gale and during the night there was a thunderstorm. The Isle of Wight Rifles War Diary states that the '*lightning was particularly vivid about 2200.*'[246]

There are no known casualties for the Isle of Wight Rifles on 15th November 1915.

16th November 1915

The storm from the night before passed and a warm day ensued.

An artillery barrage by the Turks was launched at 1000 hours which resulted in some damage to one of the parapets in the trenches held by the Isle of Wight Rifles and a further Turkish artillery barrage began at 1700 hours which targeted Hill 60 and Walkins Ridge. The Isle of Wight Rifles were able to respond to

---

[245] Isle of Wight Rifles War Diary, November 1915.
[246] Isle of Wight Rifles War Diary, November 1915.

the Turks in the evening with the arrival of a trench howitzer and three rounds were fired at 2015 hours. After two dud rounds, *'the third round exploded and stopped an enemy working party.'*[247]

Rifleman Frederick George Henry Weaving died of Jaundice. He is buried at Ari Burnu Cemetery ANZAC Cove.

17th November 1915

It was a stormy day on the 17th November 1915 with south westerly gales spreading dust around the trenches. As the afternoon progressed, the gales increased in intensity and at 2030 hours there was a *'heavy rainstorm.'*[248]

During the day, on the left of the Isle of Wight Rifles sector, four shells hit the parapet. Further enemy activity included heavy firing around 2000 hours on the right flank and a *'Turkish bomb was reported to have been thrown at No. 1 post.'*[249]

One Other Rank was wounded on 17th November 1915 however, the name of the individual was not recorded.

18th November 1915

Another day was spent in the trenches by the Isle of Wight Rifles and in the morning the parapet close to No. 8 Post was damaged by a shell.

Over in Gira near Cairo, Egypt, in the Red Cross Hospital, Rifleman Stanford Fisk wrote the following letter to his parents:

> I have been having a bit of luck lately. On Tuesday afternoon I had a visitor to see me, a Mrs Scott, from the big hospital, and she left a tin of Gold Flake cigarettes for me, which I did enjoy. Yesterday I had a parcel from home; it was dated 11th Sept, and so was just over two

---

[247] Isle of Wight Rifles War Diary, November 1915.
[248] Isle of Wight Rifles War Diary, November 1915.
[249] Isle of Wight Rifles War Diary, November 1915.

months on the trip. It had been to Gallipoli, and then came on to me here, not a thing damaged, it was a perfect God-send. It shows there is a chance of parcels getting through, though this one had been for a nice sail round anyhow!

A few days ago I went to the Zoo, which is quite near. The climate suits the animals better than London. There is a lovely collection of birds from Australia and the Pacific Islands with wonderful colours. All the large animals are represented too.

We were having a cheerful time when I left the boys in Gallipoli, four hours' sleep only in 48 hours, and two hours' rest every other afternoon, but the flies were our great torment. Every other day we were in the firing line for 24 hours, and that night we dare not close our eyes at all or even lie down. When we were off guard we had to stand or sit upright. The other night we spent half in sleeping and half in trenching. In the day-time we had rations, water, ammunition, guns, and other things to lug about. The last I heard they could not muster a company all told.[250]

Rifleman Fisk was invalided off Gallipoli on 12th October 1915 due to illness. He, along with a large number of the Isle of Wight Rifles, ended up in hospitals in Egypt and at times they were able to go out and visit the local area. His letter not only highlights the endurance required from the men at Gallipoli but also the ability of the postal service in conjunction with Army administration to find the correct recipient of a parcel despite them having moved locations from a warzone to a hospital in another country. Note

---

[250] Rifleman Stanford Fisk's letter of 18th Nov from the Red Cross Hospital, Gira, near Cairo to his parents published in the Isle of Wight County Press, 4th December 1915 p5

that all parcels would have been transported by ships as aeroplanes were in their primacy.

There are no known casualties for the 18th November 1915.

19th November 1915

On 19th November 1915, Major General Inglefield, the General Officer Commanding the 54th Division, inspected the sector during the day and in the evening the Isle of Wight Rifles put the Trench mortar into use.[251]

There were no recorded casualties for the day.

20th November 1915

The weather continued to be relatively warm. It had been generally fine since the stormy weather of the 17th November 1915.

Once again, the Isle of Wight Rifles used the Trench mortar and an enemy loophole was destroyed.[252]

There are no known casualties for the 20th November 1915.

21st November 1915

Cold weather returned to the Peninsula. Apart from an hour of drizzle, it was a clear night with bright moonlight.

No casualties have been recorded for the 21st November 1915.

22nd November 1915

It was another cold day in the trenches and the battalion began digging caverns. Both the Trench mortar and the catapult were used to good effect.[253]

---

[251] Isle of Wight Rifles War Diary, November 1915
[252] Isle of Wight Rifles War Diary, November 1915
[253] Isle of Wight Rifles War Diary, November 1915

Rifleman Alfred Ball died of dysentery in Egypt and was buried at Alexandria (Chatby) Military and War Memorial Cemetery.

23rd November 1915

One Other Rank was wounded by an enemy artillery shell whilst in a sap leading to Jamieson's Jaunt. The name of the wounded rifleman is unknown. The Isle of Wight Rifles War Diary also stated that the battalion's sniping was a *'marked success.'*[254]

24th November 1915

The weather during the day was warmer than the previous two days but the night was cold.[255]

There are no known casualties for the 24th November 1915.

25th November 1915

Rifleman Herbert John Cawston died of wounds on the 25th November 1915. After the war his grave could not be located and as such, he is commemorated on the Helles Memorial.

---

[254] Isle of Wight Rifles War Diary, November 1915
[255] Isle of Wight Rifles War Diary, November 1915

The Great Storm

26th November 1915

The 26th November 1915 saw the beginning of a period of atrocious weather on the Gallipoli Peninsula. This time in the campaign is sometimes referred to as, 'The Great Storm.' There is limited information on the conditions experienced on 26th November 1915 in the battalion's War Diary but it does state that the weather was bad with a northerly wind and there was, *'much rain and wind.'*[256] A letter written by Corporal Arthur Victor James to his parents sheds more light on what it was like that day:

> First of all we had a tremendous thunderstorm, which commenced about 4.30pm and continued up to 8pm. It was simply pitch dark, and the vivid flashes of lightning, followed by an awful crash of thunder, presented a unique although a rather weird and wet spectacle. Needless to say we were drenched to the skin in the trenches, and standing knee-deep in water and mud.[257]

On parts of the Peninsula, water flooded down the hillsides and swept into the trenches. Despite the bitter wind and cold water, the men had to remain holding the line as best as possible.

During the day the Isle of Wight Rifles were informed that the 54th Division would be sent to Mudros and that the battalion would be relieved by the New Zealand Mounted Rifles the next day at dawn.[258]

No casualties have been recorded for the 26th November 1915.

---

[256] Isle of Wight Rifles War Diary, November 1915
[257] Corporal James' letter to his parents published in the Isle of Wight County Press on 12th February 1916, p5
[258] Isle of Wight Rifles War Diary, November 1915

27th November 1915

Due to the appalling weather conditions, the relief of the Isle of Wight Rifles by the New Zealand Mounted Rifles was delayed and not completed until 1130hours. The Isle of Wight Rifles proceeded to Hatfield Park and the battalion's machine guns were passed over to the OMR:

> We were relieved by the New Zealanders after being in that part of the trenches for about a month. We went back some hundred yards, bivouacked in a gully known as Hatfield Park, stopping there until dark, when it was hoped we should be marched to the beach at ANZAC and then on board the boat, to leave the Peninsula behind for at least somewhile. However, Fate was unkind to us, for as darkness came on the rain started again, and although we began the journey walking through mud and slush almost up to our knees, we were compelled to return to our old gully, as the sea was too rough to attempt embarking that night. By this time we were nearly wet through again, and laid down by the open sides of the gully for the night.
>
> Corporal James' Letter to his parents[259]

There were no dug-outs for the men to seek cover in and they were fully exposed to the cold wind and rain.[260]

At Suvla Bay, the conditions were just as bad. Trenches were flooded and twelve unfortunate men were drowned when the corrugated iron roof of their shelter in the trenches collapsed. In the afternoon the bitter northerly wind turned into a gale and the freezing cold wind continued into the evening. Men across the

---

[259] Corporal James' letter to his parents published in the Isle of Wight County Press on 12th February 1916, p5
[260] Letter from a member of the Isle of Wight Rifles, dated 6th December 1915 at Mudros and published in the Isle of Wight County Press on 25th December 1915, p5.

Peninsula were fighting for their survival this time not from the Turks, who had gone quiet in the face of the adverse conditions, but from the elements instead.[261]

28th November 1915

Over the night of the 27th/28th November 1915 the rain turned to snow and a blizzard ensued:

> Imagine our surprise on waking up about 2 o'clock next morning to find ourselves practically snowed in, with the blankets frozen stiff over us. It continued snowing all next day and freezing with it and you can guess how rotten we felt when we were told that no rations could be got to that day as the mule tracks were impassable. However, we managed to live as has often been the case, on practically nothing that day, and then laid down again for the night.
>
> Corporal James' Letter to his parents[262]

The men must have spent a miserable day at Hatfield Park but it appears they coped well in the adversity being faced.

A temporary hospital was built at Suvla Bay out of sail covers and boxes forming a number of shelters. These shelters were *'full of men frost bitten in legs, arms and faces, who lie in great distress suffering agonies as their blood warms up and circulates to the frozen parts of their bodies.'*[263]

In addition to numerous cases of frostbite across the Peninsula, some of the men died from exposure. There are no recorded casualties for the Isle of Wight Rifles on the 28th November 1915,

---

[261] Gallipoli Diary, Major John Graham Gillan DSO, London: George Allen & Unwin Ltd, Ruskch House, 40 Museum Street WC1, p273
[262] Corporal James' letter to his parents published in the Isle of Wight County Press on 12th February 1916, p5
[263] Gallipoli Diary, Major John Graham Gillan DSO, London: George Allen & Unwin Ltd, Ruskch House, 40 Museum Street WC1, p275

however, according to a letter written by Rifleman Bert Downer to his mother in early January 1916, '*a lot were taken to hospital with frost-bite.*'[264]

29th November 1915

Although the snow had stopped, a gale was still blowing and the temperature had dropped such that the snow began to freeze. However, despite the awful weather and conditions, getting rations was a top priority for the Isle of Wight Rifles:

> The snow had ceased, and of course our first job then was to get rations up. I was one of the party and we had to go about ¾ mile for them, most of the distance through rather open land. Needless to say, John Turk, as soon as he saw we were on the move, started dropping shrapnel over. One of our chaps was killed on the downward journey, and then coming back poor Bert Coward was killed. I was with him about three minutes before he met his end, and he was saying how glad he was that we were being relieved. Alas! We little thought how soon his end would be. We got back safely with the rations, and that same night shifted to a gully [Waterfall Gully] close down to the shore.
>
> Corporal James' letter to his parents[265]

Sadly, the rations run resulted in the deaths of two men. Rifleman George Dunn was the man who was killed by a shell. Rifleman Albert Coward's cause of death was either from a shell or a sniper. Both men were buried at the 8th Hants cemetery at

---

[264] Rifleman Bert Downer's letter to his mother, early January 1916, published in the Isle of Wight County Press on 29th January 1916, p5
[265] Corporal James' letter to his parents published in the Isle of Wight County Press on 12th February 1916, p5

Rhondda Valley Cemetery. After the war, the burials at this cemetery were moved to the 7th Field Ambulance Cemetery.

30th November 1915

It remained very cold with freezing conditions at the beginning of the day. However, conditions had improved in comparison to the previous few days as the wind had dropped, the skies were clear and the sun was gradually bringing some warmth. Initially, the Isle of Wight Rifles received orders to depart Waterfall Gully, but these orders were cancelled and the battalion remained where it was.[266]

The 30th November 1915 is the likely day that Private Reginald James Brooks Butt and Private George Henry Cooper, both of the RAMC attached to the Isle of Wight Rifles, were invalided off Gallipoli. Both had fallen ill with Enteric Fever and Private Reginald James Brooks Butt also had frostbite. Many men across the Peninsula were suffering with frostbite and at Suvla Bay, the beach was *'crowded with cases of frost bite - soldiers' limbs were swathed in bundles of bandages.'*[267]

1st December 1915

The Isle of Wight Rifles remained at Waterfall Gully on 1st December 1915 and the weather continued to be freezing.

Rifleman Percy Knight was shot in the chest. The bullet broke three of his ribs and went through his lung.[268] He was invalided back to England. Rifleman Knight recovered and served with the reserve battalion of the Hampshire Regiment but had to be discharged from the Army on the 31st October 1917 due to the lasting effects of the wounding.

---

[266] Isle of Wight Rifles War Diary, November 1915
[267] Gallipoli Diary, Major John Graham Gillan DSO, London: George Allen & Unwin Ltd, Ruskch House, 40 Museum Street WC1, p280
[268] Isle of Wight County Press, 1st January 1916, p5

Rifleman William Quantrill succumbed to frost bite in his fingers and feet and initially spent time in hospitals at ANZAC Cove before being invalided to Egypt. On the 12th December 1915, he wrote the following letter on his experiences to his parents from No. 5 Canadian Stationary Hospital, Abbassia Cavalry Barracks, Cairo:

> Just a few lines to let you know I am in hospital at Cairo suffering from frost-bite in my fingers and feet. I am sorry I did not write before, but you must excuse me. I have a job to write now, as my fingers ache, and I can only just manage to hold the pencil. We had about 4in of snow on the Peninsula on the 30th November, and our blankets were wet through owing to the rain the night before, and we had nothing except a wet blanket and waterproof sheet for a bed. So you cannot wonder at our getting frost-bitten, can you? It started freezing the next day, and we had a job to get any water, as the pumps and wells were all frozen, so some of us filled our mess-tins with snow and made a drop of tea with it. All we could get to eat was bully beef, biscuits, and jam, so I was glad in a way to get away.
>
> I first went to the rest camp on the shore and stayed there for two days, and was then moved to the clearing-station hospital. We were there for four days, and then the Turks started shelling it, and we had to clear out the best way we could into the sap. I scrambled out on my hands and knees, and we then struggled on to the next hospital where we stayed two days waiting for a hospital ship. At last one came in, and we were taken off at 7'o'clock at night on December 7th [Tuesday].
>
> We started from the Peninsula on Wednesday and stopped at Lemnos all day Thursday. On Friday we started for Alexandria, arrived there on Saturday afternoon, and left by train for Cairo, where we arrived about 9.15. We completed the journey to hospital by

motor-ambulance. We were fed splendidly on the boat, and had oranges and cigarettes given out to us in the afternoon. On the train we had tea and the nurse brought round cigarettes and chocolate. Just before we arrived at the station they gave us all a mug of hot beef tea.

We did not see much of the country we passed through as it got dark soon after we started, but what we did see was very interesting, especially the villages of the natives, composed of mud huts, also flat-topped houses and the curious cabs, which look as if they are going to break in halves.

Do not worry about me, as I am having a fine time here.

Wishing you all a happy New Year.[269]

Note that Rifleman Quantrill wrote that it snowed on the 30th November 1915. Other records indicate that it did not snow then. It is likely that Rifleman Quantrill got his dates confused looking back on events and he in fact meant to write the '28th November.'

---

[269] Rifleman Quantrill's letter to his parents from Egypt on 12th December 1915 and published in the Isle of Wight County Press on 1st January 1916 p5

Evacuation

On the 2nd December 1915 and the 3rd December 1915, the Isle of Wight Rifles were located at Waterfall Gully. The battalion received orders to move to Williams Pier, ANZAC Cove, at 1830hours and later in the evening the men embarked a transport ship headed for Mudros. The following day, the Isle of Wight Rifles marched to a camp in the vicinity of Batiamas. This camp would be their base until 15th December 1915 and on the 7th December 1915 the battalion officially rejoined the 163rd Brigade.[270]

It was confirmed by a letter on 6th December 1915 by an anonymous member of the Isle of Wight Rifles that Lieutenant Stephen Ratsey, Lieutenant Kingdon and Lieutenant Sheldon had been promoted to the rank of Captain whilst those officers that had fallen sick were demoted. The soldier who wrote the letter stated that *'they well deserve it, as they have had months of the trenches, while others have only had weeks.'*[271]

Despite the Isle of Wight Rifles being away from the fighting, they still experienced the odd casualty. On 11th December 1915 Rifleman Francis Gilbert Foot passed away on a hospital ship from dysentery and was buried at sea. Either towards the end of the Gallipoli campaign or during the early stages of the battalion being at Alexandria, Rifleman Vincent fell ill with Tuberculosis. He was admitted on to HM Hospital Ship Britannic on 31st December 1915 and passed away on 9th January 1916 whilst the hospital ship was still at sea. Rifleman Vincent is buried at Netley Military Cemetery.[272][273]

---

[270] Isle of Wight Rifles War Dairy, December 1915
[271] Isle of Wight County Press, 25th December 1915, p5
[272] www.forces-war-records.co.uk: Military Hospitals Admissions and Discharge Registers WW1 - MH106/1915
[273] www.ancestry.co.uk: UK, Soldiers Died in the Great War, 1914-1919

The Isle of Wight Rifles finally left the horrors of the Dardanelles on 15th December 1915. Their transport ship, HMT 'Victorian' left harbour at 1730hours, heading for Alexandria, Egypt.

Where Next?

After docking at Alexandria, the Isle of Wight Rifles spent Christmas 1915 at Sidi Bishr. From Sidi Bishr the battalion moved to Mena Camp, by the Great Pyramids and lived in tents. They were now firmly part of the Egyptian Expeditionary Force (EEF) and had received '*a draft from the 3rd Hants and the Berkshires.*'[274] By April 1916, the 54th Division, including the Isle of Wight Rifles, were tasked with defending the Suez Canal in No. 1 (Southern) Section.

February 1917 saw the battalion march cross the Sinai Desert to take part in the Palestinian Campaign. They were held in reserve during the 1st Battle of Gaza on 26th March 1917 but saw heavy fighting in the Second Battle of Gaza on 19th April 1917 and suffered huge losses of men killed, wounded and taken prisoner. Sixty-three of those killed were veterans of the Gallipoli Campaign. These included Captain Charles Pittis M.C., Captain Charles Seely, Lieutenant Stephen Ratsey and Second Lieutenant John Parker Shelton.

The Isle of Wight Rifles took part in the Third Battle of Gaza (31st October 1917 – 7th November 1917) which saw Gaza finally being captured by the EEF. Jerusalem then fell to the EEF on 9th December 1917 but the Isle of Wight Rifles were not part of that fighting. Instead, they were operating to the north of Jerusalem and went on to take part in the Battle of Jaffa on 21st December 1917.

During the final year of the Great War, the Isle of Wight Rifles fought in the battle at Berukin on 9th April 1918 and then the Battle of Sharon, which was one of the battles of Megiddo, on 19th September 1918. The Isle of Wight Rifles then advanced on

---

[274] Sergeant William Halsey's letter to IoW County Press on 16th March 1916 and published on 8th April 1916

towards Beirut. The EEF were victorious and the armistice with Turkey took effect on 31st October 1918.

On 11th November 1918 the Great War came to an end. The Isle of Wight Rifles were brought back to Cairo, Egypt and demobilisation began. However, in 1919 the Egyptians revolted against the British and demobilisation was put on hold. The 54th Division was ordered to march through Cairo as a show of force as part of the effort to put a stop to the rebellion and when order was returned, demobilisation began again and the men returned home. A number of Isle of Wight Rifles and Colonel Marsh volunteered to deploy to Khartoum as part of the British Army's force in Sudan. These men did not return to the Isle of Wight until 24th March 1920.

As of 11th November 1918, approximately 28% of the Isle of Wight Rifles who boarded the Aquitania for Gallipoli had lost their lives during the war. Of the officers, 50% had been killed or died due to illness. A further 7 men died from 14th November 1918 to 9th February 1919 and Captain Murphy died on 20th March 1920.

The last known Isle of Wight Rifles' Gallipoli veteran to have died as a result of the war was Private George Cooper who died on 12th March 1921. He developed severe pleurisy during the German's final offensive of 1918 but could not be taken out of the line due to the extreme strain the British Army was under. The delay proved fatal and he died in a sanatorium at St. Lawrence on the Isle of Wight on 12th March 1921.

Roll of Officers, Warrant Officers, Non-Commissioned Officers and Riflemen Proceeding Overseas

List of Names Published in the Isle of Wight County Press on 24th July 1915.

Officers Serving with the Isle of Wight Rifles

Lt. Col. J E RHODES (Commanding Officer)

Lieutenant-Colonel Rhodes took over the command of the Isle of Wight Rifles in 1913 after having been recalled to the British Army from a civilian job as a bailiff for a Buckinghamshire country estate. He previously had been an army regular but had not seen combat.

During the build up to the Gallipoli deployment, Lt. Col Rhodes had hurt his leg but recovered to sail with the Isle of Wight Rifles to Gallipoli and led the battalion in their attack at Anafarta Ridge on 12th August 1915. When the attack was showing signs of faltering he led the battalion forward. The following morning, he returned to base suffering from exhaustion and shortly after this, he hurt his leg again and had to be invalided back to England.

Lt. Col Rhodes was discharged from the Army on 17th August 1917 and given the Silver War Badge.[275]

Major Ernest Hastings LEWIS

Major Ernest Lewis joined the Isle of Wight Rifles in October 1913 and took on the role of adjutant. Prior to this, he had served in the Soudan Campaign (1898), in the Ashanti Campaign (1900) and in Northern Nigeria in both 1901 and 1903.

Major Lewis was killed during the attack on Anafarta Ridge on 12th August 1915. At first, he was posted as missing and then later confirmed in the Isle of Wight County Press on 28th August

---

[275] www.ancestry.co.uk: UK, Silver War Badge Records, 1914-1920

1915 as having been killed on the 12th August 1915. He was 44 years old and is commemorated on the Helles Memorial.

Major A C T VEASEY

Major Veasey had previously served as a *'Captain with the 1st Volunteer Brigade of the Bedfordshire Rifles and was recorded as being an Honorary Lieutenant in the Army on 19th November 1901.'*[276]

At the beginning of the war, Major Veasey was based at Bembridge Fort with a number of men from the Isle of Wight Rifles.

Major Veasey took over command of the battalion in Gallipoli when Lt. Col Rhodes was invalided home. His tenure as commanding officer was short lived as on Friday 10th September 1915 he had succumbed to dysentery and was admitted into a hospital in Malta. For his work at Gallipoli, he received a Mention in Despatches.

Major Veasey became the battalion's adjutant and survived the war. In 1920 he was promoted to Lieutenant Colonel and became the Commanding Officer of the Isle of Wight Rifles.

Capt. Cecil Langdon ELLERY

Captain Cecil Ellery was recorded as being a Lieutenant in the Isle of Wight Rifles on 1st June 1910 in the UK Army List 1911.[277] He came from Ryde.

Captain Cecil Ellery was the officer in charge of 'C' Company and he took part in the advance on Anafarta Ridge. Captain Ellery had an initial bout of illness in August 1915 but returned to the frontline in September 1915. He was given the command of the battalion when Major Veasey was taken to hospital but on 14th October 1915, he became sick again and was admitted into the

---

[276] www.forces-war-records.co.uk: UK Army List 1914
[277] www.forces-war-records.co.uk: UK Army List 1911

Gizra Hospital, Cairo for treatment. Command of the Isle of Wight Rifles passed to Captain Marsh.

By the end of the war, Cecil Ellery had reached the rank of Major and had received a Mention in Despatches:

> General E.H.H. Allenby has the honour to forward herewith a list of names whom he considers worthy of mention for their services during the period from the 19th September, 1918, to the 31st January, 1919.[278]

On finishing his military career, Cecil Ellery was a Lieutenant Colonel. He had also been awarded an O.B.E.

Capt. John Gerald FARDELL

Captain John Fardell, on 9th August 1915, was left in charge of three officers and 183 NCOs and rifleman who had been selected to be held back as reserves. They remained at Mudros and landed at Gallipoli on 15th August 1915, joining their comrades who had already been involved in heavy fighting. During September 1915, Captain John Fardell was recorded as being an officer in 'B' Company. This was short lived as he fell ill with Enteric Fever and was invalided off Gallipoli on 18th September. On 25th September 1915 he was admitted to No. 21 General Hospital in Alexandria and returned to England in December for further treatment at a hospital in London.

In September 1916, 250 men from the Isle of Wight Rifles' reserve battalion, led by Captain Fardell, went to Quetta, India, detached to the 2/4th Hants. This unit then went onto Mesopotamia and then Persia in 1918.[279]

Captain Fardell survived the war and became a Major.

---

[278] www.forces-war-records.co.uk: Search Records of Soldiers Awards from the London Gazette, Gazette issue 31383, 03/06/1919, p7180
[279] The Isle of Wight Rifles, D J Quigley, Saunders, p16

Capt. Arthur HOLMES GORE

Captain Arthur Holmes Gore was killed in action during the attack on Anafarta Ridge on the 12th August 1915. He joined the Isle of Wight Rifles from the United Arts Volunteer Rifles (later known as the 1st Battalion Central London Regiment Volunteers), of which he was the Adjutant. In his civilian life he was a solicitor and actor. Captain Holmes Gore is commemorated on the Helles Memorial.

Capt. Graham Chard LOADER

Captain Graham Loader was another one of the casualties on the 12th August 1915. He was commissioned in the Isle of Wight Rifles in 1913 and promoted to Captain in the run up to Gallipoli.

News of the nature of Captain Loader's death was passed to the Isle of Wight County Press by Miss Parsons who was working at a hospital in Malta. She had been told of Captain Loader's death by a member of the Isle of Wight Rifles who had witnessed Captain Loader being struck by a bullet in the mouth whilst standing to look over his trench. He was killed instantaneously. Captain Loader was buried on the night of his death but his grave location later became unknown and as such he is commemorated on the Helles Memorial.[280]

Capt. John Francis Harrison MARSH

Captain Marsh was listed as an officer in 'A' Company in September 1915. He went on to become the Commanding Officer of the Isle of Wight Rifles in October 1915 when Captain Ellery was taken ill. Captain Marsh remained the Commanding Officer throughout the remainder of the Gallipoli campaign.

Captain Marsh once again took command of the battalion just before the Second Battle of Gaza and was promoted to the rank

---

[280] Isle of Wight County Press, 2nd October 1918, p8

of Lieutenant Colonel. He survived the war and had received two Mention in Despatches.

Capt. Clayton RATSEY

Captain Clayton Ratsey and his two brothers, Donald Ratsey and Stephen Ratsey all served with the Isle of Wight Rifles at Gallipoli. Their father, Thomas Ratsey was the principal of the famous sail making company in Cowes, Messrs. Ratsey and Lapthorn Ltd.

Captain Clayton Ratsey was killed during the Anafarta Ridge attack on 12th August 1915. He was originally posted as missing. Captain Clayton Ratsey was 29 years old and had served with the battalion for 10 years. He is commemorated on the Helles Memorial.

Capt. Donald White RATSEY

Captain Donald Ratsey was also killed on 12th August 1915 during the attack on Anafarta Ridge. Like his brother, he too was originally posted as missing. Captain Donald Ratsey was 31 years old and served with the Isle of Wight Rifles for 12 years. He is commemorated on the Helles Memorial.

Lt. Richard H CURTIS

Lieutenant Richard Curtis was recorded as a Second Lieutenant in the Isle of Wight Rifles on 15th August 1914 in the UK Army List 1914.[281]

On 10th February 1916 he *'embarked upon the ship Eboe at Devonport and sailed for the Mediterranean, travelling First Class.'*[282] He presumably was on his way to re-join the Isle of

---

[281] www.forces-war-records.co.uk: UK Army List 1914
[282] www.forces-war-records.co.uk: Embarkation Records of Servicemen WWI

Wight Rifles and on 28th July 1917 he was recorded as being a Captain in the Isle of Wight Rifles.[283]

Richard Curtis went on to serve with the Royal Berkshire Regiment and left the Army on 20th January 1919.

Lt. George GIDDENS

Lieutenant George Giddens was the battalion's Quarter Master. He remained with the Isle of Wight Rifles throughout their time at Gallipoli. After Gallipoli he was promoted to the rank of Captain. He was mentioned in despatches twice and below is the quotation in the Gazette dated 11th June 1918:

> I have the honour to forward herewith the names of those serving or who have served under my Command, whose distinguished and gallant services and devotion to duty I consider deserving of special mention.[284]

George Giddens survived the war and later in his life he was awarded an MBE (Member Of The Most Excellent Order Of The British Empire).[285]

Lt. Richard Boyd LEDWARD

Lieutenant Richard Boyd Ledward came from Bury St. Edmonds. He was listed as wounded in the Isle of Wight County Press on 2nd October 1915 and was wounded prior to 14th September 1915. On recovering from his wounds, he went on to become a Captain in the 1st Brahmans and then a Major in the Indian Army. He survived the war.

Lt. Charles Seymour PITTIS

Lieutenant Charles Pittis was the son of Seymour Pittis and lived at Hale Manor in Arreton. He was the nephew of Richard Roach

---

[283] www.forces-war-records.co.uk: UK Army List 1918
[284] www.forces-war-records.co.uk: Search Records of Soldiers Awards from the London Gazette, Gazette Issue 30746, 11/06/1918, p7053
[285] www.forces-war-records.co.uk: UK Army List 1933

Pittis who owned a law firm in Newport which became known as Roach Pittis and Co. when it was purchased by Alexander Young-James in 1913 after the death of Richard Roach Pittis. Charles Pittis had started working with his uncle in 1911 and if he were fully articled in 1913, he would have taken over the firm. He instead worked with Alexander Young-James as an articled clerk.[286]

Lieutenant Pittis was commissioned in the Isle of Wight Rifles on 20th February 1913 and was the machine-gun officer for the battalion at Gallipoli. For his actions with the machine guns at Gallipoli he received the Military Cross and a Mention in Despatches. He was invalided off Gallipoli on 6th October 1915 suffering from Enteric Fever. He was treated at a hospital in Gibraltar before being admitted into Osborne House Officers' Convalescent Home in early December 1915.

Lieutenant Pittis returned to the Isle of Wight Rifles and was promoted to the rank of Captain. He was killed, aged 21, during the Second Battle of Gaza on the 19th April 1917 and was buried next to his fallen comrades Captain Charles Seely and Lieutenant Stephen Ratsey at Gaza War Cemetery.

Lt. Walter Felix READ

Lieutenant Walter Read was commissioned in the Isle of Wight Rifles in October 1912. He was the brother-in-law of Captain Raymond. Lieutenant Read was one of the four officers held in reserve at Mudros and landed at Gallipoli on 15th August. He was very quickly invalided off Gallipoli suffering from dysentery and was transported to a hospital in Alexandria where he then suffered from appendicitis and died on 14th September 1915. He is buried at Alexandria (Chatby) Military and War Memorial Cemetery, Egypt.

---

[286] https://www.roachpittis.co.uk/about-roach-pittis/history/

Lt. Charles Grant SEELY

Lieutenant Charles Seely served with the Isle of Wight Rifles throughout their Gallipoli campaign. He became the acting adjutant in September 1915 and was the last of the officers to take on the responsibility of completing the War Diary at Gallipoli. Lieutenant Seely undertook a lot of sniping at Gallipoli using a hunting rifle that his father had given him. Reginald Brooks Butt referred to him as a *'great shot,'* and a *'good officer.'*

Like many of the officers, Lieutenant Seely did not survive the First World War. He was killed on 19th April 1917 during the Second Battle of Gaza and is buried at Gaza War Cemetery. His family paid for a memorial tomb at St Olave's Church in Gatcombe. It was sculpted by Second Lieutenant T. Brock, RA, and has the following inscription:

> WE PRAY YOU COMMEND TO THE MERCY OF GOD THE SOUL OF CHARLES GRANT SEELY, ELDEST SON OF SIR CHARLES SEELY, BARONET, AND DAME HILDA HIS WIFE. BORN ON NOV. 29, 1894. AND EDUCATED AT CHEAM, ETON AND TRINITY COLLEGE, CAMBRIDGE. HE JOINED THE ISLE OF WIGHT RIFLES AT THE OUTBREAK OF THE GREAT WAR. AND, AFTER SERVING WITH DISTINCTION IN THE GALLIPOLI AND EGYPTIAN CAMPAIGNS, FELL GLORIOUSLY, THRICE WOUNDED, AT GAZA IN PALESTINE ON APRIL 19, 1917, WHILE LEADING THE ADVANCE ON THE TURKISH POSITION.
>
> GREATLY BELOVED – FOR HE WAS A VERY GALLANT GENTLEMAN – HE LIES IN THE CEMETERY AT GAZA, SURROUNDED BY THE MEN OF HIS REGIMENT WHO FELL WITH HIM THAT DAY.
>
> MIZPAH[287]

---

[287] Memorial Tomb, Charles Grant Seely, St. Olave's Church, Gatcombe.

Lt. Alexander YOUNG-JAMES

Lieutenant Alexander Young-James was a solicitor. He moved to the Isle of Wight in 1913 and purchased the law firm owned by the late Richard Roach Pittis. Alexander Young-James called the firm Roach Pittis & Co. and took on Charles Pittis as his articled clerk.

Lieutenant Young-James joined the Isle of Wight Rifles in 1913 and was an officer in 'D' Company at Gallipoli. He was killed on the 12th August 1915 during the attack on Anafarta Ridge and Princess Beatrice brought the news of his death to his wife. Lieutenant Young-James was 30 years old and is commemorated on the Helles Memorial.[288]

2nd Lt. William Bertram BARTLETT

Second Lieutenant William Bartlett was a platoon officer in 'C' Company. He was killed by a sniper on the 18th August 1915 whilst bringing rations to the front line. He was twenty years old and a platoon commander in C Company. News of his death reached the Isle of Wight County Press by letters home from both Corporal Lambs and Lance Corporal Thorn. Second Lieutenant Bartlett is listed on the Helles Memorial.

2nd Lt. Charles Wilfred BRANNON

Second Lieutenant Charles Brannon, the son of the managing director of the Isle of Wight County Press, enlisted with the Isle of Wight Rifles on 3rd August 1914 and became a Rifleman with service number 1489. He was promoted to Corporal on 1st October 1914 and went on to be commissioned before the Gallipoli campaign.

Second Lieutenant Brannon was one of the four officers held in reserve at Mudros. He landed at Gallipoli on 15th August 1915 and shortly afterwards was taken ill, *'suffering with inflammation*

---

[288] https://www.roachpittis.co.uk/about-roach-pittis/history/

of the middle membrane of the ear, probably the effect of gun fire.[289] He was treated in the Anglo-American Hospital, Ghezireh, Egypt and then spent a few days recuperating at a base in Cyprus before re-joining the battalion at Gallipoli on 14th November 1915. At Gallipoli, Second Lieutenant Brannon was a platoon commander in 'B' Company.

Second Lieutenant Brannon reached the rank of Captain and was awarded the Military Cross during the Isle of Wight Rifles' Palestinian campaign later in the war. In 1936 he became the Commanding Officer of the Isle Wight Rifles, holding the rank of Lieutenant Colonel.

Charles Brannon in his later life lived in Wootton and in his spare time was the Scout Master for the Wootton branch.

2nd Lt. George William FOX

Second Lieutenant George Fox was a member of the Inns of Court Officers' Training Corps before joining the Isle of Wight Rifles. He was taken from the second battalion of the Isle of Wight Rifles to serve with the first battalion of the Isle of Wight Rifles.

In September, Second Lieutenant Fox was appointed as a bombing officer for the battalion and spent a period of time away from the Isle of Wight Rifles under the rank of temporary Lieutenant. He was wounded when trying to throw an enemy bomb, which had landed at his feet, out of his trench. Unfortunately, the bomb exploded when it reached the top of the parapet, severely injuring him. He survived the wounding but lost an eye. News of his wounding was published on 6th November 1915 in the Isle of Wight County Press.

He was awarded the Military Cross for, *'conspicuous gallantry and good service as bombing officer to the garrison of 'Hill 60,'*

---

[289] Isle of Wight County Press, 4th September 1915, p8.

Gallipoli peninsular, between 3rd September and 21st October 1915. He set a fine example of pluck and coolness to the bombers of the Brigade, and had considerable success as a sniper. Second Lieutenant Fox was wounded for the third time on 21st October.'[290]

2nd Lt. Herbert William KINGDON

Second Lieutenant Herbert Kingdon survived the war. In September 1915 he was recorded as being one of the officers in 'B' Company. Second Lieutenant Kingdon went on to join the Royal Flying Corps, which later became the Royal Air Force.

2nd Lt. Percy LATHAM

Second Lieutenant Percy Latham was originally in the 1st of C Officers Training Corp. He was commissioned on 14th May 1915 and became a Second Lieutenant in the Isle of Wight Rifles. He was killed on 20th August 1915 and buried. His grave could not be found after the war and so he was subsequently commemorated on the Helles Memorial.

2nd Lt. John Patrick MURPHY

Second Lieutenant Murphy was listed as one of the officers in 'C' Company in September 1915. He rose to the rank of Captain and survived the war but unfortunately, he died on the 28th March 1920 at the age of 27 years old. He is buried at Beckenham Crematorium and Cemetery.[291]

2nd Lt. Stephen Gilbert RATSEY

Second Lieutenant Stephen Ratsey initially saw active service in New Guinea with the Australian Expeditionary Force. He came back to England and joined the Isle of Wight Rifles and was

---

[290] Isle of Wight County Press, 11th December 1915, p8.
[291] https://billiongraves.com/grave/John-Patrick-Murphy/22685573

deployed to Gallipoli along with his two brothers, Clayton and Donald.

Second Lieutenant Ratsey was one of the four officers who were held in reserve at Mudros. He landed at Gallipoli on 15th August 1915. During September 1915, Second Lieutenant Stephen Ratsey was one of the remaining officers in 'B' Company. A few weeks later he succumbed to illness and was 'sent to Raz-El-Tin Military Hospital on 7th November 1915, suffering from dysentery and jaundice.'[292] Following this, he was invalided back to England and was admitted into Osborne House Officer's Convalescent Home on Sunday 19th December 1915.[293]

Second Lieutenant Stephen Ratsey remained with the Isle of Wight Rifles and was promoted to Lieutenant. He was killed during the Second Battle of Gaza on the 19th April 1917. He *'had been seen going over the top after telling his men that he was going to avenge his two brothers who had perished at Gallipoli.'*[294]

Lieutenant Stephen Ratsey's grave is in Gaza War Cemetery.

2nd Lt. Frederick Charles Motley RAYMOND

Second Lieutenant Frederick Raymond returned from Canada to join the battalion. His brother Captain Raymond was the battalion's Medical Officer. Their father, George Raymond, was the British Consul for Corfu and the Ionian Islands.

Second Lieutenant Raymond is listed on the Helles Memorial as having being killed on 21st August 1915. However, a letter from an officer in the Isle of Wight Rifles dated the 17th August 1915 and published in the Isle of Wight County Press on 4th September

---

[292] Isle of Wight County Press, 4th December 1915, p5.
[293] Isle of Wight County Press, 25th December 1915, p5.
[294] The Isle of Wight Rifles, D J Quigley, p23.

1915 suggests Second Lieutenant Raymond was actually killed during the Anafarta Ridge offensive:

> The next morning (Sunday 15th) was a bad time when we called the roll. We have lost 12 officers, including Major Lewis, who is missing. We only know of one dead – young Raymond. Two others are wounded and the others are missing.[295]

2nd Lt. John Parker SHELTON,

Second Lieutenant John Shelton was born in Tottenham, London. He was a solicitor before serving with the Isle of Wight Rifles full time. By September 1915, he was an officer in 'A' Company.

Second Lieutenant Shelton remained with the Isle of Wight Rifles after Gallipoli and was killed in action on the 19th April 1917 at the age of 29 during the Second Battle of Gaza. He is buried at Gaza War Cemetery.

2nd Lt. A G A SUTTON

Second Lieutenant A G A Sutton came from Hawkstone Park, Shrewsbury. He was wounded at Gallipoli, possibly during the Anafarta Ridge offensive. He was discharged from the Army on 9th January 1917 and received the Silver War Badge.[296]

2nd Lt. Laurence Charles WATSON

Second Lieutenant Laurence Watson was killed on 12th August 1915 during the Anafarta Ridge offensive and is commemorated on the Helles Memorial. He was 22 years old.

---

[295] Isle of Wight County Press, 4th September 1915, p6.
[296] www.ancestry.co.uk: UK, Silver War Badge Records, 1914-1920

Second Lieutenant Watson had been in the Inns of Court's Officers' Training Corps and went on to be commissioned in the Isle of Wight Rifles in April 1915.

2nd Lt. Arthur Samuel WEEDING,

Second Lieutenant Arthur Weeding was promoted from the rank of Company Sergeant Major with the Isle of Wight Rifles to the rank of Second Lieutenant in July 1915.[297]

Second Lieutenant Weeding temporarily became the officer in charge of 'B' Company after the offensive at Anafarta Ridge and by September 1915 he was one of the officers in 'A' Company. He reported sick on 26th September 1915 with Enteric Fever and was invalided off Gallipoli to Malta.

Later in the war, Second Lieutenant Weeding joined the Royal Flying Corps and reached the rank of Captain. He survived the war.

---

[297] Isle of Wight County Press, 17th July 1915

'A' Company

CSM. George Edward BRYANT, 7428

Company Sergeant Major George Bryant began his Army service in 1905 and was one of the more experienced soldiers in the Isle of Wight Rifles who set sail to Gallipoli. In 1919 he was serving in 'C' Company of the 3rd Battalion of the Hampshire Regiment as a Regimental Sergeant Major and it was recorded that he was admitted into hospital on 28th March 1919 and transferred to Brighton Grove Hospital, Newcastle on 5th April 1919.[298]

CSM. Harry Ernest SHEATH, 15

Company Sergeant Major Harry Sheath came from Cowes and joined the Isle of Wight Rifles in April 1908. He fell ill at Gallipoli and on 13th November 1915 was admitted to a hospital in Alexandria, Egypt suffering from Debility.

Company Sergeant Major Sheath was discharged from the battalion on 28th April 1916 owing to the termination of his period of Territorial Service. He had served in the Isle of Wight Rifles for 8 years.

CQMS Charles LIFE, 229

Company Quarter Master Sergeant Charles Life succumbed to Enteric Fever towards the end of September, early October 1915 and was taken to the 21st General Hospital in Cairo for treatment.

After recovering from Enteric Fever, Company Quarter Master Sergeant Life returned to serve with the Isle of Wight Rifles. He was demobilised from the battalion on 24th April 1919 under service number 330016.

---

[298] www.forces-war-records.co.uk: Military Hospitals Admissions and Discharge Registers WW1

Sgt. John 'Jack' JENKINS, 170

Sergeant John 'Jack' Jenkins came from Ventnor. He continued to serve with the Isle of Wight Rifles after their Gallipoli campaign and was promoted to the rank of Company Sergeant Major. He was given service number 330013 when the Territorials received their new service numbers.

Company Sergeant Major Jenkins was killed in action on 2nd November 1917 during the Third Battle of Gaza. He was 25 years old and a married man. Company Sergeant Major Jenkins is buried at Gaza War Cemetery.

Sgt. Arthur Richard KING, 378

Sergeant Arthur King came from Ryde and enlisted in the Isle of Wight Rifles at Ryde. He remained with the Isle of Wight Rifles after Gallipoli and was given service number 330023 with the Territorials new service numbering system.

Sergeant King was reported as having been wounded on active service in the War Office Daily List No.5428 dated the 28th November 1917.[299] He was invalided back to England where he was admitted into the Royal Victoria Country Park, Netley Hospital. Sergeant King died of his wounds on 9th April 1918 and was buried at Ryde Borough Cemetery.

Sgt. George Harvey PROUT, 1960

Sergeant George Prout came from Seaview. He was wounded at Gallipoli and news of his wounding was reported in the War Office's Casualty List on 13th September 1915.[300]

---

[299] www.forces-war-records.co.uk: First World War Daily Reports (Missing, Wounded & Prisoner of War)

[300] www.forces-war-records.co.uk: First World War Daily Reports (Missing, Wounded & Prisoner of War)

Sergeant Prout continued to serve with the Isle of Wight Rifles and was disembodied from the Army on 8th June 1919 under service number 330539.

Sgt. Raymond Joshua SIBLEY, 1025

Sergeant Raymond Sibley came from Ryde. He was seriously wounded and died overnight whilst at the Field Ambulance on 25th August 1915. He was aged 21. Although it was reported in the Isle of Wight County Press on 18th September 1915 that he was buried, Sergeant Sibley has no known grave and is commemorated on the Helles Memorial.

Sgt. Charles STEARS, 70

Sergeant Charles Stears enlisted in the Isle of Wight Rifles on 6th April 1908. He served at Gallipoli with his brother, Lance Sergeant Frank Stears (RAMC attached). Sergeant Stears received a head wound by a piece of shrapnel during October 1915. He was invalided off Gallipoli and received treatment at the Canadian Hospital in Cairo.

Sergeant Stears was discharged from the 4th (Reserve) battalion of the Hampshire Regiment on 20th September 1917 and received the Silver War Badge.

Sgt. Frederick Robert WARSAP, 997

Sergeant Frederick Warsap remained with the Isle of Wight Rifles after Gallipoli and was given service number 330050 when the Territorial Forces were given new service numbers. Sergeant Warsap was later Discharged to Commission and on 30th March 1917 held the rank of Temporary Lieutenant in the Royal Tank Corps.[301] He went on to become a Captain in the Royal Tank Corps and survived the war.

---

[301] www.forces-war-records.co.uk: UK Army List 1918

Sgt. Clarence Richard WESTMORE, 815

Sergeant Clarence Westmore served with the Isle of Wight Rifles throughout the war and reached the rank of Company Quartermaster Sergeant. He received a Mention in Despatches in General Sir Allenby's despatch on 5th March 1919.[302]

Company Quartermaster Sergeant Westmore was discharged from the Army on 10th June 1920 under service number 330044.

Sgt. Harold WISE, 235

Sergeant Harold Wise served with the Isle of Wight Rifles throughout the war and was discharged from the Army on 14th December 1918 under service number 330017.

Sgt. George Leopold WOODFORD, 594

Sergeant George Woodford enlisted in the Isle of Wight Rifles at Bembridge.[303] He was killed on 13th August 1915 and is commemorated on the Helles Memorial. His death was mentioned in a letter home from one of the RAMC attached to the Isle of Wight Rifles:

> Am sorry to say we have lost one of the 'Old Boys' in poor George Woodford. He had been doing splendid work with his machine gun in the front trench, and was shot by a sniper clean in the forehead. Fortunately the shot killed him instantaneously.[304]

QMS. Walter Sydney RUSSELL, 60

Quartermaster Sergeant Walter Russell served with the Isle of Wight Rifles at Gallipoli and was later given service number 330005. He was Discharged for Commission on 31st July 1917

---

[302] www.forces-war-records.co.uk: Gazetted Awards and Mentions in Despatches

[303] www.ancestry.co.uk: UK, Soldiers Died in the Great War, 1914-1919
[304] Isle of Wight County Press, 4th September 1915, p8.

and became an officer in the Egyptian Labour Corps, reaching the rank of Captain. He survived the war.

L/Sgt. Frank Henry BUTCHER, 981

Frank Butcher joined the Isle of Wight Rifles with his cousins; Reginald Brooks Butt, George Cooper, Will Cooper, and the Whites. On departing for Gallipoli, he had been promoted to the rank of Lance Sergeant.

Lance Sergeant Frank Butcher got through the Gallipoli campaign unscathed. He continued serving with the Isle of Wight Rifles throughout the war and reached the rank of Company Sergeant Major. He was disembodied from the Isle of Wight Rifles on 28th April 1919 under service number 330048.

L/Sgt. Alfred John WILLIAMS, 408

Lance Sergeant Alfred Williams enlisted in the Isle of Wight Rifles on 23rd November 1908. Lance Sergeant Williams continued to serve with the Isle of Wight Rifles after Gallipoli and was promoted to the rank of Sergeant and given service number 330025.

Sergeant Williams was discharged from the 4th Reserve Battalion of the Hampshire Regiment on 2nd August 1917 due to being medically unfit and was given the Silver War Badge.[305]

Cpl. William Albion BISHOP, 1099

Corporal William Bishop continued to serve with the Isle of Wight Rifles after Gallipoli. He was promoted to the rank of Sergeant and given service number 330073. He was reported as having been wounded in the War Office Daily List No.5428 on 28th November 1917.[306]

---

[305] www.ancestry.co.uk: Silver War Badge Records
[306] www.forces-war-records.co.uk: First World War Daily Reports (Missing, Wounded & Prisoner of War)

After the war, William Bishop re-joined the Isle of Wight Rifles as a Sergeant and was given service number 5488008. In May 1921 he was awarded the Territorial Force Efficiency Medal.[307]

Cpl. Frederick William BLOW, 1160

Corporal Frederick Blow continued to serve with the Isle of Wight Rifles after Gallipoli and reached the rank of Acting Warrant Officer Class II. He was disembodied from the Army on 12th April 1919.

Cpl. Alfred FLOOD, 1740

Corporal Alfred Flood was originally a regular soldier with the Dublin Fusiliers. His ten years of service saw him fight in the Boer War where he was wounded twice and taken prisoner.

Corporal Flood enlisted in the Isle of Wight Rifles on 2nd September 1915. He was reported as wounded in the Isle of Wight County Press on 4th September 1915 and it is likely that he was wounded in the advance on Anafarta Ridge on 12th August 1915.

Corporal Flood was discharged from the 4th Hants on 15th August 1917 under the rank of Lance-Sergeant and service number 330408. His Silver War Badge record states that he was discharged due to sickness.

Cpl. Arthur HUNT, 1382

Corporal Arthur Hunt continued to serve with the Isle of Wight Rifles following their Gallipoli campaign. He was disembodied from the Army on 21st February 1919 under service number 330221.

---

[307] www.forces-war-records.co.uk: Long Service Good Conduct Medal Collection

Cpl. Frank Daniel MAKER, 605

Corporal Frank Maker was wounded in the head at Gallipoli during August 1915 and received hospital treatment at St Andrew's Hospital in Malta. He was discharged from the Hampshire Regiment on 14th February 1916.

Corporal Maker decided to re-enlist in the Army, this time as a Gunner in the Royal Garrison Artillery, 443 Siege Battery and was given service number 158898.

Cpl. Harold RAYNER, 1032

Corporal Harold Rayner joined the Isle of Wight Rifles on 1st March 1911. On sailing to Gallipoli, he held the rank of Lance Sergeant.

Lance Sergeant Rayner was wounded on 14th August 1915, a couple of hours before the Isle of Wight Rifles were relieved from the front line. Four shots were aimed at him, the first just missing, the second hitting his Haverstock, the third hitting his right buttock and the fourth hitting his helmet as a comrade was trying to drag him to safety. When the battalion returned to base, Lance Sergeant Rayner was left and had to *'lie under fire all night in the company of a few dead.'*[308]

In the morning of 15th August 1915, two stretcher bearers from the Essex battalion took Lance Sergeant Rayner back to the 2nd Wessex Field Ambulance for initial treatment. He was then invalided off Gallipoli on 15th August 1915 on the same hospital ship as seven other members of the Isle of Wight Rifles; Rifleman Houghton, Rifleman Hinks, Rifleman Aylward, Rifleman A Barton, Rifleman Prince, Rifleman Wilton and Lance Corporal Cull. Lance Sergeant Rayner and Rifleman Houghton were taken back to Plymouth after their comrades had disembarked at Malta for their hospital treatment.

---

[308] Isle of Wight County Press, 18th September 1915

Lance Sergeant Rayner arrived at Plymouth on 27th August 1915 and was taken to Duchess of Connaught Canadian Red Cross Hospital in Taplow for treatment. He was discharged on 22nd April 1916 due to his wounding. His leg was permanently damaged and he was awarded an Army Pension.

Cpl. William George TILL, 1872

Corporal William Till came from Ryde. He was promoted to the rank of Sergeant at Gallipoli and was later on invalided off Gallipoli suffering with pneumonia. By November 1915, Sergeant Till had been admitted into a hospital in Alexandria, Egypt.

Sergeant Till returned to serve with the Isle of Wight Rifles and was disembodied from the battalion on 21st February 1919 under service number 330487.

Cpl. John WILKES, 1874

Corporal John Wilkes continued to serve with the Isle of Wight Rifles after their deployment to Gallipoli. He was discharged from the Army on 14th December 1918 under service number 330489.

L/Cpl. Walter John BUTCHER, 1845

Lance Corporal Walter Butcher was 22 years old when he enlisted in the Isle of Wight Rifles on 3rd September 1914 at Ryde. He was invalided off Gallipoli and died at the 21st General Hospital, Alexandria on 17th October 1915. His record in the UK, Soldiers Died in the Great War, 1914-1919 catalogue states that he 'died' rather than 'died of wounds' so it suggests that Lance Corporal Butcher died due to an illness.

Lance Corporal Butcher is buried at Alexandria (Chatby) Military and War Memorial Cemetery.

L/Cpl. Harold COMDEN, 941

Lance Corporal Harold Comden, 'received a gunshot wound in the left hand, which necessitated the amputation of one finger.'[309] His wounding occurred between August and early September 1915 and he was invalided off Gallipoli and taken to St David's Hospital in Malta for treatment.

Lance Corporal Comden was discharged from the Hampshire Regiment on 10th March 1916. According to the British War Medal and Victory Medal records, Harold Comden also served as a Private in the 1/6th Hants under service number 3798. It is not clear if this was prior to him serving with the Isle of Wight Rifles or afterwards.

L/Cpl. Harry CULL, 1404

Lance Corporal Harry Cull was shot in the right thigh on the evening of the attack on Anafarta Ridge causing a large open flesh wound. In a letter home to his mother which was published in the Isle of Wight County Press on 4th September 1915 he wrote:

> I was wounded on Thursday evening and lay about under fire until Saturday afternoon, when our clergyman found me, fetched a stretcher party and had me taken away.[310]

He embarked on a hospital ship on 14th August 1915 and was taken to Malta for treatment. Lance Corporal Cull was discharged from the Army on 14th April 1916.

L/Cpl. Eric Raymond HOLBROOK, 1245

Lance Corporal Eric Holbrook came from Bembridge and enlisted in the Isle of Wight Rifles at St. Helen's, Isle of Wight. His parents were notified by Rifleman Child that he had been wounded and was missing after the attack on Anafarta Ridge. It

---

[309] Isle of Wight County Press, 18th September 1915
[310] Isle of Wight County Press, 4th September 1915.

was later presumed that Lance Corporal Holbrook had killed in action on 12th August 1915 and he is commemorated on the Helles Memorial.

L/Cpl. Ernest Edward JOHNSON, 1801

Lance Corporal Ernest Johnson enlisted in the Isle of Wight Rifles on 2nd September 1914. He received a light wounding to his knee at Gallipoli in August 1915 and at the time was an Acting Corporal.

Lance Corporal Johnson went on to become a Corporal in the Labour Corps under service number 341870. He was discharged from the Labour Corps due to 'sickness' on 17th April 1918.

L/Cpl. Alfred <u>Oliver</u> LACEY, 1503

Lance Corporal Alfred Oliver Lacey was born on 6th August 1893. He was a blacksmith and enlisted in the Isle of Wight Rifles on 28th February 1910 at Ryde. He was also known as Oliver Lacey.

Oliver Lacey was taken ill at Gallipoli on 2nd November 1915 with dysentery and rheumatism. He was initially sent to a hospital in Malta and was then invalided back to England on 25th January 1916. Oliver Lacey then fell ill with Enteric and was in hospital from 9th February 1916 until 20th April 1916.

On 24th July 1916, Oliver Lacey was transferred to the Royal Engineers at Chatham. He was deployed to Egypt from the 26th September 1918 until 24th March 1919 and was discharged from the Royal Engineers under the rank of Lance Sergeant and with service number 188793.

Oliver Lacey joined the Royal Army Pay Corps at Chatham on 19th July 1920 but had to be discharged on 29th July 1920 due to the long-term effects of having contracted Enteric Fever. He was subsequently awarded an Army Pension.[311]

L/Cpl. Angus John LENNOX, 1569

Lance Corporal Angus Lennox was *'wounded on 1st September whilst in his dug-out by a high explosive shell which threw him 150 yards in the air causing sprains, bruises and concussion.'*[312] Lance Corporal Lennox was taken to a hospital in Malta for further treatment.

Lance Corporal Lennox returned to serve with the Isle of Wight Rifles and was later on given service number 330304. On 26th November 1917, Angus Lennox was Discharged to Commission and served as a Second Lieutenant with the Ayrshire Yeomanry and Machine Gun Corps. He survived the war.

L/Cpl. Edward George MILES, 950

Lance Corporal Edward 'Teddy' Miles came from Ryde and joined the Isle of Wight Rifles at Ryde. He was killed in action on 12th August 1915 aged 20 years old and is commemorated on the Helles Memorial.

L/Cpl. William Henry PARRACK D.C.M, 1610

Lance Corporal William Parrack continued to serve with the Isle of Wight Rifles with distinction after their Gallipoli campaign and went on to hold the rank of Lance Sergeant with service number 330301.

Lance Sergeant Parrack was Mentioned in Despatches on 28th June 1917 which was officially published in the London Gazette Issue 30474, p800, on 11th January 1918:

> I have honour to enclose here with a list of those Officers, Ladies, Non-Commissioned Officers and Men

---

[311] www.ancestry.co.uk: British Army WWI Pension Records 1914-1920
[312] Isle of Wight County Press, 2nd October 1915, p8

whose names I wish to bring to your notice for gallant or distinguished conduct in the Field, or for other valuable service.[313]

He was also awarded the Distinguished Conduct Medal and this was officially announced in the London Gazette on 3rd November 1920 on page 3081. The citation reads:

> For continuous good work and devotion to duty. He has performed the duties of orderly during the past three years. Many times under heavy fire, he has set a splendid example by his cool, methodical manner.[314]

On 28th May 1919, Lance Sergeant Parrack transferred to the Royal Army Service Corps. He was discharged from the Army on 20th April 1921 under the rank of Acting Sergeant and service number NAC/450966.

L/Cpl. Albert Emmanuel SPRAGG, 412

Lance Corporal Spragg came from Ryde. He was wounded at Gallipoli during August 1915 and was taken to a hospital in Cairo, Egypt.

Lance Corporal Spragg continued to serve with the Isle of Wight Rifles and became a Corporal. He died on 20th November 1918 aged 30 and is buried at Beirut War Cemetery. His latter service number was 330026.

L/Cpl. Walter John WARREN, 917

Lance Corporal Walter Warren served with the Isle of Wight Rifles at Gallipoli and was discharged from the Army on 29th February 1916.

---

[313] www.forces-war-records.co.uk: Gazetted Awards and Mentions in Despatches

[314] www.forces-war-records.co.uk: Gazetted Awards and Mentions in Despatches

After the war, Walter Warren re-joined the Isle of Wight Rifles and was given service number 5488109.

L/Cpl. Percy ELLAWAY, 1646

Lance Corporal Percy Ellaway came from Steventon in Berkshire, however, he enlisted in the Isle of Wight Rifles at Newport.[315] On sailing to Gallipoli he held the rank of Lance Corporal and was later promoted to Sergeant during the Gallipoli campaign. Sergeant Ellaway was on observation duty on 16th October 1915 when he was wounded. He subsequently died of his wounds later in the day and is buried at Embarkation Pier Cemetery.

L/Cpl. Edwin KINGSWELL, 2024

Lance Corporal Edwin Kingswell continued to serve with the Isle of Wight Rifles after Gallipoli. He reached the rank of Acting Sergeant and was disembodied from the Army on 31st July 1919 under service number 330585.

L/Cpl. Arthur Edward RAYNER, 1409

Lance Corporal Arthur Rayner came from Ryde. He continued serving with the Isle of Wight Rifles following their deployment to Gallipoli and was promoted to the rank of Sergeant and given service number 330227.

Sergeant Arthur Rayner was wounded, presumably during the Third Battle of Gaza, and died of his wounds on the 2nd November 1917. He was 24 years old and was serving in 'D' Company. Sergeant Rayner is buried at Deir El Belah War Cemetery.[316]

---

[315] www.ancestry.co.uk: UK, Soldiers Died in the Great War, 1914-1919
[316] https://www.cwgc.org/find-war-dead/casualty/645884/rayner,-arthur-edward/

L/Cpl. James Henry Frank RACKETT, 1863

Lance Corporal James Rackett came from Ryde and enlisted in the Isle of Wight Rifles on 3rd September 1914. He was wounded at Gallipoli on 18th August 1915 but made a swift recovery and re-joined the battalion. Lance-Corporal Rackett then fell ill with dysentery and on 5th October 1915 was admitted into the Canadian Hospital at Mudros. Following treatment at Mudros, he was invalided back to England and spent time recuperating at Graylingwell War Hospital in Chichester.[317]

Lance Corporal Rackett was discharged from the Army on 29th July 1916 owing to sickness and was given the Silver War Badge.

Bandsman Percy PURNELL, 475

Bandsman Percy Purnell came from Bembridge and enlisted in the Isle of Wight Rifles on 28th December 1908. He served with his brother, Rifleman Sydney Purnell, in the Isle of Wight Rifles at Gallipoli and they were both wounded in a similar manner and roughly in the same area of the body.

Bandsman Purnell was wounded by a piece of shrapnel on the 3rd September 1915. The shrapnel ball entered his abdomen and bounced of his pelvic bone in a downward trajectory. Private Reginald Brooks Butt (RAMC attached) recollected dressing 'Perce' Purnell's wound when speaking about his war experiences to his son.

Bandsman Purnell was discharged from the 2/8th Hants on 18th August 1916 and was given the Silver War Badge.[318]

Bugler Frederick Charles JOLLIFFE, 1303

Bugler Frederick Jolliffe continued serving with the Isle of Wight Rifles after Gallipoli and was given service number 330169. During the latter part of the war, he was transferred to the 1/4th

---

[317] Isle of Wight County Press, 11th December 1915, p8
[318] www.forces-war-records.co.uk: Silver War Badge List 1914-1918

Hants and in 1918 the 1/4th Hants were deployed to Persia from the Middle East. Frederick Jolliffe survived the war.

Bugler Leslie PAYNE, 2293

Bugler Leslie Payne was reported in the 16th October 1915 edition of the Isle of Wight County Press as having been wounded at Gallipoli.

Bugler Payne recovered from his wounding and returned to serve with the Isle of Wight Rifles and was given service number 330743 when the Territorials received new service numbers in 1917. Later in the war he was transferred to the Kings Royal Rifle Corps and given service number 49699. He survived the war.

Bugler Fred TRENT, 890

Bugler Fred Trent was reported as having been wounded at Gallipoli in the 25th September 1915 edition of the Isle of Wight County Press.

Bugler Trent was discharged from the Army on 6th March 1916.

Bugler Fred Scott WHITTINGTON, 335

Bugler Fred Whittington served in the Isle of Wight Rifles at Gallipoli with his brothers Harold and Harry. Bugler Whittington was promoted to the rank of Lance Corporal at Gallipoli. He was invalided off Gallipoli and by the beginning of December had been admitted to Hazelwood Ryde following treatment at Fawcett Road Hospital in Southsea.

Fred Whittington went on to become a Corporal in the Machine Gun Corps under service number 88021. He was disembodied from the Army on 24th February 1919 but decided to re-enlist with the Isle of Wight Rifles, holding the rank of Corporal and with service number 548807. His brother, Harold, was killed in the Battle of Langemarck on 16th August 1917. Harry survived the war.

Rfn. Christopher ARNOLD, 2380

Rifleman Christopher Arnold came from Cowes and enlisted in the Isle of Wight Rifles at Newport. He served with his brother, Rifleman Fred Arnold, in the Isle of Wight Rifles at Gallipoli.

Rifleman Christopher Arnold was wounded between August 1915 and early September 1915. He was, *'shot in the hand and lost a finger.'*[319] Rifleman Arnold was invalided off Gallipoli and taken to a hospital in Alexandria. He later picked up pneumonia and passed away on the 2nd November 1915. He is buried at Alexandria (Chatby) Military and War Memorial Cemetery.

Rfn. Charles Albert ASH, 1658

Rifleman Charles Ash enlisted in the Isle of Wight Rifles on 31st August 1914 and was wounded at Gallipoli on 10th August 1915. He, 'took a ricocheted bullet in the left shoulder at Suvla Beach, Gallipoli.'[320] Rifleman Ash was invalided off Gallipoli prior to the Isle of Wight Rifles advance on Anafarta Ridge on 12th August 1915.

Rifleman Ash was discharged from the Army on 10th August 1918 at the age of 26. His service number was 380074 and he was given the Silver War Badge due to 'wounds.'[321]

Rfn. Alexander ATTRILL, 1381

Rifleman Alexander Attrill continued to serve with the Isle of Wight Rifles after their deployment to Gallipoli. He was disembodied from the battalion on 2nd April 1919 under service number 330210.

---

[319] Isle of Wight County Press, 18th September 1915, p8.
[320] https://livesofthefirstworldwar.org/lifestory/74803#stories
[321] www.ancestry.co.uk: Silver War Badge Records

Rfn. Augustus Francis ATTRILL, 1823

Rifleman Augustus Attrill enlisted in the Isle of Wight Rifles on 3rd September 1914. At some point after the deployment to Gallipoli he was transferred to the Labour Corps as a Private.

Augustus Attrill was discharged from the Army on 14th June 1919 and was awarded the Silver War Badge due to 'sickness.'

Rfn. Richard Henry ATTRILL, 1277

Rifleman Richard Attrill enlisted in the Isle of Wight Rifles on 26th March 1913 and following the Gallipoli deployment continued to serve with the Isle of Wight Rifles. A wounding later in the war led to Rifleman Attrill being discharged from the Army on 22nd May 1918 and given the Silver War Badge. His latter service number was 330157.

Rfn. Herbert AYLING, 1723

Rifleman Herbert Ayling continued to serve with the Isle of Wight Rifles after their Gallipoli campaign. He was disembodied from the battalion on 23rd July 1919 under service number 330401.

Rfn. R. L. AYLWARD, 1396

Rifleman Aylward came from Ryde. He fell victim to dysentery and was invalided off Gallipoli on the 14th August 1915 and taken to a hospital in Malta with a few other members of the Isle of Wight Rifles.

Rifleman Aylward later joined the RFC/RAF and survived the war. His service number was 403813.

Rfn. Henry John AYRES, 2391

Rifleman Henry Ayres enlisted in the Isle of Wight Rifles on 20th April 1915 and at some point, following serving with the battalion at Gallipoli and in Egypt, he was transferred to the 2/4th

Hants and given service number 205466. By the end of April 1917, the 2/4th Hants had arrived in Palestine from India and the battalion fought in the Palestinian campaign until it was transferred to France on 22nd May 1918.[322]

Rifleman Ayres was discharged from the Army on 24th December 1919 and was given the Silver War Badge for 'sickness.'

Rfn. Thomas BAKER, 2146

Rifleman Thomas Baker was residing at Kipson Bank, Hunston, Chichester, Sussex when he enlisted in the Isle of Wight Rifles on 1st January 1915.[323] Following Gallipoli, he remained with the Isle of Wight Rifles but was discharged from the Army on 8th September 1916 due to 'sickness' and was given the Silver War Badge.

Rfn. John BALLARD, 1829

Rifleman John Ballard came from Lake and enlisted in the Isle of Wight Rifles at Shanklin.[324]

At some point after the Gallipoli campaign, Rifleman Ballard was transferred to the 2/4th Hants as a Private and was given service number 205455. Following serving with the 2/4th Hants, Private Ballard was transferred to the 2/5th Hants. He was killed in action during the successful Battle of Nabi Samweil and is buried at Jerusalem War Cemetery.

Rfn. Walter BALLARD, 2453

Rifleman Walter Ballard came from Ryde and enlisted in the Isle of Wight Rifles in June 1915 at Newport. He was killed in action

---

[322] https://www.longlongtrail.co.uk/army/regiments-and-corps/the-british-infantry-regiments-of-1914-1918/hampshire-regiment/
[323] www.forces-war-records.co.uk: Silver War Badge List 1914-1918
[324] www.ancestry.co.uk: UK, Soldiers Died in the Great War, 1914-1919

on 12th August 1915 aged 24 and is commemorated on the Helles Memorial.

Rfn. Jesse James BARNES, 1399

Rifleman Jesse Barnes received wounds to his body and arm at Gallipoli during August 1915.

Rifleman Barnes later went on to serve with the 2/4th Hants and then the 2/5th Hants under service number 205445. He was killed in action on the 20th November 1917 during the Battle of Nabi Samweil and is buried at Jerusalem War Cemetery.

Rfn. Thomas BARTLETT, 1505

Rifleman Thomas Bartlett enlisted into the Isle of Wight Rifles at Ryde. After Gallipoli he continued to serve with the Isle of Wight Rifles. He was promoted to the rank of Lance Corporal and was given service number 330273.

Lance Corporal Bartlett was listed as missing after the Isle of Wight Rifles took part in the Second Battle of Gaza on 19th April 1917.[325] It was later assumed that Lance Corporal Bartlett had been killed in action on 19th April 1917. He was 24 years old and has no known grave. Lance Corporal Bartlett is commemorated on the Jerusalem Memorial.

Rfn. Albert Ernest BARTON, 1504

Rifleman Albert Barton enlisted in the Isle of Wight Rifles at Ryde in 1914. He quickly became ill with dysentery at Gallipoli and was taken by hospital ship to Malta on 14th August 1915.

Later in the war, Rifleman Barton was promoted to the rank of Corporal and served in the 214th Company of the Machine Gun Corps with the service number 50254. The 214th Company of the Machine Gun Corps fought in the Third Battle of Ypres during

---

[325] www.forces-war-records.co.uk: British Red Cross and Order of St John Enquiry List 1917 (Wounded and Missing)

1917 and Corporal Barton was killed in action on 20th September 1917. He is commemorated on the Tyne Cot Memorial.

Rfn. Charles James BARTON, 2481

Rifleman Charles Barton joined the Isle of Wight Rifles in June 1915. He was wounded at Gallipoli and died on a hospital ship headed for Malta on 25th August 1915. Rifleman Barton was buried at sea and is commemorated on the Helles Memorial.

Rfn. George BARTON, 2102

Rifleman George Barton enlisted in the Isle of Wight Rifles on 21st December 1914. He was wounded in the arm and side on 12th August 1915 and was invalided off Gallipoli and taken to St Andrew's Hospital in Malta. He was then sent to Wharncliffe War Hospital in Sheffield. Rifleman Barton was discharged from the British Army on 22nd June 1916 due to the effect of his wounding.

Rfn. Jack BARTON, 1438

Rifleman Jack Barton enlisted into the Isle of Wight Rifles on 28th January 1914. Following the Gallipoli campaign, Jack Barton was transferred to the 1/5th battalion of the Duke of Cornwall's Light Infantry as a Private soldier. He was given service number 260060. He was later transferred to the 1st battalion of the Duke of Cornwall's Light Infantry and was wounded whilst fighting on the Western Front. Jack Barton was subsequently discharged from the Army on 23rd September 1918 and given the Silver War Badge.[326] [327]

Rfn. Charles BAYLIS, 1824

Rifleman Charles Baylis was transferred to the Somerset Light Infantry at some point after the Isle of Wight Rifles Gallipoli campaign. He was given service number 34511 and reached the

---

[326] www.ancestry.co.uk: UK, Silver War Badge Records, 1914-1920
[327] www.ancestry.co.uk: UK, WWI Service Medal and Award Rolls, 1914-1920

rank of Lance Corporal. Charles Baylis was disembodied from the Army on 2nd April 1919 and at a later date re-enlisted into the Isle of Wight Rifles as a Lance Corporal under service number 5488105.[328]

Rfn. James BEARD, 1403

Rifleman James Beard came from Ryde and enlisted into the Isle of Wight Rifles on 14th January 1914. Either at Gallipoli or after Gallipoli, in Egypt, Rifleman Beard became ill. He was subsequently discharged from the Army on 6th September 1916 and was given the Silver War Badge as he was deemed to be unfit for further military service due to 'sickness.'[329]

Rfn. John BEAUMONT, 2366

Rifleman John Beaumont came from St Leonards, Sussex and enlisted into the Isle of Wight Rifles on 16th March 1915. He only spent a short amount of time at Gallipoli as on 8th September 1915, at the age of 19, he was admitted on to Her Majesty's Hospital Ship Assaye suffering with a *'disordered action of the heart.'*[330] As a result of this, he was subsequently discharged from the Army on 11th July 1916 and was given the Silver War Badge for 'sickness.'[331]

Rfn. George BEAVER, 2345

Rifleman George Beaver was transferred to the 2/4th Hants at some point after the Isle of Wight Rifles' deployment to Gallipoli. He served under service number 330772 and held the rank of Private. George Beaver was later transferred to the 2/5th Hants and then on to the 1/4th battalion of the Wiltshire Regiment.

---

[328] www.ancestry.co.uk: British Army WWI Medal Rolls Index Cards, 1914-1920
[329] www.forces-war-records.co.uk: Silver War Badge List 1914-1918
[330] www.forces-war-records.co.uk: Military Hospitals Admissions and Discharge Registers WW1
[331] www.forces-war-records.co.uk: Silver War Badge List 1914-1918

Both of these battalions were part of the Egyptian Expeditionary Force.

George Beaver was discharged from the Army and placed onto the Class Z reserve list on 8th May 1919.

Rfn. Charles BERRY, 2362

Rifleman Charles Berry was wounded at Gallipoli and was *'listed as "Wounded" on the Casualty List issued by the War Office on 20th October 1915.'*[332]

Rifleman Berry recovered from his wounding and continued to serve with the Isle of Wight Rifles under service number 330788 until the 21st August 1918 when he enlisted into the Royal Air Force.

Rfn. Reginald BOARD, 1815

Rifleman Reginald Board came from Upton Pyne in Devon and enlisted in the Isle of Wight Rifles at Newport.[333]

Rifleman Board continued to serve with the Isle of Wight Rifles after their Gallipoli deployment and was given service number 330451. He was killed in action during the Second Battle of Gaza on 19th April 1917 and is commemorated on the Jerusalem Memorial.

Rfn. W. BOWERS, 2343

Rifleman Bowers joined the Royal Flying Corps at some point after serving with the Isle of Wight Rifles at Gallipoli and was given service number 406126. He survived the war.

---

[332] www.forces-war-records.co.uk: First World War Daily Reports (Missing, Wounded & Prisoner of War)
[333] www.ancestry.co.uk: UK, Soldiers Died in the Great War, 1914-1919

Rfn. William BRADING, 1841

Rifleman William Brading resided at "Sunnyside", Weeks Road, Ryde, and enlisted into the Isle of Wight Rifles on 3rd September 1914.[334] At some point either at Gallipoli or afterwards in Egypt, Rifleman Brading became ill. He was subsequently discharged from the Army on 29th July 1916 and was given the Silver War Badge.

Rfn. Henry Dean BREWER, 2337

Rifleman Henry Brewer was wounded at Gallipoli and was 'listed as "Wounded" on the Casualty List issued by the War Office on 24th September 1915.'[335]

Rifleman Brewer was discharged from the Army on 20th July 1916.

Rfn. Frederick BROADBRIDGE, 2148

Rifleman Frederick Broadbridge was reported as having been wounded at Gallipoli in the 25th September 1915 edition of the Isle of Wight County Press.

Rifleman Broadbridge continued to serve with the Isle of Wight Rifles after being wounded and was disembodied from the battalion on 28th July 1919 under service number 330658.

Rfn. Henry BROWN, 2484

Rifleman Henry Brown served with the Isle of Wight Rifles throughout the war and was disembodied from the Army on 21st August 1919 under service number 330861.

---

[334] www.forces-war-records.co.uk: Silver War Badge List 1914-1918
[335] www.forces-war-records.co.uk: First World War Daily Reports (Missing, Wounded & Prisoner of War)

Rfn. William Henry BUCKETT, 1020

Rifleman William Buckett became ill with dysentery between the middle of August and early September 1915. He was invalided off Gallipoli and taken to a hospital in Liverpool for further treatment.

On returning to full health, Rifleman Buckett re-joined the Isle of Wight Rifles and served with them for the remainder of the war. He was disembodied from the Army on the 15th July 1919 under service number 330052.

Rfn. Stanley BURDEN, 741

Rifleman Stanley Burden came from St Helen's and enlisted into the Isle of Wight Rifles at the age of 18 on 4th March 1909. He was promoted to the rank of Lance Corporal at Gallipoli on 28th September 1915 and then promoted to the rank of Acting Sergeant on 12th December 1915. Stanley Burden sailed with the Isle of Wight Rifles to Alexandria but due to his service period coming to an end, he sailed for England on 22nd March 1916 and arrived home on 4th April 1916. He was discharged from the Army on 17th April 1916 after having served with the Isle of Wight Rifles for 7 years and 45 days.[336]

Rfn. Sydney Ernest BUTT, 1844

Rifleman Sydney Butt served with the Isle of Wight Rifles at Gallipoli and for some of the battalion's time in the Egyptian Expeditionary Force where he was given service number 330467 when the Territorial Forces received new service numbers. Later in the war, Sydney Butt transferred to the Royal Engineers as a Sapper and was given service number 624704. He was disembodied from the Army on 24th July 1919.

---

[336] www.ancestry.co.uk: British Army WWI Pension Records 1914-1920

Rfn. Gordon CHAMBERS, 1828

Rifleman Gordon Chambers came from Shanklin and enlisted into the Isle of Wight Rifles at Shanklin. At some point after the Gallipoli campaign, Rifleman Chambers was transferred to the Suffolk Regiment under service number 330344 and then later on was posted to the 1st Battalion of the Cambridgeshire Regiment with the rank of Private.

Private Chambers died at the General Hospital in Sheffield on 14th August 1917.[337] He is buried at Sheffield Burngreave Cemetery.

Rfn. Philip Evershed CHAPMAN, 2364

Rifleman Philip Chapman came from Hereford. He originally enlisted into the RAMC at Maidstone in Kent and was given service number 2681 however he was transferred to the Isle of Wight Rifles and became a rifleman.

Rifleman Chapman was wounded on 26th August 1915 and was invalided off Gallipoli to Malta for further treatment where he was treated by his Godfather, Charles Symonds who was a surgeon.[338] Rifleman Chapman died of his wounds on the 5th September 1915 aged 21 years old and is buried at Pieta Military Cemetery.[339]

Rfn. Alan Napier CHILDS, 1287

Rifleman Alan Childs was transferred to the Machine Gun Corps after the Gallipoli campaign. He was promoted to the rank of Corporal and given service number 104440 and on 26th July 1917

---

[337] www.ancestry.co.uk: UK, Army Registers of Soldiers' Effects, 1901-1929 for Gordon Chambers
[338] https://livesofthefirstworldwar.iwm.org.uk/story/83453
[339] https://www.cwgc.org/find-war-dead/casualty/115008/chapman,-philip-evershed/#&gid=null&pid=3

officially became a Second Lieutenant in the Machine Gun Corps. He survived the war.[340]

Rfn. Frederick Arthur CHIVERTON, 2317

Rifleman Frederick Chiverton came from Newport. He continued to serve with the Isle of Wight Rifles after Gallipoli and reached the rank of Sergeant with service number 330759. Sergeant Chiverton was killed in action on 2nd November 1917 during the Third Battle of Gaza. He was 24 years old and is commemorated on the Jerusalem Memorial.

Rfn. Walter Henry CLARKE, 1385

Rifleman Walter Clarke came from Bembridge. Following Gallipoli, he continued to serve with the Isle of Wight Rifles and was given service number 330213 when the Territorial Forces received new service numbers. He was wounded and taken prisoner during the Second Battle of Gaza and subsequently died of his wounds on 7th August 1917. Rifleman Clarke was 20 years old and is buried at Damascus Commonwealth War Cemetery.

Rfn. Herbert Thomas COLLIS, 543

Rifleman Herbert Collis was reported as having been wounded at Gallipoli in the Isle of Wight County Press on 4th September 1915. Given the time it took news to reach England and the high number of casualties taken on 12th August 1915, it is likely that Rifleman Collis was wounded during the action at Anafarta Ridge.

Rifleman Collis was discharged from the Army on 21st January 1916.

---

[340] www.ancestry.co.uk: 1914-15 Star records

Rfn. H COMDEN, 1734

Rifleman H Comden became ill with Enteric Fever between the middle of September and early October 1915. He was invalided off Gallipoli to Shruba Military Hospital in Cairo.

Later on in the war, Rifleman Comden joined the Royal Flying Corps which later became the Royal Air Force and was given service number 103287. He survived the war.

Rfn. John Stanley COMPTON, 1615

Rifleman John Compton continued serving with the Isle of Wight Rifles after Gallipoli and was given service number 330336 when the Territorial Forces received new service numbers.

John Compton applied to become an officer and was Discharged to Commission on 8th December 1917 and served in the Royal Field Artillery as a Second Lieutenant.[341]

Rfn. George Charles Thomas COOKE, 2115

Rifleman George Cooke came from Newport. During August 1915 at Gallipoli he received a wounding to his side.

Rifleman Cooke continued to serve in the Isle of Wight Rifles and was disembodied from the Army on 29th March 1919 under service number 330640.

Rfn. Albert Ernest COOMBES, 1846

Rifleman Albert Coombes had previously served in the Isle of Wight Rifles and re-joined the battalion at Ryde when war broke out. He was wounded on 14th August 1915 and subsequently died on 24th August 1915 whilst on a hospital ship. He was buried at sea and is commemorated on the Helles Memorial.

---

[341] www.ancestry.co.uk: British Army WWI Medal Rolls Index Cards, 1914-1920

Rfn. Harold Roy COOPER, 1619

Rifleman Harold Cooper enlisted in the Isle of Wight Rifles on 21st August 1914. He continued to serve with the Isle of Wight Rifles after Gallipoli and was promoted to the rank of Lance Corporal. He was given service number 330337 when the Territorial Forces received new service numbers in 1917.

Lance Corporal Cooper was wounded during the fighting in Palestine and as a result was discharged from the Army on 17th July 1918 at the age of 25.[342]

Rfn. Thomas Charles COOPER, 2105

Rifleman Thomas Cooper served with the Isle of Wight Rifles throughout the war and survived the war. His latter service number was 330635.

Rfn. Charles James COUSINS, 2007

Rifleman Charles Cousins served with the Isle of Wight Rifles throughout the war and reached the rank of Corporal. He was disembodied from the Army on 31st July 1919 under service number 330570.

Rfn. Archibald Beaconsfield CRABB, 2236

Rifleman Archibald Crabb came from Ryde. He remained with the Isle of Wight Rifles following their deployment to Gallipoli and was given service number 330174 when the Territorial Forces received new service numbers in 1917. Rifleman Crabb took part in the Second Battle of Gaza on 19th April 1917 and was killed in action during the battle. He was 29 years old and is commemorated on the Jerusalem Memorial.[343]

---

[342] www.forces-war-records.co.uk: Silver War Badge List 1914-1918
[343] https://www.cwgc.org/find-war-dead/casualty/1644823/crabb,-archibald-beaconsfield/

Rfn. A J CRANEFIELD, 1276

Rifleman Cranefield enlisted into the Isle of Wight Rifles on 26th March 1913. Following Gallipoli, he joined the Royal Flying Corps, which later became the Royal Air Force, and was given service number 406058. His Royal Air Force record states that he was a sailmaker with the Royal Flying Corps and when transferred to the Royal Air Force, his trade was as a fabric maker.[344]

Rfn. George Ernest CREASY, 1708

Rifleman George Creasy was transferred to the 1/6th Hants at some point after his time with the Isle of Wight Rifles at Gallipoli and was given service number 281801. The 1/6th Hants were based in India. They deployed to Basra in September 1917 and remained in Mesopotamia to the war's conclusion.

Rifleman Creasy was disembodied from the Army on 30th October 1919.

Rfn. Cyril CROOK, 2309

Rifleman Cyril Crook was one of the men recruited by Lieutenant Colonel Rhodes. He came from High Wycombe and enlisted in the Isle of Wight Rifles at Newport on 2nd February 1915.

Rifleman Crook was initially reported as missing on 22nd August 1915 but he had in fact been taken ill and had been sent to 54th Division Base Depot on West Mudros. On 7th September 1915, Rifleman Crook was admitted into Nasrieh School Military Hospital, Cairo suffering from consumption. He was then transferred to a rest camp at Abbassia on 15th October 1915. Rifleman Crook boarded Hospital Ship 'Salta' on 1st November 1915 and set foot back on English soil on 16th November 1915.

---

[344] www.forces-war-records.co.uk: RAF Formations List 1918

Due to his illness, he was discharged from the 3/8th Hants at Parkhurst Barracks on 4th February 1916.[345]

Rifleman Crook chose to re-enlist into the 2/8th Hants on 22nd September 1916 and was given service number 357379. Later in the war, he became ill with bacillary dysentery which led to him being physically unfit for military service. Rifleman Crook was discharged from the Army on 2nd February 1918 and was given a 26 week pension.[346]

Rfn. William CRUMP, 2469

Rifleman William Crump came from High Wycombe in Buckinghamshire and was one of the men recruited by Lieutenant Colonel Rhodes. After Gallipoli he fought in Palestine with the Isle of Wight Rifles and was killed in action during the Third Battle of Gaza on 2nd November 1917 at the age of 21. His service number was 330852. Rifleman Crump is buried at Gaza War Cemetery.[347]

Rfn. Reginald Sidney DALLIMORE, 1429

Rifleman Reginald Dallimore was transferred to the Machine Gun Corps following Gallipoli. He was given service number 50270 and the rank of Private. Reginald Dallimore was disembodied from the Army on 4th October 1919.

Rfn. Frank DAVIS, 1799

Rifleman Frank Davis transferred to the Royal Engineers after serving with the Isle of Wight Rifles at Gallipoli. He became a Sapper and was given service number 233545. Frank Davis then went on to work in the Railways section of the Royal Engineers under service number WR/195050.

---

[345] www.ancestry.co.uk: British Army WW1 Pension Record 1914-1920
[346] www.ancestry.co.uk: British Army WW1 Pension Record 1914-1920
[347] https://www.cwgc.org/find-war-dead/casualty/649818/crump,-/

After the war, Frank Davis re-enlisted into the Isle of Wight Rifles. He held the rank of Corporal and his service number was 5488090.[348]

Rfn. James DEVEREAUX, 2294

Rifleman James Devereaux came from High Wycombe, Buckinghamshire. He was wounded at Gallipoli and subsequently died on 14th August 1915. Rifleman Devereaux was 19 years old and is commemorated on the Helles Memorial.

Rfn. Sidney Charles Henry DOWNER, 909

Rifleman Sidney Downer came from Ryde and joined the Isle of Wight Rifles in 1909. He received a gunshot wound to his chest and subsequently died of his wounds on 23rd August 1915 aged 22 whilst on a hospital ship. He was buried at sea and is commemorated on the Helles Memorial.

Rfn. George Henry DRURY, 1496

Rifleman George Drury came from Clapham in London and enlisted in the Isle of Wight Rifles on 3rd August 1914. He was *'listed as "Wounded" on the Casualty List issued by the War Office on 17th September 1915.'*[349]

Rifleman Drury was discharged from the Army on 16th June 1916 and given the Silver War Badge due to 'sickness.'[350]

Rfn. George DUNN, 1731

Rifleman George Dunn came from Sandown. He was killed at Gallipoli by a shell on 29th November 1915 at the age of 21 and is buried at 7th Field Ambulance Cemetery.[351] Rev H K Bond, an

---

[348] www.ancestry.co.uk: UK, WWI Service Medal and Award Rolls, 1914-1920
[349] www.forces-war-records.co.uk: First World War Daily Reports (Missing, Wounded & Prisoner of War)
[350] www.forces-war-records.co.uk: Silver War Badge List 1914-1918
[351] https://www.cwgc.org/find-war-dead/casualty/605472/dunn,-/

Army Chaplain, notified Rifleman Dunn's mother of the death of her son by a letter:

> He died almost at once. I buried him the same day in the Hants' burial-ground...We erected a cross over his grave just like the others.[352]

Rfn. Edward DYER, 962

Rifleman Edward Dyer enlisted into the Isle of Wight Rifles at St Helen's on 25th October 1910 at the age of 15 years and 4 months. He was recorded as being 4 foot and 11 ½ inches on attesting and at the time, his full-time job was working as a Caddie at the Royal Isle of Wight Golf Club.[353]

Rifleman Dyer fell ill at Gallipoli with Enteritis and on 30th October 1915 was admitted into the Red Cross Hospital at Giza. On 2nd February 1916 Rifleman Dyer was posted to 54th Infantry Base Depot at Alexandria and then on 22nd March 1916 he embarked on H.T. Tunisian to return to England for discharge from the Army due to completing his period of service. He was officially discharged on 24th April 1916.[354]

Rfn. Frederick DYER, 1400

Rifleman Frederick Dyer continued serving with the Isle of Wight Rifles after Gallipoli and was disembodied from the battalion on 28th July 1919 under service number 330222.

Rfn. William DYER, 1206

Rifleman William Dyer was transferred to the Machine Gun Corps following Gallipoli and reached the rank of Sergeant. He was disembodied from the Army on 4th August 1919 under service number 50251.

---

[352] Isle of Wight County Press, 29th January 1916, p5
[353] www.ancestry.co.uk: British Army WWI Pension Records 1914-1920
[354] www.ancestry.co.uk: British Army WWI Pension Records 1914-1920

Rfn. Harold Edward ESCOTT, 2382

Rifleman Harold Escott enlisted into the Isle of Wight Rifles on 15th April 1915. At some point after the Gallipoli campaign, he was transferred to the 1/6th Hants as a Private and was given service number 281802. He served with the Light Trench Mortar Battery within the 1/6th Hants. From September 1917 the 1/6th Hants operated in Basra and wider Mesopotamia.

Medical records for H.M. Hospital Ship Assaye state that in September 1919, Harold Escott boarded the ship at Alexandria, which was headed for Marseille, suffering with *'valvular disease of the heart.'*[355] As a result, he was discharged from the Army on 10th December 1919 and given the Silver War Badge for 'sickness.' He was 36 years old.[356]

Rfn. William FAGAN, 1625

Rifleman William Fagan enlisted into the Isle of Wight Rifles on 25th August 1914. He remained with the battalion after Gallipoli and was discharged on 19th July 1919 under service number 330341 due to illness. He was given the Silver War Badge.[357]

Rfn. William FLITNEY, 2123

Rifleman William Flitney enlisted in the Isle of Wight Rifles on 29th December 1914. He was reported as having been wounded at Gallipoli in the 25th September 1915 edition of the Isle of Wight County Press.

Rifleman Flitney was discharged from the Army on 7th March 1916 due to illness and was given the Silver War Badge.

---

[355] www.forces-war-records.co.uk: Military Hospitals Admissions and Discharge Registers WW1
[356] www.forces-war-records.co.uk: Silver War Badge List 1914-1918
[357] www.ancestry.co.uk: Silver War Badge Records, 1914-1920

Rfn. Percy William FLUX, 2440

Rifleman Percy Flux was transferred to the 1st battalion of the Hampshire Regiment at some point after he served with the Isle of Wight Rifles at Gallipoli and his service numbers were 330835 and then 010287. The 1st battalion of the Hampshire Regiment spent the First World War fighting on the Western Front.

Rifleman Flux survived the war.

Rfn. Francis Gilbert FOOT, 1849

Rifleman Francis Foot came from Ryde. He was taken ill with dysentery at Gallipoli and was admitted into hospital. He was then transferred onto a hospital ship to return to England but unfortunately, he passed away on the journey home on 11th December 1915. Rifleman Foot was buried at sea and is commemorated on the Helles Memorial.[358]

Rfn. William Stanley FORD, 1848

Rifleman William Ford was reported in the 16th October 1915 edition of the Isle of Wight County Press as having been wounded at Gallipoli.

On recovering from his wounding, Rifleman Ford continued to serve with the Isle of Wight Rifles and reached the rank of Corporal. He survived the war and his latter service number was 330649.

Rfn. Reginald GILBERT, 1626

Rifleman Gilbert came from Hitchen in Hertfordshire.[359] He remained serving with the Isle of Wight Rifles after Gallipoli and was later given service number 330342.

---

[358] Isle of Wight County Press, 1st January 1916, p5
[359] www.forces-war-records.co.uk: Soldiers Died in the Great War 1914-1919

Rifleman Gilbert took part in the Second Battle of Gaza and was originally listed as missing in action.[360] He had however been killed in action and his body was later found and buried at Gaza War Cemetery. Rifleman Gilbert was 21 years old.[361]

Rfn. Barrington GRAY MM, 1831

Rifleman Barrington Gray came from Beckenham. He continued to serve with the Isle of Wight Rifles after Gallipoli and reached the rank of Sergeant. He was awarded the Military Medal for *'bravery in the field'* and this was officially published in the London Gazette on 25th September 1917.[362]

Sergeant Gray was disembodied from the Army on 1st September 1919 under service number 330461.

Rfn. Maurice GRAY, 1460

Rifleman Maurice Gray came from Ryde and enlisted in the Isle of Wight Rifles on 4th April 1914. His service record states that he was wounded on 18th August 1915 and was back on English soil on 10th September 1915 for further treatment.

Rifleman Gray went on to become an acting corporal in the 2nd Bedfords with service number 205775 and survived the war. On 4th July 1921, Maurice Gray re-enlisted into the Isle of Wight Rifles at Parkhurst and was promoted to Sergeant.

Rfn. E M GREEN, 1957

Rifleman Green went on to serve in the Royal Flying Corps after Gallipoli under service number 406069.[363]

---

[360] www.forces-war-records.co.uk: British Red Cross and Order of St John Enquiry List 1917 (Wounded and Missing)
[361] https://www.cwgc.org/find-war-dead/casualty/650128/gilbert,-/
[362] www.forces-war-records: Gazetted Awards and Mentions in Despatches – London Gazette Issue 30312, p10026.
[363] www.forces-war-records.co.uk: Nominal index of all service personnel serving in a theatre of war 1914-1919

Rfn. Harry GRINHAM, 1671

Rifleman Harry Grinham and his brother Rifleman Ivan Grinham came from Ryde and both served at Gallipoli with the Isle of Wight Rifles. Rifleman Harry Grinham continued to serve with the Isle of Wight Rifles after Gallipoli and was disembodied from the battalion on 27th March 1919 under service number 330370.

Rfn. Ivan Augustus GRINHAM, 1850

Rifleman Ivan Grinham came from Ryde and enlisted in the Isle of Wight Rifles on 3rd September 1914. He was wounded in the right wrist at Gallipoli on the 17th August 1915 by a shrapnel ball. By 27th August 1915 he was in hospital and Malta and was then sent home to England for further treatment at The Abbotts Hospital in Cheltenham where he was admitted on 15th September 1915.[364]

On 30th June 1917, Rifleman Ivan Grinham was transferred to the Labour Corps and given service number 279716. He then became a Lance Corporal in 319 Coy, Royal Defence Corps with service number 83755 and survived the war.

Rfn. Walter GUSTAR, 2111

Rifleman Walter Gustar came from Newport and enlisted in the Isle of Wight Rifles on 26th December 1914. Rifleman Gustar was one of the many men invalided off Gallipoli due to illness and by November 1915, he had been *'admitted to hospital at Alexandria suffering from nephritis.'*[365]

After serving with the Isle of Wight Rifles, Walter Gustar was transferred to the Royal Army Service Corps as a private and was given service number T/443561. He was discharged from the

---

[364] www.ancestry.co.uk: British Army WWI Service Records, 1914-1920 – Territorial Attestation Form
[365] Isle of Wight County Press, 27th November 1915, p5

Army on 7th May 1919 due to sickness and was given the Silver War Badge.

Rfn. James HALSEY, 2384

Rifleman James Halsey continued to serve with the Isle of Wight Rifles after their deployment to Gallipoli. He was discharged from the battalion on 14th December 1918 under service number 330801.

Rfn. Thomas HAWES, 2388

Rifleman Thomas Hawes came from High Wycombe in Buckinghamshire and was one of the men recruited by Lieutenant Colonel Rhodes. He continued to serve with the Isle of Wight Rifles after Gallipoli and was killed in action during the Second Battle of Gaza. He is commemorated on the Jerusalem War Memorial and his latter service number was 330805.[366]

Rfn. Edgar Hubert HAYLES, 3811

Rifleman Edgar Hayles and his brother, Rifleman William Hayles, came from Newport. They both avoided being wounded whilst serving with the Isle of Wight Rifles at Gallipoli and both survived the war.

In the Isle of Wight County Press on 12th February 1916, Rifleman Edgar Hayles was reported to have had a haemorrhage and had recently been admitted into No. 5 Southern Hospital, Portsmouth. Prior to this, Rifleman Hayles had spent time at a convalescent home close to Cairo, followed by a short period of time at Eastleigh Hospital.[367]

Rifleman Hayles was transferred to the 1/6th Hants and was given service number 281803. He remained with the battalion for the remainder of the war. The 1/6th Hants arrived at Basra on 16th

---

[366] www.ancestry.co.uk: UK, Soldiers Died in the Great War, 1914-1919
[367] Isle of Wight County Press, 12th February 1916, p5

September 1917 and operated in Mesopotamia until the end of the war.[368]

Rfn. Francis C HAYWARD, 1386

Rifleman Francis Hayward was transferred to the Machine Gun Corps after the Isle of Wight Rifles' deployment to Gallipoli. He was disembodied from the Army on 5th May 1919 under service number 120519.

Rfn. Joseph Steven HENNING, 1741

Rifleman Joseph Henning enlisted in the Isle of Wight Rifles on 2nd September 1914. He was reported as having been wounded at Gallipoli in the 25th September 1915 edition of the Isle of Wight County Press.

Rifleman Henning returned to serve with the Isle of Wight Rifles and was discharged from the battalion on 24th April 1919 under service number 330409. His Silver War Badge record states that he was discharged from the Army due to 'wounds.'

Rfn. Sydney HERRINGTON, 1743

Rifleman Sydney Herrington came from Crockerhill in Sussex and enlisted in the Isle of Wight Rifles at Newport. He remained serving with the Isle of Wight Rifles after Gallipoli and was given service number 330410.

Rifleman Herrington fought in the Second Battle of Gaza on 19th April 1917 and afterwards he was initially reported as wounded and missing in action and then later he was presumed to have been killed during the battle. Rifleman Herrington was 19 years old. He has no known grave and is commemorated on the Jerusalem Memorial.

---

[368] http://www.longlongtrail.co.uk/army/regiments-and-corps/the-british-infantry-regiments-of-1914-1918/hampshire-regiment/

Rfn. Francis George HILLS, 1023

Rifleman Francis Hills continued with serving with the Isle of Wight Rifles and was given service number 330053 when the Territorial Forces received new service numbers. Rifleman Hills survived the war.

Rfn. George HILLS, 1414

Rifleman George Hills came from Ryde. He was killed, at the age of 20, on 12th August 1915 along with many of his comrades during the advance on Anafarta Ridge. Rifleman Hills has no known grave and is commemorated on the Helles Memorial.

Rfn. William Walter HINKS, 1508

Rifleman William Hinks came from Lake. He was invalided off Gallipoli on 14th August 1915 suffering from dysentery and was transported on a hospital ship to Malta. On recovering, he rejoined the Isle of Wight Rifles and served with them throughout the Great War. He was disembodied from the Army on 4th March 1919 under service number 330275 and the rank of Lance Corporal.

Rfn. George Henry HOBBS, 1283

Rifleman George Hobbs was hit in the leg by shrapnel during August 1915 at Gallipoli. It was reported in the Isle of Wight County Press on 27th November 1915 that Rifleman Hobbs *'was in hospital at Cairo for 8 weeks. He still has the bullet in his groin, and the doctors think it would be dangerous to extract it.'*[369]

Later in the war, Rifleman Hobbs was given service number 330161 and served in the 11th Hampshire Regiment reaching the rank of Corporal. He then went on to serve in the Hampshire Regiment Depot under service number 9449. Corporal Hobbs

---

[369] Isle of Wight County Press, 27th November 1915, p5.

died on 7th October 1917 and is buried in Newport (St. Paul's) Cemetery, Isle of Wight.

Rfn. George William HOBGEN, 1401

Rifleman George Hobgen served in the Isle of Wight Rifles at Gallipoli with his brother Rifleman Arthur Hobgen.

After Gallipoli, Rifleman George Hobgen was transferred to the Devonshire Regiment and served with the regiment until he was disembodied from the Army on 12th May 1919 under service number 50697 and rank of Private.

Rfn. Fred HOOPER, 2170

Rifleman Fred Hooper enlisted into the Isle of Wight Rifles on 4th January 1915. He continued to serve with the Isle of Wight Rifles after Gallipoli and was later given service number 330677.

Rifleman Hooper was discharged from the Army on 29th January 1918 due to having been wounded. He was 22 years and was given the Silver War Badge.

Rfn. George Henry HOUGHTON, 1742

Rifleman George Houghton was originally from Chichester. He enlisted with the Isle of Wight Rifles on 2nd September 1914 and deployed with them to Gallipoli.

In the first few days of being at Gallipoli, Rifleman Houghton was shot through the thigh. He was invalided off Gallipoli on 14th August 1915 along with Lance Sergeant Rayner and six other members of the Isle of Wight Rifles. He and Lance Sergeant Rayner were taken back to England and arrived at Plymouth on 27th August 1915. After hospital treatment, Rifleman Houghton was discharged on 11th August 1916.

Rfn. John HOUSE, 2307

Rifleman John House continued to serve with the Isle of Wight Rifles after Gallipoli. He was disembodied from the battalion on 20th March 1919 under service number 330751.

Rfn. Harry HUNNYBUN, 2074

Rifleman Harry Hunnybun enlisted in the Isle of Wight Rifles on 9th December 1914. He was wounded in the right hand at Gallipoli during August 1915 and was treated at Government Hospital, Damanhour, Egypt. On 26th October 1915 in a letter to his mother, he wrote:

> My hand is healed now, but I still have to have it in splints. I have been booked for the lines of communication – that means a job of some description down at the base.[370]

Rifleman Hunnybun was discharged from the Army on 6th September 1916 and received the Silver War Badge due to sickness.

Rfn. Cyril HUNT, 1958

Rifleman Cyril Hunt remained with the Isle of Wight Rifles after their Gallipoli campaign and was disembodied from the battalion on 24th July 1919 under service number 330537.

Rfn. William JACKSON, 1605

Rifleman William Jackson enlisted in the Isle of Wight Rifles on 18th August 1914. He received a number of wounds to his thigh during August 1915 and was invalided off Gallipoli and taken to a hospital in Malta for treatment.

---

[370] Isle of Wight County Press, 27th November 1915, p5.

Rifleman Jackson was discharged from the Army on 26th October 1916 under service number 330326. He received the Silver War Badge for sickness.

Rfn. Stanley Walter JEFFERY, 1387

Rifleman Stanley Jeffery came from Bembridge and enlisted in the Isle of Wight Rifles at St Helen's.[371] He was wounded during the attack on Anafarta Ridge. News of his wounding was published in the Isle of Wight County Press on 4th September 1915 when Rifleman R. H. Attrill's letter to his parents, dated 15th August 1915, was included in the paper:

> Stanley Jeffery, Boyd and R Warne are wounded…… Stanley had a bullet through the head but I do not think it is very dangerous.[372]

Due to the wounding, Rifleman Jeffery was taken to a hospital in Malta where he received treatment there for 7 weeks. He was then invalided back to England.

Rifleman Jeffery returned to the Isle of Wight Rifles and reached the rank of Corporal. He was killed in action on 19th April 1917 when the Isle of Wight Rifles took part in the Second Battle of Gaza. He was 21 years old. Rifleman Jeffery has no known grave and is commemorated on the Jerusalem Memorial.

Rfn. Charles Alfred JERRAM, 1428

Rifleman Charles Jerram came from Binstead. He became ill at Gallipoli between the middle of August 1915 and early September 1915 and was taken to hospital for treatment.

Rifleman Jerram returned to serve with the Isle of Wight Rifles for the rest of the war and was disembodied from the Army on 16th August 1919 under service number 330240.

---

[371] www.ancestry.co.uk: UK, Soldiers Died in the Great War, 1914-1919
[372] Isle of Wight County Press, 4th September 1915, p6.

Rfn. Gordon Hazell JOHNCOX, 1608

Rifleman Gordon Johncox was reported as having been missing since 22nd August in the Isle of Wight County Press on 11th September 1915. However, on 29th August 1915, Rifleman Johncox wrote home to let his parents know that he was safe and well.

On 24th March 1917, Rifleman Johncox, under service number 330329, was discharged for commission. He became a Second-Lieutenant in the Machine Gun Corps and survived the war.

Rfn. Joseph H JOHNS, 1853

Rifleman Joseph Johns enlisted into the Isle of Wight Rifles in September 1915. He fell ill at Gallipoli with Enteritis and was admitted on to H.M. Hospital Ship Assaye on 4th October 1915 for treatment.

Rifleman Johns was later on transferred to the 11th battalion of the King's (Liverpool) Regiment who were operating in France. He reached the rank of Lance Corporal and was demobilised from the Army under service number 87709.

Rfn. Richard W JOHNS, 1854

Rifleman Richard Johns came from Penzance and moved to the Isle of Wight for work. When Rifleman Johns enlisted into the Isle of Wight Rifles at Ryde on 3rd September 1914, he was working as a Steward and was residing at Haversham House in Ryde.

Rifleman Richard Johns was promoted to the rank of Lance Corporal whilst at Gallipoli on 1st October 1915. Several weeks later, he fell with Jaundice and was admitted to No. 5 Canadian Hospital in Cairo on 21st November 1915. Following time in hospital, Richard Johns spent time at a convalescent camp in Cyprus where he then fell ill with rheumatic fever. This delayed his return to the Isle of Wight Rifles until 31st July 1916 and at this point the battalion was based at Suez. Richard Johns was promoted to the rank of Corporal on 28th August 1916 and when the Territorial Forces received new service numbers, he was given service number 330473.

Corporal Johns was shot in the right shoulder during the 3rd Battle of Gaza on 2nd November 1917 and after initial medical treatment in Egypt, he was invalided back to England on 14th December 1917 and was admitted to the Southern General Hospital in Bristol on 28th December 1917. Corporal Johns spent further time in hospitals in Penzance and Belfast recovering from his wounding. He was then posted to the 4th Hants in August 1918.

Corporal Johns was discharged from the Army on 2nd September 1918 as a result of his wounding and also due to having fallen ill with Tuberculosis. He was given the Silver War Badge and an Army Pension. Unfortunately, Richard Johns did not recover from having Tuberculosis and he passed away at Burton Court in Chelsea on 14th May 1920. He was 29 years old and is buried at Penzance (Paul) Cemetery.[373]

Rfn. Sydney JOLLIFFE, 1855

Rifleman Sydney Jolliffe came from Ryde and enlisted in the Isle of Wight Rifles on 3rd September 1914. He was discharged from the battalion on 7th April 1916 due to sickness and was given the Silver War Badge.

Rfn. Arthur JUPE, 1890

Rifleman Arthur Jupe was born in Carrickfergus in Antrim. At the time of enlisting in the Isle of Wight Rifles on 4th September 1914 at Newport, Arthur Jupe was working as a gardener and was residing at Milford on Sea. He had recently turned 17 years old.

Rifleman Jupe fell ill with dysentery at Gallipoli and on 6th October 1915 he was admitted to No. 19 General Hospital in

---

[373] www.ancestry.co.uk: British Army WWI Pension Records 1914-1920

Alexandria. He was then invalided back to England on 28th October 1915 for convalescence.[374]

Once Rifleman Jupe had been deemed fit for active service again, he was posted back to the Isle of Wight Rifles. He took part in the Second Battle of Gaza on 19th April 1917 and was initially listed as missing. However, the Isle of Wight Rifles received notification on 2nd May 1917 that he had been wounded on 19th April 1917. He had received a gunshot wound to his left leg. This wounding resulted in Rifleman Jupe being discharged from the Army on 14th April 1919 under service number 330498. He was given the Silver War Badge and a pension.[375]

Rfn. George JUPE, 1891

Rifleman George Jupe continued serving with the Isle of Wight Rifles after Gallipoli. He was disembodied from the Army on 24th July 1919 under service number 330499.

Rfn. Arthur William KARLEY, 1856

Rifleman Arthur Karley came from Ryde and enlisted in the Isle of Wight Rifles at Ryde on 3rd September 1914. He became ill with dysentery at Gallipoli and was admitted into a hospital at Mudros on 3rd September 1915. Rifleman Karley was then invalided back to England on 18th September 1915 aboard the Aquitania which was now operating as a hospital ship.

Rifleman Karley sailed from Southampton on 20th October 1916 to re-join the Isle of Wight Rifles in Egypt. He disembarked at Alexandria on 1st November 1916 and on 6th November 1916 he re-joined the battalion at Suez. Rifleman Karley was transferred to the 21st Rifle Brigade on 19th December 1917 and his service number was changed from 330474 to 212159. He went on to

---

[374] www.forces-war-records.co.uk: Military Hospitals Admissions and Discharge Registers WW1 - MH106/226 No. 19 General Hospital Alexandria 27/09/1915 – 11/10/1915
[375] www.ancestry.co.uk: British Army WWI Pension Records 1914-1920

deploy with the 21st Rifle Brigade to India in late October 1918 and returned to England in November 1919, where he was discharged from the Army on 1st January 1920.[376]

Rfn. Arthur KELSON, 1397

Rifleman Arthur Kelson continued serving with the Isle of Wight Rifles after Gallipoli and was given service number 330220 when the Territorial Forces received new service numbers.

Arthur Kelson went on to serve in the Royal Air Force under service number 337775.

Rfn. Frederick John KENT, 887

Rifleman Frederick Kent enlisted in the Isle of Wight Rifles in 1908 when he was 18. He was promoted to Lance Corporal at Gallipoli and during August 1915, received a slight wound to his head. Lance Corporal Kent was taken to a hospital in Egypt and then spent a period of convalescence at Mansoura prior to being discharged from the Army on the 22nd October 1915.

Rfn. S KING, 1893

Rifleman King came from Arreton. He was admitted into a hospital in Malta on 1st October 1915 due to an illness he had picked up Gallipoli.

Rfn. William Harold LACEY, 1318

Rifleman William Lacey continued to serve in the Isle of Wight Rifles following their deployment to Gallipoli. He reached the rank of Acting Sergeant and was latterly given service number 330175. William Lacey survived the war.

---

[376] www.ancestry.co.uk: British Army WW1 Service Records, 1914-1919 – Cover for Discharge Documents

Rfn. Arthur Robert LAMBERT, 1120

Rifleman Arthur Lambert remained with the Isle of Wight Rifles after Gallipoli and was latterly given service number 330083. At some point between 1917 and 1918 he was transferred to the 1/4th Hants who were deployed initially in Mesopotamia and then in 1918 in Persia.

Rifleman Lambert was disembodied from the Army on 5th August 1919.

Rfn. Herbert LANE, 2125

Rifleman Herbert Lane was transferred to the 2/4th Hants at some point after the Isle of Wight Rifles' deployment to Gallipoli and was given service number 205459. By the end of April 1917, the 2/4th Hants had moved from India to take part in the Palestinian campaign and their last battle in Palestine was in April 1918. On 22nd May 1918 the battalion left Egypt for France.

Rifleman Lane was disembodied from the Army on 16th February 1919.

Rfn. Isaac LANE, 1510

Rifleman Isaac Lane was working at a farm in Bembridge before he enlisted in the Isle of Wight Rifles. He was mistakenly reported as killed in action in the 11th September 1915 edition of the Isle of Wight County Press.

At some point after the Isle of Wight Rifles' Gallipoli campaign, Isaac Lane was transferred to the Labour Corps. He was disembodied from the Labour Corps on 16th July 1919 under service number 621710.

Rfn. William James LANE, 1711

Rifleman William Lane came from Binstead. He remained with the Isle of Wight Rifles after their deployment to Gallipoli and reached the rank of Corporal. He was given service number

330384 when the Territorial Forces received new service numbers.

Corporal Lane took part in the Second Battle of Gaza on 19th April 1917. He was originally reported as *'wounded and missing'* however he had in fact been killed during the battle.[377] Corporal Lane was 38 years old and a married man. He has no known grave and is commemorated on the Jerusalem Memorial.

Rfn. William Edwin LANGDON, 1747

Rifleman William Langdon was reported in the Isle of Wight County Press and in the 1914/1915 Star report to have been killed in action on 12th August 1915. He is however, recorded by the Commonwealth War Graves Commission as having been killed on 14th August 1915. Rifleman Langdon was aged 18 and came from Ryde. He is commemorated on the Helles Memorial.

Rfn. Harold LAWRENCE, 2239

Rifleman Harold Lawrence continued to serve with the Hampshire Regiment after Gallipoli and was given service number 205418. He was disembodied from the Army under the rank of Lance Corporal on 16th July 1919.

Rfn. Ernest LAY, 2203

Rifleman Ernest Lay enlisted in the Isle of Wight Rifles on 7th January 1915. He was seriously wounded at Gallipoli at some point between the battalion's landing at Suvla Bay and the end of September 1915 and as a result was discharged from the Army on 24th April 1916. Rifleman Lay was awarded the Silver War Badge.

---

[377] www.forces-war-records.co.uk: British Red Cross and Order of St John Enquiry List 1917 (Wounded and Missing)

Rfn. Ernest Harry LOCKE, 1681

Rifleman Ernest Locke came from Ryde. He was reported as having fallen sick at Gallipoli in the Isle of Wight County Press on 11th September 1915.

Rifleman Locke returned to serve with the Isle of Wight Rifles and was later given service number 330379. On 29th January 1918, Ernest Locke was Discharged to Commission and became a Second Lieutenant in the Dorset Regiment. He survived the war.

Rfn. Frederick Sirdar LOVE, 1494

Rifleman Frederick Love came from Sandown and enlisted in the Isle of Wight Rifles at Sandown. He reached the rank of Lance Corporal but sadly passed away on 9th September 1916 at the age of 18 years. He is buried at Ismailia War Memorial Cemetery in Egypt.

Rfn. Alfred MABEY, 1613

Rifleman Alfred Mabey was one of the designated signallers in the Isle of Wight Rifles whilst at Gallipoli. He fell ill with dysentery between the middle of September and early October and was invalided off Gallipoli to Imtarfa Hospital in Malta. Rifleman Mabey re-joined the battalion at Gallipoli in November 1915.

Rifleman Mabey continued to serve with the Isle of Wight Rifles throughout the war and reached the rank of Lance Corporal. He was disembodied from the Army on the 1st May 1919 under service number 330334.

Rfn. Frederick MATTHEWS, 1833

Rifleman Frederick Matthews came from Shanklin and enlisted in the Isle of Wight Rifles at Shanklin on 2nd September 1914. He was 26 years old at the time of enlisting.

Rifleman Matthews was invalided off Gallipoli due to illness and arrive back in England on 25th October. He did not recover from his illness to a level deemed to be fit enough for active service and he was subsequently discharged from the Army on 26th September 1916 and given the Silver War Badge.

Frederick Matthews moved to Brighton and worked as a Fish Monger. He volunteered to serve in the 1st Home Counties Brigade, RFA (Territorial Force) at Brighton on 19th May 1920 and was accepted and given service number 723742. He was discharged from the unit on 4th July 1921.[378]

Rfn. William MERRYWEATHER, 1179

Rifleman William Merryweather was reported in the 16th October 1915 edition of the Isle of Wight County Press as having been wounded at Gallipoli. He returned to serve with the Isle of Wight Rifles and was disembodied from the battalion on 8th July 1919 under service number 330113.

Rfn. Albert Charles MILLS, 1502

Rifleman Albert Mills came from Ryde. He served at Gallipoli from the beginning of the Isle of Wight Rifles' campaign and kept a diary. He was officially a Pioneer and on 2nd September 1915 he joined the Headquarters in the role of Pioneer. Albert Mills fell ill with suspected Diptheria on 4th October 1915 and was sent to a hospital at Gallipoli. He spent 6 days in isolation on the shore at Gallipoli and was discharged from hospital on Sunday 10th October 1915 and returned to the battalion. When the battalion moved from Gully to the trenches, Albert Mills wrote in his diary that he *'stayed behind up to November 28th'*

---

[378] www.ancestry.co.uk: British Army Pension Records 1914-1920 - Territorial Force Attestation

and on Friday 29th he *'went to Anzac and stayed to December 1st.'*[379]

Albert Mills continued serving with the Isle of Wight Rifles after Gallipoli. He was disembodied from the battalion under service number 330272.

Rfn. John MOREY, 1858

Rifleman John Morey enlisted in the Isle of Wight Rifles at Ryde, his home town. He was reported as missing in the Isle of Wight County Press on 25th September 1915 but he had in fact fallen ill with dysentery at Gallipoli and by November 1915, he had been admitted to the Bombay PG Hospital in Alexandria, Egypt.

John Morey continued serving with the Isle of Wight Rifles and rose to the rank of Sergeant. He was given service number 330476 when the Territorial Forces were issued new service numbers. Sergeant Morey took part in the Second Battle of Gaza on 19th April 1917 and was presumed to have been killed during it. He was 22 years old and is commemorated on the Jerusalem Memorial.

Rfn. Thomas MUMFORD, 2198

Rifleman Thomas Mumford was transferred to the Army Service Corps at some point after having served with the Isle of Wight Rifles at Gallipoli. He was given the rank of Private and service number NAC/450976 and served with the Army Service Corps until he was discharged from the Army on 27th May 1920.

Rfn. William Alfred MUNDELL, 1712

Rifleman William Mundell enlisted in the Isle of Wight Rifles on 1st September 1914. He was reported as having been wounded at

---

[379] A C Mills diary: https://sites.google.com/site/iowrifles/rifleman-mills-diary/the-diary-transcript

Gallipoli in the Isle of Wight County Press on 18th September 1915.

Rifleman Mundell transferred to the Royal Army Medical Corps and served as a Private in the 1st E. General Hospital under service number 481391. Private Mundell was discharged from the Army on 26th February 1919 due to sickness and was given the Silver War Badge.

Rfn. Stanley NIGHTINGALE, 1511

Rifleman Stanley Nightingale was transferred to the Machine Gun Corps at some point after the Isle of Wight Rifles Gallipoli campaign and reached the rank of Lance Corporal. He was disembodied from the Army on 6th April 1919 under service number 52059.

Rfn. Leslie E J NORRIS, 1688

Rifleman Leslie Norris remained serving with the Isle of Wight Rifles after Gallipoli and was later given service number 330385. Leslie Norris then went onto serve in the Royal Engineers. He was given service number 521654 and the rank Pioneer.

Rfn. Henry James ORCHARD, 1402

Rifleman Henry Orchard continued to serve with the Isle of Wight Rifles after Gallipoli and reached the rank of Corporal. He was placed on the reserve list on 20th March 1919 under service number 330223.

Rfn. Fred OSMAN, 1860

Rifleman Fred Osman was one of the group of men who were held back from the Isle of Wight Rifle's landing at Gallipoli on 10th August 1915. Rifleman Osman and the rest of the men who did not land at Suvla Bay on 10th August 1915, were reunited with their depleted battalion on 15th August 1915.

Rifleman Osman fought with the Isle of Wight Rifles in the Second Battle of Gaza on 19th April 1917 and was killed in action. He has no known grave and is commemorated on the Jerusalem Memorial. His service number was 330478.

Rfn. William OXLADE, 2308

Rifleman William Oxlade remained with the Isle of Wight Rifles after Gallipoli and reached the rank of Lance Corporal. He was disembodied from the battalion on 7th August 1919 under service number 330752.

Rfn. Charles David PALMER, 1161

Rifleman Charles Palmer enlisted in the Isle of Wight Rifles on 21st June 1912. He was reported to have been wounded at Gallipoli in the 25th September 1915 edition of the Isle of Wight County Press. Following his wounding, he later became sufficiently ill to be discharged from the Army on 3rd April 1916 and given the Silver War Badge for 'sickness.'

Rfn. Horace Henry PALMER, 2480

Rifleman Horace Palmer continued to serve with the Isle of Wight Rifles following Gallipoli. He was disembodied from the battalion on 5th August 1919 under service number 330859.

Rfn. Edward PEACH, 1065

Rifleman Edward Peach enlisted in the Isle of Wight Rifles at Sea View. He continued to serve with the Isle of Wight Rifles after Gallipoli, was promoted to the rank of Corporal, and was given service number 330056 when the Territorial Forces received their new service numbers.

Corporal Peach died of wounds on 19th September 1918 as a result of wounds he received during the successful Battle of Megiddo – Battle of Sharon on 19th September 1918. He is buried at Ramleh War Cemetery.

Rfn. Joseph William PEARSON D.C.M., 1692

Rifleman Joseph Pearson continued to serve with the Isle of Wight Rifles after Gallipoli and was given service number 330388 when the Territorial Forces received their new service numbers.

Joseph Pearson had been promoted to the rank of Sergeant by the time of the Second Battle of Gaza on 19th April 1917. He fought with distinction during the battle and was awarded the Distinguished Conduct Medal:

> For conspicuous gallantry and devotion to duty. He displayed the utmost fearlessness in fighting his way into an enemy redoubt and capturing twenty of the enemy single handed. He successfully conducted them to the rear and then returned to the firing line.[380]

Joseph Pearson was promoted to the rank of Company Sergeant Major and survived the war. He was disembodied from the Army on 18th April 1919.

Rfn. Henry PERKIS, 1861

Rifleman Henry Perkis remained with the Isle of Wight Rifles after their Gallipoli deployment. He was disembodied from the battalion on 18th April 1919 under service number 330479.

Rfn. Arthur PHILLIPS, 1839

Rifleman Arthur Phillips was transferred to the Labour Corps at some point after the Isle of Wight Rifles' deployment to Gallipoli. He served as Private in the Labour Corps for the remainder of the war and was disembodied from the Labour Corps on 22nd March 1919 under service number 360919.

---

[380] www.forces-war-records.co.uk: Gazetted Awards and Mentions in Despatches – London Gazette 16/08/1917, p8408

Rfn. Claude <u>Ernest</u> PHILLIPS, 1748

Rifleman Ernest Phillips came from Nettlestone and enlisted in the Isle of Wight Rifles at Newport. He remained with the Isle of Wight Rifles after their Gallipoli campaign and was given service number 330411.

Rifleman Phillips was killed in action on 19th April 1917 during the Second Battle of Gaza. He was 24 years old and has no known grave. Rifleman Phillips is commemorated on the Jerusalem Memorial.

Rfn. Ernest PHILLIPS, 1536

Rifleman Ernest Phillips enlisted in the Isle of Wight Rifles at Sandown Barracks on 7th August 1914. He was 17 years and 9 months old and had left his job as a labourer.

Rifleman Phillips was invalided off Gallipoli and arrived back in England on 20th November 1915. He was assessed to be *'no longer physically fit for war service'* and was discharged from the Army on 14th January 1916.[381]

Rfn. Frederick Samuel PINK, 1543

Rifleman Frederick Pink continued serving with the Isle of Wight Rifles after their deployment to Gallipoli. He was disembodied from the battalion on 16th July 1919 under service number 330292.

Rfn. Claude PONSFORD, 1542

Rifleman Claude Ponsford came from Southampton and enlisted in the Isle of Wight Rifles at Newport. Following Gallipoli, he remained with the battalion, reaching the rank of Sergeant and was given service number 330291.

---

[381] www.ancestry.co.uk: British Army WWI Pension Records 1914-1920 - Territorial Force Attestation

Sergeant Ponsford died of wounds on 6th November 1917 after being wounded at some point during the Third Battle of Gaza. He was 20 years old and is buried at Deir El Belah War Cemetery in Gaza.

Rfn. A L POTTER, 2483

Rifleman Potter was invalided off Gallipoli due to illness. He spent time in hospital at Alexandria before being transferred to a convalescent camp in Egypt during the beginning of November 1915.

Rifleman Potter went on to join the Royal Flying Corps, which latterly became the Royal Air Force. He survived the war and his service number was 409967.

Rfn. Arthur PRICE, 1751

Rifleman Arthur Price remained with the Isle of Wight Rifles following their campaign in Gallipoli. He was disembodied from the battalion on 3rd April 1919 under service number 330413.

Rfn. Harry PRICE, 1862

Rifleman Harry Price continued serving with the Isle of Wight Rifles after Gallipoli and reached the rank of Corporal. He was disembodied from the battalion on 8th July 1919 under service number 330480.

Rfn. Percy PRIESTLY, 1611

Rifleman Percy Priestly enlisted in the Isle of Wight Rifles on 19th August 1914 and reached the rank of acting Corporal. He was wounded and taken prisoner but where and when has not been documented.

Acting Corporal Priestly was discharged from the Army on 15th July 1919 under service number 330332 due the effect of his wounding. He was 24 years old and was given the Silver War Badge.³⁸²

Rfn. Sydney PURNELL, 1031

Rifleman Sydney Purnell enlisted in the Isle of Wight Rifles on 1ˢᵗ March 1911. He served at Gallipoli with his brother, Bandsman Percy Purnell. They were both wounded within a couple weeks of each other, in a similar manner and roughly in the same area of the body by shrapnel. Both of their wounds were recalled by Private Brooks Butt to his son.

Rifleman Purnell was discharged from the Army on 23ʳᵈ November 1915 and was given the Silver War Badge. His Silver War Badge record states that he was discharged due to 'sickness.'³⁸³

Rfn. Robert RASHLEY, 1466

Rifleman Robert Rashley came from Ryde. He re-enlisted in the Isle of Wight Rifles on 29ᵗʰ April 1914 after having previously served with the battalion for 5 years.

Rifleman Rashley was wounded on 12ᵗʰ August 1915 during the advance on Anafarta Ridge and was invalided off Gallipoli. He reached England on 8ᵗʰ September 1915 and remained in England until his discharge from the Army on 28ᵗʰ April 1916. Rifleman Rashley has completed a further two years' service with the Isle of Wight Rifles.³⁸⁴

Rfn. Robert Frank RAYNER, 1183

Rifleman Robert Rayner continued serving with the Isle of Wight Rifles after Gallipoli. He was disembodied from the battalion on 2ⁿᵈ April 1919 under service number 330200.

---

³⁸² www.forces-war-records.co.uk: Silver War Badge List 1914-1918
³⁸³ www.ancestry.co.uk: Silver War Badge Record
³⁸⁴ www.ancestry.co.uk: British Army WWI Pension Records 1914-1920

Rfn. William Joseph RAYNER, 1803

Rifleman William Rayner enlisted in the Isle of Wight Rifles on 2nd September 1914. Following Gallipoli, he was transferred to the 1st Garrison Battalion of the Northamptonshire Regiment as a Private and was given service number 31412. The battalion was stationed in Egypt, Palestine and then in late October 1918 moved to Salonika.

Private Rayner was discharged from the Army on 8th January 1919 and given the Silver War Badge as he was 'no longer fit for war service.'[385]

Rfn. Archibald READ, 1606

Rifleman Archibald Read remained with the Isle of Wight Rifles after Gallipoli and was given service number 330327 when the Territorial Forces received new service numbers. Rifleman Read survived the war.

Rfn. Ernest T REEVES, 2240

Rifleman Ernest Reeves was transferred to the 2/5th Hants after Gallipoli. He was then posted to the 1/4th Wilts as a Private and given service number 204023. Both the 2/5th Hants and 1/4th Wilts were part of the Egyptian Expeditionary Force and took part in the Palestinian campaign.

Ernest Reeves was classified as Class Z Reserve on 6th May 1919.

Rfn. George REYNOLDS, 2376

Rifleman George Reynolds came from Cowes. He was wounded between August 1915 and early September 1915.

Rifleman Reynolds recovered from his wounding and returned to serve with the Isle of Wight Rifles for the remainder of the war.

---

[385] www.forces-war-records.co.uk: Silver War Badge List 1914-1918

He was disembodied from the Army on 8th August 1919 under service number 330798.

Rfn. Reginald RIDDETT, 1465

Rifleman Reginald Riddett was transferred to the 1/6th Hants after Gallipoli and was given service number 281812. The 1/6th Hants were initially based in India and were posted to Basra in September 1917.

Reginald Riddett survived the war and was demobilised from the Army on 10th December 1919.

Rfn. Alexander ROGERS, 1753

Rifleman Alexander Rogers came from Sandown and enlisted in the Isle of Wight Rifles at Newport. He continued serving with the Isle of Wight Rifles after Gallipoli and was given service number 330414 when the Territorials received their new service numbers.

By September 1918, Alexander Rogers had been promoted to the rank of Acting Corporal. He was killed in action on 19th September 1918, at the age of 20, during the Battle of Sharon and is buried at Ramleh War Cemetery.

Rfn. James ROGERS, 2081

Rifleman Rogers was *'listed as "Wounded" on the Casualty List issued by the War Office on 17th September 1915.'*[386]

Later in the war, James Rogers was transferred to the Machine Gun Corps as a Private and was given service number 50265. He survived the war and was disembodied from the Army on 5th April 1919.

---

[386] www.forces-war-records.co.uk: First World War Daily Reports (Missing, Wounded & Prisoner of War)

Rfn. William ROGERS, 1443

Rifleman William Rogers was transferred to the Labour Corps at some point after the Isle of Wight Rifles deployment to Gallipoli. He held the rank of Private and was given service number 341659. Williams Rogers survived the war and was disembodied from the Army on 1st May 1919.

Rfn. Ernest RUSSELL, 1694

Rifleman Ernest Russell was transferred to the Machine Gun Corps following Gallipoli and was given service number 50268. He survived the war and was disembodied from the Army on 24th July 1919.

Rfn. H RUSSELL, 1426

Rifleman H Russell came from Carisbrooke. He was reported as having been wounded at Gallipoli in the Isle of Wight County Press on 4th September 1915 and was officially *'listed as "Wounded" on the Casualty List issued by the War Office on 24th September 1915.'* [387]

Rfn. H G RUSSELL, 2087

Rifleman H G Russell came from Freshwater and was reported as 'sick' in the Isle of Wight County Press on 27th November 1915. He was admitted to a hospital in Woolwich for further treatment.

Rfn. John Thomas RUSSELL, 1380

Rifleman John Thomas Russell was invalided off Gallipoli between the middle of August and early September 1915 and taken to a hospital in Cairo suffering from deafness and Enteric.

---

[387] www.forces-war-records.co.uk: First World War Daily Reports (Missing, Wounded & Prisoner of War)

Rifleman John Thomas Russell returned to serve with the Isle of Wight Rifles and was given service number 330209. He fought in and was killed in the Second Battle of Gaza on 19th April 1917 and is buried at Gaza War Cemetery.

Rfn. Arthur Frederick SADLER, 2319

Rifleman Arthur Sadler was transferred to the Labour Corps later on in the war and was promoted to the rank of Lance Corporal. He was disembodied from the Army on 12th April 1919.

Rfn. Hector Rhodes SALMON, 1866

Rifleman Hector Salmon served in the Isle of Wight Rifles with his brother, Rifleman Arthur Salmon.

Rifleman Hector Salmon remained with the Isle of Wight Rifles throughout the war and reached the rank of Lance Corporal. He was disembodied from the Army on 2nd April 1919 under service number 330482. His brother, Arthur, also survived the war.

Rfn. Charles SAUNDERS, 1138

Rifleman Charles Saunders continued to serve with the Isle of Wight Rifles after Gallipoli and reached the rank of Lance Corporal. He was disembodied from the battalion on 10th April 1919.

Rfn. Frank SAUNDERS, 1366

Rifleman Frank Saunders came from Porchfield. He received a gunshot wound to his leg at Gallipoli during August 1915 and was invalided off the peninsular and admitted in to a hospital in Cairo.

Rifleman Saunders continued to serve with the Isle of Wight Rifles and was disembodied from the Army on 2nd April 1919 under service number 330200.

Rfn. Lawrence Douglas Geoffrey SEARLE, 1383

Rifleman Lawrence Searle came from Ryde and enlisted in the Isle of Wight Rifles at Ryde. He was killed in action on 17th August 1915 at the age of 18 and is commemorated on the Helles Memorial.

Rfn. Alfred SHALES, 744

Rifleman Alfred Shales enlisted in the Isle of Wight Rifles on 4th March 1909. Following Gallipoli, he went on to serve in the Duke of Edinburgh's (Wiltshire) Regiment as a Private. He was discharged from the Army under service number 33694 on 16th October 1917 due to sickness and was given the Silver Badge.

Rfn. Harry SHEPPARD, 1696

Rifleman Harry Sheppard came from Ryde and had married before deploying to Gallipoli. He was killed in action on 18th August 1915 at the age of 22 and is commemorated on the Helles Memorial.

Rfn. Victor Harold SHERGOLD, 1633

Rifleman Victor Harold Shergold came from Ashey. He was wounded at Gallipoli during August 1915.

Rifleman Shergold survived the war.

Rfn. Douglas SHINAR, 1456

Rifleman Douglas Shinar came from Ryde. Following Gallipoli, he spent a period of time with the 2/8th Hants based at Sandown Barracks. On 11th March 1916 he *'was charged with the offence of "Quitting their Post" and was sentenced to 42 days detention.'*[388]

---

[388] www.forces-war-records.co.uk: British Army Court Martials 1914-1950 (WO86/69)

Rifleman Shinar was later given service number 330251 whilst serving with the 8th Hants. During 1917 he was transferred as a Private to the 2nd Hants and joined the battalion on the Western Front. The 2nd Hants took part in the Battle of Cambrai on 20th November 1917 and were caught up in the German counter-attacks on 30th November 1917. Douglas Shinar was taken prisoner by the Germans in the aftermath of the German counter-attacks and his official Prisoner of War record held by the International Committee of the Red Cross was dated the 4th December 1917.

After being released from captivity, Private Shinar returned to the Hampshire Regiment and was posted to the 1st Hants, D Company, with service number 04160. He was taken ill in September 1919 and was admitted to Catterick Military Hospital on 13th September 1919. On 22nd October 1919 he was *'discharged back to duty with 7 days of light duty.'*[389]

Rfn. Wilfred SHOTTER, 1406

Rifleman Wilfred Shotter came from Ryde. He became ill at Gallipoli and was admitted to No. 17 General Hospital, Alexandria on 6th October 1915.

Later in the war Wilfred Shotter was transferred to the Devonshire Regiment. He was disembodied from the Devonshire Regiment on 14th April 1919 holding the rank of Private and service number 205516.

Rfn. Arthur George SILSBURY, 2234

Rifleman Arthur Silsbury came from Brading and enlisted in the Isle of Wight Rifles at Newport. He was killed in action on 18th September 1915 at the age of 28 years old. The War Diary for the 18th September 1915 states that the Turks launched an attack at

---

[389] www.forces-war-records.co.uk: Military Hospitals Admissions and Discharge Registers WW1 - MH106/1814 Medical Records of Catterick Camp Military Hospital: 12/08/1919-04/11/1919

4.30pm and so it is likely that he was killed during this attack. Rifleman Silsbury is buried at the 7th Field Ambulance Cemetery, Gallipoli.

Rfn. Reginald SIMMONDS, 1756

Rifleman Reginald Simmonds came from Shanklin and enlisted in the Isle of Wight Rifles on 2nd September 1914. He fell ill after Gallipoli and was subsequently discharged from the 2/8th Hants on 18th August 1916 and give the Silver War Badge.[390]

Rfn. Frederick SIVIER, 2297

Rifleman Frederick Sivier was transferred to the Labour Corps later in the war and was disembodied from the Labour Corps on 23rd February 1919 under service number 360864. Frederick Sivier went on to re-join the Isle of Wight Rifles and was given the rank of Lance Corporal and service number 5488257.

Rfn. William John SMITH, 371

Rifleman William Smith was reported under the list of wounded personnel serving with the Isle of Wight Rifles at Gallipoli in the 25th September 1915 edition of the Isle of Wight County Press.

Rifleman Smith continued to serve with the Isle of Wight Rifles after his wounding and was later given service number 330021. After the war, Rifleman Smith re-enlisted into the battalion and received service number 05247.

Rfn. Allen James SPANTON, 1506

Rifleman Allen Spanton enlisted in the Isle of Wight Rifles on 4th August 1914. He was discharged from the Army on 20th July 1916 due to 'sickness' and was given the Silver War Badge.

---

[390] www.forces-war-records.co.uk: Silver War Badge List 1914-1918

Rfn. Leonard Charles SPENCER, 1836

Rifleman Leonard Spencer came from Shanklin and enlisted in the Isle of Wight Rifles on 2nd September 1914. He fell ill at Gallipoli with dysentery between the middle of August and the middle of September 1915 and was brought back to England for treatment at the University War Hospital in Southampton.

Rifleman Spencer went on to serve with the 15th Hants under service number 330462. He was discharged from the Army on 20th May 1919 with his Silver War Badge record stating that he was discharged due to 'wounds.'

Rfn. Charles Daniel SPRINGER, 2199

Rifleman Charles Springer came from Ryde. He continued to serve with the Isle of Wight Rifles after Gallipoli and was disembodied from the battalion on 4th August 1919 under service number 330693.

Rfn. Reginald STONE, 1838

Rifleman Reginald Stone came from Shanklin. He had served with the Isle of Wight Rifles for 4 years prior the beginning of the First World War One and on 2nd September 1914 he re-enlisted into the battalion at Shanklin. Following Gallipoli, he was transferred to the Labour Corps and was discharged from the Army on 7th May 1919 under service number 646667.

Rfn. Victor STREET, 1698

Rifleman Victor Street came from Brading and enlisted in the Isle of Wight Rifles at Newport. He was reported as having been wounded at Gallipoli in the 25th September 1915 edition of the Isle of Wight County Press.

Rifleman Street returned to serve with the Isle of Wight Rifles and with the new Territorial Forces service numbering, he was given service number 330391. Rifleman Street took part in the

Second Battle of Gaza on 19th April 1917 whilst serving in 'F' Company and was presumed to have been killed during the battle on 19th April 1917. He is commemorated on the Jerusalem Memorial.

Rfn. Albert George STRONG, 1868

Rifleman Albert Strong came from Ryde. He became ill with dysentery at Gallipoli and was invalided to Malta where he received treatment at St Andrew's Hospital. By November 1915, Rifleman Strong had been admitted to a hospital in Newport, Wales.

Rifleman Strong served with the Isle of Wight Rifles for the remainder of the war. He was disembodied from the battalion on 24th July 1919 under service number 330484.

Rfn. Sydney Frank TAYLOR, 1544

Rifleman Sydney Taylor served with the Isle of Wight Rifles throughout the war and his latter service number was 330293. At the end of the war he re-enlisted into the battalion and was given service number 05283.

Rfn. Alfred TESTER, 1714

Rifleman Alfred Tester and his brother Rifleman George Tester came from Ryde. They both served at Gallipoli with the Isle of Wight Rifles. Following Gallipoli, Rifleman Alfred Tester was posted to the 1/7th Hants and was given service number 4337. The 1/7th Hants were based in India throughout the war and Alfred Tester remained with the battalion until he was disembodied from the Army on 8th May 1919 under service number 307599.

Rfn. George Henry TESTER, 1871

Rifleman George Tester and his brother Rifleman Alfred Tester served together at Gallipoli with the Isle of Wight Rifles. Rifleman George Tester was transferred to the Machine Gun

Corps after Gallipoli. He was disembodied from the Machine Gun Corps on 13th February 1919 under service number 50275.

Rfn. Albert TROTT, 1760

Rifleman Albert Trott was wounded early on during the Isle of Wight Rifles' deployment to Gallipoli. He sent a field card home on 15th August 1915 confirming he had been wounded and was at hospital. This news was published in the Isle of Wight County Press on 4th September 1915. He had been wounded in his right shoulder and was at a hospital in Alexandria.

Rifleman Trott continued to serve with the Isle of Wight Rifles throughout the rest of the war and was disembodied on 2nd April 1919 under service number 330413.

Rfn. Edmund Richard TRUEMAN, 1700

Rifleman Edmund Trueman served at Gallipoli with his brother Rifleman William Trueman. They came from Shanklin.

Rifleman Edmund Trueman was promoted to the rank of Lance Corporal in the Isle of Wight Rifles. He was killed in action on 19th April 1917, aged 20, during the Second Battle of Gaza and is buried at Gaza War Cemetery. His brother, William, survived the war.

Rfn. James TUCKWELL, 1252

Rifleman James Tuckwell came from Ryde. He was promoted to Lance Corporal and was later given service number 330144. He was wounded during the Second Battle of Gaza, and died of his wounds on 5th May 1917 in a hospital at Port Said. He was 22 years old and is buried in Port Said War Memorial Cemetery.[391]

---

[391] https://www.cwgc.org/find-war-dead/casualty/110772/tuckwell,-/

Rfn. William Edward VANNER, 1873

Rifleman William Vanner enlisted in the Isle of Wight Rifles during August 1914. He fell ill with Enteric at Gallipoli and was admitted to No. 19 General Hospital, Alexandria on 14th November 1915. He was 18 years old at the time. On 24th November 1915, Rifleman Vanner embarked on Hospital Ship Neuralia for England.[392]

Rifleman Vanner reached the rank of Lance Corporal and was given service number 330488. In the latter part of the war he served with the 2nd Hants on the Western Front. He survived the war and was placed on the reserve list on 7th May 1919.

Rfn. George Frederick WALKER, 1546

Rifleman George Walker came from Nettlestone. He had previously served with the Isle of Wight Rifles for a four-year term prior to the Great War and re-joined after war was declared. In the early stages of the war, he spent some of his time with the Isle of Wight Rifles manning Bembridge Fort.

Rifleman Walker was killed at Gallipoli on 9th October 1915 and is buried at the 7th Field Ambulance Cemetery. He was 22 years old.

Rfn. Jack WALKER, 1574

Rifleman Jack Walker was wounded in the head at Gallipoli during August 1915.

On recovering from his wounding, Rifleman Walker returned to active service and was given the service number 330306. He was disembodied from the Hampshire Regiment on 18th April 1919.

---

[392] www.forces-war-records.co.uk: Military Hospitals Admissions and Discharge Registers WW1 - MH106/1228 No. 19 General Hospital: 29/10/1915 to 21/11/1915

Rfn. Arthur WARNE, 1703

Rifleman Arthur Warne came from Bembridge and enlisted in the Isle of Wight Rifles at Newport on 31st August 1914 at the age of 22 years old. On attesting, he put his trade as 'at sea.'[393]

Rifleman Warne was wounded in the left hand at Gallipoli on 12th August 1915 during the advance on Anafarta Ridge and on 17th August 1915 was admitted into a hospital in Malta. Rifleman Warne was then invalided back to England and was admitted into the 5th Northern General Hospital in Leicester on 24th September 1915.[394]

On 14th January 1916, Rifleman Warne went before a medical board. As well as stating that Rifleman Warne's character was 'very good' his medical report stated:

> In action 12th August 1915 at Gallipoli, Man was struck by two bullets in left hand, one penetrating palm, middle and ring fingers, and the other striking his little finger. Left hand presents extremely restricted movements of any kind and limited to 1st and 3rd digits. Moves thumb fairly well. Semi-flexion of 2nd digit firmly towards palm......Hand is practically useless. Arm movements natural.[395]

As a result of the damage to Rifleman Warne's left hand, Rifleman Warne was discharged from the Army on 18th February 1916. He was given a funds from the Army and the Silver War

---

[393] www.ancestry.co.uk: British Army WWI Pension Records 1914-1920 – Rifleman Arthur Warne
[394] www.ancestry.co.uk: British Army WWI Pension Records 1914-1920 – Rifleman Arthur Warne
[395] www.ancestry.co.uk: British Army WWI Pension Records 1914-1920 – Rifleman Arthur Warne

Badge. By June 1916, Arthur Warne was, *'serving as deckhand H.M. Transport.'*[396]

Rfn. Reginald Henry WARNE, 1275

Rifleman Reginald Warne remained with the Isle of Wight Rifles after Gallipoli and was given service number 330155 when the Territorials received new service numbers. He survived the war.

Rfn. Ernest WARREN, 2378

Rifleman Ernest Warren came from Ryde. He was reported to have been wounded at Gallipoli in the Isle of Wight County Press on 11th September 1915.

Rifleman Warren returned to serve with the Isle of Wight Rifles and was given service number 330799. He was wounded for the second time during 1917 and this was officially reported in the War Office Daily List on 2nd August 1917.[397]

Rifleman Ernest Warren survived the war.

Rfn. George WARREN, 2377

Rifleman George Warren and his brother Harry Warren were both wounded at Gallipoli between 12th August 1915 and the middle of September 1915 and were taken to a hospital in Egypt.

Rifleman George Warren continued to serve in the Army after recovering from his wounds and went on to serve in the Machine Gun Corps under service number 50274. He was disembodied from the Machine Gun Corps on 10th April 1919.

---

[396] www.ancestry.co.uk: British Army WWI Pension Records 1914-1920 – Rifleman Arthur Warne
[397] www.forces-war-records.co.uk: First World War Daily Reports (Missing, Wounded & Prisoner of War) - War Office Daily List No.5327, NLS 1917_WList01

Rfn. Harry WARREN, 2379

Rifleman Harry Warren and his brother George Warren were both wounded at Gallipoli between 12th August 1915 and the middle of September 1915 and were taken to a hospital in Egypt.

Rifleman Harry Warren was discharged from the Army on 31st July 1916.

Rfn. Ronald Alfred WEAVER, 1279

Rifleman Ronald Weaver came from Bembridge. According to the diary of an officer in the Isle of Wight Rifles which was printed in the Isle of Wight County Press on 25th September 1915, Rifleman Weaver was killed by a sniper whilst in the trenches on the 4th September 1915. However, a contradictory letter from Captain Marsh to Rifleman Weaver's parents dated 15th September 1915 and also published in the Isle of Wight County Press on 25th September 1915 stated that Rifleman Weaver had been instantaneously killed by an enemy shell on 4th September 1915. Rifleman Weaver's parents received news of their son's death on his 19th birthday.[398]

Rifleman Weaver is buried at the 7th Field Ambulance Cemetery, Turkey.

Rfn. Alfred George WEEKS, 2098

Rifleman Alfred Weeks came from Bullen, Ryde. He contracted dysentery at Gallipoli and by November 1915 had been admitted to the Military Hospital in Gibraltar.

Rifleman Weeks spent the remainder of the war with the Isle of Wight Rifles. He was disembodied from the battalion on 31st July 1919 under service number 330631.

---

[398] Isle of Wight County Press, 25th September 1915

Rfn. Ernest WHEATLEY, 2077

Rifleman Ernest Wheatley came from Finchley and enlisted in the Isle of Wight Rifles at Newport. Following Gallipoli, Rifleman Wheatley continued to serve with the Isle of Wight Rifles and was given service number 330616 when the Territorials received their new service numbers.

Rifleman Wheatley was killed in action on 19th April 1917 during the Second Battle of Gaza at the age of 21 years. He has no known grave and is commemorated on the Jerusalem Memorial.

Rfn. William Henry WHITNEY, 1654

Rifleman William Whitney was listed as having been wounded in the left hand in the Isle of Wight County Press on 4th September 1915. It is likely that he received this wound during the advance on Anafarta Ridge.

Later in the war, Rifleman Whitney served in the 1st Garrison Worcester Regiment under service number 37293 and then in the 2nd Hampshire Regiment under service number 32685. Rifleman Whitney died on 11th December 1917 and is buried at Tincourt New British Cemetery which is located in the Somme area.

Rfn. Harold James WHITTINGTON, 1458

Rifleman Harold Whittington served in 'A' Company of the Isle of Wight Rifles at Gallipoli with his brothers Fred and Harry. Whilst at Gallipoli, Rifleman Harold Whittington fell ill and by November 1915 was *'in hospital in Cairo with Enteric Fever and a septic hand.'*[399]

Rifleman Harold Whittington was transferred to the 2nd Hants later in the war under service number 330252. He was killed in the Battle of Langemarck on 16th August 1917 aged 19 years old

---

[399] Isle of Wight County Press, 4th December 1915, p5

and is buried at Cement House Cemetery, Belgium. Fred and Harry survived the war.

Rfn. Harry WHITTINGTON, 1563

Rifleman Harry Whittington served in 'A' Company of the Isle of Wight Rifles at Gallipoli with his brothers Fred and Harold. On 4th December 1915, the Isle of Wight County Press published that Rifleman Harry Whittington was 'still with the battalion at the front.'[400]

Rifleman Harry Whittington survived the war and was disembodied from the Army on 6th May 1919. His brother, Fred, also survived the war but Harry was killed on 16th August 1917 during the Battle of Langemarck.

Rfn. Bertie Gordon WILLIAMS, 1247

Rifleman Bertie Williams was transferred to the Labour Corps later in the war and was given service number 360305. He was disembodied from the Army on 6th May 1919.

Rfn. Reginald Harry WOLFE, 1607

Rifleman Reginald Wolfe enlisted in the Isle of Wight Rifles on 18th August 1914. At some point after Gallipoli, he was transferred to the 3rd Wessex Field Ambulance (26th Field Ambulance) and saw service on the Western Front. He held the rank of Private and his service number was 461592.

Reginald Wolfe was discharged from the Army on 12th March 1919 due to being medically unfit for service and was given the Silver War Badge.[401]

---

[400] Isle of Wight County Press, 4th December 1915, p5
[401] www.ancestry.co.uk: Silver War Badge Records 1914-1919

Rfn. Alfred Victor George WOODFORD, 1632

Rifleman Alfred Woodford came from Ryde and enlisted in the Isle of Wight Rifles at Newport. He was wounded at Gallipoli and subsequently died of his wounds on 11th September 1915 at the age of 18 years old. Rifleman Woodford is commemorated on the Helles Memorial.

Rfn. Charles Hannaman WOODFORD, 1280

Rifleman Charles Woodford came from Bembridge and enlisted in the Isle of Wight Rifles at Bembridge. He rose to the rank of Acting Corporal with the Isle of Wight Rifles before being transferred to the 1st Battalion of the Somerset Light Infantry. Charles Woodford was given service number 235008 and was promoted to the rank of Corporal.

Corporal Woodford was killed in action during the Third Battle of the Scarpe on 3rd May 1917 at the age of 21 years. He has no known grave and is commemorated on the Arras Memorial.

Rfn. George Henry WOODNUTT, 2439

Rifleman George Woodnutt enlisted in the Isle of Wight Rifles on 21st May 1915. He was transferred to the Machine Gun Corps after Gallipoli and was given service number 139122 as well as the rank of Private. George Woodnutt was discharged from the Army on 22nd April 1919 due to 'sickness' and was given the Silver War Badge.[402]

Rfn. William WOODWARD, 1208

Rifleman William Woodward enlisted in the Isle of Wight Rifles on 12th November 1912. He was transferred to the Labour Corps later in the war as a Private and was given service number 453889. Private Woodward was discharged from the Army on

---

[402] www.ancestry.co.uk: Silver War Badge Records 1914-1919

12th October 1918 due to 'sickness' and was given the Silver War Badge.[403]

Rfn. Harold Ernest WRIGHT, 1462

Rifleman Harold Wright came from Ryde. He became ill at Gallipoli with dysentery and by early November 1915 had been admitted to a hospital in Cardiff.

Rifleman Wright re-enlisted into the Royal Flying Corps on 24th September 1916 and was given service number 39544. He survived the war.

Rfn. Reginald Henry WRIGHT, 1875

Rifleman Reginald Wright was wounded at Gallipoli between the middle of August and the middle of September 1915 and received further treatment at a hospital in Malta. His brother, Rifleman Donald Wright was also sent to the same hospital in Malta around the same time suffering with dysentery.

Later in the war, Rifleman Reginald Wright was transferred to the Labour Corps and given the rank of Private. He was disembodied from the Labour Corps on 4th August 1919 under service number 622777. His brother, Donald, did not survive the war. He died on 23rd October 1917.

Rfn. Charles William YOUNG, 1963

Rifleman Charles Young enlisted in the Isle of Wight Rifles on 4th October 1914. Later in the war he was transferred to the Labour Corps with the rank of Private and service number 341882. Private Young served in the Labour Corps until his discharge on 21st November 1917 due to 'sickness.' For this he was given the Silver War Badge.[404]

---

[403] www.ancestry.co.uk: Silver War Badge Records 1914-1919
[404] www.ancestry.co.uk: Silver War Badge Records 1914-1919

Rfn. Frederick YOUNG, 1717

Rifleman Frederick Young served with the Isle of Wight Rifles throughout the war and survived the war. His latter service number was 330396.

Rfn. Ward YOUNG, 1716

Rifleman Ward Young came from Brading and was reported to have been wounded at Gallipoli in the 25th September 1915 edition of the Isle of Wight County Press. He was subsequently discharged from the Army on 15th April 1916 at the age of 21 years old.

On 12th July 1917, Ward Young was recalled to the Army and on 13th July 1917 and was posted to the 8th Training Reserve Brigade at Winchester. He was given service number 8/14034 along with the rank of Private and his military fitness was classified as C1. Ward Young was then posted to 36th Training Reserve Battalion on 15th July and on his request, was discharged from the Army on 11th August 1917.[405]

---

[405] www.ancestry.co.uk: British Army WW1 Pension Records 1914-1920

'B' Company

CSM. Walter George PURKIS, 1475

CSM Walter Purkis came from Newport and was the Captain of Newport Rowing Club. His wife received notification on 9th September 1915 that he was missing in action. However, he had in fact been killed in action on 12th August 1915 during the advance on Anafarta Ridge. CSM Purkis was 38 years old and is commemorated on the Helles Memorial.

CQMS. John Francis DENHAM, 44

Company Quarter Master Sergeant John Denham held the rank of Sergeant with the Isle of Wight Rifles in 1908. He was *'listed as "Wounded" on the Casualty List issued by the War Office on 2nd January 1916.'*[406] This means that it is likely that he was wounded towards the end of the Isle of Wight Rifles' Gallipoli campaign.

Later in the war John Denham was transferred to the Labour Corps. He was given service number 347236 and held the rank of Colour Sergeant when he was disembodied from the Labour Corps on 11th January 1920. John Denham decided to re-enlist in the Isle of Wight Rifles and he returned to the battalion with the rank of Company Quarter Master Sergeant and service number 5489096.

Sgt. Charles John BARHAM, 1165

Sergeant Charles Barham enlisted in the Isle of Wight Rifles on 25th June 1912. He fell ill at Gallipoli and wrote about it in a letter dated 10th November 1915 to the Registrar of the St Paul's Brotherhood whilst recuperating in hospital at Alexandria:

---

[406] www.forces-war-records.co.uk: First World War Daily Reports (Missing, Wounded & Prisoner of War) - DT03011916

I started with a nervous breakdown, and then contracted fever and bronchitis but I have almost got rid of it, though it has left me with asthma.[407]

Sergeant Barham was discharged from the Army on 26th September 1916 due to sickness and was given the Silver War Badge. After the war, he re-enlisted in the Isle of Wight Rifles and was given service number 5488018.

Sgt. Ernest Frank BARNES, 644

Sergeant Ernest Barnes was wounded on Monday 16th August 1915 by a piece of shrapnel. It smashed his big toe on his left foot. Earlier that day he had been hit on the helmet by a spent shrapnel ball, luckily with no damage to him. The wound to his left foot saw him invalided off Gallipoli.

Later in the war, Sergeant Ernest Barnes was promoted to a Company Sergeant with the Isle of Wight Rifles. He then went on to serve with the Duke of Edinburgh's (Wiltshire) Regiment as a Company Quarter Master Sergeant under service number 02159 and finally served with the Labour Corps with the service number 285901.

Sgt. Albert William BISHOP, 482

Sergeant Albert Bishop was serving with the Isle of Wight Rifles before the Great War began. He survived the war and during his time at Gallipoli and the aftermath he kept a diary. His diary entry on Friday 13th August 1915 states that he was wounded during the advance on 12th August 1915:

> Wounded in the neck at 6.30pm yesterday……..I crawled back to a field dressing tent and was bound up. Stayed there the night. Was carried down to the sea this morning. Am writing this sitting on a stretcher waiting for a boat to take me off to a hospital ship…. Besides the

---

[407] Isle of Wight County Press, 4th December 1915, p5

one through the neck, I had one through my helmet and one through my haversack. Thank God I am here. I never expected to get out of it. [408]

Sergeant Bishop spent his 24th birthday on Monday 16th August 1915 at Madross Harbour, Lemnos waiting to be taken to either Malta or England. He wrote that many of his comrades died on the ship before they set sail and that the first ship he was on was infested with rats. On the 24th August a further 500 wounded soldiers boarded his ship after the recent offensive on 21st August.

He finally left Lemnos on Thursday 26th August 1915 and arrived in Devonport, England on Wednesday 8th September 1915 after stops at Malta and Gibraltar. He was then treated at a hospital in London and had a period of leave in Newport, Isle of Wight.

Sergeant Bishop returned to serve with the Isle of Wight Rifles and was discharged from the Army on 14th December 1918 under service number 330033.

Sgt. Patrick Augustine COONEY, 2325

Sergeant Patrick Cooney was the Manager for Messrs Besson's Military Department which was based in Euston Road, London. He joined the Isle of Wight Rifles and became the Bandmaster for the battalion.[409]

Either during Gallipoli or afterwards, Patrick Cooner was promoted to the rank of Warrant Officer Class I and in 1917 he was given service number 330765. On 31st July 1917, Patrick Cooney was Discharged to Commission. He was killed on 22nd February 1918 whilst serving as a Second Lieutenant with the General List attached to the Egyptian Labour Corps. Second

---

[408] Sgt A W Bishop's Diary: https://www.sites.google.com/site/iowrifles/sgt-bishop-diary
[409] http://www.hertfordshire-genealogy.co.uk/data/occupations/military/military-hampshire-reg.htm

Lieutenant Cooney is buried at Kantara War Memorial Cemetery in Egypt.

Sgt. John Bernard FLUX, 1355

Sergeant John Flux served with the Isle of Wight Rifles throughout the war and survived the war. He reached the rank of Colour Sergeant and his latter service number was 330194.

Sgt. Harry Wallace HALL, 61

Sergeant Harry Hall enlisted in the Isle of Wight Rifles on 4th May 1908. In late September 1915 he became ill with dysentery and spent a period of time at a hospital near the beach at Gallipoli before returning to the front line.

Sergeant Hall continued to serve with the Isle of Wight Rifles until his discharge on 17th June 1918 due to sickness. He had spent just over 10 years in the Territorial Force.

Sgt. Robert Talbot LAWN, 163

Sergeant Robert Lawn originally came from Bermondsey. He began his military service with the Croydon Volunteers and in 1900 he 'volunteered for the active service company of Queen's Regiment and joined the regiment's second battalion to take part in the South African War.'[410]

Robert Lawn moved to the Isle of Wight in 1904 and began work with the Isle of Wight County Press. He went on to become the Isle of Wight County Press' chief machinist at their Newport Office.

Robert Lawn joined the Isle of Wight Rifles on 1st April 1905 and was promoted to Sergeant on 1st September 1914. In September 1915 he became ill with Enteritis and was invalided off Gallipoli. His Territorial Force attestation papers state that on 25th September he was admitted to Kasr-el-Ainy Hospital in Cairo

---

[410] Isle of Wight County Press, 29th July 1972

and on 13th October 1915 he was transferred to a convalescent home. Sergeant Lawn was then moved to the Base Depot at Mustapha on 19th November 1915.

On 31st December 1915, Sergeant Lawn sailed from Alexandria to England as he was nearing the end of his service period. He landed in England on 16th January 1916 and was discharged from the 3/8th Hants on 31st March 1916.

Sgt. Arthur Henry MARLOW, 1609

Sergeant Arthur Marlow was attached to the Brigade HQ at Gallipoli during the middle of September 1915 as a chef for the staff officers. On 18th September 1915 he wrote, *'I have been attached to Brigade Headquarters to practise my culinary knowledge on bully beef and biscuits and I guess it would require a chef de cuisine à la Ritz and Cecil combined to do a full course dinner, including dessert, out of it.'*[411]

Sergeant Marlow fought with the Isle of Wight Rifles during the Second Battle of Gaza on 19th April 1917 and was killed in action on that day. He was 30 years old and his service number was 330330. Sergeant Marlow has no known grave and is commemorated on the Jerusalem Memorial.

Sgt. William NEWMAN, 466

Sergeant William Newman enlisted in the Isle of Wight Rifles on 16th December 1908. He was an 'old campaigner, having seen active service in India and South Africa.'[412]

Sergeant Newman received a slight shrapnel wound to his leg at Gallipoli on 16th August 1915. He also became ill with dysentery. By the end of October 1915, Sergeant Newman was being treated in a hospital in Bristol and towards the end of November had returned home to Newport, Isle of Wight.

---

[411] Isle of Wight County Press, 16th October 1915, p8
[412] Isle of Wight County Press, 27th November 1915, p5

Sergeant Newman continued to serve with the Isle of Wight Rifles and was discharged from the Army on 4th May 1918 due to sickness. He was given the Silver War Badge.

Sgt. Harry SUTTON, 620

Sergeant Harry Sutton fell ill at Gallipoli with dysentery and by the middle of October 1915 he was in a hospital in Birmingham.

Sergeant Sutton returned to serve with the Isle of Wight Rifles and was disembodied from the Army on 25th February 1919 under service number 330035.

Sgt. Clement John VILLAR, 1189

Sergeant Clement Villar was invalided off Gallipoli towards the end of September 1915 suffering with Enteric Fever. After a period of time in hospital, he was given extended leave and returned to the Isle of Wight.[413]

Clement Villar returned to serve with the Isle of Wight Rifles after fully recovering from Enteric Fever. He was promoted to the rank of Company Sergeant Major and his new service number was 330119. At the Second Battle of Gaza on 19th April 1917 he was wounded in the right arm and back but recovered to re-join the battalion.[414]

On 7th December 1917 Clement Villar was 'Discharged to Commission' and became an officer in the Isle of Wight Rifles, rising to the rank of Captain.[415] He was killed by a sniper during the Battle of Megiddo on 19th September 1918 and is buried at Ramleh War Cemetery.

---

[413] Isle of Wight County Press, 12th February 1916, p5
[414] http://www.wightatwar.org.uk/island-stories/captain-clement-villar
[415] www.ancestry.co.uk: UK, WWI Service Medal and Award Rolls, 1914-1920, 1914-15 Star

Sgt. Herbert Edward WHITTINGTON, 106

Sergeant Herbert Whittington was a member of the Isle of Wight Rifles before the outbreak of war. He was wounded during the attack on Anafarta Ridge and taken prisoner. He was originally held in Constantinople. Later in the war Sergeant Whittington was given the service number 330011. He died on 22nd February 1917, presumably still as a prisoner of war, and was buried at Baghdad (North Gate) War Cemetery.

L/Sgt. Harry Maurice LEAL, 1488

Lance Sergeant Harry Leal was expecting to be commissioned just before departing for Gallipoli. He was killed during the attack on Anafarta Ridge on 12th August 1915, aged 30 years old. CQMS Clark, in a letter to his wife dated 18th August 1915, confirmed the nature of Lance Sergeant Leal's death:

> Sgt Leal was killed about a yard from me. He was shot in the stomach. He only lived about two minutes after he was hit.[416]

Lance Sergeant Leal was reported to have been buried by his comrades but he has no known grave and is commemorated on the Helles Memorial.

L/Sgt. Cecil Hastings WALES, 1341

Lance Sergeant Cecil Hastings Wales came from Carisbrooke and was already serving with the Isle of Wight Rifles when war broke out. At Gallipoli he was promoted to the rank of Sergeant but soon afterwards fell ill with Typhoid. He died on 23rd September, aged 20, at a hospital in Malta and is buried at Pieta Military Cemetery.

---

[416] Isle of Wight County Press, 4th September 1915, p6

Cpl. John BARTON, 521

Corporal John Barton came from Wooton Bridge and had been serving with the Isle of Wight Rifles prior to the outbreak of war. He was a member of the *'Civilian Rifle Club, was a crack shot and winner of many trophies.'*[417]

Corporal Barton was killed on the 12th August 1915 during the advance on Anafarta Ridge. He was 35 years old and is commemorated on the Helles Memorial.

Cpl. George JAMES, 288

Corporal George James came from Newport. Before the war he worked in a boot shop and his pastimes included boxing.

Corporal James' bravery was noted in a letter home by Lance Corporal T Alexander on 16th August 1915:

> He crawled out of the trenches under a hail of bullets and rescued a wounded man who was helpless.[418]

By the beginning of October 1915, Corporal James had fallen ill with influenza was invalided off Gallipoli to Malta.

On 17th April 1916, Corporal James was discharged to be commissioned. He became a Second Lieutenant in the 3rd Battalion of the Hampshire Regiment and was attached to the 2nd Hants when he was wounded. He was taken to a hospital at Etaples in France and subsequently died on 8th May 1917.

Cpl. John Reginald SCOTT, 1804

Corporal John Scott was wounded in the knee by a piece of shrapnel on 31st October 1915. The same shell killed wounded

---

[417] Isle of Wight County Press, 29th July 1916, p4
[418] Isle of Wight County Press, 4th September 1915, p6

Rifleman Chandler as well as an artilleryman from the New Zealand Army.[419]

Corporal Scott recovered from his wounding and returned to active service with the Isle of Wight Rifles. He was given service number 330447 when the Territorial Forces received new service numbers in early 1917. At some point in 1917/1918, Corporal Scott was promoted to Sergeant and transferred to the 1/4th Hants with whom he served with until being disembodied from the Army on 12th June 1919. In 1918 the 1/4th Hants were deployed to Persia from the Middle East.

Cpl. Frederick William SMALL, 697

Corporal Frederick Small enlisted in the Isle of Wight Rifles on 8th March 1909. Previously he had served in the 5th Hants. Corporal Small also worked for the Isle of Wight County Press in their Composing Department prior to deploying to Gallipoli. He became ill at Gallipoli during October 1915 with dysentery and a breakdown and was admitted into a hospital at Malta.

Corporal Small was discharged from the Army on 28th April 1916 after completing his service period. He had served with the Isle of Wight Rifles for just over 7 years.

Cpl. Charles Frederic WHITTICOM, 400

Corporal Whitticom came from Cowes and enlisted in the Isle of Wight Rifles on 30th October 1908. He was invalided off Gallipoli on Saturday 23rd October 1915 suffering from jaundice and was taken to Egypt on the Hospital Ship Glenart Castle. Corporal Whitticom was then admitted in to Giza Hospital.

Corporal Whitticom went on to join the Royal Flying Corps, which later became the Royal Air Force and was given service number 403626. At the end of the war, Corporal Whitticom was serving at 'X' Aircraft Depot but he sadly died on 22nd November

---

[419] Isle of Wight County Press, 20th November 1915, p5

1918 and is buried at St. Germain-Au-Mont-D'Or Communal Cemetery Extension, France.[420]

Cpl. William Herbert WITHAM, 1530

Corporal William Witham came from Newport and enlisted in the Isle of Wight Rifles at Newport. He was killed in action on 12th August 1915, at the age of 30, during the advance on Anafarta Ridge and official notification of his death was published in the Isle of Wight County Press on 29th July 1916. He is commemorated on the Helles Memorial.

Cpl. Percy George WILLS, 986

Corporal Percy Wills was in the Isle of Wight Rifles' machine gun section at Gallipoli. He served with the Isle of Wight Rifles throughout the war and was disembodied from the Army on 3rd August 1919 under service number 330049 and with the rank of Lance Sergeant.

L/Cpl. Thomas Edgar ALEXANDER, 1186

Lance Corporal Thomas Alexander came from Newport. He was serving in the Isle of Wight Rifles when war broke out and was part of the battalion's machine gun section.

Lance Corporal Alexander became ill with cellulitis in his right foot and his hand and was invalided off Gallipoli to a hospital in Malta where he subsequently passed away on 29th October 1915. He is buried at Pieta Military Cemetery.

L/Cpl. Harold George BEVERTON, 1089

Lance Corporal Harold Beverton served at Gallipoli with his brother Rifleman Wallis Beverton. Both became ill at Gallipoli

---

[420] Commonwealth War Graves Commission: https://www.cwgc.org/find-war-dead/casualty/326105/whitticom,-charles-frederic/

during September 1915 – Harold with dysentery and Wallis with Enteric, and both were taken to Malta for treatment.

Lance Corporal Harold Beverton returned to serve with the Isle of Wight Rifles but his brother was discharged from the battalion on 10th December 1915. Harold Beverton was promoted to the rank of Sergeant and survived the war. His latter service number was 330068.

L/Cpl. William FLUX, 1185

Lance Corporal William Flux enlisted in the Isle of Wight Rifles on 5th July 1912. Following Gallipoli, he was transferred to the Labour Corps with whom he held the rank of Sergeant and service number 353965.

William Flux was discharged from the Army on 25th January 1918 due to sickness and was given the Silver War Badge.

L/Cpl. B LAMB, 1254

Lance Corporal Lamb fell ill at Gallipoli with dysentery between the middle of September and the beginning of October 1915.

Lance Corporal Lamb reached the rank of Corporal with the Isle of Wight Rifles before joining the Royal Flying Corps. He survived the war.

L/Cpl. Leonard John LEDICOTT, 956

Lance Corporal Leonard Ledicott enlisted in the Isle of Wight Rifles on 3rd March 1910. He reached the rank of Corporal with the Isle of Wight Rifles before being transferred to the Second Battalion of the Devonshire Regiment at some point after the Gallipoli campaign. The Second Battalion of the Devonshire Regiment was in the 8th Division and fought on the Western Front.

Leonard Ledicott was discharged from the Army on 18th June 1919 due to 'sickness' and was given the Silver War Badge. He was a Lance Sergeant at the time and his service number was 204944.[421]

L/Cpl. Horace Roland MEECH, 905

Lance Corporal Horace Meech was taken ill with a fever whilst at Gallipoli and as a result was hospitalised. He returned to his home town, Newport, at the beginning of December 1915 and was discharged from the Army on 10th December 1915.

L/Cpl. Herbert George PEACHEY, 1900

Lance Corporal Herbert Peachey served in the Isle of Wight Rifles with his younger brother Bugler Reginald Peachey. Lance Corporal Peachey continued to serve with the Isle of Wight Rifles after Gallipoli and reached the rank of Regimental Quartermaster Sergeant. He received a Mention in Despatches in Gazette Issue 30746 on 11th June 1918:

> I have the honour to forward herewith the names of those serving or who have served under my Command, whose distinguished and gallant services and devotion to duty I consider deserving of special mention.[422]

Regimental Quartermaster Sergeant Herbert Peachey survived the war and was disembodied from the Isle of Wight Rifles on 19th March 1919 under service number 330504.

L/Cpl. Harry PERKINS, 1096

Lance Corporal Harry Perkins enlisted in the Isle of Wight Rifles on the 1st January 1912 and was a member of the borough Fire Brigade at Newport.

During the advance on Anafarta Ridge, he was wounded four times. In a letter to Town Sergeant, B. Osborn, he wrote:

---

[421] www.ancestry.co.uk: Silver War Badge Records 1914-1919
[422] www.forces-war-records.co.uk: Gazetted Awards and Mentions in Despatches - Gazette Issue 30746, 11/06/1918, p7053.

They had to hit me four times before I was finished, so I fell, as I said, right in the thick of it.[423]

Lance Corporal Perkins initially received a light wound to his forehead and shortly afterwards he was shot in the arm. Despite this, he continued to advance but was hit by shrapnel in his leg.[424] Sgt Barnes and fellow soldiers tried to carry Lance Corporal Harry Perkins back but as he was in too much pain, they had to leave him under a tree and request a stretcher. Lance Corporal Perkins was taken onto a hospital ship however, the ship caught fire and he, along with many men, had to be transferred to another hospital ship which was bound for England.

Lance Corporal Perkins unfortunately had to have his leg amputated at a hospital in Manchester. He was discharged from the Army on the 19th August 1916 and was also unable to return to his civilian job as a firefighter.

L/Cpl. Edward William RACKETT, 1190

Lance Corporal Edward Rackett was wounded in the hand during August 1915 and was invalided off Gallipoli to a hospital in Malta.

Lance Corporal Rackett re-joined the Isle of Wight Rifles on returning to fitness and remained with B Company. He was later promoted to the rank of Corporal and when the Isle of Wight Rifles received new service numbers, was given service number 330120.

Lance Corporal Rackett was captured during the Second Battle of Gaza on 19th April 1917 and was taken to a prisoner of war camp at Yarbaschi. He died on 27th November 1917 and is buried at Baghdad (North Gate) War Cemetery.

---

[423] Isle of Wight County Press, 4th September 1915, p6
[424] Isle of Wight County Press, 9th October 1915, p8

L/Cpl. Hubert Victor REDSTONE, 1977

Lance Corporal Hubert Redstone was transferred to the 1st Garrison Battalion, Devonshire Regiment as a Private later in the war and was given service number 241659. This battalion performed garrison duties in Egypt followed by Palestine.

Private Hubert Redstone was disembodied from the 1st Garrison Battalion of the Devonshire Regiment on 29th June 1919.

L/Cpl. Albert SANGER, 1342

Lance Corporal Albert Sanger came from Newport and enlisted in the Isle of Wight Rifles at Newport. He continued serving with the Isle of Wight Rifles after Gallipoli and was killed in action during the Second Battle of Gaza on 19th April 1917 at the age of 25 years old. Lance Corporal Sanger's service number at the time was 330190. He is buried at Gaza War Cemetery.

L/Cpl. Percy STAY, 1021

Lance Corporal Percy Stay came from Carisbrooke. He enlisted in the Isle of Wight Rifles on 15th February 1911 under his full name Denniss Percival Stay.

Lance Corporal Stay became ill at Gallipoli with dysentery and an enlarged Thyroid Gland and had to leave the peninsula on 9th September 1915. His attestation papers state that he was admitted to the Convalescent Depot, Citadel, Cairo on 10th September 1915. Lance Corporal Stay embarked on the Hospital Ship 'Ghoorka' on 6th November and returned to England. He spent from the 19th November 1915 to 18th February 1916 at Shirley Warren Hospital, Southampton. On 17th March 1916, Lance Corporal Stay went before the Medical Board at Parkhurst Military Hospital, Isle of Wight and according to his attestation papers was recommended for discharge as he was *'permanently medically unfit.'* However, he was discharged from the Isle of Wight Rifles' reserve battalion (2/8th Hants) on 12th April 1916 and his attestation papers state that he was discharged due to *'the termination of his period of engagement.'*[425]

At the age of 31 years old, on 18th June 1920, Lance Corporal Stay re-enlisted with the Isle of Wight Rifles. He was given the rank of Sergeant and service number 5488015.[426]

L/Cpl. Albert Bernard WHEELER M.M., 1575

Lance Corporal Albert Wheeler came from Wooton. He continued to serve with the Isle of Wight Rifles after Gallipoli and was promoted to the rank of Sergeant and given service number 330307.

It was reported in the London Gazette on 25th September 1917 that Sergeant Albert Wheeler had been awarded the Military Medal for 'bravery in the field.'[427] This was likely awarded for Sergeant Wheeler's actions during the Second Battle of Gaza on 19th April 1917.

Albert Wheeler survived the war and was disembodied from the Isle of Wight Rifles on 24th July 1919 holding the rank of Acting Company Quartermaster Sergeant.

Bugler Albert Edward DOWNER, 675

Bugler Albert Downer came from Calbourne and enlisted in the Isle of Wight Rifles at Calbourne a few years before the onset of war. He was killed by a sniper whilst *'polishing his boots on 31st October 1915'* and is buried at the 7th Field Ambulance Cemetery.[428]

---

[425] www.ancestry.co.uk: British Army WWI Pension Records 1914-1920
[426] www.ancestry.co.uk: British Army WWI Pension Records 1914-1920
[427] www.forces-war-records.co.uk: Gazetted Awards and Mentions in Despatches - Gazette Issue 30312, p10037
[428] Isle of Wight in the Great War, M. J. Trow, Pen & Sword Military

Bugler William James FINCH, 1052

Bugler William Finch came from Cowes and was serving in the Isle of Wight Rifles at the outbreak of war. Like many of his comrades, he was posted as missing after the advance on Anafarta Ridge and was later presumed to have been killed in action on 12th August 1915. Official notification of his death was published in the Isle of Wight County Press on 29th July 1916. Bugler Finch was 21 years old and is commemorated on the Helles Memorial.

Bugler Sidney KEMP, 1058

Bugler Sidney Kemp joined the Isle of Wight Rifles on 24th May 1911 at the age of 15 years and 11 months old. He made it through the Gallipoli campaign without being wounded or becoming seriously ill and was appointed to the rank of Lance Corporal on 12th December 1915. He then went with the battalion to Alexandria.

Sidney Kemp was promoted to Corporal on 6th January 1916. His time as a Corporal was short lived as on 29th April 1916 he embarked on H.T. 'Northland' to return to England for his pending discharge from the Army for having completed his service period. Corporal Kemp was formally discharged from the Army on 26th May 1916.[429]

Bugler Reginald Frank PEACHEY, 1901

Bugler Reginald Peachey served in the Isle of Wight Rifles alongside his brother Lance Corporal Herbert Peachey. Reginald Peachey was the bugler for Lt. Col Rhodes and he was shot in the leg on 12th August 1915 straight after he *'sounded the advance.'*[430]

---

[429] www.ancestry.co.uk: British Army WW1 Pension Records 1914-1920
[430] The Isle of Wight Rifles, DJ Quigley, p8. Saunders, The Printers.

After being wounded, Bugler Peachey was taken onto a hospital ship which later caught fire. The wounded, included Bugler Peachey were transferred to another hospital ship. He safely made it back to England and spent some leave back on the Isle of Wight.

Bugler Peachey returned to serve with the Isle of Wight Rifles and reached the rank of Corporal. Later in the war he was transferred to the 1/4th Hants. In 1918 the 1/4th Hants were deployed to Persia from the Middle East. Corporal Peachey was disembodied from the 1/4th Hants on 22nd May 1919.

Rfn. Charles George ASH, 1171

Rifleman Charles George Ash lived in Shide and enlisted in the Isle of Wight Rifles at Newport. He served with the battalion at Gallipoli and afterwards under service number 330109. Rifleman Ash was killed in action during the Second Battle of Gaza on 19th April 1917 at the age of 24 years old. He has no known grave and is commemorated on the Jerusalem Memorial.

Rfn. George Henry ASH, 1286

Rifleman George Henry Ash came from Newport and enlisted at Newport. He fell ill at Gallipoli with enteric and pneumonia and subsequently died on 2nd October 1915 at a hospital in Malta. He was 23 years old. Rifleman Ash is buried at Pieta Military Cemetery.

Rfn. Harold ATTRILL, 1359

Rifleman Harold Attrill enlisted in the Isle of Wight Rifles on 25th October 1913. He was wounded in the arm at Gallipoli during August 1915 and taken to a hospital at Malta. As a result of the wounding, Rifleman Attrill was discharged from the Army on 24th April 1916 and received the Silver War Badge.

Rfn. John William BAKER, 1707

Rifleman John Baker came from Wroxhall. He was reported as missing in the Isle of Wight County Press on 11th September 1915 and was later presumed to have been killed during the advance on Anafarta Ridge on 12th August 1915. Official notification of his death was published in the Isle of Wight County Press on 29th July 1916. Rifleman Baker was 21 years old and is commemorated on the Helles Memorial.

Rfn. Alfred BALL, 2444

Rifleman Alfred Ball came from Ryde and enlisted in the Isle of Wight Rifles at Newport in May 1915. He fell ill with dysentery at Gallipoli and as a result passed away at a hospital in Alexandria on 22nd November 1915.[431] Rifleman Ball is buried at Alexandria (Chatby) Military and War Memorial Cemetery in Egypt.

Rfn. Leonard Frank BALL, 2066

Rifleman Leonard Ball was one of the Buckinghamshire men recruited by Lieutenant Colonel Rhodes in 1915. He came from Wooburn Green.

Rifleman Ball was reported missing after the advance on Anafarta Ridge on 12th August 1915 and was later presumed to have been killed during that fighting. He is commemorated on the Helles Memorial and was 18 years old.

Rfn. Frederick George BARBER, 1149

Rifleman Frederick Barber joined the Isle of Wight Rifles on 11th June 1912. He was wounded in the hand by a bullet at Gallipoli during August 1915 and was treated at hospitals in Malta and Leicester.

---

[431] www.ancestry.co.uk: UK, Army Registers of Soldiers' Effects, 1901-1929 for Alfred Ball

Later in the war, Frederick Barber served with the Labour Corps under service number 357683. He was discharged on 7th April 1919 due to sickness but later re-joined the 8th Hants under service number 5488628.

Rfn. Hilton BARNES, 2398

Rifleman Hilton Barnes lived at Totland and enlisted in the Isle of Wight Rifles at Newport. He continued serving with the Isle of Wight Rifles after Gallipoli and was given service number 330814.

Rifleman Barnes was killed in action on 2nd November 1917 during the Third Battle of Gaza. He was 21 years old and is buried at Gaza War Cemetery.

Rfn. George BARTLETT, 1075

Rifleman George Bartlett came from Newport and enlisted in the Isle of Wight Rifles on 1st September 1914. He was reported to be ill at Gallipoli with dysentery in the Isle of Wight County Press on 4th September 1915.

Rifleman George Bartlett continued to serve with the Isle of Wight Rifles. He was discharged from the Army on 18th June 1919 under service number 330060 due to a wounding and was given the Silver War Badge.

Rfn. Arthur Thomas BARTON, 1158

Rifleman Arthur Barton enlisted in the Isle of Wight Rifles on the 13th February 1915. He was invalided off Gallipoli and taken to a hospital in Malta suffering from dysentery. In a letter home on 20th August 1915 he wrote:

> It is a treat to get away from the firing line. I had a week there and on the third day when we made a big advance it was like hell. I had a narrow escape from a bullet, for

it took my Hants badge on my shoulder strap and nearly pulled it in two pieces.[432]

Rifleman Barton was discharged from the Army on the 19th August 1916 due to sickness and as a result was awarded the Silver War Badge.

Rfn. William A. BENNETT, 1164

Rifleman William Bennett remained serving with the Isle of Wight Rifles after Gallipoli and was given service number 330104 when the Territorial Forces were given new service numbers. William Bennett transferred to the Royal Engineers later in the war and was disembodied from the Army on 26th August 1919 under service number 521699.

Rfn. Wallis James BEVERTON, 902

Rifleman Wallis Beverton enlisted in the Isle of Wight Rifles on 25th November 1909. He served with the battalion at Gallipoli alongside his brother, Lance Corporal Harold Beverton. Both became ill at Gallipoli towards the end of September 1915 and on 1st October 1915, Wallis was admitted to a hospital in Malta suffering with Enteritis.

According to Rifleman Beverton's service record, he returned to England during November 1915 on board the Empress of Britain and was discharged from the Army on 10th December 1915 due to completing his service period. However, Rifleman Beverton's Silver War Badge record states that he was discharged due to sickness. His brother, Harold, survived the war.

Rfn. William John BRAMBLE, 1358

Rifleman William Bramble reached the rank of Acting Sergeant with the Isle of Wight Rifles. He was invalided off Gallipoli on 9th September 1915, however, the records do not indicate whether

---

[432] Isle of Wight County Press, 4th September 1916, p6

he was wounded or ill. His records state that the next time he served abroad was with the 8th London Regiment (Post Office Rifles) on the Western Front from the 11th October 1917 until the 25th October 1918 as a Lance Corporal under service number 374474.[433]

Lance Corporal Bramble survived the war.

Rfn. Frank BRETT, 1509

Rifleman Frank Brett came from Calbourne and enlisted in the Isle of Wight Rifles at Newport. He was reported as missing after the advance on Anafarta Ridge and was later presumed to have been killed during the advance on 12th August 1915. He is commemorated on the Helles Memorial.

Rfn. Christopher BUCKETT, 1178

Rifleman Christopher Buckett served in the Isle of Wight Rifles at Gallipoli with his brother Hubert Buckett.

When the soldiers in the Territorial forces received new service numbers in 1917, Rifleman Christopher Buckett was given service number 330112. Later on in 1917, he was transferred from the Isle of Wight Rifles to the 2nd Hants. He was wounded during the Battle of Cambrai and died of his wounds on 22nd November 2017. He is buried at Flesquieres Hill British Cemetery, France.

Rfn. Hubert BUCKETT, 1131

Rifleman Hubert Buckett served in the Isle of Wight Rifles at Gallipoli with his brother Christopher Buckett. Hubert was one of the designated signallers in the Isle of Wight Rifles.

Rifleman Hubert Buckett was given service number 330087 when the Territorial forces service numbers were renumbered in

---

[433] www.ancestry.co.uk: UK, WWI Service Medal and Award Rolls, 1914-1920 – British War Medal and Victory Medal

1917. At some point after this, Hubert joined the Royal Flying Corps/Royal Air Force and was given service number 406128. He survived the war.

Rfn. Percy BUCKETT, 2181

Rifleman Percy Buckett served at Gallipoli with his brother Rifleman William Harold Buckett. They came from Ryde.

Rifleman Percy Buckett served with the Isle of Wight Rifles throughout the war and was disembodied from the Army on 3rd April 1919 under service number 330684. His brother, William, was killed during the advance on Anafarta Ridge on 12th August 1915.

Rfn. William Harold BUCKETT, 2370

Rifleman William Buckett came from Ryde and served at Gallipoli with his brother Rifleman Percy Buckett. Rifleman William Buckett was reported as missing after the advance on Anafarta Ridge. On 6th May 1916 the Isle of Wight County Press published the following in their 'Information Desired' section:

> No official news has been received of the death of Rifleman W. H. Buckett, 2370, 1/8th Hants, missing since August 12th, at Gallipoli; there is therefore some hope of his having been taken prisoner.[434]

Unfortunately, Rifleman Buckett had not been taken prisoner and it was later presumed that he had been killed on 12th August 1915. He was 19 years old and is commemorated on the Helles Memorial. His brother, Percy, survived the war.

Rfn. George William BUDDEN, 2447

Rifleman George Budden was transferred to the 2nd Hants at some point after Gallipoli and was given service number 31279.

---

[434] Isle of Wight County Press, 6th May 1916, p3

He would have fought on the Western Front with the 2nd Hants. Rifleman Budden survived the war.

Rfn. Alfred W. BULL, 1514

Rifleman Alfred Bull remained with the Isle of Wight Rifles throughout the war and survived it. His latter service number was 330278.

Rfn. Arthur Frank BURGESS, 1297

Rifleman Arthur Burgess enlisted in the Isle of Wight Rifles at Newport. He became sick with dysentery at Gallipoli during August 1915.

Later in the war, Arthur Burgess was transferred to the 2/4th Hants and served in C Company under service number 205448. He reached the rank of Lance Sergeant and was killed in action on 1st December 1917 during the Battle of Nabi Samweil. Lance Sergeant Burgess is buried at Ramleh War Cemetery.

Rfn. Frederick CAREY, 1733

Rifleman Frederick Carey came from Newport. He was shot in the thumb at Gallipoli during August 1915. On recovering, he rejoined the Isle of Wight Rifles and continued to serve with them throughout the war. He was disembodied from the Army on 12th March 1919 under service number 330403.

Rfn. Frank CASS, 1376

Rifleman Frank Cass came from Newport and joined the Isle of Wight Rifles in 1913. He served in the Isle of Wight Rifles at Gallipoli along with his brother, Rifleman George Cass. At Gallipoli, Rifleman Frank Cass was wounded in the legs and, *'taken prisoner at Art Burnu on August 12th'*.[435]

---

[435] Isle of Wight County Press, 11th September 1915, p8.

Rifleman Cass died on 27th January 1917 and is buried at Baghdad (North Gate) War Cemetery. His latter service number was 330205. His brother, Rifleman George Cass, was killed during the Third Battle of Gaza.

Rfn. Frederick George CASSFORD, 2331

Rifleman Frederick Cassford came from Sandown and enlisted in the Isle of Wight Rifles at Newport. In the confusion of the early stages of the Isle of Wight Rifles campaign at Gallipoli, Rifleman Cassford was initially reported as missing in the 25th September 1915 edition of the Isle of Wight County Press. However, Rifleman Cassford was actually not missing.

Rifleman Cassford continued serving with the Isle of Wight Rifles after Gallipoli and was given service number 330769. He was killed in action during the Second Battle of Gaza on 19th April 1917 and is buried at Gaza War Cemetery.

Rfn. Archibald CHANDLER, 1074

Rifleman Archibald Chandler came from Newport. He was wounded in the foot at Gallipoli by a piece of shrapnel and the below extract from a letter written by Rifleman Chandler was published in the Isle of Wight County Press on 20th November 1915:

> I am very thankful to say that although the piece of shrapnel went right through the foot it never touched the bone at all and so the wound is healing nicely.[436]

Corporal Scott was also wounded in the same incident.

By November 1915, Rifleman Chandler was receiving treatment at South 6 General Military Hospital in Gibraltar. He had been invalided to Gallipoli aboard Hospital Ship Somali along with Riflemen Jack Hamilton, Trickett and Creasey.

---

[436] Isle of Wight County Press, 20th November 1915, p5

Rifleman Chandler returned to serve with the Isle of Wight Rifles and was promoted to the rank of Corporal. He was disembodied from the Army on 12th August 1919 under service number 330059.

Rfn. Frederick CHIVERTON, 1336

Rifleman Frederick Chiverton enlisted in the Isle of Wight Rifles at Newport. Following Gallipoli, he remained with the battalion and was given service number 330187 when the Territorial Forces received new service numbers.

Rifleman Chiverton was killed in action during the Second Battle of Gaza on 19th April 1917 at the age of 23 years. He is buried at Gaza War Cemetery.

Rfn. Edward Victor CHURCH, 1348

Rifleman Edward Church came from Ryde and enlisted in the Isle of Wight Rifles on 24th October 1913. He was taken prisoner during the Second Battle of Gaza on 19th April 1917 and was held prisoner at Adana Yarbaschi.[437]

Rifleman Church was discharged from the Army on 18th March 1919 under service number 330192 due to illness and was given the Silver War Badge. He was also awarded the Territorial Force War Medal.

Rfn. Edward CLARKE, 1655

Rifleman Edward Clarke came from Carisbrooke and enlisted in the Isle of Wight Rifles on 31st August 1914. During August 1915, he was invalided off Gallipoli due to sunstroke and a slight shrapnel wound and was taken back to Southampton.

---

[437] From research undertaken by Ian Meadows

Rifleman Clarke returned to the Isle of Wight Rifles and was discharged on 16th August 1919 under service number 330359 and given the Silver War Badge due to wounds.

Rfn. Charles Alfred George COFFEN, 1621

Rifleman Charles Coffen came from Wooton and enlisted in the Isle of Wight Rifles on 29th August 1914. He was discharged from the Army on 17th September 1916 owing to illness and was given the Silver War Badge.

Rfn. William Basil COLE, 1151

Rifleman William Cole came from Newport. He served with the Isle of Wight Rifles throughout the war and reached the rank of Sergeant. He fell ill with Influenza in December 1918 whilst with the Isle of Wight Rifles in Beirut and was transferred to a hospital in Alexandria where he managed to recover.[438]

Sergeant Cole was demobilised from the Army on 27th May 1919 under service number 330095.

Rfn. Arthur Charles COLEMAN, 1516

Rifleman Arthur Coleman came from Brighstone and enlisted in the Isle of Wight Rifles at Newport. Rifleman Coleman remained with the battalion after Gallipoli and was given service number 330280. He was killed in action during the Second Battle of Gaza on 19th April 1917 at the age of 27 years and is commemorated on the Jerusalem Memorial.

Rfn. Wallace Edmund Leonard COOPER, 1518

Rifleman Wallace Cooper came from Newport. He was invalided off Gallipoli suffering from dysentery and admitted into the 5th

---

[438] www.forces-war-records.co.uk: Military Hospitals Admissions and Discharge Registers WW1 - MH106/1941

Canadian Stationary Hospital in Abbasia, Cairo during November 1915.

Once fit again, Rifleman Cooper returned to serve with the Isle of Wight Rifles for the rest of the war. He was disembodied from the battalion on 5th May 1919 under service number 330281.

Rfn. Charles COURTNEY, 1363

Rifleman Charles Courtney was invalided off Gallipoli between late September and early October 1915 suffering from dysentery. He was treated at St. George's Hospital in Malta.

Rifleman Courtney continued serving with the Isle of Wight Rifles for the remainder of the war and was disembodied from the battalion on 1st August 1919 under service number 330198.

Rfn. Albert Charles COWARD, 1371

Rifleman Albert Coward came from Carisbrooke. He had gone through the Gallipoli campaign unscathed up to the point when he was killed in action on 29th November 1915 whilst returning from collecting rations. His death was mentioned in a letter from Corporal James, to Corporal James' parents:

> Coming back poor Bert Coward was killed. I was with him about 3 minutes before he met his end and he was saying how glad he was that we were being relieved.[439]

Rifleman Coward is buried in the 7th Field Ambulance Cemetery at Gallipoli.

Rfn. Ernest Alfred DALLIMORE, 1520

Rifleman Ernest Dallimore came from Ventnor. He was wounded at Gallipoli during August 1915.

---

[439] Isle of Wight County Press, 12th February 1916, p5

Rifleman Dallimore continued to serve with the Isle of Wight Rifles on recovering from his wounds and was given service number 330282. He was killed in action on 19th April 1917 during the Second Battle of Gaza and is buried at Gaza War Cemetery.

Rfn. John DAVIS, 1338

Rifleman John Davis continued to serve with the Isle of Wight Rifles after Gallipoli and was given service number 330189. Later in the war he transferred to the Royal Engineers and was given service number 521672. After the war, John Davis re-enlisted into the Royal Engineers under service number 315074.

Rfn. Gustave William DORE M.C., 1173

Rifleman Gustave Dore came from Newport and joined the Isle of Wight Rifles in June 1912. He was taken ill at Gallipoli and by November 1915 had been admitted into Ghezireh Hospital, Cairo.

Rifleman Dore rose through the ranks to become a Sergeant with the Isle of Wight Rifles and was given service number 330110 when the Territorials received their new service numbers. Gustave Dore was then Discharged to Commission on 17th December 1917 and he became a Second Lieutenant in the Isle of Wight Rifles.[440]

For his actions on the night of the 18th-19th September 1918 whilst commanding a patrol at Merj Kesfa, Gustave Dore was awarded the Military Cross. He survived the war and deployed with a number of the Isle of Wight Rifles to Khartoum, Sudan in 1919.[441]

---

[440] www.ancestry.co.uk: British Army WWI Medal Rolls Index Cards, 1914-1920
[441] https://www.stpaulsbarton.co.uk/content/pages/documents/1542300370.pdf

Rfn. Arthur DOWNER, 1362

Rifleman Arthur Downer enlisted in the Isle of Wight Rifles on 25th October 1913. He was wounded during the attack at Anafarta Ridge and taken prisoner. He was treated at a hospital in Constantinople and spent time as a prisoner of war at Croisant War Rouge Hospital, Pera.[442]

Rifleman Downer was discharged on 5th May 1919 due to his wounds and awarded the Silver War Badge. His service number on being discharged was 330197.

Rfn. George H. DOWNER, 1114

Rifleman George Downer was transferred to the Machine Gun Corps following his deployment to Gallipoli with the Isle of Wight Rifles. He was disembodied from the Army on 24th July 1919 under service number 50273.

Rfn. William George Morris DUNSTAN, 1636

Rifleman William Dunstan died on 18th August 1915, aged 34, as a result of the wounds he received at Gallipoli. He is buried at Hill 10 Cemetery, Gallipoli. His brother, Gordon, also served with the Isle of Wight Rifles and was wounded at Gallipoli but survived the war.

Rfn. Frank DYER, 2103

Rifleman Frank Dyer was invalided off Gallipoli with dysentery between late September and early October 1915. He was taken to Malta and treated at Tigne Military Hospital.

Rifleman Dyer returned to serve with the Isle of Wight Rifles and at some point in 1917/1918 he was transferred to the 1/4th Hants. In 1918 the 1/4th Hants were deployed to Persia from the Middle

---

[442] Research undertaken by Ian Meadows

East. Rifleman Dyer survived the war and was disembodied from the Army on 27th March 1919 under service number 330633.

Rfn. Sidney George EARLY, 854

Rifleman Sidney Early enlisted in the Isle of Wight Rifles at Newport on 3rd August 1909. He was 16 years and 2 months old. His elder brothers, Rifleman William James Early and Rifleman Charles Arthur Early also served with the Isle of Wight Rifles. Although Rifleman Sidney Early was listed in the men of the Isle of Wight Rifles that were deploying to Gallipoli, he in fact did not go to Gallipoli. His Army pension record states that he was discharged from the 2/8th Hants on 3rd August 1915 after 6 years' service with the Isle of Wight Rifles.[443]

Rfn. William James EARLY M.M., 1461

Rifleman William Early was wounded in the arm at the beginning of October 1915 by shrapnel whilst he was behind the firing line. The shrapnel missed his bone but caused a large flesh wound causing him to be invalided off Gallipoli to a hospital in Cairo, Egypt. In a letter to Mr Eldridge written at Alexandria and dated the 9th December, he stated that his wound had healed.[444]

Rifleman Early continued to serve with the Isle of Wight Rifles and reached the rank of Sergeant. He was awarded the Military Medal for 'bravery in the field' and his award was officially reported in the London Gazette on 25th September 1917.[445]

Rifleman Early was disembodied from the Army on 16th May 1919 under service number 330253.

---

[443] www.ancestry.co.uk: British Army WWI Pension Records 1914-1920
[444] Isle of Wight County Press, 1st January 1916, p5
[445] www.forces-war-records.co.uk: Gazetted Awards and Mentions in Despatches – Gazette Issue 30312, 25/09/1917, p10025

Rfn. Leonard ELDRIDGE, 1669

Rifleman Leonard Eldridge enlisted with the Isle of Wight Rifles on 3rd August 1914. He was wounded in the left eye during the Anafarta Ridge advance and was invalided to St Andrew's hospital at Malta.

On 9th October 1915, the Isle of Wight County Press reported that Rifleman Eldridge had been receiving treatment at a military hospital in Southampton but was on a period of leave and was *'still unable to see with his left eye.'*[446]

Due to his wounding, Rifleman Eldridge was discharged from the 2/8th Hants on 22nd April 1916 and awarded the Silver War Badge. He went on to work for the Manchester Guardian as a sports journalist.

Rfn. Percy E FILLENHAM, 2424

Rifleman Percy Fillenham enlisted in the Isle of Wight Rifles on 7th May 1915. He was reported to have been wounded at Gallipoli in the 25th September 1915 edition of the Isle of Wight County Press on 25th September 1915.

Rifleman Fillenham was discharged from the Army on 23rd September 1916. His Silver War Badge record states that he was discharged due to 'sickness.'

Rfn. Stanford James FISK, 1205

Rifleman Stanford Fisk fell ill at Gallipoli and boarded a hospital ship at Anzac Cove on 12th October 1915. On the 18th October 1915 he was admitted to the Red Cross Hospital at Gizeh which is close to Cairo. In a letter to his parents written on the 19th October 1915, he wrote:

---

[446] Isle of Wight County Press, 9th October 1915, p8

You need not worry, I am not wounded, just absolutely done up to the world. With a decent rest and treatment I hope soon to be fit again.[447]

Rifleman Fisk returned to the Isle of Wight Rifles following a further stint in hospital back in England at the London Hospital. He took part in the Isle of Wight Rifles' campaign in Palestine and was killed in action on 2nd November 1917 during the Third Battle of Gaza, aged 24 years old. Rifleman Fisk is commemorated on the Jerusalem Memorial. His latter service number was 330125.

Rfn. Edgar FLEMING, 517

Rifleman Edgar Fleming was one of the Isle of Wight Rifles' bandsmen and a member of the stretcher squad. He was shot in the right hand by a sniper on the evening of 18th August at Gallipoli whilst fetching water. Within an hour of being wounded, his hand had been dressed and he was taken to a hospital ship. After 3 days in harbour, the hospital ship sailed to Alexandria which took a couple of days. There, Rifleman Fleming received further hospital treatment.

Rifleman Fleming was discharged from the Army on 28th April 1916.

Rfn. Osman FORD, 2401

Rifleman Osman Ford was transferred to the Machine Gun Corps after Gallipoli and was given service number 149440. Later in the war, he was transferred to the Somerset Light Infantry and was given service number 235002. After the war, Osman re-enlisted in the Isle of Wight Rifles under service number 5488094 and became a Corporal in the battalion.

---

[447] Isle of Wight County Press, 6th November 1915, p5

Rfn. Isaac FOSS, 1566

Rifleman Isaac Foss came from Whippingham. He was initially reported as missing and then presumed to have been killed in action on 22nd August 1915. Official notification of his death was published in the Isle of Wight County Press on 29th July 1916. Rifleman Foss was 24 years old and is commemorated on the Helles Memorial.

Rfn. Edward George FOSTER, 1315

Rifleman Edward Foster came from Newport and joined the Isle of Wight Rifles in 1913. He was killed during the advance on Anafarta Ridge on 12th August 1915. He was 28 years old and is commemorated on the Helles Memorial.

Rfn. George Walter FRY, 1305

Rifleman George Fry was 17 years old when he was wounded at Gallipoli during August 1915. Rifleman J Davis, in a letter to Mrs Davis that was published in the Isle of Wight County Press on 9th October, wrote that his *'pal Geo Fry got hit in the hand with a piece of shrapnel but it was not very serious. It only just went under the skin.'*

Rifleman Fry went on to serve with the 1/6th Hants in Mesopotamia under service number 330170 and reached the rank of Lance Corporal. He died on 14th November 1918 and is buried at Amara War Cemetery, Iraq.

Rfn. Arthur Charles Stansfield GALE, 982

Rifleman Arthur Gale came from Carisbrooke and enlisted in the Isle of Wight Rifles at Newport on 10th October 1910 at the age of 17 years and 4 months. Rifleman Gale came through the Gallipoli campaign unscathed and sailed with the battalion to Alexandria. He returned home in January 1916 and was discharged from the Army on 28th January 1916 after completing his service period.

Rfn. William GEORGE, 2347

Rifleman William George was reported as having been wounded at Gallipoli in the Isle of Wight County Press' 2nd October 1915 edition.

Rifleman George recovered from his wounding and continued to serve with the Isle of Wight Rifles. He reached the rank of Acting Sergeant and was disembodied from the Army on 3rd August 1919 under service number 330779.

Rfn. Sidney Charles GINGER, 2026

Rifleman Sidney Ginger came from Carisbrooke and enlisted in the Isle of Wight Rifles at Newport shortly after the declaration of war. He was killed on the 9th October 1915 at the age of 19 and is buried at 7th Field Ambulance Cemetery, Gallipoli.

Rfn. Frank GRAVES, 1521

Rifleman Frank Graves came from Ventnor and enlisted in the Isle of Wight Rifles on 6th August 1914. He was discharged from the Army on 20th July 1916 due to 'sickness' and was given the Silver War Badge.[448]

Rfn. Frank GREEN, 1104

Rifleman Frank Green came from Parkhurst and enlisted in the Isle of Wight Rifles at Newport. He was reported as missing after the advance on Anafarta Ridge on 12th August 1915 and was later presumed to have died on 12th August 1915. Rifleman Green was 19 years old and is commemorated on the Helles Memorial.

Rfn. Arthur John GREENHAM, 1495

Rifleman Arthur Greenham came from Wooton Bridge and enlisted in the Isle of Wight Rifles at Wooton Bridge. He became seriously ill with dysentery whilst at Gallipoli and was taken to

---

[448] www.forces-war-records.co.uk: Silver War Badge List 1914-1918

Imtarfa Hospital in Malta where he passed away on 19th September 1915 at the age of 25 years old. Rifleman Greenham is buried at Pieta Military Cemetery.

Rfn. William GRIFFIN, 2371

Rifleman William Griffin served with the 2/4th Hants and 2/5th Hants under service number 330794 following his period of time with the Isle of Wight Rifles. In the latter part of the war, William Griffin was transferred to the 1/4th Duke of Edinburgh's (Wiltshire) Regiment who were also part of the Egyptian Expeditionary Force. He held the rank of Private with service number 204015.

Private Griffin was categorised as a Class Z reservist on 6th May 1919.

Rfn. Alfred Thomas GROVES, 2300

Rifleman Alfred Groves served with the Isle of Wight Rifles throughout the war and was demobilised from the battalion on 8th August 1919 under service number 330747.

Rfn. Charles Henry GUY, 1337

Rifleman Charles Guy fell ill with Enteric and dysentery at Gallipoli and was admitted on to HM Hospital Ship Assaye on 3rd October 1915.[449]

Rifleman Guy returned to serve with the Isle of Wight Rifles and was disembodied from the Army on 12th August 1919 under service number 330188.

Rfn. George GUY, 1167

Rifleman George Austen Rice Guy came from Newport and enlisted in the Isle of Wight Rifles at Newport. He was killed in

---

[449] www.forces-war-records.co.uk: Military Hospitals Admissions and Discharge Registers WW1 – MH106/1913 Records of H.M.A.T Ship Assaye: 02/10/1915 - 11/10/1915

action on 12th August 1915 during the advance on Anafarta Ridge at the age of 18 and is commemorated on the Helles Memorial.

Rfn. George HAGGER, 1334

Rifleman George Hagger came from Newport. He was reported to have been wounded at Gallipoli in the Isle of Wight County Press on 11th September 1915.

Rifleman George Hagger returned to serve with the Isle of Wight Rifles and was promoted to the rank of Lance Corporal. He was disembodied from the Army on 31st July 1919 under service number 330186.

Rfn. Arthur Thomas HALE, 1197

Rifleman Arthur Hale came from Newport. He was reported as missing in action after the advance on Anarfarta Ridge on 12th August 1915 and was later presumed to have been killed in action on the 12th August 1915. Official notification of his death was published in the Isle of Wight County Press on 29th July 1916. Rifleman Hale was 19 years old and is commemorated on the Helles Memorial.

Rfn. Hilton Charles HALL, 1150

Rifleman Hilton Hall came from Newport. He enlisted in the Isle of Wight Rifles on 11th June 1912 and went to Gallipoli with the battalion. Rifleman Hall was invalided off Gallipoli towards the end of November 1915 due to dysentery and was taken to a hospital in Egypt where he suffered shortness of breath, exhaustion on walking and palpitations.[450]

Rifleman Hall was discharged from the Army on 8th May 1916 due to the lasting side effects he experienced from falling ill with dysentery. He was given an Army pension and the Silver War Badge.

---

[450] www.ancestry.co.uk: British Army WWI Pension Records 1914-1920

Rfn. Bertram Charles HAMILTON, 1157

Rifleman Bertram Hamilton served at Gallipoli with his brother Rifleman Leonard Hamilton. Rifleman Bertram Hamilton was reported as missing after the advance on Anafarta Ridge and was later presumed to have died on 12th August 1915 during the advance. Official notification of his death was published in the Isle of Wight County Press on 29th July 1916. He was 17 years old and is commemorated on the Helles Memorial. His brother survived the war.

Rfn. Leonard <u>Jack</u> HAMILTON, 1155

Rifleman Jack Hamilton and his brother Rifleman Bertram Hamilton served together at Gallipoli. Rifleman Leonard Hamilton escaped significant wounding in August 1915. A bullet struck his cigarette tin and he was also bruised on the arm by a piece of shrapnel.

Towards the end of October 1915, Rifleman Hamilton fell ill with dysentery. He was taken to Gibraltar on the Hospital Ship Somali and by November 1915 had been admitted to a hospital on Gibraltar. Rifleman Leonard Hamilton was on the same hospital ship as Rifleman Chandler and Rifleman Trickett.[451]

Rifleman Hamilton was later promoted to Corporal. He was disembodied from the Hampshire Regiment on 16th May 1919 under service number 330098. His brother was killed on 12th August 1915 during the advance on Anafarta Ridge.

Rfn. Oliver HARDING, 1141

Rifleman Oliver Harding came from Calbourne and enlisted in the Isle of Wight Rifles at Locksgreen. He was wounded at Gallipoli and died of his wounds on 23rd August 1915 whilst on

---

[451] Isle of Wight County Press, 20th November 1915, p5

a hospital ship. Rifleman Harding was aged 22 and was buried at sea.[452] He is commemorated on the Helles Memorial.

Rfn. Charles HARFIELD, 2025

Rifleman Charles Harfield was born on 21st April 1899 in Newport. He enlisted in the Isle of Wight Rifles on 3rd December 1914 stating that he was 18 years and 9 months old. He was in fact 15 years and 7 months old. The age to serve abroad at the time was 19 years old.

Despite being underage, Rifleman Harfield deployed to Gallipoli with the Isle of Wight Rifles. He fell ill with dysentery in October 1915 and was admitted into a hospital in Malta. He was then invalided back to England aboard Hospital Ship Soudan on 28th November 1915. On recovering, Rifleman Harfield was sent to the 3/8th Hants at Parkhurst.

Rifleman Harfield was living with his aunt and uncle before the war and they were effectively his next of kin. On 2nd March 1916 they enclosed Rifleman Harfield's birth certificate and wrote the following to the Commanding Officer of the 3/8th Hants:

> Sir,
>
> Enclosed please find my nephew's Birth Certificate, we wish to claim him out of the army as he is not old enough or strong enough to do any more military work. He had been to the Dardanelles and has only just recovered from Dysentery. The Reverend at Malta Hospital advised him to come out of the Army as soon as possible for he wants somebody to look after him.
>
> By seeing to this you would oblige your faithful servants

---

[452] www.ancestry.co.uk: UK, Soldiers Died in the Great War, 1914-1919

R & A Smith[453]

Rifleman Harfield's Territorial Force Attestation papers state that he was discharged from the 3/8th Hants on 14th March 1916 due to *'having made a misstatement as to age on enlistment.'*[454]

Rfn. Sydney James HARFIELD, 1349

Rifleman Sydney Harfield continued serving with the Isle of Wight Rifles after Gallipoli and was disembodied from the battalion on 5th May 1919 under service number 330193.

Rfn. Arthur HARRIS, 2341

Rifleman Arthur Harris came from Watford and is recorded as having enlisted in the Isle of Wight Rifles at Newport.[455] It is probable that he joined the Isle of Wight Rifles when they were training in Watford.

After Gallipoli, Rifleman Harris was posted to the 2/5th Hants and given service number 2054632. He was then transferred to the 1/4th Duke of Edinburgh's (Wiltshire) Regiment as a Private with service number 204016. It was with this battalion that he took part in the Battle of Sharon on 19th September 1918 and was killed in action. He was 21 years old and is buried at Ramleh War Cemetery.

Rfn. Herbert Daniel John HARVEY, 2118

Rifleman Herbert Harvey and his brother, Rifleman Cecil Harvey, both served at Gallipoli with the Isle of Wight Rifles.

Rifleman Herbert Harvey was reported in the Isle of Wight County Press on 27th November 1915 as having been missing since 22nd August 1915 and his 1914/1915 Star Medal record

---

[453] www.ancestry.co.uk: British Army WW1 Pension Records 1914-1920 – Territorial Force Attestation
[454] www.ancestry.co.uk: British Army WW1 Pension Records 1914-1920 – Territorial Force Attestation
[455] www.ancestry.co.uk: UK, Soldiers Died in the Great War, 1914-1919

states that his death was presumed to have been on 22nd August 1915. However, contrary to this, Rifleman Herbert Harvey is recorded as having died on 12th August 1915 with the Commonwealth War Graves Commission. Official notification of his death was published in the Isle of Wight County Press on 29th July 1916. Rifleman Harvey was 19 years old and is commemorated on the Helles Memorial. His brother survived the war.

Rfn. Francis HATCHER, 2013

Rifleman Francis Hatcher came from Lake, Sandown and enlisted in the Isle of Wight Rifles on 2nd December 1914 at Sandown Barracks. He was 24 years and 7 months old and had 3 and a half years of previous military experience from serving with the Territorial Force of the Hampshire Royal Field Artillery.

Rifleman Hatcher started to have trouble with his vision in November 1915 and was invalided off Gallipoli and admitted into the Red Cross Hospital at Cairo on 23rd November 1915. He re-joined the battalion at Sidi Bishr, Alexandria on 27th December 1915.

On 12th April 1917 he was seen by the 26th Casualty Clearing Station due to suffering with Myopia and on 15th April 1917 he was admitted into Citaldel North Hospital in Cairo. He was diagnosed with having a myopic astigmatism on 23rd April 1917 and was discharged to duty on 30th April 1917. Around this time, Francis Hatcher was transferred to the 1/4th Northants as a Private and his service number changed from 330576 to 205170. Then, on 24th May 1917 he was posted to the 1st Garrison Battalion of the Northamptonshire Regiment.[456]

Private Hatcher went with the 1st Garrison Battalion of the Northamptonshire Regiment to Salonika, arriving on 31st

---

[456] www.ancestry.co.uk: British Army WW1 Service Records, 1914-1920 – Territorial Force Attestation Papers.

October 1918. The battalion left Salonika on 8th January 1919 and Private Hatcher was disembodied from the 3rd Northants on 22nd April 1919.

Rfn. Laurence Norman HATCHER, 1497

Rifleman Laurence Hatcher came from Newport. He was reported to have been wounded on 12th August 1915 in the 11th September 1915 edition of the Isle of Wight County Press. He in fact died on 12th August 1915. He was 21 years old and is commemorated on the Helles Memorial.

Rfn. William Henry HAYDEN, 2028

Rifleman William Hayden came from Sandown and enlisted in the Isle of Wight Rifles at Sandown Barracks. After Gallipoli he remained with the Isle of Wight Rifles, reaching the rank of Lance Sergeant with service number 330586.

Lance Sergeant Hayden was killed in action on 19th April 1917 during the Second Battle of Gaza. He was 28 years old and is commemorated on the Jerusalem Memorial.

Rfn. Robert HAYLES, 1345

Rifleman Robert Hayles joined the Isle of Wight Rifles in 1913. He was taken prisoner at Gallipoli in August 1915 after having been slightly wounded by a bayonet and was held prisoner at Constantinople, Anyora, Bilemedik-Pusanti.[457]

Rifleman Hayles was disembodied from the Isle of Wight Rifles on 1st April 1919 under service number 330191.

Rfn. Frank HOLBROOK, 1288

Rifleman Frank Holbrook enlisted in the Isle of Wight Rifles on 22nd April 1913. Between the middle of September and early

---

[457] Research undertaken by Ian Meadows

October 1915, Rifleman Holbrook was taken sick. He was invalided off Gallipoli to a hospital in Cairo.

Rifleman Holbrook returned to the Isle of Wight Rifles after his illness. He was discharged from the battalion on 23rd March 1919 under service number 330164. His Silver War Badge Record states that he was discharged due to 'sickness.'

Rfn. Percy John Denness HOLBROOK, 1140

Rifleman Percy Holbrook was wounded in the leg during August 1915 at Gallipoli. On recovering from his wounds, he continued to serve with the Isle of Wight Rifles throughout the rest of the war and was disembodied from the Army on 11th April 1919 under service number 330091.

Rfn. Frederick William HOLLIS, 2119

Rifleman Frederick Hollis enlisted in the Isle of Wight Rifles at Newport. He was killed in action on 3rd September 1915 and was buried by his brother Rifleman John Hollis the following morning. Captain Fardell was near to Rifleman Frederick Hollis when he was killed and wrote the following kind words to Rifleman Hollis' wife:

> Everyone regrets the loss of your husband, as he was one of the very best soldiers I have ever served with. However hard the task has been here, I have never known him complain or do anything but try to cheer his comrades. I am afraid we shall all miss him very much. We shall always remember him as an example of what a soldier should be. [458]

Rifleman Hollis left behind a wife and three children. Unfortunately, the location of his grave was unknown at the end of the war and so he is commemorated on the Helles Memorial.

---

[458] Isle of Wight County Press, 2nd October 1915 p8

Rfn. John Charles HOLLIS, 2386

Rifleman John Hollis served in the Isle of Wight Rifles at Gallipoli with his brother Rifleman Frederick Hollis. He buried his brother after his brother was killed on 3rd September 1915.

Rifleman John Hollis continued to serve with the Isle of Wight Rifles after Gallipoli and rose to the rank of Sergeant. He survived the war and his final service number was 330803.

Rfn. Henry HORSCROFT, 1148

Rifleman Henry Horscroft came from Thornley and was serving in the Isle of Wight Rifles before the outbreak of war. He was wounded on the 20th August 1915 and died of his wounds on the same day. Rifleman Horscroft is buried at Hill 10 Cemetery.

Rfn. Charles Robert HORSECROFT, 1369

Rifleman Charles Horsecroft came from Hunny Hill and enlisted in the Isle of Wight Rifles at Newport. He remained with the battalion after Gallipoli and was killed in action on 19th April 1917 during the Second Battle of Gaza. Rifleman Horsecroft 330201 has no known grave and is commemorated on the Jerusalem Memorial.

Rfn. Albert HUMBER, 1612

Rifleman Albert Humber and his brother Rifleman Reginald Humber both served with the Isle of Wight Rifles at Gallipoli. Rifleman Albert Humber *'was wounded in the thumb just after the attack commenced on August 12th.'*[459] He was invalided off Gallipoli and taken to a hospital at Malta.

Rifleman Albert Humber returned to serve with the Isle of Wight Rifles throughout the rest of the war. He was disembodied from the Army on 3rd April 1919 under service number 330333.

---

[459] Isle of Wight County Press, 4th September 1915, p8

Rfn. Reginald William HUMBER, 1170

Rifleman Reginald Humber came from Carisbrooke and enlisted in the Isle of Wight Rifles at Newport. After Gallipoli he was transferred to the 2/4th Hants as a Private and was given service number 205441.

Private Humber died on the 25th June 1918 at the age of 24 years. Depending on which official record, Private Humber either died of wounds or died of accidental injuries. He is buried at Gezaincourt Communal Cemetery Extension which is located in the Somme area of France.

Rfn. Alfred HUNNYBUN, 2008

Rifleman Alfred Hunnybun came from Newport and enlisted in the Isle of Wight Rifles at Newport. He continued to serve with the battalion after Gallipoli and was given service number 330571 when the Territorial Forces received new service numbers. Rifleman Hunnybun was killed in action on 19th April 1917 during the Second Battle of Gaza. He was 20 years old and is commemorated on the Jerusalem Memorial.

Rfn. John Augustus (Jack) HURRY, 1354

Rifleman Jack Hurry came from Newport. He was originally reported as missing but was later presumed to have been killed during the advance on Anafarta Ridge on 12th August 1915. He was 19 years old and is commemorated on the Helles Memorial.

Rfn. Arthur Victor JAMES, 1677

Rifleman Arthur James had become ill with dysentery at Gallipoli by the middle of September 1915 and required hospital treatment. He returned to serve with the Isle of Wight Rifles at Gallipoli and had reached the rank of Corporal prior to the battalion leaving the Gallipoli peninsula.

Arthur James was given service number 330375 under the new Territorials' service numbering system. He was promoted to Sergeant and fought with the Isle of Wight Rifles in the Second Battle of Gaza on the 19th April 1917 where he was killed in action on that day. Sergeant Arthur James is commemorated on the Jerusalem Memorial. He was 21 years old.

Rfn. Leslie Victor Frank JAMES, 1156

Rifleman Leslie James was hit three times during the Anafata Ridge offensive, including in the right hand and right thigh. He was sent to a hospital in Malta for treatment and convalescence.

After recovering from his wounding, Rifleman James returned to serve with the Isle of Wight Rifles and was given service number 330099. He was killed in action on the 19th April 1917, aged 23, during the Second Battle of Gaza and is commemorated on the Jerusalem Memorial.

Rfn. Thomas William JOLLIFFE, 1002

Rifleman Thomas Jolliffe came from Whippingham and enlisted in the Isle of Wight Rifles on 27th January 1911 with Rifleman Vernon Jolliffe. Census records indicate that the two are not brothers. They are likely to be cousins.

Rifleman Thomas Jolliffe fell ill with diarrhoea at Gallipoli and was admitted into a hospital in Malta on 24th October 1915. He was invalided to England on 26th December 1915 aboard Hospital Ship Italia and was then admitted in to Graylingwell War Hospital in Chichester on 2nd January 1916 for 6 days of convalescence after suffering with dysentery.[460]

On 4th February 1916 Rifleman Jolliffe was discharged from the Army for completing his service period.

---

[460] www.ancestry.co.uk: British Army WWI Pension Records 1914-1920 – Territorial Force Attestation

Rfn. Vernon JOLLIFFE, 1003

Rifleman Vernon Jolliffe joined the Isle of Wight Rifles on 27th January 1911. He was shot in the hand on 12th August 1915 during the advance on Anafarta Ridge and received initial treatment by the 30th Field Ambulance. On 25th August 1915 he was admitted to a hospital at Malta and on recovering from his wound returned to the Base Depot at Mudros on 28th October 1915. Rifleman Jolliffe then re-joined the Isle of Wight Rifles on 14th November.

Rifleman Jolliffe left the Isle of Wight Rifles at Alexandria on 15th January 1916 to return to England and was formally discharged from the Army on 14th February 1916 after having completed his service period.

Rfn. Charles Edward KELLEWAY, 1018

Rifleman Charles Kelleway joined the Isle of Wight Rifles in 1911. He received a gunshot wound to his hand at Gallipoli during August 1915.

Charles Kelleway was discharged from the Army on 28th February 1916 with the rank of acting Lance Corporal.

Rfn. Ernest KERLEY, 1019

Rifleman Ernest Kerley came from Gatcombe and enlisted in the Isle of Wight Rifles at Newport.[461] He was reported as missing in the Isle of Wight County Press on 18th September 1915 and was later presumed to have died on 22nd August 1915. Rifleman Kerley has no known grave and is commemorated on the Helles Memorial.

Rfn. Clifford Roy KING, 2045

Rifleman Clifford King came from Ventnor. He was killed in action on 13th August 1915, the day after the advance on Anafarta

---

[461] www.ancestry.co.uk: UK, Soldiers Died in the Great War, 1914-1919

Ridge, when the Isle of Wight Rifles were holding the ground they had taken. Rifleman King had originally been reported as missing and his death was finally confirmed in the Isle of Wight County Press on 4th March 1916. Rifleman King is commemorated on the Helles Memorial and was 18 years old when he died.[462]

Rfn. George Henry KNIGHT, 2358

Rifleman George Knight served with the Isle of Wight Rifles throughout the war and reached the rank of Corporal. He was disembodied from the Army on 1st September 1919 under service number 330785.

Rfn. John William KNIGHT, 2339

Rifleman John Knight enlisted in the Isle of Wight Rifles during February 1915. He was married with seven children. His brothers, Percy and Charles Knight, also served with the Isle of Wight Rifles at Gallipoli.

On 12th August 1915, Rifleman Knight took part in the advance on Anafarta Ridge and was reported as missing. He was later presumed to have been killed on 12th August 1915 and official notification of his death was published in the Isle of Wight County Press on 29th July 1916. Rifleman Knight was 37 years old and is commemorated on the Helles Memorial. Percy and Charles Knight survived the war.

Rfn. Percy KNIGHT, 2116

Rifleman Percy Knight enlisted in the Isle of Wight Rifles on 28th December 1914. He served with the battalion at Gallipoli alongside his brothers John and Charles Knight and was wounded on 13th August 1915 when the Isle of Wight Rifles were holding the territory that they had taken during the advance on

---

[462] Isle of Wight County Press, 4th March 1916, p8

Anafarta Ridge. His brother, John Knight, is presumed to have been killed on 12th August 1915 during the advance.

Rifleman Percy Knight recovered from his wounding and once again found himself with the Isle of Wight Rifles in the trenches at Gallipoli. He was wounded a second time and news of this was published in the Isle of Wight County Press on 25th December 1915 along with news that his brother, John Knight, was missing and his brother, Charles Knight, had also been wounded. Rifleman Percy Knight had been shot in the chest on 1st December 1915. The bullet broke 3 ribs and went through his lung.[463] He was invalided back to England and was admitted into Reading War Hospital on 25th December 1915.

Rifleman Percy Knight remained with the Hampshire Regiment but was restricted to home service duties and was given service number 380749. On 31st October 1917 it was decided that due to his gunshot wound from Gallipoli that he was no longer fit for further service and so he was discharged from the 17th Reserve Hants.[464]

His brother, Charles Knight, survived the war.

Rfn. James Arthur LOCKYER, 1163

Rifleman James Lockyer came from Newport. He was reported as having fallen ill at Gallipoli and being in hospital in the Isle of Wight County Press' newspaper on 18th September 1915.

Rifleman Lockyer returned to the Isle of Wight Rifles and was given service number 330103 when the Territorial Forces received new service numbers. Rifleman Lockyer died of wounds on the 21st April 1917. It is likely that he was wounded on 19th April 1917 during the Second Battle of Gaza. He is buried

---

[463] Isle of Wight County Press, 1st January 1916, p5
[464] www.ancestry.co.uk: British Army WWI Pension Records 1914-1920

at Deir El Belah War Cemetery which in April 1917 was the site of Casualty Clearing Stations and the 69th General Hospital.[465]

Rfn. Cecil MARSH, 2110

Rifleman Cecil Marsh came from Ventnor. He was reported as having fallen ill at Gallipoli and being admitted into a hospital in the 18th September 1915 edition of the Isle of Wight County Press.

Rifleman Marsh returned to serve with the Isle of Wight Rifles. Later in the war he was transferred to the 1/4th Hants who were deployed in the Middle East followed by Persia towards the end of the war. Rifleman Marsh was disembodied from the Army on 5th August 1919 under service number 330637.

Rfn. William Henry MARTIN, 1778

Rifleman William Martin came from Newport. He became ill with dysentery at Gallipoli and was admitted to a hospital in Malta during October 1915. He was then invalided back to England and treated at Fawcett Road Hospital in Southsea. By December 1915, Rifleman Martin had been moved to Hazlewood in Ryde.

At some point later in the war, Rifleman Martin was transferred to the 2/4th Hants and given service number 205454. By the end of April 1917, the 2/4th Hants had moved from India to take part in the Palestinian campaign. The 2/4th Hants last battle in Palestine was in April 1918 and on 22nd May 1918 the battalion left Egypt for France.

Rifleman Martin was disembodied from the Army on 26th April 1919.

---

[465] Commonwealth War Graves Commission: https://www.cwgc.org/find-a-cemetery/cemetery/71200/deir-el-belah-war-cemetery/

Rfn. Arthur MATTHEWS, 1098

Rifleman Arthur Matthews continued to serve with the Isle of Wight Rifles after Gallipoli and was given service number 330072. Arthur Matthews was Discharged to Commission on 12th April 1917 and became a Lieutenant in the Hampshire Regiment. He survived the war.

Rfn. James MEW, 1370

Rifleman James Mew remained with the Isle of Wight Rifles throughout the war and reached the rank of Sergeant. He received a Mention in Despatches which was officially published in the London Gazette on 11th June 1918:

> I have the honour to forward herewith the names of those serving or who have served under my Command, whose distinguished and gallant services and devotion to duty I consider deserving of special mention.[466]

Sergeant James Mew was disembodied from the Army on 20th April 1919 under service number 330202.

Rfn. William John MEW, 2338

Rifleman William Mew served with the Isle of Wight Rifles throughout the war and reached the rank of Sergeant. He was disembodied from the Army on 28th March 1919 under service number 330773.

Rfn. Stanley MILLGATE, 1182

Rifleman Stanley Millgate was wounded in August 1915 at Gallipoli. He was *'shot through the elbow and had a fractured arm in addition.'*[467] Rifleman Millgate was treated in hospital at Malta and on recovery re-joined the Isle of Wight Rifles. He rose

---

[466] www.forces-war-records.co.uk: Gazetted Awards and Mentions in Despatches - Gazette Issue 30746, 11/06/1918, p7053
[467] Isle of Wight County Press, 4th September 1915, p6

to the rank of Sergeant (service number 330115) before becoming a Warrant Officer Class II in the Machine Gun Corps under service number 85768.

Rfn. Frank MORGAN, 1523

Rifleman Frank Morgan was shot in the leg by a sniper at Gallipoli on Tuesday 25th August 1915.[468]

Rifleman Morgan continued to serve in the Hampshire Regiment under service number 330284. On 25th April 1917, he was Discharged to Commission in the Hampshire Regiment and became a Second Lieutenant. He survived the war.

Rfn. Oliver James Frank MORGAN, 1169

Rifleman Oliver Morgan came from Newport and enlisted in the Isle of Wight Rifles on 26th June 1912. He was wounded at Gallipoli on 28th September 1915 receiving a gunshot wound to his right foot. It appears that he had a swift recovery from the wound as he was promoted to acting Corporal on 12th December 1915 and was then officially promoted to the rank of Corporal on 6th January 1916 with the Isle of Wight Rifles.

Oliver Morgan was promoted to Sergeant on 27th March 1916. He was wounded for the second time during the Second Battle of Gaza on 19th April 1917. Despite being wounded twice and having served with the battalion for 5 years, Sergeant Morgan was *'retained in service on 26th June 1917.'*[469]

In December 1917, Oliver Morgan fell ill with Malaria but he recovered from it and on 12th February 1918, he was promoted to acting Company Quarter Master Sergeant. This promotion was made permanent on 14th June 1918. He had a second attack of

---

[468] Letter by Cpl G James on 26th August 1915, published in the Isle of Wight County Press, 18th September 1915 p6
[469] www.ancestry.co.uk: British Army WWI Pension Records 1914-1920 - Cover for Discharge Documents

Malaria in January 1919 and was treated in Mile End Military Hospital between the 12th January 1919 and 25th January 1919.[470]

Company Quartermaster Sergeant Morgan was discharged from the Isle of Wight Rifles on 22nd February 1919 under service number 330107. He was 24 years old.

Rfn. Frank Arthur MORRIS, 1300

Rifleman Frank Morris went onto serve with the 1/5th Hants at some point after the Isle of Wight Rifles' Gallipoli campaign. He was given service number 330168 and survived the war.

Rfn. Reginald MOWBRAY, 509

Rifleman Reginald Mowbray came from Newport. He was reported in the Isle of Wight County Press on 1st January 1916 as being in Citadel Hospital, Egypt suffering from dysentery. On 3rd March 1916 Rifleman Mowbray was *'granted discharge on completion of his engagement.'*[471]

Reginal Mowbay re-enlisted into the 2nd Hants and was given service number 203929. During the latter part of the war, until the Armistice, Reginald Mowbray served with the 6th Somerset Light Infantry under service number 29288. Both the 2nd Hants and the 6th Somerset Light Infantry fought on the Western Front between 1916 and 1918.

Rfn. Walter James George NEW, 1526

Rifleman Walter New served with the Isle of Wight Rifles up until his transfer to the Royal Army Service Corps on 3rd November 1917. He was discharged from the Royal Army Service Corp on 31st March 1920 under service number S/365470 and a few months later on 21st August 1920, Walter New re-

---

[470] www.ancestry.co.uk: British Army WWI Pension Records 1914-1920 - Cover for Discharge Documents
[471] Isle of Wight County Press, 4th March 1916, p8

enlisted in the Isle of Wight Rifles and was given service number 5488050.

Rfn. Arthur NEWHAM, 1316

Rifleman Arthur Newham remained with the Isle of Wight Rifles after Gallipoli and was given service number 330174 when the Territorial Forces received new service numbers. Rifleman Newham survived the war.

Rfn. Alfred PARSONS, 2287

Rifleman Alfred Parsons was transferred to the Devonshire Regiment at some point after his time at Gallipoli with the Isle of Wight Rifles. Later in the war he was transferred to the Royal Army Medical and his service number was changed from 241555 to 457527. Alfred Parsons spent the remainder of the war with the Royal Army Medical Corps and survived the war.

Rfn. Ernest William PARSONS, 1524

Rifleman Ernest Parsons came from Newport. He was initially reported as missing in action and was later presumed to have been killed in action on 12th August 1915 during the advance on Anafarta Ridge. Official notification of his death was published in the Isle of Wight County Press on 29th July 1916. Rifleman Parsons was 22 years old and is commemorated on the Helles Memorial.

Rfn. Benjamin Edward PIMM, 2090

Rifleman Benjamin Pimm was reported as having been wounded at Gallipoli in the Isle of Wight County Press' 2nd October 1915 edition.

On recovering from his wounding, Rifleman Pimm returned to serve with the Isle of Wight Rifles and reached the rank of Sergeant. He was disembodied from the Army on 2nd April 1919 under service number 330624.

Rfn. James Henry POCOCK, 1812

Rifleman James Pocock came from Arreton. He was officially reported missing following the advance on Anafarta Ridge. He was later presumed to have been killed during the advance on Anafarta Ridge on 12th August 1915 and official notification of Rifleman Pocock's death was published in the Isle of Wight County Press on 29th July 1916. Rifleman Pocock is commemorated on the Helles Memorial.

Rfn. Latimer Frederick PRATCHETT, 702

Rifleman Latimer Pratchett enlisted in the Isle of Wight Rifles at Newport on 24th February 1909. He was 24 years and 4 months old.

Rifleman Pratchett came through Gallipoli unscathed and went with the battalion to Alexandria. In February 1916 he set sail for England for discharge from the Army and returned home on 24th February 1916. He was formally discharged from the Army on 10th March 1916 due to the *'termination of his period of engagement.'*[472]

Rfn. George PRINCE, 2035

Rifleman George Prince was shot in the right side early in the Isle of Wight Rifles' Gallipoli campaign. He was invalided off Gallipoli on the 14th August 1915 and taken to a hospital in Malta for treatment of his, 'large superficial wound.'[473]

At some point during the war, Rifleman Prince was transferred to the Labour Corps. His rank changed to Private and he was given the service number 247074. He was disembodied from the Labour Corps on 9th May 1919.

---

[472] www.ancestry.co.uk: British Army WWI Pension Records 1914-1920 – Territorial Force Attestation
[473] Isle of Wight County Press, 4th September 1915, p6

Rfn. James PUNCH, 2215

Rifleman James Punch came from Merston. He was officially reported as missing after the advance on Anafarta Ridge and then later presumed to have died during the advance on Anafarta Ridge on the 12th August 1915. Official notification of his death was published in the Isle of Wight County Press on 29th July 1916. Rifleman Punch is commemorated on the Helles Memorial.

Rfn. Frederick RACKETT, 1198

Rifleman Frederick Rackett was invalided off Gallipoli on 30th September 1915 but it is unknown if he was wounded or ill.

Rifleman Rackett was transferred to the 21st Rifle Brigade, a battalion used for garrison duties, and given service number 207276. Between the 4th January 1917 and 17th September 1918 Rifleman Rackett was with the 21st Rifle Brigade in Egypt. He then went with the battalion to India for the remainder of the war.[474]

Rfn. Arthur Alfred RANN, 1343

Rifleman Arthur Rann served in the Isle of Wight Rifles with his brother, Rifleman Edwin Rann. They came from Newport.

The Commonwealth War Graves Commission has Rifleman Rann's date of death as the 11th August 1915. However, the Army's 1914/15 Star record and the UK, Soldiers Died in the Great War, 1914-1919 record state that Rifleman Arthur Rann *'died on or after 12th August 1915.'*[475] In addition, the War Diary does not state that any casualties were taken on the 11th August and the Isle of Wight County Press initially published that Rifleman Arthur Rann had been taken prisoner. Therefore, it is

---

[474] www.ancestry.co.uk: UK, WWI Service Medal and Award Rolls, 1914-1920 - British War Medal and Victory Medal

[475] www.ancestry.co.uk: British Army 1914/15 Star records and UK, Soldiers Died in the Great War, 1914-1919.

more likely that Rifleman Arthur Rann was killed on 12th August 1915 during the advance on Anafarta Ridge and during the ensuing chaos, there was uncertainty regarding his fate. Official notification of his death was published in the Isle of Wight County Press on 29th July 1916.

Rifleman Rann is commemorated on the Helles Memorial.

Rfn. Edwin RANN, 1525

Rifleman Edwin Rann came from Newport. He served in the Isle of Wight Rifles with his brother, Rifleman Arthur Rann.

Rifleman Edwin Rann was invalided off Gallipoli and taken to a hospital with a foot injury at some point between August and early September 1915.

Later in the war Rifleman Edwin Rann was transferred to the 1/6th Hants, B Company. He was given service number 281881 and the rank of Private. Edwin Rann died on 4th November 1918 aged 23 and is buried at Baghdad (North Gate) War Cemetery.

Rfn. Albert Edward READ, 2340

Rifleman Albert Read enlisted in the Isle of Wight Rifles on 22nd February 1915. He was wounded at Gallipoli and was invalided off the peninsular on 16th August 1915. Rifleman Read returned to active service on 9th October 1915 and remained with the Isle of Wight Rifles until being transferred to the 19th Rifle Brigade on 27th November 1916.[476] The 19th Rifle Brigade were also part of the Egyptian Expeditionary Force operating in Egypt and Palestine.

Rifleman Read was discharged from the 19th Rifle Brigade on 18th April 1919 under service number 208690. His Silver War

---

[476] www.ancestry.co.uk: UK, WWI Service Medal and Award Rolls, 1914-1920, British War and Victory Medal Records

Badge record states that he was discharged due to wounds received.

Rfn. Edwin READ, 1296

Rifleman Edwin Read lived in Newport and enlisted in the Isle of Wight Rifles in 1913. His family came from Southampton. He was reported as missing in action after the advance on Anafarta Ridge and was later presumed to have been killed on 12th August 1915. He was 21 years old and is commemorated on the Helles Memorial.

Rfn. James Richard George READ, 1063

Rifleman James Read served in the Isle of Wight Rifles with his brother Harry Read. Rifleman Read had joined the Isle of Wight Rifles in 1910. After the advance on Anafarta Ridge, Harry Read wrote home to his parents to let them know that James was missing. James was later presumed to have died on 12th August 1915 and official notification of his death was published in the Isle of Wight County Press on 29th July 1916. He is commemorated on the Helles Memorial. His brother, Harry, survived the war.

Rfn. Archie READER, 2292

Rifleman Archie Reader remained with the Isle of Wight Rifles throughout the war and was disembodied from the battalion on 2nd August 1919 under service number 330742.

Rfn. William George REDSTONE, 2443

Rifleman William Redstone came from Ryde and enlisted in the Isle of Wight Rifles at Newport. He continued serving with the Isle of Wight Rifles after Gallipoli and was given service number 330838 when the Territorial Forces received new service numbers.

Rifleman Redstone died on 6th October 1917 at the age of 19. He is buried at Oakfield (St. John) Church cemetery on the Isle of Wight.

Rfn. Arthur REED, 2219

Rifleman Arthur Reed served with the Isle of Wight Rifles throughout the war and reached the rank of acting Lance Corporal with service number 330703.

Rfn. Fred REYNARD, 1311

Rifleman Fred Reynard was in the Isle of Wight Rifle's machine gun section. He suffered a minor wounding at Gallipoli as well as a short bout of dysentery but despite this, remained with the battalion throughout the whole of their Gallipoli campaign and rose to the rank of Sergeant.[477]

In November 1916, Sergeant Fred Reynard received notice that he had been selected to become an Army Officer and embarked on the SS Minnewaska at Alexandria to make his way back to England. The SS Minnewaska struck a German mine on 29th November 1916 near Suda Bay, Crete but all passengers and crew survived, and Sergeant Fred Reynard managed to get back to England.[478]

Sergeant Fred Reynard was given service number 330172 prior to being formally discharged to Commission on 12th April 1917. He became a Second Lieutenant in the Hampshire Regiment and then a Lieutenant in the 18th battalion of the Corps of Cyclists with whom he saw active service on the Western Front.[479]

---

[477] Fred Reynard's memoirs: http://fightingthroughpodcast.co.uk/16-gallipoli-ww1-memoir/4593981882
[478] Fred Reynard's memoirs: http://fightingthroughpodcast.co.uk/16-gallipoli-ww1-memoir/4593981882
[479] www.ancestry.co.uk: 1914-1915 Star Records and British Army WWI Medal Rolls Index Cards, 1914-1920

During World War Two, Fred Reynard was involved in the Dunkirk Evacuation in 1940 as a crew member of the MV Bee.[480]

Rfn. William RICHARDSON, 1347

Rifleman William Richardson came from Newport and was the brother-in-law of Rifleman Edward Urry. Rifleman Richardson was listed as missing in action after the advance on Anafarta Ridge. On 23rd September 1916, the Isle of Wight County Press reported that he was presumed to have been killed in action on 12th August 1915. He was 21 years old and is commemorated on the Helles Memorial.[481]

Rfn. Charles James ROLF, 1360

Rifleman Charles Rolf and his brother Rifleman Percy Rolf came from Newport. Both went to Gallipoli with the Isle of Wight Rifles. Rifleman Charles Rolf had served with the Isle of Wight Rifles before the outbreak of war but Rifleman Percy Rolf enlisted in the battalion on 5th May 1915.

Rifleman Charles Rolf was killed in action on 12th August 1915 during the advance on Anafarta Ridge and official notification of his death was published in the Isle of Wight County Press on 29th July 1916. He was 23 years old and is commemorated on the Helles Memorial. His brother, Rifleman Percy Rolf, was wounded at Gallipoli during August 1915 and was discharged from the Army on 29th July 1916 due to sickness.

Rfn. Harry SAIT, 523

Rifleman Harry Sait came from Wootton and enlisted in the Isle of Wight Rifles at Wootton on 11th January 1909. He came through Gallipoli unscathed and went with the battalion to Alexandria. Rifleman Sait landed back in England on 29th

---

[480] http://www.iowtodunkirk.com/the-bee-goes-to-war/the-crew-of-the-bee/engineer-fred-reynard/
[481] Isle of Wight County Press, 23rd September 1916, p4

January 1916 and was discharged from the Army on 14th February 1916 as he had completed his period of service.[482]

Rfn. Henry Charles SALTER, 1312

Rifleman Henry Salter came from Carisbrooke and enlisted in the Isle of Wight Rifles at Newport on 23rd September 1913 at the age of 17 years and 2 months.

Rifleman Salter fell ill at Gallipoli on 17th August 1915 with dysentery and trench fever which led him to him being invalided home and landing in England on 27th November 1915. Rifleman Salter spent a further 4 months in hospital before returning to light duties. His illness had lasting effects and he was discharged from the Army on 27th September 1916 as he was found to be unfit for further military service. Rifleman Salter was given the Silver War Badge and on 22nd May 1918 received a final sum of £60 from the Army.[483]

Rfn. Bert SAMPSON, 1357

Rifleman Bert Sampson served with the Isle of Wight Rifles throughout the war and his latter service number was 331571. After the war, Rifleman was transferred to the Military Foot Police as a Private with service number P/5842. Bert Sampson then went on to re-join the Hampshire Regiment and was given service number 5488600. He ended his military career with the Royal Field Artillery.[484]

Rfn. Albert SAUNDERS, 1137

Rifleman Albert Saunders enlisted in the Isle of Wight Rifles in 1911 at Locks Green and was 14 years old. According to the Commonwealth War Graves records and the Army's 'UK,

---

[482] www.ancestry.co.uk: British Army WWI Pension Records 1914-1920 - Territorial Force Attestation
[483] www.ancestry.co.uk: British Army WWI Pension Records 1914-1920 - Territorial Force Attestation
[484] www.ancestry.co.uk: British Army WWI Medal Rolls Index Cards, 1914-1920

Soldiers Died in the Great War, 1914-1919' records, Rifleman Saunders was killed on the 10th August 1915. However, the Isle of Wight Rifles' War Diary does not indicate that the battalion suffered any fatalities on 10th August 1915 and Rifleman Saunders' 1914-1915 Star record states that he *'died on or after 12th August 1915.'*[485] In addition, the Isle of Wight County Press on 18th September 1915 reported that Rifleman Saunders was missing. It therefore seems more likely that Rifleman Saunders was killed during the advance on Anafarta Ridge.

Rifleman Saunders is commemorated on the Helles Memorial.

Rfn. Frank SAUNDERS, 1135

Rifleman Frank Saunders enlisted in the Isle of Wight Rifles on 1st June 1912. He was wounded early on whilst at Gallipoli and on 16th August 1915 sent a field post card to his father *'stating that he was in hospital with wounds and going on well.'*[486]

Rifleman Saunders was discharged from the Army on 28th April 1916 and given the Silver War Badge.

Rfn. Sidney John SHEATH, 2155

Rifleman Sidney Sheath came from Sandown. He enlisted in the Isle of Wight Rifles on 2nd January 1915. His discharge documents state that he was 5'10" tall with dark hair and blueish grey eyes.[487]

Rifleman Sheath received a gunshot wound just above his left knee during the advance on Anafarta Ridge on 12th August 1915. He was initially treated by the 31st Field Ambulance and was then admitted into the 26th Casualty Clearing Station on 13th August

---

[485] www.ancestry.co.uk: UK, Soldiers Died in the Great War, 1914-1919 and 1914-1915 Star Records
[486] Isle of Wight County Press, 11th September 1915, p8
[487] www.ancestry.co.uk: British Army WWI Pension Records 1914-1920 (Discharge Documents)

1915. On the 26th August 1915, Rifleman Sheath boarded HS Franconia at Mudros to return to England for further treatment.

The severity of Rifleman Sheath's wound meant he had a medical assessment at Parkhurst Barracks on 14th April 1917. In addition to the wounding of his left knee, Rifleman Sheath was also suffering from varicose of his right leg. He was subsequently *'transferred to Class W or W(T) of the reserve.'*[488] Rifleman Sheath was formally discharged from the Army on 14th December 1918.

Rfn. Arthur SHEPARD, 1248

Rifleman Arthur Shepard came from Newport and enlisted at Newport. Rifleman Shepard fell ill with dysentery between the middle of August and the middle of September 1915 and was invalided off Gallipoli back to a hospital in Birmingham.

Later in the war, Arthur Shepard was transferred to the 4th Hants under service number 330142. He rose to the rank of Quartermaster Sergeant and was attached to the 3rd/2nd King's Africa Rifles in Tanzania when he died on 4th July 1918. He is buried at Dar Es Salaam (Upanga Road) Cemetery.

Rfn. Charlie Hart SHIER, 2029

Rifleman Charlie 'Chas' Shier enlisted in the Isle of Wight Rifles on 2nd December 1914. He was admitted to St. George's Hospital, Malta between late September and early October 1915 suffering with dysentery.

Rifleman Shier was discharged from the Army on 18th October 1916. His Silver War Badge record stated that he was *'physically unfit.'*

---

[488] www.ancestry.co.uk: British Army WWI Pension Records 1914-1920 (Discharge Documents)

Rfn. Reginald Robert SIBBICK, 1301

Rifleman Reginald Sibbick was officially reported as missing after the advance on Anafarta Ridge and was later presumed to have been killed on 12th August 1915. He was 20 years old and from Carisbrooke. Rifleman Sibbick is commemorated on the Helles Memorial.

Rfn. Arthur James SIMMONDS, 736

Rifleman Arthur Simmonds came from Newport. He was initially posted as missing and then later presumed to have died on 12th August 1915 during the advance on Anafarta Ridge. He was 22 years old and is commemorated on the Helles Memorial.

Rfn. Frederick Benjamin SIMMONDS, 1109

Rifleman Frederick Simmonds served with the Isle of Wight Rifles throughout the war. He was disembodied from the Army on 10th August 1919 under service number 330078.

Rfn. Harry SMART, 1310

Rifleman Harry Smart enlisted in the Isle of Wight Rifles at Newport. After the advance on Anafarta Ridge, he was reported as missing in action. It was later presumed that he was killed in action on 12th August 1915. He was 22 years old and is commemorated on the Helles Memorial.

Rfn. Charles SMITH, 2120

Rifleman Charles Smith came from Newchurch and enlisted in the Isle of Wight Rifles at Newport. He continued to serve with the Isle of Wight Rifles after Gallipoli and reached the rank of Sergeant under service number 330641.

Sergeant Smith was initially reported as missing after the Second Battle of Gaza on 19th April 1917.[489] He had unfortunately been killed during the battle. Sergeant Smith has no known grave and is commemorated on the Jerusalem Memorial.

Rfn. Frank SMITH, 1974

Rifleman Frank Smith came from Sandown and enlisted in the Isle of Wight Rifles at Newport. He was killed in action during the Second Battle of Gaza on 19th April 1917 and is commemorated on the Jerusalem Memorial. His latter service number was 330549.

Rfn. Frederick SMITH, 1306

Rifleman Frederick Smith came from Newport and enlisted in the Isle of Wight Rifles at Newport. His father served in the reserve battalion of the Isle of Wight Rifles.

Rifleman Smith was killed by a shell on 31st October 1915. Shrapnel from the shell also wounded Corporal Scott, Rifleman Chandler and a soldier from the New Zealand Artillery. Rifleman Smith was 19 years and is buried at the 7th Field Ambulance Cemetery.[490]

Rfn. Ronald SMITH, 507

Rifleman Ronald Smith enlisted in the Isle of Wight Rifles at Wootton on 11th January 1909. He came through Gallipoli without being wounded or suffering from a serious illness and sailed with the battalion to Alexandria. Rifleman Smith landed back in England on 29th January 1916 and was discharged from

---

[489] www.forces-war-records.co.uk: British Red Cross and Order of St John Enquiry List 1917 (Wounded and Missing)
[490] Isle of Wight County Press, 20th November 1915, p5

the Army on 14th February 1916 after completing his period of service.[491]

Rfn. Charley SPRAKE, 1332

Rifleman Charley Sprake came from Yarmouth. He served with the Isle of Wight Rifles throughout the war and was demobilised from the Army on 12th April 1919 under service number 330184.

Rfn. Wallace STUBBS, 1339

Rifleman Wallace Stubbs came from Newport. He enlisted in the Isle of Wight Rifles on 24th October 1913. During August 1915 he was invalided off Gallipoli with an injured knee and was also suffering from *'nervous shock.'*[492]

Rifleman Stubbs was discharged from the Army on the 19th May 1916 and given the Silver War Badge due to sickness.

Rfn. Frank SWADLING, 2329

Rifleman Frank Swadling came from Marlow in Buckinghamshire and was one of the men recruited by Lieutenant Colonel Rhodes. He continued to serve with the Isle of Wight Rifles after Gallipoli and was given service number 330768.

Rifleman Swadling was taken prisoner by the Turks during the Second Battle of Gaza on 19th April 1917. He died on 12th August 1917 at Jarbache and is buried at Baghdad (North Gate) Cemetery.

Rfn. Charles SWEATMAN, 1308

Rifleman Charles Sweatman enlisted in the Isle of Wight Rifles on 9th September 1913. During August 1915 he became ill due to heart disease and was invalided off Gallipoli. On 29th August

---

[491] www.ancestry.co.uk: British Army WWI Pension Records 1914-1920 – Territorial Force Attestation
[492] Isle of Wight County Press, 11th September 1915, p8

1915 he was admitted to a hospital in Malta and left Malta for England on 15th September 1915. Rifleman Sweatman was discharged from the Army on 15th April 1916.

Rfn. William Henry TAYLOR, 265

Rifleman William Taylor was transferred to the 1/6th Hants and given service number 281800 at some point after Gallipoli. He remained with this battalion until he was demobilised from the Army on 16th December 1919. The 1/6th Hants arrived at Basra on 16th September 1917 and operated in Mesopotamia until the end of the war.[493]

Rfn. Arthur John TEE, 1078

Rifleman Arthur Tee continued serving with the Isle of Wight Rifles after Gallipoli. He was disembodied from the Army on 1st August 1919 under service number 330058.

Rfn. John Frederick THOMAS, 1486

Rifleman John Thomas came from Newport and enlisted in the Isle of Wight Rifles on 3rd August 1914. He was shot in the left thigh and injured his back between August 1915 and early September 1915 whilst at Gallipoli. By November 1915, Rifleman Thomas had been admitted into Northwood House Red Cross Hospital. His wounding was serious enough for him to be discharged from the Army on 29th July 1916 and given the Silver War Badge.

Rfn. Alfred George THOMPSON, 1328

Rifleman Alfred Thompson was transferred to the 2/4th Hants at some point after Gallipoli but later in the war he returned to serve with the Isle of Wight Rifles. He was disembodied from the Army on 31st July 1919 under service number 205447.

---

[493] http://www.longlongtrail.co.uk/army/regiments-and-corps/the-british-infantry-regiments-of-1914-1918/hampshire-regiment/

Rfn. John THOMSON, 1299

Rifleman John Thomson enlisted in the Isle of Wight Rifles on 23rd June 1913. At Gallipoli, he was in the Transport Section of the Isle of Wight Rifles and was wounded in the left knee by a bullet during August 1915. Rifleman Thomson was treated at a hospital in Manchester and later discharged from 2/8th Hants on 11th August 1916, receiving the Silver War Badge due to sickness.

Rfn. George Mark TOOGOOD, 1321

Rifleman George Toogood came from Newport. He was reported as missing in action on the 22nd August 1915 and was later presumed to have died on 22nd August 1915. He was 18 years old. Official notification of his death was published in the Isle of Wight County Press on 19th July 1916 in which Rifleman Toogood was included in a list of riflemen who had originally been reported as missing *'since the great attack which the Island regiment, with other troops, made at Suvla Bay, Gallipoli, on August 12th 1915.'* The article continued, stating that 'these gallant men are now presumed to be dead, having been killed in action on or about that day.'[494]

Rifleman Toogood is commemorated on the Helles Memorial.

Rfn. Harold Ernest TRELOAR, 1172

Rifleman Harold Treloar fell ill with Enteric between late September and early October 1915 and was invalided off Gallipoli to Alexandria, Egypt. He was then admitted to Lady Howard de Walden's Convalescent Home, Alexandria on 18th November 1915.[495]

Later in the war, Rifleman Treloar was transferred to the Army Service Corps and given service number S4/186201. He then

---

[494] Isle of Wight County Press, 29th July 1916, p4
[495] Isle of Wight County Press, 18th December 1915, p6

went on to join the Royal Tank Corps as a Private and was given service numbers 302340/302240. Harold Treloar survived the war.

Rfn. Arthur Ralph TRICKETT, 1327

Rifleman Arthur Trickett came from Arreton. He was invalided off Gallipoli in August 1915 suffering with a fever.

Rifleman Trickett went on to serve as a Private in the Machine Gun Corps under service number 114085. He was disembodied from the Army on 24th June 1919.

Rfn. Edward TROTT, 1614

Rifleman Edward Trott served with the Isle of Wight Rifles throughout the war. He was disembodied from the Army on 6th March 1919 under service number 330335.

Rfn. Harry TROWBRIDGE, 1335

Rifleman Harry Trowbridge came from Newport and was initially reported as missing after the advance on Anafarta Ridge. He was however killed in action on 12th August 1915 at the age of 17. Official notification of his death was published in the Isle of Wight County Press on 29th July 1916. Rifleman Trowbridge is commemorated on the Helles Memorial.

Rfn. Edward George URRY, 670

Riflemen Edward, Frederick and William Urry were brothers from Newport and enlisted in the Isle of Wight Rifles at some point after the declaration of war. However, Rifleman Edward Urry had previously served with the 5th Hampshire Volunteers followed by a short period of time in the Corps of Royal Engineers in 1904.[496]

---

[496] http://www.jacksontree.co.uk/RememberThemFrame1.htm?

Riflemen Edward, Frederick and William Urry were reported missing after the advance on Anafarta Ridge which was confirmed in a letter from Lance Corporal Thorn to his mother, dated the 19th August 1915:

> Comic Urry's Platoon went charging at the Turks singing, 'We are the Hants boys' and they haven't been seen or heard since.[497]

The three brothers had tragically all been killed during the advance on Anafarta Ridge on 12th August 1915 and official notification of their deaths was published in the Isle of Wight County Press on 29th July 1916. It is thought that they are the only instance of three brothers having been killed on the same day in the same action during the First World War.[498] In addition, Rifleman Edward Urry's brother-in-law, Rifleman William Richardson (B Company, Isle of Wight Rifles), was also killed during the advance on 12th August 1915.

Riflemen Edward, Frederick and William Urry have no known graves and are commemorated on the Helles Memorial. Edward was 35 years old, Frederick was 21 years old and William was 26 years old.

Rfn. Frederick Albert URRY, 853

Please see above.

Rfn. William Henry URRY, 2032

Please see above.

Rfn. Charles George VINCENT, 1191

Rifleman Charles Vincent enlisted in the Isle of Wight Rifles at Newport. Either towards the end of the Gallipoli campaign or

---

[497] Isle of Wight County Press, 4th September 1915, p6
[498] https://onthewight.com/fascinating-story-of-isle-of-wight-brothers-who-fought-the-gallipoli-campaign/

during the early stages of the battalion being at Alexandria, Rifleman Vincent fell ill with Tuberculosis. He was admitted on to HM Hospital Ship Britannic on 31st December 1915 and passed away on 9th January 1916 whilst the hospital ship was still at sea. Rifleman Charles Vincent is buried at Netley Military Cemetery.[499] [500]

Rfn. Walter William VINCENT, 2346

Rifleman Walter Vincent enlisted in the Isle of Wight Rifles at Newport. He was originally reported as missing after the advance on Anafarta Ridge and as late as 6th May 1916, his wife had still not had official news of his fate. She asked for any news on him to be passed on to her in the Isle of Wight County Press.[501]

Rifleman Vincent had in fact been killed in action during the attack on Anafarta Ridge on 12th August 1915 and this was confirmed in the Isle of Wight County Press on 29th July 1916:

> Mrs Vincent heard from a comrade in May that her husband was mortally wounded in the retirement after the big advance.[502]

Rifleman Vincent has no known grave and is commemorated on the Helles Memorial.

Rfn. William Robert WALLACE, 1153

Rifleman William Wallace came from Carisbrooke and enlisted in the Isle of Wight Rifles at Newport. He became ill at Gallipoli and spent time at a hospital in Malta during October 1915 before returning to serve with the Isle of Wight Rifles.

---

[499] www.forces-war-records.co.uk: Military Hospitals Admissions and Discharge Registers WW1 - MH106/1915
[500] www.ancestry.co.uk: UK, Soldiers Died in the Great War, 1914-1919
[501] Isle of Wight County Press, 6th May 1916, p3
[502] Isle of Wight County Press, 29th July 1916, p4

Rifleman Wallace died of wounds on 2nd May 1917 and is buried at Alexandria (Hadra) War Memorial Cemetery. He was possibly wounded on 19th April 1917 during the Second Battle of Gaza when the Isle of Wight Rifles suffered very high casualties.

Rfn. Charles WAPSHOTT, 1365

Rifleman Charles Wapshott came from Newport. He was reported as missing in the Isle of Wight County Press on 11th September 1915 and was later presumed to have died on the 22nd August 1915. Official notification of his death was published in the Isle of Wight County Press on 29th July 1916. Rifleman Wapshott was 26 years old and is commemorated on the Helles Memorial.

Rfn. Alfred WARD, 1143

Rifleman Alfred Ward was living in Freshwater when he enlisted in the Isle of Wight Rifles at Newtown. He was killed in action on the 12th August 1915, at the age of 22, during the advance on Anafarta Ridge and is commemorated on the Helles Memorial.[503]

Rfn. Hubert Alexander WATSON, 1548

Rifleman Hubert 'Dink' Watson came from Wootton and was good friends with Fred Reynard. Rifleman Watson was killed in action at Gallipoli and both the Commonwealth War Graves Commission and official Army records have recorded Rifleman Watson's death at Gallipoli as the 22nd August 1915. However, on 4th September 1915, the Isle of Wight County Press published a letter dated 18th August 1915 from Rifleman Fred Reynard to his father that stated that *'Dink Watson was killed whilst giving a wounded man a drink.'*[504] In addition to this information, Fred Reynard's memoir indicated that 'Dink' Watson had been killed

---

[503] www.ancestry.co.uk: UK, Soldiers Died in the Great War, 1914-1919
[504] Isle of Wight County Press, 4th September 1915, p6

by a sniper on the day after the advance on Anafarta Ridge i.e. 13th August 1915 and was buried by an olive tree.[505]

Rifleman Watson is commemorated on the Helles Memorial.

Rfn. Frederick WEARNE, 2422

Rifleman Frederick Wearne was transferred to the 1/4th Hants later in the war and was given service number 281822. In 1918 the 1/4th Hants were deployed to Persia from the Middle East. Rifleman Wearne survived the war and was disembodied from the Army on 5th August 1919.

Rfn. Charles Edward WESTMORE, 2363

Rifleman Charles Westmore served with the Isle of Wight Rifles after Gallipoli and was transferred to the 21st Rifle Brigade, a battalion used for garrison duties, on 19th September 1917. Rifleman Westmore went with the 21st Rifle Brigade to India and his records state that he was in India from 1st October 1918 until 12th October 1919.[506]

Rfn. Christine (Christopher) Augustus WESTMORE, 665

Rifleman Christopher Westmore came from Newport and joined the Isle of Wight Rifles on 16th February 1909 at the age of 17. He became ill with Enteritis and was admitted on 30th October 1914 to the Red Cross Hospital in Giza. Rifleman Westmore was still recovering in Egypt when the Isle of Wight Rifles reached Alexandria. On 4th April 1916 Rifleman Westmore landed back at England as his period of service had been completed and he was discharged from the Isle of Wight Rifles on 17th April 1916.[507]

---

[505] Fred Reynard's memoirs: http://fightingthroughpodcast.co.uk/16-gallipoli-ww1-memoir/4593981882
[506] www.ancestry.co.uk: UK, WWI Service Medal and Award Rolls, 1914-1920 – British War Medal and Victory Medal
[507] www.ancestry.co.uk: Rifleman C A Westmore's Pension Record.

Rifleman Westmore re-enlisted in the Isle of Wight Rifles on 13th August 1920. He was discharged from the battalion on 29th April 1924 under service number 5488033 and holding the rank of Sergeant.

Rfn. William George WHATLEY, 1159

Rifleman William Whatley served with the Isle of Wight Rifles throughout the war and reached the rank of Corporal. He was disembodied from the Army on 6th May 1919.

Rfn. Fred WHEELER, 1649

Rifleman Fred Wheeler came from Wooton. He was reported as having been wounded at Gallipoli in the Isle of Wight County Press on 4th September 1915. It is likely that he was wounded during the fighting at Anafarta Ridge when the battalion suffered a large number of casualties.

Rifleman Wheeler returned to serve with the Isle of Wight Rifles and was disembodied from the Army on 21st March 1919 under service number 330354.

Rfn. George WHEELER, 1377

Rifleman George Wheeler came from Newport and enlisted in the Isle of Wight Rifles on 4th November 1913. He fell ill with diarrhoea at Gallipoli and on 13th August 1915 he was reported as being back at base. On 8th September 1915, Rifleman Wheeler was admitted to a hospital on Malta and on 20th September 1915 he was transferred to Ghain Tuffeiha in Malta. Rifleman Wheeler re-joined the battalion at Gallipoli on 14th November 1915 after a period of time from the 23rd October at the Base Depot in Mudros.

Rifleman Wheeler was promoted to Sergeant on 12th January 1917 and when the Territorial Forces received their new service numbers, he was given service number 330206. He took part in the Second Battle of Gaza on 19th April 1917 and was wounded in his right thigh by a piece of shrapnel. Exactly a month afterwards, he returned to the Isle of Wight Rifles.

Sergeant Wheeler was withdrawn from the battalion on 6th November 1917 and was diagnosed with Neurasthenia – an illness which is now referred to as Chronic Fatigue Syndrome. Sergeant Wheeler was able to recover sufficiently enough to be able to re-join the Isle of Wight Rifles on 16th December 1917.

During November 1918 Sergeant Wheeler fell ill with Pyrexhia and in January 1919, he fell ill with Malaria. His Army service came to an end on 6th May 1919.[508]

Rfn. William Henry WHEELER, 1203

Rifleman William Wheeler enlisted in the Isle of Wight Rifles on 16th September 1912. During August 1915 he was *'badly wounded, being shot through both legs.'*[509] He was invalided off Gallipoli and taken to a hospital in Alexandria, Egypt.

Rifleman Wheeler was discharged from the Army on 15th April 1916 due to the wounds he received at Gallipoli and was given the Silver War Badge.

Rfn. Herbert Sidney WHITE, 1451

Rifleman Herbert White came from Shide and enlisted in the Isle of Wight Rifles at Arreton. He served with the Isle of Wight Rifles at Gallipoli with his brother Rifleman William Charles White.

Rifleman Herbert White continued to serve with the Isle of Wight Rifles after Gallipoli and was given service number 330249. He died in an accident from drowning on 22nd July 1918 and is buried

---

[508] www.ancestry.co.uk: British Army WWI Pension Records 1914-1920 – Cover for discharge documents
[509] Isle of Wight County Press, 4th September 1915, p8

at Ramleh War Cemetery. His brother, William, died on 9th February 1919.

Rfn. Sidney George WHITE, 1490

Rifleman Sidney White came from Newport. He received a wound to his right shoulder between August and early September 1915.

Rifleman White returned to serve with the Isle of Wight Rifles and when the Territorials received new service numbers, he was given the service number 330265. Rifleman White survived the war.

Rfn. William Charles WHITE, 1166

Rifleman William White served with the Isle of Wight Rifles with his brother at Gallipoli. Rifleman White served with the Isle of Wight Rifles throughout the war and his latter service number was 330105. He died whilst serving with the Isle of Wight Rifles in Cairo on 9th February 1919, presumably from an illness and was 23 years old. Rifleman White is buried at Cairo War Memorial Cemetery. His brother, Herbert, died on 22nd July 1918.

Rfn. Wilfred WHITTINGTON, 2180

Rifleman Wilfred Whittington enlisted in the Isle of Wight Rifles on 5th January 1915. He was wounded at Gallipoli and this was officially reported in the *'Casualty List issued but the Home Office on the 19th September.'*[510]

Following recovering from his wounds, Wilfred Whittington returned to serve with the Isle of Wight Rifles and reached the rank of Acting Sergeant. He was discharged from the Army on

---

[510] www.forces-war-records.co.uk: First World War Daily Reports (Missing, Wounded & Prisoner of War) - DT20091915

15th July 1919 under service number 330683 due to 'wounds' and was given the Silver War Badge.[511]

Rfn. William WHITTINGTON, 1656

Rifleman William Whittington continued to serve with the Isle of Wight Rifles after Gallipoli. He was disembodied from the Army on 28th April 1919 under service number 330360.

Rfn. Alfred Frank WILLIAMS, 1176

Rifleman Alfred Williams came from Newport. He enlisted in the Isle of Wight Rifles on 28th June 1912. Rifleman Williams fell ill at Gallipoli with dysentery and during October 1915 was admitted to St George's Hospital in Malta.

Rifleman Williams served with the Isle of Wight Rifles throughout the Great War and was discharged from the Army on 22nd July 1919 under service number 330111. His Silver War Badge record states that he was discharged due to sickness.

Rfn. Christopher Henry William WILLIAMS, 2112

Rifleman Christopher Williams enlisted in the Isle of Wight Rifles on 28th December 1914. He continued to serve with the battalion after Gallipoli and was subsequently given the new service number of 330638 but later in the war he was transferred to the 1/4th Hants and served with them in Persia.

Rifleman Williams was discharged from the Army on 30th July 1919 at the age of 36 due to sickness. [512]

Rfn. Albert Edward WILTON, 1529

Rifleman Albert Wilton was shot through both legs at Gallipoli and was invalided off the peninsula on 14th August 1915. He was taken by hospital ship to Malta for treatment. As a result of the

---

[511] www.ancestry.co.uk: Silver War Badge Records, 1914-1919
[512] www.forces-war-records: Silver War Badge Records, 1914-1919

wounding, he had to have one of his legs amputated below the knee.

Rifleman Wilton went on to serve at the Hampshire Regiment Depot under service number 330286. He died on 23rd March 1918 and is buried at Carisbrooke Cemetery.

Rfn. Harry WOODFORD, 1320

Rifleman Harry Woodford joined the Isle of Wight Rifles before war broke out. He was wounded in the thigh at Gallipoli during September 1915.

Rifleman Harry Woodford returned to serve with the Isle of Wight Rifles and continued to serve with them throughout the rest of the war. He was disembodied from the battalion on 28th March 1919 under service number 330176. However, Rifleman Woodford decided to re-join the Isle of Wight Rifles and was service number 5488012.

Rfn. Harry William WOODFORD, 1309

Rifleman Harry William Woodford served in the Isle of Wight Rifles at Gallipoli with his two brothers; Rifleman George Henry Woodford and Rifleman Charles Albert Woodford. At the same time, their youngest brother, Frank, was in the reserve battalion (2/8th Hants). Rifleman Harry Woodford was invalided off Gallipoli with dysentery towards the end of their deployment there.

Rifleman Harry William Woodford reached the rank of Corporal with the Isle of Wight Rifles. He was then transferred to the 15th Hants and fought in Belgium. He was killed on the 7th June 1917 and is buried at Bus House Cemetery, Ypres.

Rifleman Charles Albert Woodford survived the war but Rifleman George Henry Woodford was killed on 4th October 1917 during the Third Battle of Ypres.

Rfn. Reginald WOODFORD, 1330

Rifleman Reginald Woodford was captured during the Second Battle of Gaza on 19th April 1917 and was held as a prisoner at Baghtche Amanus.[513]

Rifleman Woodford was discharged from the Army on 31st March 1920 under service number 330182. Rifleman Woodford decided to re-enlist in the Isle of Wight Rifles and was given service number 5488013.

Rfn. Arthur Frederick WOODMAN, 1322

Rifleman Arthur Woodman enlisted in the Isle of Wight Rifles at Newport on 14th October 1913 at the age of 17 years. He remained with the Isle of Wight Rifles throughout the war and reached the rank of Corporal. During this time Arthur Woodman had a short spell in hospital at the 27th General Hospital in Cairo due to getting Malaria from a mosquito bite.[514]

Corporal Woodman was disembodied from the Army on 4th August 1919 under service number 330177.

Rfn. Ernest Isaac WOODMAN, 1644

Rifleman Ernest Woodman's British War Medal and Victory Medal Record states that he first served abroad with the Isle of Wight Rifles on 20th February 1916. His British Army WWI Medal Rolls Index Card makes no mention of him being awarded the 1914-15 Star Medal and there is not 1914-15 Star record for him. Although Rifleman Ernest Woodman was listed as one of the men of the battalion heading overseas in the Isle of Wight County Press on 24th July 1915, it appears that Rifleman Woodman did not go to Gallipoli.

---

[513] Research undertaken by Ian Meadows.
[514] www.ancestry.co.uk: British Army WWI Pension Records 1914-1920 - Cover for Discharge Documents

Rifleman Woodman was transferred from the Isle of Wight Rifles to the 19th Rifle Brigade on 16th August 1918 and was given service number 212885. He remained with this battalion on Garrison duties in Egypt, until the end of the war.[515]

Rfn. William WOODMORE M.M., 1132

Rifleman William Woodmore remained with the Isle of Wight Rifles and was given service number 330088. He was awarded the Military Medal and received a Mention in Despatches in the London Gazette on 11th January 1918 for *'gallant or distinguished conduct in the Field, or for other valuable services.'*[516]

Rifleman Woodmore was reported wounded in the War Office Daily List on 8th August 1918.[517] The last Isle of Wight Rifles' offensive prior to the 8th August 1918 was on the 9th April 1918 at Berukin. Therefore, Rifleman Woodmore would have been wounded either whilst holding the line or on a trench raid.

William Woodmore was disembodied from the Army on 10th March 1919.

Rfn. Bertie Howard WRAY, 1988

Rifleman Bertie Wray had been with the Isle of Wight Rifles for 4 years prior to the outbreak of war and re-enlisted shortly after hostilities began. He was a keen sportsman and rowed for Newport Rowing Club.

Rifleman Wray was wounded during the offensive action at Anafarta Ridge. He was carried back by Sergeant Barnes and another member of the Isle of Wight Rifles and died shortly

---

[515] www.ancestry.co.uk: UK, WWI Service Medal and Award Rolls, 1914-1920 - British War Medal and Victory Medal
[516] www.forces-war-records.co.uk: Gazetted Awards and Mentions in Despatches - Gazette Issue 30474, 11/01/1918, p800
[517] www.forces-war-records.co.uk: First World War Daily Reports (Missing, Wounded & Prisoner of War) - NLS 1918_WList54

afterwards. He was buried at Hill 10 Cemetery with his date of death listed as the 13th August 1915.

News of Rifleman Wray's death was published in the Isle of Wight County Press on 21st August 1915 and was the first news received from Gallipoli, raising suspicions with the Islanders that the Isle of Wight Rifles had been on the offensive.

Rfn. Frank YEATES, 1184

Rifleman Frank Yeates came from Newport. He was initially reported as missing after the advance on Anafarta Ridge on 12th August 1915 but had in fact been killed in action on 12th August 1915. Official notification of his death was published in the Isle of Wight County Press on 29th July 1916. Rifleman Yeates was 20 years old and is commemorated on the Helles Memorial.

Rfn. Arthur YOUNG, 2426

Rifleman Arthur Young served with the Isle of Wight Rifles throughout the war and was disembodied from the Army on 28th March 1919 under service number 330828.

'C' Company

CSM. Walter Ormonde MINNS, 304

Company Sergeant Major Walter Minns enlisted with the Isle of Wight Rifles on 1st April 1908. He was promoted to Company Sergeant Major on the 5th January 1915.

On Monday 16th August 1915, CSM Minns was wounded in the left shoulder, 'by shrapnel fire in a ravine.'[518] In a letter to his wife by Rifleman Denness, which was published on 6th November 1915 in the Isle of Wight County Press, Rifleman Denness wrote that CSM Minns would not and did not leave his men for two days after being wounded.

CSM Minns' wound was treated in Nasrith School Military Hospital in Cairo. As it was not a serious wounding, he was able to re-join the Isle of Wight Rifles on 25th October 1915. He remained with them through the Gallipoli evacuation and re-deployment to Egypt and returned to England on HT Tunisian for his discharge on 22nd March 1916 due to completing his service period.

CQMS. Evelyn James GATRALL, 377

Company Quartermaster Sergeant Evelyn Gatrall served with the Isle of Wight Rifles throughout the war. His latter service number was 330022.

Sgt. Paul CHAMBERS, 42

Sergeant Paul Chambers came from Lake. He was taken ill with Enteric at Gallipoli and by November 1915 had been admitted into a hospital at Malta.

---

[518] Isle of Wight County Press, 4th September 1915, p6.

Towards the end of the war, Sergeant Chambers went on to serve in the 34th (County of London) Battalion, London Regiment, which deployed to France in August 1918 as a Corporal with service number 897352. Following this, he served with the 1st Cambridgeshire Regiment on the Western Front as a Corporal with service number 330345 and he survived the war.

Sgt. Lewin CHANNING, 805

Sergeant Lewin Channing served with the Isle of Wight Rifles throughout the war. He was disembodied from the battalion on 28th May 1919 under service number 330043.

Sgt. Arthur Charles EARLY, 291

After Gallipoli, Sergeant Arthur Charles Early continued to serve with the Isle of Wight Rifles and by April 1917 he held the rank of Company Sergeant Major (CSM) and had service number 330019. He was wounded during the Second Battle of Gaza on 19th April 1917 and despite being wounded, helped to get aid to Lieutenant Harper who had also been wounded. CSM Early survived the war.

Sgt. Ernest Stanley ELLIOTT, 152

Sergeant Ernest Elliott *'served in the old Island Volunteers from November 21st, 1904, to April 7th, 1908, and re-joined the regiment on its change to the Territorial Force'*[519] on April 8th 1908.

Sergeant Elliott was wounded at Gallipoli on 13th August 1915 resulting in injury to his thigh and a fractured leg. He was left on the battlefield for several hours before being picked up and taken back for treatment. Sergeant Elliott was then invalided off Gallipoli and was admitted to Netley Hospital on Friday 3rd

---

[519] Isle of Wight County Press, 4th September 1915, p6.

September 1915. He was discharged from the Army on 27th June 1916 due to sickness.

Sgt. Hugh Leopold LOVE, 1680

Sergeant Hugh Love enlisted in the Isle of Wight Rifles on 31st August 1914. He was wounded in the leg on 13th August 1915 and was invalided off Gallipoli and taken back to England where he was admitted to Netley Hospital for further treatment. Sergeant Love was discharged from the 4th Hants on 31st August 1917 under service number 330378 due to being medically unfit.

Sgt. John Wilfred RAYNER, 1580

Sergeant John Rayner fell ill with dysentery sometime between the middle of September and October 1915. He then subsequently became ill with rheumatism. By the beginning of November 1915 Sergeant Rayner had been posted to serve with the 1st Garrison Battalion, Essex Regiment at the Intermediate Base in the Eastern Mediterranean and was given service number 34225.

Sergeant Rayner was later transferred back to the Isle of Wight Rifles. He was disembodied from the battalion on the 17th March 1919 under service number was 331573.

Sgt. T. WOOLTORTON, 1603

Sergeant T Wooltorton survived the war.

L/Sgt. Joseph Michael Stephen CLARKE, 1015

Lance Sergeant Joseph Clarke enlisted in the Isle of Wight Rifles on 8th February 1911 at the age of 25 years old. He had previous military experience with the Gloucestershire Regiment and at the time of joining the Isle of Wight Rifles, was a school teacher. Lance Sergeant Clarke became ill at Gallipoli with diarrhoea and was admitted into St Patrick's Hospital, Malta on 24th November 1915. He was then invalided back to England on 25th January

1916 and discharged from the Army on 24th March 1916 after having completed his period of service.[520]

L/Sgt. William Gardner SILVESTER, 162

Lance Sergeant William Silvester came from Ryde. He died of heart failure on 14th August 1915 at the age of 27 years. He is commemorated on the Helles Memorial.

Cpl. Thomas Frank BOYCE, 1479

Corporal Thomas Boyce came from Sandown and enlisted into the Isle of Wight Rifles at Sandown. He was reported as missing after the advance on Anafarta Ridge and as indicated by Rifleman Edward Denness' letter that was published in the Isle of Wight County Press on 6th November 1915, the men from 'C' Company thought that he had been taken prisoner. However, he had been killed during the advance on 12th August 1915 and official notification of his death was published in the Isle of Wight County Press on 29th July 1916.

Corporal Boyce was 28 years old. He has no known grave and is commemorated on the Helles Memorial.

Cpl. Sidney BUNCE, 1588

Corporal Sidney Bunce came from Shanklin. He was reported as missing in action in the Isle of Wight County Press on 11th September 1915 and later was presumed to have died on 22nd August 1915. Corporal Bunce was 20 years and is commemorated on the Helles Memorial.

Cpl. Joseph Alex MABB, 1895

Corporal Joseph Alex Mabb re-joined the Isle of Wight Rifles at the outbreak of war, having served previously. After the advance on Anafarta Ridge, he was reported missing. He had been wounded in the legs and captured by the Turks at Ari Burnu. He

---

[520] www.ancestry.co.uk: British Army WWI Pension Records 1914-1920

was taken to Constantinople, as a prisoner of war. In a letter to a friend, written whilst at Constantinople and published in the Isle of Wight County Press on 1st January 1916, Corporal Mabb wrote:

> My leg was a long-time healing. It is quite sound now. I am still in hospital nursing the sick. We have some very bad cases.[521]

Corporal Mabb spent the final years of the war at Yarbaschi as a prisoner of war. He was disembodied from the Army on 11th March 1919.

Cpl. George H. MUMFORD, 325

Corporal George Mumford was reported to have been wounded *'on the Casualty List issued by the War Office on 24th September 1915.'*[522]

Later in the war, George Mumford transferred to the Royal Engineers. He was given the rank of Sapper and service number 144765. On 26th August 1919 he was placed on the Z Reserve list.

Cpl. Edward William RIDGWAY, 2137

Corporal Edward Ridgway enlisted in the Isle of Wight Rifles on 31st December 1914. He was wounded on 21st August 1915 and gave details of his wounding in a letter home to his wife, written at Reading Hospital:

> I was the first man to get hit when we started to advance, but I saw them falling a little further on. I have four wounds, one in the back of the hand, one in the palm (the bullet coming out near the wrist), one half way between

---

[521] Isle of Wight County Press, 1st January 1916, p5
[522] www.forces-war-records.co.uk: First World War Daily Reports (Missing, Wounded & Prisoner of War) - DT25091915

my wrist and elbow, and one in the elbow (which broke the bone). The bullet is still there.[523]

His Silver War Badge record states that he was discharged on 29th July 1916 due to sickness.

Cpl. William Ernest WICKS, 1794

Corporal William Wicks was transferred to the Machine Gun Corps after Gallipoli and was given service number 50250. He reached the rank of Company Sergeant Major before going on to be commissioned as a Second Lieutenant in the Machine Gun Corps on 28th April 1917.

On 21st March 1918, the first day of the German Army's Spring Offensive, Second Lieutenant Wicks was taken prisoner whilst serving with the 61st Battalion of the Machine Gun Corps. He was repatriated on 6th December 1918.[524]

Cpl. Herbert POWELL, 1623

Corporal Herbert Powell came from Cowes and had previously served in the Army as a regular. He was reported as holding the rank of sergeant and having been wounded in the Isle of Wight County Press on 4th September 1915. It is likely that he was wounded during the advance on Anafarta Ridge.

Herbert Powell remained with the Isle of Wight Rifles throughout the war and was discharged from the Army on 14th December 1918 under service number 330339 and the rank of Lance Sergeant.

---

[523] Isle of Wight County Press, 18th September 1915, p6
[524] www.ancestry.co.uk: UK, British Officer Prisoners of War, 1914-1918

L/Cpl. Charles Henry ADAMS, 1512

Lance Corporal Charles Adams became ill with a fever at Gallipoli and by late October 1915 was at the Red Cross Hospital at Studley Court in Stourbridge.

Lance Corporal Adams returned to serve with the Isle of Wight Rifles and was disembodied from the battalion on 28th April 1919 under service number 330277.

L/Cpl. William HALSEY D.C.M, 1888

Lance Corporal William Halsey enlisted in the Isle of Wight Rifles at Newport on 4th September 1914. At the time he was living in Gurnard and was 45 years and 8 months old. He had previously served in the Kings Royal Rifles for 12 years.

William Halsey was promoted to the rank of Lance Sergeant on 1st October 1915 and then to the rank of Sergeant on 12th December 1915. He came through the Gallipoli campaign without being wounded or becoming seriously ill.[525] For his soldering at Gallipoli, Sergeant Halsey received a Mentioned in Despatches in the London Gazette, No. 29541, on 10th April 1916 *'for distinguished and gallant services during the period of General Sir Charles Monro's Command of the Mediterranean Expeditionary Force.'*[526]

Further to receiving a Mention in Despatches, Sergeant Halsey was awarded the Distinguished Conduct Medal, *'for conspicuous gallantry and good work under fire'* and the citation in the London Gazette on 21st June 1916 also stated that Sergeant Halsey is *'a fine sniper and patrol leader.'*[527]

---

[525] www.ancestry.co.uk: British Army WW1 Service Records, 1914-1920 – Territorial Force Attestation
[526] www.forces-war-records.co.uk: Gazetted Awards and Mentions in Despatches – London Gazette No. 29541, 10/04/1916 *and* London Gazette, 07/11/1916, p6949
[527] www.forces-war-records.co.uk: Gazetted Awards and Mentions in Despatches - London Gazette, 21/06/1916, p6144

Sergeant Halsey was transferred to the 1/4th Northants on 24th May 1917 and was then subsequently posted to the 1st Garrison Battalion of the Northamptonshire Regiment on 15th July 1917 who were on Garrison duties in Egypt/Palestine followed by Salonika from the 31st October 1918. On 8th December 1918, Sergeant Halsey was discharged from the Army due to Gastritis. He received an Army pension and was given the Silver War Badge.[528]

L/Cpl. Alfred William PLUMRIDGE, 1782

Lance Corporal Alfred Plumridge continued to serve with the Isle of Wight Rifles after Gallipoli and was given service number 330433. He was taken prisoner by the Turks, most likely during the Second Battle of Gaza on 19th April 1917 and was held at Afion Kara Hissar.[529]

Lance Corporal Alfred Plumridge was disembodied from the Army on 16th March 1919.

L/Cpl. Leonard SYMES, 1757

Lance Corporal Leonard Symes came from Chichester and enlisted in the Isle of Wight Rifles on 2nd September 1914. His brother, Rifleman Ernest Symes, also joined the battalion and they both went to Gallipoli. Unfortunately, Rifleman Ernest Symes was killed in action on 22nd August 1915.

Lance Corporal Leonard Symes was discharged from the Army on 5th October 1916 due to 'sickness' and was given the Silver War Badge.[530]

---

[528] www.ancestry.co.uk: British Army WW1 Service Records, 1914-1920 – Territorial Force Attestation

[529] *List of prisoners provided by Ian Meadows*

[530] www.forces-war-records.co.uk: Silver War Badge List 1914-1918

L/Cpl. Harry Lester TRUEMAN, 1573

Lance Corporal Harry Trueman was transferred to the 1/6th Hants after his time at Gallipoli with the Isle of Wight Rifles. He was given service number 3800 followed by service number 281792. The 1/6th Hants were deployed to India in October 1914 and were moved to Mesopotamia in September 1917.

Lance Corporal spent the last part of the war with the 2nd Garrison Battalion of the Northumberland Fusiliers who were based in India. He was disembodied from the Army under service number 206556.[531]

L/Cpl. Albert Victor WATSON, 1909

Lance Corporal Albert Watson joined the Isle of Wight Rifles on 5th September 1915. He was shot in the foot during the attack on Anafarta Ridge and was taken back to Lemnos followed by Cairo for treatment. Lance Corporal wrote to his parents on 14th August 1915 telling them that he had been wounded:

> Just a line or two to let you know I am alive and well, though not very nimble, for I have got a bullet wound in the foot. It is only a flesh wound…..I saw Ern a few minutes before I was 'clicked' and he was alright.[532]

Lance Corporal Watson returned to the Isle of Wight Rifles and was later promoted to Sergeant. He survived the war and was disembodied from the army on 2nd April 1919.

L/Cpl. George WHITE, 1631

Lance Corporal George White came from Lake. His father had previously served in the Isle of Wight Rifles. Lance Corporal White was friends with Adolphus Ballard and Fred Shave.

---

[531] www.ancestry.co.uk: UK, WWI Service Medal and Award Rolls, 1914-1920 - British War Medal and Victory Medal
[532] Isle of Wight County Press, 4th September 1915, p6

Lance Corporal White survived the advance on Anafarta Ridge and became ill in September 1915. By the 16th October 1915, Lance Corporal White was in hospital at No. 17 General Hospital, Alexandria suffering with Rheumatism and suspected Enteric Fever. Lance Corporal White was then taken to England for further rehabilitation and recovery and in April 1916 he was staying at an Enteric Convalescent Camp in Surrey.[533]

Later in the war, Lance Corporal White was transferred to the 14th Hants and given service number 27756. He served at the Somme and at Ypres and was promoted to the rank of Corporal. On 26th September 1917, at Passchendaele, George White was acting as a Platoon Sergeant and was killed by a shell shortly after going over the top from 'Tower Hamlet' trench.[534]

George White is listed on Tyne Cott Memorial as Private George White.

L/Cpl. Alfred James WHITTINGTON, 1704

Lance Corporal Alfred Whittington had served with a Territorial Army unit in Southampton for four years before the Great War and he was also the Deputy Captain of Newport Fire Brigade. On the outbreak of war, he joined the Isle of Wight Rifles.

Following the advance on Anafarta Ridge on 12th August 1915, Lance Corporal Whittington was posted as missing. He had however, been killed and official notification of his death was published in the Isle of Wight County Press on 29th July 1916. Lance Corporal Whittington was 32 years old and is commemorated on the Helles Memorial.[535]

---

[533] Isle of Wight Rifles: www.wwwight.co.uk
[534] Isle of Wight Rifles: www.wwwight.co.uk
[535] Isle of Wight Fire Brigades Federation http://www.iwfbf.co.uk/439511031

L/Cpl. Frank George WOODING, 1911

Lance Corporal Frank Wooding was reported as having been wounded at Gallipoli in the 2nd October 1915 edition of the Isle of Wight County Press.

Lance Corporal Wooding recovered from his wounding and rejoined the Isle of Wight Rifles. He was disembodied from the Army on 22nd July 1919 under service number 330510.

L/Cpl. Alfred R. JEWELL, 1482

Lance Corporal Alfred Jewell was transferred to the 1/6th Hants after his time with the Isle of Wight Rifles at Gallipoli. He was given service number 3797 followed by 281789. Alfred Jewell was later transferred to the Royal Engineers as a Sapper. He was placed on the Z Reserve List on 8th November 1919 under service number 574389.[536]

L/Cpl. Frederick John WESTMORE, 1648

Lance Corporal Frederick Westmore enlisted in the Isle of Wight Rifles on 28th August 1914. He served with the Isle of Wight Rifles up until his discharge from the Army on 19th March 1919 due to 'sickness.' Frederick Westmore had reached the rank of Sergeant with service number 330353 and was 31 years old when he was discharged from the Army. He was given the Silver War Badge.[537]

Bandsman James WESTMORE, 1953

Bandsman James Westmore served in the Isle of Wight Rifles with his two brothers. One of whom was Lance Corporal Frederick Westmore. As a Bandsman, James Westmore would have also been given the role as a stretcher bearer during the

---

[536] www.ancestry.co.uk: UK, WWI Service Medal and Award Rolls, 1914-1920 - British War Medal and Victory Medal
[537] www.forces-war-records.co.uk: Silver War Badge Lists 1914-1918

fighting. In a letter to his parents after the Anafarta Ridge offensive, he wrote:

> They have taken the names of a few of us who went straight up to the very front trench to collect the wounded. I happened to be one of them.[538]

Between the middle of August and the middle of September 1915, Bandsman Westmore fell ill with dysentery and went to a hospital in Malta for treatment.

Bandsman Westmore returned to serve with the Isle of Wight Rifles and was disembodied from the battalion on 27th March 1919 under service number 330534.

Br. Francis Edwin HARVEY, 1771

Bugler Francis Harvey was transferred to the Machine Gun Corps after Gallipoli and was given service number 50253. Francis Harvey reached the rank of Lance Sergeant before being Commissioned in the Hampshire Regiment on 17th March 1918. Francis Harvey survived the war and ended his Army career as a Second Lieutenant.

Br. Frank Stroud HARVEY, 260

Bugler Frank Harvey joined the 5th Volunteer Battalion of the Hampshire Regiment, the predecessor to the Isle of Wight Rifles, on 5th November 1907. He was just 13 and a half years old and was given the rank of 'Boy.' On the 8th April 1908, Frank Harvey officially enlisted in the Isle of Wight Rifles at East Cowes, having just turned 14 years old.[539]

Bugler Frank Harvey came through the Gallipoli deployment without getting wounded or becoming seriously ill and went with the battalion to Alexandria. He landed back in England on 14th

---

[538] Isle of Wight County Press, 4th September 1915, p6
[539] www.ancestry.co.uk: British Army WWI Pension Records 1914-1920 – Territorial Force Attestation

April 1916 and was discharged from the Army on 28th April 1916 for having completed his service period.

Br. Percy HUMPHRIES, 315

Bugler Percy Humphries came from Ventnor. He became ill with dysentery and by November 1915 was being treated in a hospital in Cairo, Egypt.

Bugler Humphries was transferred to the 15th Hants later in the war and was given service number 380191. The 15th Hants served on the Western Front and had a brief deployment to Italy towards the end of 1917 and early 1918 before returning to France.[540] Bugler Humphries was disembodied from the Army on 3rd May 1919.

Br. Frederick George SCOVELL, 1001

Bugler Frederick Scovell came from Sandown and enlisted in the Isle of Wight Rifles at Sandown on 18th January 1911 at the age of 17 years old. He was officially appointed as a Bugler on 19th July 1915.

Bugler Scovell fell ill at Gallipoli with Pyrexia of Unknown Origin and was admitted into a hospital in Malta on 23rd September 1915. He was then transferred to Ghain Tuffieha on 8th October 1915 and on 26th October 1915 he embarked on Hospital Ship Braemar Castle to return to England for further treatment.[541]

After completing his period of service, Bugler Scovell was discharged from the Army on 28th January 1916.

---

[540] https://www.forces-war-records.co.uk/maps/units/674/hampshire-regiment/15th-service-battalion-2nd-portsmouth/
[541] www.ancestry.co.uk: British Army WWI Pension Records 1914-1920 – Territorial Force Attestation

Bugler Sydney John SMEES, 874

Bugler Sydney Smees came from Cowes. His Army Pension Record states that he enlisted in the Isle of Wight Rifles on 6th October 1909 at the age of 15 and 9 months and on the 19th July 1915, he officially became a Bugler in the battalion.

Bugler Smees was wounded in the head by a piece of shrapnel on 4th September 1915 and was subsequently admitted into Bombay PG Hospital in Alexandria, Egypt on 9th September 1915. Bugler Smees returned to England in November 1915 and was discharged from the Army on 10th December 1915 after having completed his period of service.

Rfn. Percy ADAMS, 2204

Rifleman Percy Adams served with the Isle of Wight Rifles throughout the war and was disembodied from the Army on 3rd April 1919 under service number 330695.

Rfn. Robert Dobbie AITKEN, 1041

Rifleman Robert Aitken enlisted in the Isle of Wight Rifles at Cowes on 28th February 1911. He was 17 years and 10 months old and the attesting officer was Donald Ratsey.

Rifleman Aitken was appointed Temporary Acting Lance Corporal on 1st October 1915. He made it through the Gallipoli campaign without being wounded or becoming seriously ill and went with the battalion to Alexandria. Rifleman Aitken landed back in England on 9th February 1916 and was discharged from the Army on 13th March 1916 due to *'the termination of his period of engagement.'*[542]

---

[542] www.ancestry.co.uk: British Army WWI Pension Records 1914-1920 – Territorial Force Attestation

Rfn. Charles ALLEN M.M., 2327

Rifleman Charles Allen continued to serve with the Isle of Wight Rifles after Gallipoli and was promoted to the rank of Sergeant with service number 330766.

On 16th October 1917 it was reported in the London Gazette that Sergeant Allen had been awarded the Military Medal for *'bravery in the field.'*[543] It is likely that he was awarded the Military Medal for his actions during the Second Battle of Gaza on 19th April 1917.

Charles Allen was disembodied from the Army on 7th August 1919 holding the rank of Warrant Officer Class 2.

Rfn. A. ALLINGHAM, 2193

Rifleman Allingham was transferred to the Military Police Corps - Foot Branch later on in the war and was promoted to Lance Corporal. He was disembodied from the Army on 21st March 1919 under service number P.14118.

Rfn. W. ANTHONY, 1513

Rifleman Anthony was admitted to Cottomera Hospital, Malta on 17th September 1915 suffering with Enteric and Influenza.

Rifleman Anthony joined the Royal Flying Corps in 1916 and was given service number 39452. He survived the war.

Rfn. George ARMSTRONG, 1722

Rifleman George Armstrong served with the Isle of Wight Rifles throughout the war and was disembodied from the Army on 2nd August 1919 under service number 330400.

---

[543] www.forces-war-records.co.uk: Gazetted Awards and Mentions in Despatches - Gazette issue 30340, 16/10/1917, p10715

Rfn. Frederick ARNOLD, 2427

Rifleman Frederick Arnold and his brother Rifleman Christopher Arnold both served with the Isle of Wight Rifles at Gallipoli. Rifleman Christopher Arnold was wounded and then later died due to an illness on 2nd November 1915.

Later in the war Rifleman Frederick Arnold was transferred to the Royal Army Service Corps as a Private and was given service number T/289816. He finished the war serving with the Royal Engineers as a Pioneer with service number WR307876.

Rfn. James Thomas AUSTIN, 1762

Rifleman James Austin enlisted in the Isle of Wight Rifles on 2nd September 1914. He was wounded at Gallipoli between the battalion's landings on the 10th August 1915 and the end of September 1915.

Rifleman Austin returned to serve with the Isle of Wight Rifles and was later given service number 330417. He was discharged from the Army on 27th July 1918 owing to sickness and awarded the Silver War Badge.

Rfn. George BAILEY, 2147

Rifleman George Bailey came from North Mundham, Chichester. He enlisted in the Isle of Wight Rifles on 1st January 1915 and was discharged from the Army on 22nd September 1916 due to 'sickness.'[544]

Rifleman Bailey died as a result of his war service on 6th December 1918 at the age of 21 years old. He is buried at North Mundham (St. Stephen) Churchyard Extension.[545]

---

[544] www.forces-war-records.co.uk: Silver War Badge List 1914-1918
[545] https://www.cwgc.org/find-war-dead/casualty/402759/bailey,-george/

Rfn. Herbert Arthur BAKER, 2472

Rifleman Herbert Baker's family came from Dorking in Surrey but around the outbreak of war, Rifleman Baker was living in Ryde and he decided to enlist in the Isle of Wight Rifles at Newport. Rifleman Baker was reported as missing after the advance on Anafarta Ridge and was later presumed to have been killed on 12th August 1915. Rifleman Baker like many others from the Isle of Wight Rifles has no known grave. He is commemorated on the Helles Memorial and is also commemorated on Dorking's War Memorial.

Rfn. Adolphus BALLARD, 1659

Rifleman Adolphus Ballard came from Sandown. He was friends with George White and Fred Shave and was dating George White's sister. Rifleman Ballard enlisted in the Isle of Wight Rifles on 25th August 1914.[546]

Rifleman Ballard was originally thought to have been wounded on 12th August and missing.[547] However, he had been killed in action on 12th August 1915 during the advance on Anafarta Ridge. Rifleman Ballard is commemorated on the Helles Memorial.

Rfn. Alfred Henry BATCHELOR, 1372

Rifleman Alfred Batchelor continued to serve with the Isle of Wight Rifles after Gallipoli. He reached the rank of Corporal and was disembodied from the Army on 7th April 1919 under service number 330203.

Rfn. Albert BEALE, 1798

Rifleman Albert Beale enlisted in the Isle of Wight Rifles on 1st September 1914. He was reported to have been wounded at Gallipoli in the 25th September 1915 edition of the Isle of Wight

---

[546] Isle of Wight County Press, 9th October 1915, page 8.
[547] Isle of Wight Rifles: www.wwwight.co.uk

County Press. Rifleman Beale's wounds were serious enough for him to be medically discharged from the Army on 22nd April 1916 and as a result, he was awarded the Silver War Badge.

Rfn. Robert BENFIELD, 1718

Rifleman Robert Benfield came from Newport. He was wounded in his right leg during August 1915 and was invalided off Gallipoli and taken to a hospital in Malta. On recovering from his wound, Rifleman Benfield continued to serve with the Isle of Wight Rifles.

Rifleman Benfield was promoted to the rank of Corporal and was given service number 330397. He was wounded for a second time and this was officially reported in the War Office Daily List on 28th November 1917.[548] It is likely that Robert Benfield was wounded at some point during the Third Battle of Gaza which lasted from the 31st October to 7th November.

Robert Benfield returned to serve with the Isle of Wight Rifles and was promoted to the rank of acting Quarter Master Sergeant. He was disembodied from the Army on 24th July 1919.

Rfn. Bernard BENNETT, 1765

Rifleman Bernard Bennett came from East Cowes. He fell ill with dysentery at Gallipoli and was invalided back to England where he was admitted into Northwood House, Red Cross Hospital on Wednesday 1st December 1915.

Rifleman Bennett continued serving with the Isle of Wight Rifles. He was discharged from the battalion on 14th December 1918 under service number 330420.

---

[548] www.forces-war-records.co.uk: First World War Daily Reports (Missing, Wounded & Prisoner of War) - War Office Daily List No.5428, 28/11/1917

Rfn. William BILLINGHURST, 1766

Rifleman William Billinghurst served with the Isle of Wight Rifles throughout the war and was disembodied from the Army on 6th May 1919 under service number 330421.

Rfn. Arthur F BLOW, 1067

Rifleman Arthur Blow was with Rifleman Edward Denness during the Anafarta Ridge fighting. They both came out of it unscathed. As well as being a fighting soldier, Rifleman Blow was one of the Isle of Wight Rifles' cooks.

Later in the war, Rifleman Blow transferred to the Military Mounted Police Corps and reached the rank of Acting Corporal. He was disembodied from the Army on 14th August 1919 under service number P/6308.

Rfn. Alfred Frank BLOW, 1551

Rifleman Alfred Blow served with the Isle of Wight Rifles throughout the war and was discharged from the Army on 14th December 1918 under service number 330356.

Rfn. William Henry BLOW, 2381

Rifleman William Blow was reported in the 16th October 1915 edition of the Isle of Wight County Press as having been wounded at Gallipoli.

Later in the war, possibly due to the effects of his wounding, Rifleman William Blow was transferred to the Labour Corps. He was disembodied from the Labour Corps on 7th May 1919 under service number 247075.

Rfn. Thomas BOWDREY, 1767

Rifleman Thomas Bowdrey came from Bourne End in Buckinghamshire and in enlisted in the Isle of Wight Rifles on 2nd September 1914. He was one of the men recruited by

Lieutenant Colonel Rhodes and was 20 years old at the time of joining the battalion.

Rifleman Bowdrey remained with the Isle of Wight Rifles until he was transferred on 27th January 1917 to the 1st Garrison Battalion of the Notts and Derby Regiment who were based in Egypt. Thomas Bowdrey was then transferred to the Labour Corps on 18th January 1918. He was given service number 361205 with the rank of Private.

On 8th April 1919, Thomas Bowdrey reported to the London District Labour Centre. During his time abroad he had reported of heart trouble with his Cover of Discharge Documentation reporting that he had an enlarged heart. Thomas Bowdrey applied for a pension based on him having Valvular Disease of the Heart but his pension application was rejected. He was disembodied from the Army on 14th May 1919.[549]

Rfn. George BOWLER, 1660

Rifleman George Bowler continued to serve with the Isle of Wight Rifles after Gallipoli and was given service number 330362 when the Territorial Forces received new service numbers. In either 1917 or 1918, he was transferred to the Rifle Brigade and given service number 211298. George Bowler was then transferred to the Royal Engineers and given the rank of Pioneer. He was placed on the Z Reserve List on 28th June 1919 under service number 559900.[550]

Rfn. W BOWLER, 1661

Rifleman Bowler enlisted in the Isle of Wight Rifles on 31st August 1914. He was reported to have been wounded at Gallipoli

---

[549] www.ancestry.co.uk: British Army WWI Service Records, 1914-1920 - Cover for Discharge Documents
[550] www.ancestry.co.uk: British Army WWI Medal Rolls Index Cards, 1914-1920

in the 25th September 1915 edition of the Isle of Wight County Press.

Later in the war, Rifleman Bowler joined the Royal Flying Corps which went on to form the Royal Air Force. He was given service number 404228, held the rank of Air Mechanic 3rd Class and his trade was a Fitter (General).[551] He survived the war.

Rfn. David BROOKS, 2306

Rifleman David Brooks enlisted in the Isle of Wight Rifles on 2nd February 1915. He continued to serve with the battalion after Gallipoli and was given service number 330750.

Rifleman David Brooks was wounded and taken prisoner during the Second Battle of Gaza on 19th April 1917 and was subsequently held as a Prisoner of War at Damascus. He was discharged from the Army on 10th April 1919 at the age of 24 years old. Rifleman Brooks was given the Silver War Badge for 'wounds.'[552]

Rfn. John Thomas BROOKS, 2320

Rifleman John Brooks came from Marlow in Buckinghamshire and was one of the men recruited by Lieutenant Colonel Rhodes. He joined the battalion at the age of 16 in February 1915.

Rifleman Brooks fell ill with dysentery at Gallipoli and was invalided back to England where he spent time in a hospital in London. By January 1916, he was back with the Isle of Wight Rifles and when the Territorial Forces received new service numbers, he was given service number 330762. Rifleman Brooks was appointed as the batman to Captain Vincent.

During the Second Battle of Gaza on 19th April 1917, Rifleman Brooks was shot whilst attending to the wounds that Captain Vincent had received and he immediately died. Rifleman Brooks

---

[551] www.forces-war-records.co.uk: RAF Formations List 1918 - AIR 1/819/204/4/1316
[552] www.forces-war-records.co.uk: Silver War Badge List, 1914-1918

was 19 years old. His body was not recovered from the battlefield and subsequently he is commemorated on the Jerusalem Memorial.[553]

Rfn. Frank BROWN, 1012

Rifleman Frank Brown enlisted in the Isle of Wight Rifles at Sandown on 1st February 1911. He was 17 years old.

Rifleman Brown made it through the Gallipoli deployment without being wounded or becoming seriously ill and he went to Alexandria with the Isle of Wight Rifles. He landed back in England on 29th January 1916 and was discharged from the Army on 14th February 1916 due to completing his service period.[554]

Rfn. Charles BURT, 1725

Rifleman Charles Burt came from Chale and enlisted in the Isle of Wight Rifles on 2nd September 1915. He fell ill with Dysentery and Enteric at Gallipoli and was invalided back to a hospital in Scotland. By late November 1915 he was on a period of sick leave back at the Isle of Wight.

Rifleman Burt was discharged from the Army on 1st June 1916 due to sickness and was awarded the Silver War Badge.

Rfn. Gordon BURT, 1935

Rifleman Gordon Burt was reported as wounded in the 25th September 1915 edition of the Isle of Wight County Press.

Rifleman Burt was transferred to the 2/4th Hants later in the war. From the end of April 1917, the 2/4th Hants had moved from India to take part in the Palestinian campaign and on 22nd May 1918 the battalion left Egypt for France. Gordon Burt continued

---

[553] http://www.marlowsociety.org.uk/MRWW1/userfiles/file/Rifleman-John-Brooks.pdf
[554] www.ancestry.co.uk: British Army WWI Pension Records 1914-1920 - Territorial Force Attestation

serving with the 2/4th Hants until he was disembodied from the Army on 28th March 1919 under service number 205456.

Rfn. George BURTON, 1769

Rifleman George Burton was transferred to the Duke of Edinburgh's (Wiltshire) Regiment later on in the war. He was given the rank Private and service number 204013. George Burton was placed on the Class Z List on 2nd April 1919.

Rfn. Albert E. BUTLER, 1539

Rifleman Albert Butler enlisted in the Isle of Wight Rifles on 8th August 1914. He was transferred to the Machine Gun Corps after Gallipoli and was given service number 50277 along with the rank of Private. He was discharged from the Army on 11th April 1919 at the age of 22 years and 11 months due to 'sickness' and was given the Silver War Badge.[555]

Rfn. George CASS, 2367

Rifleman George Cass came from Newport and enlisted in the Isle of Wight Rifles at Newport. He served in the Isle of Wight Rifles at Gallipoli with his brother, Rifleman Frank Cass. Rifleman Frank Cass was taken prisoner at Gallipoli and died on 27th January 1917.

Rifleman George Cass continued serving with the Isle of Wight Rifles after Gallipoli and was given service number 330791. He was killed in action during the Third Battle of Gaza on 2nd November 1917 and is buried at Gaza War Cemetery.[556]

Rfn. Albert James Ruffin CHESSELL, 1515

Rifleman Albert Chessell came from Northwood and enlisted in the Isle of Wight Rifles at Newport in October 1914. He remained with the battalion after Gallipoli and was given service

---

[555] www.ancestry.co.uk: Silver War Badge Records, 1914-1920
[556] https://www.cwgc.org/find-war-dead/casualty/649665/cass,-/

number 330279. Rifleman Chessell was killed in action during the Second Battle of Gaza on 19th April 1917 at the age of 19 years and is buried at Gaza War Cemetery.[557]

Rfn. Sidney CHESSELL, 1517

Rifleman Sidney Chessell came from Northwood and enlisted in the Isle of Wight Rifles on 6th August 1914 at the age of 17 years old.[558]

On 25th July 1916, Sidney Chessell joined the Royal Flying Corps as a Coppersmith and held the rank of Air Mechanic 3rd Class with service number 39543.[559] He survived the war.

Rfn. William G COLENUTT, 1270

Rifleman William Colenutt came from Shanklin. He was wounded on 12th August 1915 during the advance on Anafarta Ridge and was invalided back to England. He received further treatment at a hospital in Manchester.

Later in the war, Rifleman Colenutt was transferred to the Machine Gun Corps and given service number 50256. He survived the war and reached the rank of Acting Sergeant.

Rfn. Charles William COOPER, 1666

Rifleman Charles Cooper served with the Isle of Wight Rifles throughout the war and was disembodied from the Army on 19th July 1919 under service number 330366.

---

[557] http://www.isle-of-wight-fhs.co.uk/Northwoodmemorials/chessell_ajr.pdf
[558] www.ancestry.co.uk: UK, Royal Air Force Airmen Records, 1918-1940
[559] www.forces-war-records.co.uk: RAF Formations List 1918 - AIR 1/819/204/4/1316

Rfn. Ernest COOPER, 1665

Rifleman Ernest Cooper served with the Isle of Wight Rifles throughout the war and was disembodied from the Army on 2nd April 1919 under service number 330365.

Rfn. William Charles COOPER, 1938

Rifleman William Cooper worked for Timothy White Chemists and as part of his job he had designed a hair cream which was later purchased by Brylcreem - Brylcreem came into existence in 1928.

Rifleman William Cooper joined the Isle of Wight Rifles on 4th September 1914 with his brother, George Cooper, and cousins; Reginald Brooks Butt, Frank Butcher, and the two Whites, one of whom was Charlie White. They all went to Gallipoli and only William Cooper and Frank Butcher lasted through the whole campaign. George Cooper, was invalided off Gallipoli along with Reginald Brooks Butt after the winter storm. Both had fallen ill with Enteric Fever with Reginald also having frostbite. Charlie White had sadly passed away from dysentery in September 1915.

Rifleman William Cooper continued to serve with the Isle of Wight Rifles after Gallipoli and by October 1917 he had reached the rank of Company Quartermaster Sergeant with service number 330526. He was reported as wounded in the War Office Daily List No.5390 on 15th October 1917.[560] Prior to this report, the Isle of Wight Rifles' last major offensive was during the Second Battle of Gaza on 19th April 1917. Therefore, William Cooper would have been wounded whilst holding the line or on a trench raid.

William Cooper returned to the Isle of Wight Rifles on recovering from his wounds. Shortly after the armistice, William Cooper became seriously ill with influenza and broncho-

---

[560] www.forces-war-records.co.uk: First World War Daily Reports (Missing, Wounded & Prisoner of War) - War Office Daily List No.5390, 15/10/1917

pneumonia and passed away on 10th December 1918 at the 3rd General Hospital, Alexandria aged 26 years old. He is buried at Cairo War Memorial Cemetery.[561]

George Cooper passed away on 12th March 1921 as a result of developing severe pleurisy during the German's final offensive of 1918. He could not be taken out of the line due to the extreme strain the British Army was under and the delay proved fatal as he died in a sanatorium at St. Lawrence on the Isle of Wight on 12th March 1921. He was 27 years old and is buried in Sandown churchyard.

Frank Butcher and Reginald Brooks Butt were the only two of the group of six who were still alive in 1922.

Rfn. George Henry CORNEY, 1564

Rifleman George Corney was transferred to the Machine Gun Corps after Gallipoli and held the rank of Private. He was disembodied from the Army on 6th April 1919 under service number 50260.

Rfn. Charles Owen COULBERT, 1622

Rifleman Charles Coulbert and Rifleman Edward Roberts were good friends. Rifleman Coulbert was invalided off Gallipoli on 23rd September 1915 with dysentery and fever, shortly before Rifleman Roberts was wounded. Rifleman Coulbert returned to England and by the beginning of December was at The Orchard Convalescent Home in Dartford, Kent.[562]

Rifleman Coulbert was transferred to the 1/6th Hants and given service number 281800. He remained with the battalion until he was disembodied from the Army on 10th December 1919. The

---

[561] Isle of Wight County Press, 21st December 1918, p1
[562] Isle of Wight County Press, 11th December 1915, p8

1/6th Hants arrived at Basra on 16th September 1917 and operated in Mesopotamia until the end of the war.[563]

Rfn. Harry CROSS, 1719

Rifleman Cross came from Newport. He was promoted to the rank of Lance Corporal at Gallipoli. He was taken ill at some point between October 1915 and November 1915 and by December 1915 he had been admitted into the *'Convalescent Hospital at Woodcote Park, Epsom, Surrey, suffering with rheumatism.'*[564]

Harry Cross continued to serve with the Isle of Wight Rifles and reached the rank of Sergeant. He was disembodied from the Army on 26th February 1919 under service number 330398.

Rfn. Harry Reginald DAVIS, 1056

Rifleman Harry Davis had been in the Isle of Wight Rifles for four years prior to going to Gallipoli. He was wounded in the hand during August 1915. At some point, Rifleman Davis was promoted to Lance Corporal. He was discharged from the Army on 12th May 1916.

Rfn. Harry DENNESS, 1076

Rifleman Harry Denness continued to serve with the Isle of Wight Rifles after Gallipoli and when the Territorial Forces received new service numbers, he was given service number 330061.

Later in the war, Harry Denness was transferred to the Royal Engineers and was given the rank of Sapper. His initial service number was 521662 and when he was then transferred to the

---

[563] http://www.longlongtrail.co.uk/army/regiments-and-corps/the-british-infantry-regiments-of-1914-1918/hampshire-regiment/
[564] Isle of Wight County Press, 25th December 1915, p5

Railway Section of the Royal Engineers he was given service number WR194508.

Rfn. Edward James DENNIS (DENNESS), 1667

Rifleman Edward Denness took part in the advance on Anafarta Ridge. He spent a lot of his time during the fighting at Anafarta Ridge alongside his friend Rifleman Arthur Blow. Both came out of it unharmed. By early September 1915, Rifleman Denness was feeling the strain of the extreme conditions faced at Gallipoli and in a letter home to his wife he wrote:

> I have been pretty badly run down lately, and my nerves or something have gone wrong. All the chaps are like it. We have had enough of this.[565]

Rifleman Denness served with the Isle of Wight Rifles throughout the war and re-enlisted in the battalion after the Great War. He was given service number 05249.

Rfn. Lawrence George DEPTFORD, 1592

Rifleman Lawrence Deptford came from Whitwell. He was reported as being in hospital in the Isle of Wight County Press on 11th December 1915 but it was not stated if he had been wounded at Gallipoli or taken ill.

Rifleman Deptford was transferred to the 2/4th Hants and given service number 205444 and the rank of Private. He then went on to serve in the 2/5th Hants and was killed in action during the capture of Junction Station on 13th November 1917. Private Deptford has no known grave and is commemorated on the Jerusalem Memorial.

Rfn. Harry Lawrence DODSWORTH, 2019

Rifleman Harry Dodsworth came from Newport and enlisted in the Isle of Wight Rifles in Newport. He remained in 'C'

---

[565] Isle of Wight County Press, 6th November 1915, p5

Company of the Isle of Wight Rifles after Gallipoli and was given service number 300582.

Rifleman Dodsworth was 20 years old when he took part in the Second Battle of Gaza on 19th April 1917. He was part of a Lewis Gun Section in 'C' Company and following the battle was reported as missing.[566] Sometime later it was presumed that he died on 19th April 1917. Rifleman Dodsworth has no known grave and is commemorated on Jerusalem Memorial.

Rfn. Jack DOLLERY, 1450

Rifleman Jack Dollery served with the Isle of Wight Rifles throughout the war and was disembodied from the Army on 5th May 1919 under service number 330248.

Rfn. Sidney DOWNER, 1920

Rifleman Sidney Downer came from Newport and enlisted in the Isle of Wight Rifles on 4th September 1914. He became ill at Gallipoli and by October 1915 was at *'a convalescent home at Alexandria recovering from rheumatic fever.'*[567]

Rifleman Downer was discharged from the Army on 8th August 1916 due to sickness and was given the Silver War Badge.

Rfn. Frank DRAPER, 1565

Rifleman Frank Draper came from Chale. He became ill with jaundice whilst at Gallipoli and by November 1915 had been admitted into a hospital in Giza.

On recovering from illness, Rifleman Draper returned to serve with the Isle of Wight Rifles throughout the rest of the war. He was disembodied from the Army on 18th April 1919 under service number 330302.

---

[566] www.forces-war-records.co.uk: British Red Cross and Order of St John Enquiry List 1917 (Wounded and Missing)
[567] Isle of Wight County Press, 30th October 1915, p5

Rfn. Ernest Gordon DUNFORD, 1121

Rifleman Ernest Dunford was transferred to the Machine Gun Corps after Gallipoli and was given the rank of Private. He was disembodied from the Army on 14th December 1918 under service number 50272.

Rfn. Gordon DUNSTAN, 2326

Rifleman Gordon Dunstan enlisted with the Isle of Wight Rifles on 15th February 1915. He was shot through his left arm at some point in August 1915 at Gallipoli and a year later on 8th August 1916, he was discharged from the Army due to sickness.

Rifleman Gordon Dunstan's brother, William also served with the Isle of Wight Rifles and he died on 18th August 1915.

Rfn. William EAST, 2333

Rifleman William East came from Marlow in Buckinghamshire and was one of the men recruited by Lieutenant Colonel Rhodes. He continued serving in the Isle of Wight Rifles with 'C' Company after Gallipoli and was given service number 330770.

Rifleman East was killed in action at the age of 19 on 2nd November 1917 during the Third Battle of Gaza and is buried at Gaza War Cemetery.[568]

Rfn. Douglas EDMUNDS, 1579

Rifleman Douglas Edmunds enlisted in the Isle of Wight Rifles on 12th August 1914. In September 1915 he was invalided off Gallipoli suffering with dysentery and was taken to a hospital in Malta. By October 1915, Rifleman Edmunds had been sent back to England for convalescence at the Royal Victoria Convalescent Hospital, Netley.

---

[568] https://www.cwgc.org/find-war-dead/casualty/649955/east,-/

Rifleman Edmunds was discharged from the Army on 18th August 1916. His Silver War Badge record states that he was discharged due to 'sickness.'

Rfn. Arthur ELDRIDGE, 1594

Rifleman Arthur Eldridge came from Godshill and enlisted in the Isle of Wight Rifles on 15th August 1914. He was severely wounded in his right wrist on 13th September 1915 and had to be invalided back to England where he was treated in a hospital in Manchester. The severity of the wounding meant that Rifleman Eldridge had to be discharged from the Army on 24th April 1916.

Rfn. Clarence Albert FALLICK, 1637

Rifleman Clarence Fallick continued to serve with the Isle of Wight Rifles after Gallipoli and was given service number 330348. He was reported as having been wounded in the War Office Daily List on 28th November 1917.[569] It is likely that he was wounded during the Third Battle of Gaza.

Rifleman Fallick was disembodied from the Army on 15th July 1919.

Rfn. Colin FINLAY, 1582

Rifleman Colin Finlay came from Shanklin and enlisted in the Isle of Wight Rifles at Newport. He was wounded at Gallipoli during August 1915 and on recovering from his wounds he rejoined the Isle of Wight Rifles. Latterly he was given service number 330309.

Rifleman Finlay was killed in action on 19th April 1917 during the Second Battle of Gaza. He was 19 years old and is buried at Gaza War Cemetery.

---

[569] www.forces-war-records.co.uk: First World War Daily Reports (Missing, Wounded & Prisoner of War) - War Office Daily List No.5428, 28/11/1917

Rfn. Horace FLUX, 1922

Rifleman Horace Flux fell ill at Gallipoli with Jaundice and in November 1915 was being treated in a hospital in Malta.

Rifleman Flux continued to serve with the Isle of Wight Rifles. He was disembodied from the battalion on 22nd July 1919 under service number 330517.

Rfn. Charles FORD, 2323

Rifleman Charles Ford served with the Isle of Wight Rifles throughout the war and was disembodied from the Army on 11th March 1919 under service number 330763.

Rfn. Robert William Henry FOX, 1011

Rifleman Robert Fox enlisted in the Isle of Wight Rifles at Sandown on 1st February 1911. He was 17 years and 2 months old. He served with the battalion throughout their Gallipoli campaign and went with the battalion to Alexandria. Rifleman Fox landed back in England on 29th January 1916 and was discharged from the Army on 14th February 1916 for having completed his period of service.[570]

Rfn. William FRITH, 1770

Rifleman William Frith went on to become a Private in the Machine Gun Corps after Gallipoli. He was disembodied from the Army on 22nd April 1919 under service number 120518.

Rfn. Reginald GLADWIN, 1808

Rifleman Reginald Gladwin came from Cowes and enlisted in the Isle of Wight Rifles on 3rd September 1914. During August 1915 at Gallipoli, he was taken sick and received treatment in hospital. Rifleman Gladwin was then *'admitted to 5th Canadian*

---

[570] www.ancestry.co.uk: British Army WWI Pension Records 1914-1920

Stationary Hospital, Abbasia on November 15th suffering from dysentery.[571]

Rifleman Gladwin returned to serve with the Isle of Wight Rifles and under the new service numbering system he was given the service number: 330449. Later in the war Rifleman Gladwin was transferred to the Rifle Brigade (service number: 211944) and then to the Royal Army Medical Corps where he served with the London Mounted Brigade Field Ambulance until being discharged from the Army on 3rd April 1919 under service number 533143 due to sickness.

Rfn. John Hamilton GLOVER, 1670

Rifleman John Hamilton Glover enlisted in the Isle of Wight Rifles between September and October 1914. He fell ill at Gallipoli with dysentery and was so weak he had to be carried to get medical assistance. Rifleman Glover was subsequently invalided off Gallipoli and was admitted to No. 19 General Hospital in Alexandria on 8th November 1915. It was feared that he would he died but he managed to recover and was sent back to England on Hospital Ship Nevasa on 6th December 1915.[572]

Rifleman Glover returned to serve with the Isle of Wight Rifles and was in 9 Platoon, 'C' Company when he was wounded during the Second Battle of Gaza on 19th April 1917. He recovered from his wounding and continued serving with the battalion. During his time in Palestine, he also fell ill with Malaria.[573]

Rifleman Glover was disembodied from the Army on 15th July 1919 under service number 330369.

---

[571] Isle of Wight County Press, 11th December 1915, p8
[572] https://www.iwm.org.uk/collections/item/object/80031373
[573] www.forces-war-records.co.uk: Military Hospitals Admissions and Discharge Registers WW1 - MH106/1228: No. 19 General Hospital: 29/10/1915 to 21/11/1915.

Rfn. Harold Leslie GYMER, 1285

Rifleman Harold Gymer was transferred to the Labour Corps at some point after the Isle of Wight Rifles' deployment to Gallipoli. He was given the rank of Private and service number 311537 and was disembodied from the Army on 28th February 1919.

Rfn. Frederick John HARVEY, 1006

Rifleman Frederick Harvey served at Gallipoli and was discharged from the Army on 28th January 1916. He was not awarded a Silver War Badge which suggests that he was discharged after completing his service period.

Rfn. Maurice HARWOOD, 1123

Rifleman Maurice Harwood came from Cowes. He took part in the Isle of Wight Rifles' advance on Anafarta Ridge and by the end of August/early September 1915 had succumbed to dysentery. He was invalided back to England where he spent around two months at St Bartholomew's hospital recovering.

Rifleman Harwood went on to serve in another battalion in the Hampshire Regiment under service number 281786 and was discharged from the Army on 12th March 1917.

Rfn. Hubert HAWARD, 2183

Rifleman Hubert Haward came from Chiswick and enlisted in the Isle of Wight Rifles at Newport. He was killed in action on 18th August 1915 at the age of 27 years old and is commemorated on the Helles Memorial.

Rfn. Clarence HAYDEN, 1449

Rifleman Clarence Hayden and his brother Rifleman Harold Hayden came from Sandown. They both enlisted in the Isle of Wight Rifles at Sandown and went to Gallipoli with the battalion. Rifleman Clarence Hayden was reported in the Isle of Wight

County Press on 25th September 1915 as having been wounded at Gallipoli. His brother, Harold Hayden, was killed by a sniper on 29th August 1915.

After Gallipoli, Rifleman Clarence Hayden went on to serve in the 163rd Company of the Machine Gun Corps as a Private and was given service number 50258. He was killed in action during the 3rd Battle of Gaza on 2nd November 1917 and is buried at Gaza War Cemetery.

Rfn. Harold HAYDEN, 1448

Rifleman Harold Hayden served in the Isle of Wight Rifles at Gallipoli with his brother Rifleman Clarence Hayden. They lived in Sandown and enlisted in Sandown.

Rifleman Harold Hayden was shot by a sniper on 29th August 1915 and passed away that evening. The circumstances surrounding his death was written in a letter by Rifleman Edward Denness:

> Poor young Harold Hayden was killed last week, he was hit in the head in the morning, and died at sunset. He died quite peacefully, and never regained consciousness. Poor chap, he had only just come in the trench and taken over guard when he was struck. I saw him just as he was going in and he said to me, 'I have put my blanket in your dug-out, Happy; look after it for me.' He was just handing a periscope to the Captain and said, 'I can see three or four working over there' (meaning Turks) when a bullet came through the loop-hole and struck him; he fell back and never spoke again.[574]

Rifleman Haydon is buried at the 7th Field Ambulance Cemetery. His brother, Clarence Hayden, was killed in action on 2nd November 1917.

---

[574] Isle of Wight County Press, 6th November 1915, p5

Rfn. A. HEALEY, 1674

Rifleman Healey was reported as having been wounded at Gallipoli in the Isle of Wight County Press on 18th September 1915.

Rifleman Healey transferred to the Military Mounted Police Corps later in the war and reached the rank of Lance Corporal. He was disembodied from the Army on 5th May 1919 under service number P14898.

Rfn. William HESTER, 1673

Rifleman William Hester enlisted in the Isle of Wight Rifles on 31st August 1914. He continued to serve with the Isle of Wight Rifles after Gallipoli and was given service number 330371. Rifleman Hester was discharged from the Army on 16th May 1918 due to 'wounds' and was given the Silver War Badge.[575]

Rfn. William HICKENS, 2441

Rifleman William Hickens enlisted in the Isle of Wight Rifles at Ventnor. He remained with the battalion after Gallipoli and was given service number 330836. Rifleman Hickens was killed in action on 19th April 1917 during the Second Battle of Gaza and is buried at Gaza War Cemetery.

Rfn. Thomas HODDINOTT, 1773

Rifleman Thomas Hoddinott received a gunshot wound to his abdomen at Gallipoli during August 1915 and was taken to a hospital in Cairo.

Later in the war, Thomas Hoddinott transferred to the Royal Engineers becoming a Sapper in the Inland Waterways and Docks (Transportation) Unit. His service number was WR.551114.

---

[575] www.ancestry.co.uk: Silver War Badge Records, 1914-1919

Rfn. George Frederick HOLBROOK, 1941

Rifleman George Holbrook came from Sandown and enlisted in the Isle of Wight Rifles at Sandown. He took part in the advance on Anafarta Ridge on 12th August 1915 and was originally thought to have been wounded. However, at a later date, Rifleman Holbrook was presumed to have been killed during the action on the 12th August 1915. He was 22 years old and is commemorated on the Helles Memorial.

Rfn. William HOLLOWAY, 2328

Rifleman William Holloway served with the Isle of Wight Rifles throughout the war. He was disembodied from the Army on 7th August 1919 under service number 330767.

Rfn. Walter HOLMES, 1774

Rifleman Walter Holmes came from Cowes and enlisted in the Isle of Wight Rifles at Newport. He remained serving with the Isle of Wight Rifles after Gallipoli and was given service number 330426 when the Territorial Forces received new service numbers.

Walter Holmes was a Lance Sergeant when he fought with the Isle of Wight Rifles during the Second Battle of Gaza on 19th April 1917. After the battle he was initially reported as *'wounded and missing'*[576] but unfortunately, he had been killed in action on 19th April 1917. Confirmation of Lance Sergeant Walter Holmes' death was officially reported in the *'War Office Daily List No. 5488 on 9th February 1918.'*[577]

Lance Sergeant Holmes is buried at Gaza War Cemetery.

---

[576] www.forces-war-records.co.uk: British Red Cross and Order of St John Enquiry List 1917 (Wounded and Missing)
[577] www.forces-war-records.co.uk: First World War Daily Reports (Missing, Wounded & Prisoner of War) - War Office Daily List No. 5488, NLS 1918_WList28

Rfn. Edward Reginald HOME-GALL M.C., 2193

Rifleman Edward Home-Gall was born in 1897. In 1914 he was working as an office-boy for the Amalgamated Press and despite being underage he managed to join the Isle of Wight Rifles. He went on to serve at Gallipoli and fell ill with Enteric.[578]

Rifleman Home-Gall applied to become an Army Officer after serving with the Isle of Wight Rifles at Gallipoli. He was Commissioned on 22nd November 1916 and served as a Second Lieutenant in the Royal Fusiliers (London Regiment). It was with the Royal Fusiliers (London Regiment) that Edward Home-Gall was awarded the Military Cross. The citation for the award was printed in the London Gazette on 24th August 1917:

> For conspicuous gallantry and devotion to duty as Battalion Signalling Officer. He personally superintended the laying of wires under heavy shell fire, and was most successful in obtaining and maintaining communication throughout the action.[579]

Edward Home-Gall was promoted to Lieutenant on 22nd May 1918 and served on the Western Front with the 10th (Service) Battalion (Battersea) of the Queen's (Royal West Surrey Regiment).[580]

Lieutenant Home-Gall served as a Lieutenant with the Royal Regiment of Artillery during World War Two.

In his civilian life, Edward Home-Gall was a successful author.

Rfn. Herbert HUMBY, 2403

Rifleman Herbert Humby came from Shirley, Southampton and enlisted in the Isle of Wight Rifles on 27th April 1915. He fell ill

---

[578] https://bearalley.blogspot.com/2010/12/edward-r-home-gall.html
[579] www.forces-war-records.co.uk: Gazetted Awards and Mentions in Despatches, Gazette Issue No. 30251, 24/08/1917, p8811
[580] www.forces-war-records.co.uk: UK Army List 1918

with Enteritis at Gallipoli and was admitted to No. 19 General Hospital in Alexandria on 9th September 1915. He was 18 years old at the time. On 29th September 1915 Rifleman Humby was admitted on to Hospital Ship Salta which was bound for England.[581]

Rifleman Humby was discharged from the Army on 15th April 1916 due to 'sickness' and was given the Silver War Badge.[582]

Rfn. Stanley Thomas IVORY, 1042

Rifleman Stanley Ivory came from Cowes and enlisted in the Isle of Wight Rifles at Cowes at on 28th February 1911. He was 17 years and 9 months old.

Rifleman Ivory received medical treatment for diarrhoea at Mudros beginning on 8th October 1915. He returned to the Isle of Wight Rifles on 14th November 1915 and went with the battalion to Alexandria when they were evacuated from the Gallipoli Peninsula.

On 11th February 1916 Rifleman Ivory embarked on HT Empress of Britain to return to England. He was discharged from the Army on 10th March 1916 on completion of his period of service.[583]

Stanley Ivory applied for an Army Pension in 1917 as he was suffering with his mental health and was unable to work. It is likely that Stanley Ivory had Post Traumatic Stress Disorder from his military service. This is a condition that was not well understood during the First World War and the years afterwards.

---

[581] www.forces-war-records.co.uk: Military Hospitals Admissions and Discharge Registers WW1 - MH106/1225 No. 19 General Hospital: 01/09/1915 to 27/09/1915
[582] www.forces-war-records.co.uk: Silver War Badge List 1914-1918
[583] www.ancestry.co.uk: British Army WWI Pension Records 1914-1920

Rfn. Leonard William JACKMAN, 1583

Rifleman Leonard Jackman came from Shanklin. He was wounded at Gallipoli during August 1915 and was taken to Alexandria for treatment.

Rifleman Jackman was disembodied from the Hampshire Regiment under service number 330310 on 28th March 1919.

Rfn. Reginald JACKMAN, 1924

Rifleman Reginald Jackman came from Newport and enlisted in the Isle of Wight Rifles early on in the war. He made it *'through the Dardanelles campaign without being wounded or sick.'*[584]

It was reported in the Isle of Wight County Press on 12th February 1916 that Rifleman Jackman had had his appendix taken out at the 17th General Hospital in Alexandria. After recovering from the operation, he returned to the Isle of Wight Rifles and served with the battalion for the remainder of the war. His latter service number was 330518.

Rfn. Arthur William JACOBS, 2410

Rifleman Arthur Jacobs enlisted in the Isle of Wight Rifles on 1st May 1915. He continued to serve with the battalion after Gallipoli and was given service number 330821. Later in the war Rifleman Jacobs was wounded which led to him being discharged from the Army 6th November 1918. He was 22 years old and was given the Silver War Badge.[585]

Rfn. Albert JAMES, 2194

Rifleman Albert James suffered from heat stroke at Gallipoli during August 1915 and was treated on a hospital ship.

---

[584] Isle of Wight County Press, 12th February 1916, p5.
[585] www.forces-war-records.co.uk: Silver War Badge List 1914-1918

Rifleman James continued to serve in the Isle of Wight Rifles and was disembodied from the Army on 3rd April 1919 under service number 330688.

Rfn. Archibald JAMES, 1678

Rifleman Archibald James served at Gallipoli with the Isle of Wight Rifles alongside his younger brother, Rifleman George James. Rifleman Archibald James became ill towards the end of the battalion's Gallipoli campaign and as a result was hospitalised. His brother came through Gallipoli unscathed.

Rifleman Archibald James continued to serve with the Isle of Wight Rifles and was promoted to Lance Corporal. He was wounded and taken prisoner during the Second Battle of Gaza on 19th April 1917 and was held at Baghtche Amanus.[586]

Archibald James was disembodied from the Army on 9th March 1919 under service number 330376. His brother, George James, also survived the war.

Rfn. George JAMES, 1676

Rifleman George James and his older brother, Rifleman Archibald James, both served at Gallipoli with the Isle of Wight Rifles. Rifleman George James came through the Gallipoli campaign unscathed but towards the end of their time at Gallipoli, Rifleman Archibald James became ill and was taken to hospital.

Rifleman George James was given service number 330374 during the renumbering of the Territorials' service numbers. He served with the Isle of Wight Rifles up until 20th March 1918 when he was transferred to the 20th Rifle Brigade who were based in Egypt. George James was disembodied from the Army on 2nd

---

[586] Research undertaken by Ian Meadows

April 1919 under service number 212229. He held the rank of Private. His brother, Archibald, also survived the war.

Rfn. Norman Walker JAMES, 2298

Rifleman Norman James was transferred to the Machine Gun Corps after Gallipoli and was given service number 50267. He was commissioned in the Army Cyclist Corps on 13th April 1917 and reached the rank of Lieutenant. Norman James survived the war.

Rfn. Harold Sydney JANES, 1447

Rifleman Harold Sydney Janes came from Sandown and enlisted in the Isle of Wight Rifles at Sandown. Either at Gallipoli or afterwards, he was promoted to the rank of Lance Corporal. Lance Corporal Janes died on 12th November 1916 at the age of 18 and is buried at Ismailia War Memorial Cemetery in Egypt.[587]

Rfn. Ernest Edward JOHNSON, 2051

Rifleman Ernest Johnson enlisted in the Isle of Wight Rifles on 7th December 1914. After Gallipoli he was transferred to the Machine Gun Corps as a Private and was given service number 50271. Ernest Johnson was discharged from the Army on 3rd August 1919, at the age of 23 years and 8 months, due to 'sickness.' He was given the Silver War Badge.[588]

Rfn. Ernest Clifford KENT, 922

Rifleman Ernest Kent served with the Isle of Wight Rifles at Gallipoli and was discharged from the Army on 13th March 1916. Rifleman Kent did not receive the Silver War Badge so it is likely that he was discharged from the Army for completing his period of service.

---

[587] https://www.cwgc.org/find-war-dead/casualty/110999/janes,-sydney-harold/
[588] www.ancestry.co.uk: Silver War Badge Records, 1914-1920

Rfn. Sydney Barton KENT, 1679

Rifleman Sydney Kent enlisted in the Isle of Wight Rifles on 31st August 1914. He was transferred to the Labour Corps later on in the war and was given the rank of Private and service number 360541. Sydney Kent was discharged from the Army on 19th March 1919 due to 'sickness' and was given the Silver War Badge.[589]

Rfn. Albert Edward KEYNES, 2445

Rifleman Albert Keynes came from Ryde. He quickly fell ill with dysentery at Gallipoli and was admitted to a hospital in Malta on 18th August 1915. By November 1915 he was back in England at Eastleigh for a period of recuperation.

Rifleman Keynes returned to serve with the Isle of Wight Rifles and was disembodied from the battalion on 5th April 1919 under service number 330839.

Rfn. Henry Frederick KINGSWELL, 1378

Rifleman Henry Kingswell was transferred to the 2/5th Hants after his time at Gallipoli and was given service number 205445 along with the rank of Private. He was then transferred to the 2/4th Hants before being posted to the Duke of Edinburgh's (Wiltshire) Regiment – 1/4th Wilts. These three battalions were originally in India and moved to Palestine later in the war. They all took part in the Third Battle of Gaza.

Henry Kingswell survived the war and was placed on the Class Z list on 27th July 1919 under service number 204038.

Rfn. Herbert KITSON, 2100

Rifleman Herbert Kitson continued to serve with the Isle of Wight Rifles after Gallipoli and was given service number 330632. Between 1917 and 1918 he transferred to the Royal

---

[589] www.ancestry.co.uk: Silver War Badge Records, 1914-1920

Engineers and became a Sapper with service number 521059. Herbert Kitson spent the last part of the war with the Railways Section of the Royal Engineers and his service number was WR17741.

Rfn. Fred LAMBOURNE, 2318

Rifleman Fred Lambourne enlisted in the Isle of Wight Rifles on 7th February 1915. Later in the war he was transferred to the Labour Corps receiving service number 621144 and the rank of Private. Fred Lambourne was discharged from the Army due to 'sickness' on 11th April 1919 and was given the Silver War Badge.[590]

Rfn. Thomas Frederick LANE, 1045

Rifleman Thomas Lane enlisted in the Isle of Wight Rifles at the age of 18 at Cowes on 28th February 1911. He made it through Gallipoli without being wounded or becoming seriously ill and was appointed Acting Lance Corporal on 12th December 1915. Thomas Lane landed back in England on 30th April 1916 and on 12th May 1916 he was 'discharged in consequence of the termination of period of engagement.'[591]

Rfn. George LEACH, 2151

Rifleman George Leach came from Chichester and enlisted in the Isle of Wight Rifles in Newport. He continued serving with the Isle of Wight Rifles in 'C' Company and was given service number 330661. Rifleman Leach was killed in action at the age of 19 during the Third Battle of Gaza on 2nd November 1917. He is buried at Gaza War Cemetery.[592]

---

[590] www.ancestry.co.uk: Silver War Badge Records, 1914-1920
[591] www.ancestry.co.uk: British Army WWI Pension Records 1914-1920, Territorial Force Attestation
[592] https://www.cwgc.org/find-war-dead/casualty/650564/leach,-george/

Rfn. Raymond Walter LEACH, 1682

Rifleman Raymond Leach was originally reported as missing in the Isle of Wight County Press on 25th September 1915. However, he had not been killed or taken prisoner.

At some point after the Isle of Wight Rifles' Gallipoli campaign Rifleman Leach was transferred to the 1/6th Hants and was given service number 281810. He served with the battalion in Mesopotamia and was disembodied from the Army on 25th September 1919.

Rfn. John LEGG, 1629

Rifleman John Legg came from Shanklin and enlisted in the Isle of Wight Rifles at Shanklin. He remained with the Isle of Wight Rifles after Gallipoli and was given service number 330344. Rifleman Legg was killed in action during the Second Battle of Gaza on 19th April 1917. He has no known grave and is commemorated on the Jerusalem Memorial.

Rfn. Eugene Gladston LINDSAY, 137

Rifleman Eugene Lindsay came from Cowes and enlisted in the Isle of Wight Rifles on 3rd April 1908. He was discharged from the Army on 18th August 1916 due to 'sickness' and was given the Silver War Badge.[593]

Rfn. Gilbert LIPSCOMBE, 1776

Rifleman Gilbert Lipscombe served with the Isle of Wight Rifles throughout the war and was disembodied from the Army on 8th April 1919 under service number 330428.

Rfn. William LUNNON, 1777

Rifleman William Lunnon came from Bourne End in Buckinghamshire and was one of the men recruited by

---

[593] www.forces-war-records.co.uk: Silver War Badge Lists 1914-1918

Lieutenant Colonel Rhodes. Rifleman Lunnon had his Army medical on 31st August 1914 in Marlow and officially enlisted in the Isle of Wight Rifles on 2nd September 1914 at Newport. He was 22 years old at the time of enlisting.

On 27th August 1915 Rifleman Lunnon was admitted to a hospital in Mudros with a sprained back. He was then transferred to No. 3 Australian Stationary Hospital at Lemnos for convalescence and on 21st October 1915, Rifleman Lunnon was invalided back to England aboard the Aquitania. Rifleman Lunnon was admitted into Graylingwell War Hospital on 27th October 1915 with Enteric, Dysentery and Diphtheria and was a patient there until the 21st December 1915.

Once Rifleman Lunnon had recovered he was posted to the 2/8th Hants and was given service number 330429. He was discharged from the Army on 9th June 1917 as he was deemed to be *'no longer fit for war service'* and was given the Silver War Badge.[594]

Rfn. Leonard MABEY, 2251

Rifleman Leonard Mabey enlisted in the Isle of Wight Rifles on 13th January 1915. He was wounded at Gallipoli at some point between the battalion's landings at Gallipoli and the end of September 1915. Rifleman Mabey was invalided home and was reassigned to the 2/8th Hants where he was then declared medically unfit for the Army. Rifleman Mabey was discharged from the Army on 18th August 1916 and was awarded the Silver War Badge.

Rfn. John Edmund MACE, 2281

Rifleman John Mace continued serving with the Isle of Wight Rifles after Gallipoli and was given service number 330735. He reached the rank of Lance Corporal with the Isle of Wight Rifles before being Discharged to Commission on 25th September 1917.

---

[594] www.ancestry.co.uk: British Army WWI Pension Records 1914-1920, Territorial Force Attestation

John Mace became a Second Lieutenant and served with the Royal Engineers followed by the Royal West Kent Regiment. He survived the war.

Rfn. Sidney Victor MARINER, 1685

Rifleman Sidney Mariner was 17 years and 3 months old when he enlisted in the Isle of Wight Rifles on 31st August 1914 at Newport. He resided in Shanklin.

Rifleman Mariner fell ill with Dysentery and between the 4th November 1915 and 21st January 1916 he was back in England convalescing. Once Rifleman Mariner had recovered, he was sent to the Hampshire Base Depot and he spent his time there until being deployed back to the Isle of Wight Rifles in Palestine on 27th April 1917.

In late October 1917 Rifleman Mariner fell ill with Bronchitis and spent three weeks in hospital before returning back to the battalion. He then spent from the 8th February 1918 to 7th March 1918 in convalescence as he was suffering with his feet due to being flat footed. For this, Rifleman Mariner was given specialist boots.

On 1st May 1918, Rifleman Mariner deployed to France, joining the 1st Hants as a Private. He was wounded at La Bassee on 25th June 1918, receiving a gunshot wound to his right thigh. Private Mariner was subsequently invalided back to England for further treatment which lasted for several months. In 1919 it was deemed that the wound had not caused any permanent disability to Private Mariner. He was denied a pension and was disembodied from the Army on 3rd March 1919 under service number 330382.[595]

---

[595] www.ancestry.co.uk: British Army WWI Pension Records 1914-1920, Cover for Discharge Documents

Rfn. John MARTIN, 2109

Rifleman John Martin served with the Isle of Wight Rifles throughout the war and his latter service number was 330636. He survived the war.

Rfn. Alfred Edward MASSER, 1750

Rifleman Alfred Masser was transferred to the Machine Gun Corps as a Private after Gallipoli. He was disembodied from the Army on 4th April 1919 under service number 50261.

Rfn. William Alfred MAYO, 1779

Rifleman William Mayo came from Flackwell Heath in Buckinghamshire and was one of the men recruited by Lieutenant Colonel Rhodes.

Rifleman Mayo was originally listed as missing after the advance on Anafarta Ridge and was later presumed to have been killed during the advance on the 12th August 1915. He was 19 years old and is commemorated on the Helles Memorial.

Rfn. Arthur J. MEADOWS, 2242

Rifleman Arthur Meadows came from High Wycombe and enlisted in the Isle of Wight Rifles on 11th January 1915. He went with the battalion to Gallipoli. Rifleman Meadows was discharged from the Army on 16th September 1916 due to 'sickness' and was given the Silver War Badge.[596]

Rfn. George MEECHAM, 2417

Rifleman George Meecham came from Carisbrooke and enlisted in the Isle of Wight Rifles at Newport. He was reported as missing after the advance on Anafarta Ridge and was later presumed to have been killed during the advance on 12th August

---

[596] www.forces-war-records.co.uk: Silver War Badge List 1914-1918

1915. Rifleman Meecham was 20 years old and is commemorated on the Helles Memorial.

Rfn. Albert Henry MILLER, 2209

Rifleman Albert Miller remained with the Isle of Wight Rifles after Gallipoli and reached the rank of Acting Corporal. He was disembodied from the Army on 3rd August 1919.

Rfn. Frederick Cecil MILLER, 1430

Rifleman Frederick Cecil Miller originally came from East Cowes but later resided in Portsmouth. He was killed in action on 16th August 1915 and is commemorated on the Helles Memorial.

Rfn. Ernest George MILLIGAN, 2451

Rifleman Ernest Milligan continued to serve with the Isle of Wight Rifles after Gallipoli. He was disembodied from the Army on 3rd April 1919 under service number 330844.

Rfn. William Thomas Henry MOGER, 1498

Rifleman William Moger became ill with dysentery and Enteric between the middle of August and early September 1915 and spent a short period of time in hospital on one of the islands close to Gallipoli. He was then moved to a hospital in Egypt for further treatment. Rifleman Moger was then moved *'to another hospital there for treatment for an affection of the ear, due to shell concussion.'*[597]

Prior to falling ill at Gallipoli, Rifleman Moger *'had a very narrow escape of being wounded by a large piece of shrapnel which struck his valise....a piece of the metal is in his father's possession.*[598]

---

[597] Isle of Wight County Press, 27th November 1915, p5
[598] Isle of Wight County Press, 1st January 1916, p5

Rifleman Moger returned to serve with the Isle of Wight Rifles after a period of recuperation at Highfield Red Cross Hospital, Southampton. He remained with the battalion throughout the war and was disembodied from the Army on 1st August 1919 under service number 330269.

Rfn. Edgar MOREY, 1811

Rifleman Edgar Morey joined the Isle of Wight Rifles on 3rd September 1914 with his brother, Sidney Morey. They came from Cowes.

Rifleman Edgar Morey was wounded in the right hand between August and early September 1915 causing him to lose three fingers. He was subsequently classified as medically unfit and was discharged from the Army on 26th November 1915. Rifleman Morey was given the Silver War Badge.[599]

Rifleman Edgar Morey's brother, Sidney, survived the war.

Rfn. Alfred Thomas MORGAN, 1204

Rifleman Alfred Morgan came from Cowes. He took part in the advance on Anafarta Ridge on 12th August 1915 and in a letter to his parents that was published in the Isle of Wight County Press on 9th October 1915 he wrote that he *'brought three snipers out of a tree.'*

Rifleman Morgan was wounded in the foot on 6th September by a piece of shrapnel. He was taken to a hospital in Cairo and then fell ill with tonsillitis. Once back to fitness, Rifleman Morgan rejoined the Isle of Wight Rifles. He was demobbed on 2nd May 1919 with the rank of Sergeant and service number 330124.

---

[599] Isle of Wight County Press, 11th December 1915, p8

Rfn. Henry G. MORGAN, 2296

Rifleman Henry Morgan continued to serve with the Isle of Wight Rifles after Gallipoli. He was disembodied from the Army on 2nd May 1919 under service number 330744.

Rfn. Charles MORRIS, 1686

Rifleman Charles Morris remained with the Isle of Wight Rifles after Gallipoli and was disembodied from the Army on 3rd April 1919 under service number 330383.

Rfn. William George MOWBRAY D.C.M., 2083

Rifleman William Mowbray enlisted in the Isle of Wight Rifles on 12th December 1914. He was awarded two medals for bravery during the war after Gallipoli. The first medal was the Obilitch Medal for Bravery – In Gold, which was confirmed in the Gazette on 15th February 1917.[600] This medal is awarded by Serbia and it suggests that Rifleman Mowbray may have spent time with either the 10th Hants or 12th Hants at Salonika in 1916.

It was confirmed in the Gazette on 26th January 1918 that Rifleman Mowbray had been awarded the Distinguished Conduct Medal for 'gallantry in the field in the face of the enemy.'[601] Unfortunately the record states that he was serving with the Hampshire Regiment but does not identify the battalion he was in. He could have been with the Isle of Wight Rifles or another battalion in the Hampshire Regiment. The citation for his DCM is as follows:

> For conspicuous gallantry and devotion to duty as a stretcher bearer. He displayed the greatest pluck and coolness in helping to rescue the wounded crew of a disabled Tank under heavy shell fire. Although wounded

---

[600] www.forces-war-records.co.uk: Gazetted Awards and Mentions in Despatches – Gazette 15/02/1917, p1611
[601] www.forces-war-records.co.uk: Gazetted Awards and Mentions in Despatches – Gazette 26/01/1918

two days later he remained on duty, setting a splendid example of devotion to all ranks. (26.1.18)[602]

Rifleman Mowbray was discharged from the Hampshire Regiment on 4th November 1918 at the age of 35 under service number 330619 due to illness. He was given the Silver War Badge.[603]

Rfn. James Herbert Denness MUMFORD, 1117

Rifleman James Mumford came from Cowes and enlisted in the Isle of Wight Rifles at Cowes on 13th March 1912. He was 19 years and 10 months old and was working as an apprentice boiler maker.

Rifleman Mumford fell ill at Gallipoli with diarrhoea and haemorrhoids and was admitted into a hospital in Gibraltar during October 1915. He was invalided back to England and was admitted into Beaufort War Hospital in Bristol on 31st October 1915 and after this hospital admission he remained in England until October 1916 with the 2/8th Hants holding the rank of acting Lance Corporal.

On 20th October 1916 James Mumford set sail for Alexandria from Southampton and his rank had reverted back to Rifleman. He re-joined the Isle of Wight Rifles at Suez on 6th November 1916 and took part in the Second Battle of Gaza on 19th April 1917 with the battalion. During the battle he received gunshot wounds to his *'right arm and shoulder'* and consequently spent the next few months in hospitals receiving treatment and

---

[602] www.ancestry.co.uk: UK, Citations of the Distinguished Conduct Medal, 1914-1920: Original data: Walker, R. W., and Chris Buckland, compilers. Citations of the Distinguished Conduct Medal, 1914–1920. 4 sections. Uckfield, East Sussex, United Kingdom: Naval and Military Press, 2007.
[603] www.forces-war-records.co.uk: Silver War Badge List 1914-1918

convalescing. Rifleman Mumford was able to re-join the Isle of Wight Rifles on 13th August 1917.[604]

Rifleman Mumford was discharged from the Army on 14th December 1918 under service number 330081 due to 'sickness' and was given the Silver War Badge.[605]

Rfn. Arthur NEWBERY, 1640

Rifleman Arthur Newbery came from Ventnor and enlisted in the Isle of Wight Rifles on 27th August 1914. He served at Gallipoli and was discharged from the Army on 13th July 1916 due to 'sickness' and given the Silver War Badge.[606]

Rfn. Stanley NEWMAN, 1898

Rifleman Stanley Newman was given service number 330502 when the Territorial Forces received new service numbers. He survived the war.

Rfn. Thomas Walter NEWMAN, 1647

Rifleman Thomas Newman's family came from Mereworth in Kent. However, Rifleman Newman moved to Sandown and enlisted in the Isle of Wight Rifles at Newport.

Rifleman Newman was wounded at Gallipoli and was invalided off the peninsular. He succumbed to his wounds whilst on a hospital ship on 14th August 1915 and was buried at sea.[607] Rifleman Newman was 20 years old and is commemorated on the Helles Memorial.

---

[604] www.ancestry.co.uk: British Army WWI Pension Records 1914-1920 - Territorial Force Attestation
[605] www.forces-war-records.co.uk: Silver War Badge Lists 1914-1918
[606] www.forces-war-records.co.uk: Silver War Badge List 1914-1918
[607] www.ancestry.co.uk: UK, Soldiers Died in the Great War, 1914-1919

Rfn. Charles J. NEWNHAM, 1959

Rifleman Charles Newnham joined the Royal Flying Corps/Royal Air Force later in the war and was given service number 410035. He was transferred to the 'G' Reserve List on 2nd April 1919.

Rfn. William NORTH, 2354

Rifleman William North came from Marlow in Buckinghamshire and was one of the riflemen recruited by Lieutenant Colonel Rhodes. Rifleman North fell ill with Enteric at Gallipoli and as a result died of it on 30th September 1915 whilst he was still at Gallipoli.[608] He was 18 years old. Rifleman North is commemorated on the Helles Memorial as the whereabouts of his grave is unknown.

Rfn. Bertie Harold Reuben OATLEY, 1046

Rifleman Bertie Oatley came from Cowes and enlisted in the Isle of Wight Rifles at Cowes on 28th February 1911 at the age of 17 years and 6 months. His Territorial Force Attestation Papers has limited information on his service but it does record that he landed back in England from his deployment to Gallipoli on 11th November 1915.

Rifleman Oatley was discharged from the Army on 27th February 1916 due to completing his period of service. It was not recorded why Rifleman Oatley returned to England early. He may have been sent home from Gallipoli as his period of service was coming to an end but it is most likely that he was ill or had suffered an injury. It is unlikely that Rifleman Oatley was wounded as this was not recorded.[609]

---

[608] www.ancestry.co.uk: UK, Army Registers of Soldiers' Effects, 1901-1929
[609] www.ancestry.co.uk: British Army WWI Pension Records 1914-1920 – Territorial Force Attestation

Rfn. Charles ORCHARD, 2172

Rifleman Charles Orchard came from Godshill and enlisted in the Isle of Wight Rifles on 4th January 1915 at Newport. He was shot in the right hand during the advance on Anafarta Ridge on the 12th August 1915 and was invalided off Gallipoli.

In December 1915 Rifleman Orchard was attached to the Essex Garrison Battalion in Egypt. He was then transferred to the Essex Regiment as Private and was given service number 34227. Private Charles Orchard served with the Essex Regiment for the rest of the war and his service record states that he joined the Salonica Force on 25th October 1918. He then sailed back to the UK on 9th December 1918.

Private Orchard was discharged from the 3rd Essex on 20th March 1919 due to the effects of his previous wounding and was given the Silver War Badge. The gunshot wound to Charles Orchard's right hand on 12th August 1915 was judged to have caused him a 20% disability and so at the end of the war, he was awarded a weekly pension.[610]

Rfn. Jack PATMORE, 1690

Rifleman Jack Patmore came from Wooburn Green in Buckinghamshire and was one of the men recruited by Lieutenant Colonel Rhodes. He enlisted in the Isle of Wight Rifles on 31st August 1914 at Newport and his brother, Rifleman William Patmore, also joined the battalion.

Rifleman Jack Patmore fell ill with Jaundice at Gallipoli and on 13th November 1915 he was admitted into a hospital in Cairo. He returned to serve with the Isle of Wight Rifles and was transferred to the 163rd Brigade's Machine Gun Corps on 10th August 1916. Jack Patmore remained with this unit until 19th March 1918 when he was posted to the 54th Division's battalion

---

[610] www.ancestry.co.uk: British Army Service Records, 1914-1920

of the Machine Gun Corps. With this unit he held the rank of Driver.

Jack Patmore contracted Malaria on 21st November 1918 and was admitted to the 31st General Hospital in Cairo. He was disembodied from the Machine Gun Corps on 8th May 1919 under service number 50269.[611]

Rfn. William PATMORE, 1689

Rifleman William Patmore came from Buckinghamshire and worked as a gamekeeper. He enlisted in the Isle of Wight Rifles with his brother Rifleman Jack Patmore and they both served at Gallipoli with the battalion.

Rifleman William Patmore remained with the Isle of Wight Rifles throughout the war and was disembodied from the Army on 17th July 1919 under service number 330386.

Rfn. Herbert PEACH, 1010

Rifleman Herbert Peach came from Shanklin and enlisted in the Isle of Wight Rifles at Sandown. He was killed in action on 12th August 1915 during the advance on Anafarta Ridge and is commemorated on the Helles Memorial.

Rfn. Archie Thomas PEPPER, 1781

Rifleman Archie Pepper came from High Wycombe, Buckinghamshire and was one of the men recruited by Lieutenant Colonel Rhodes.

The Isle of Wight County Press on the 18th September 1915 reported that Rifleman Pepper had been wounded at Gallipoli. Rifleman Pepper recovered from his wounds and continued to serve with the Isle of Wight Rifles and was given service number

---

[611] www.ancestry.co.uk: British Army Service Records, 1914-1920

330432. Rifleman Pepper was killed on 19th April 1917 during the Second Battle of Gaza and is buried at Gaza War Cemetery.

Rfn. Walter Percival PERKIN, 1691

Rifleman Walter Perkin was reported to have been wounded at Gallipoli in the Isle of Wight County Press, 18th September 1915 edition.

On recovering from being wounded, Rifleman Perkin returned to serve with the Isle of Wight Rifles. He was disembodied from the Army on 10th April 1919 under service number 330387.

Rfn. Charles Henry PERRIMENT, 1457

Rifleman Charles Perriment came from East Cowes and enlisted in the Isle of Wight Rifles on 11th March 1914. He served at Gallipoli and was discharged from the Army on 16th June 1916 due to 'sickness.' For this Rifleman Perriment was given the Silver War Badge.[612]

Rfn. Stanley J PIERCE, 2412

Rifleman Stanley Pierce served in the Isle of Wight Rifles with his brother Sydney Pierce.

Later in the war, Stanley Pierce transferred to the Royal Engineers and was given service number WR195053 and the rank of Private. He then went on to serve with the Royal Engineer Railway Operating Division under service number 233694 until the end of the war.

Rfn. Sydney Joseph PIERCE, 2414

Rifleman Sydney Pierce came from Newport and enlisted in the Isle of Wight Rifles on 5th May 1915. He and his brother, Rifleman Stanley Pierce, served with the Isle of Wight Rifles at

---

[612] www.forces-war-records.co.uk: Silver War Badge List 1914-1918

Gallipoli. On 17th September 1915, Rifleman Sydney Pierce was admitted to hospital with dysentery.

Rifleman Sydney Pierce was discharged from the Army on 29th July 1916 due to sickness and was given the Silver War Badge.

Rfn. Edward PLUMRIDGE, 1784

Rifleman Edward Plumridge came from Maidenhead, Berkshire and enlisted in the Isle of Wight Rifles at Newport.

Rifleman Plumridge was reported as having been wounded at Gallipoli in the 9th October 1915 edition of the Isle of Wight County Press. Following recovery from his wounds, Rifleman Plumridge returned to serve with the Isle of Wight Rifles and he was promoted to the rank of Lance Corporal. He was given service number 330435 when the Territorial Forces received new service numbers.

Lance Corporal Plumridge was killed in action on 19th April 1917 during the Second Battle of Gaza. He is buried at Gaza War Cemetery.

Rfn. Edwin POPE, 2342

Rifleman Edwin Pope came from High Wycombe. He had his Army medical at Marlow on 21st February 1915 and on 22nd February 1915 he officially enlisted in the Isle of Wight Rifles at Newport.

Rifleman Pope was invalided off Gallipoli due to illness and landed back in England on 16th September 1915. He remained in England until re-joining the Isle of Wight Rifles in Egypt on 5th June 1916. Rifleman Pope was given service number 330775 and took part in the Second Battle of Gaza on 19th April 1917 in which he received a slight wounding.

On 22nd March 1918, Edwin Pope was transferred to the Labour Corps and was given the rank of Private and service number

362665. He developed valvular disease of the heart and was discharged from the Army at Connaught Hospital, Aldershot on 3rd June 1919.[613]

Rfn. S. G. PULLEN, 1108

Rifleman Pullen came from Cowes and enlisted in the Isle of Wight Rifles on 6th March 1912. He took part in the advance on Anafarta Ridge on 12th August 1915 and on the 19th August 1915, he wrote a letter home to his mother which included his experience during the advance on Anafarta Ridge:

> Just after we started into action I got lost, and in company with a few of our fellows found ourselves mixed with the Norfolks. When our regiment was relieved we were left behind, but I cannot speak too highly of the way Lieut. Beck, of the Norfolks, treated us.[614]

Later in the war, Rifleman Pullen joined the Royal Flying Corps/Royal Air Force. He held the rank of Air Mechanic 1st Class with service number 403520 and survived the war.[615]

Rfn. W. PYM, 1785

Rifleman Pym served with the Essex Regiment under service number 34226 following Gallipoli. He was disembodied from the Army on 5th March 1919.

Rfn. William QUANTRILL, 1925

Rifleman William Quantrill came from Newport and enlisted in the Isle of Wight Rifles underage in September 1914. He went through the Gallipoli campaign unscathed until he got frost bite in the big storm at the end of November 1915. In a letter home to his parents on the 12th December 1915 he wrote about his

---

[613] www.ancestry.co.uk: British Army WWI Service Records, 1914-1920
[614] Isle of Wight County Press, 4th September 1915, p6
[615] www.forces-war-records.co.uk: RAF Formations List 1918 - AIR 1/819/204/4/1316

eventful final days at Gallipoli and stated that his fingers were still hurting from the frost bite, making it difficult to write.[616]

On 1st December 1915, when the freeze set in, Rifleman Quantrill succumbed to frost bite in his fingers and feet. He was initially sent to a rest camp for a couple of days and was then admitted in to a Casualty Clearing Station where he spent 4 days. On the fourth day, the Turks shelled the hospital and Rifleman Quantrill managed to escape by crawling out of the hospital to another hospital close by. He then boarded a hospital ship on 7th December 1915 at 7pm which took him to Egypt where he was admitted into No. 5 Canadian Stationary Hospital, Abbassia, Cavalry Barracks, Cairo.[617]

Rifleman Quantrill continued to serve with the Isle of Wight Rifles and was wounded in the thigh during the Second Battle of Gaza. 'He recovered from this but was greatly weakened by attacks of malaria, enteric and relapsing fever.'[618]

Rifleman Quantrill was disembodied from the Army on 24th July 1919 under service number 330519 but unfortunately passed away at the age of 21 on 21st October 1919 after a recurrence of 'malaria and relapsing fever that he contracted on active service.'[619] He is buried at Newport Borough Cemetery.

Rfn. George E. RAYNER, 2435

Rifleman George Rayner joined the Royal Tank Corps later in the war and was given service number 318867. He reached the rank of Lance Sergeant and survived the war.

---

[616] Isle of Wight County Press, 1st January 1916, p5
[617] Isle of Wight County Press, 1st January 1916, p5
[618] Isle of Wight County Press, 25th October 1919 & http://www.isle-of-wight-memorials.org.uk/war-graves/npt/newport_quantrill_wc.htm
[619] Isle of Wight County Press, 25th October 1919

Rfn. Percy H. REED, 2411

Rifleman Percy Reed came from Shanklin. He had his medical for the Isle of Wight Rifles at Sandown Barracks on 2nd May 1915 and officially enlisted in the battalion on 4th May 1915 at Newport. He was 25 years and 8 months old at the time of enlisting.

Rifleman Reed suffered from Heat Stroke at Gallipoli and was admitted to 25th Casualty Clearing Station on 12th September 1915. He was subsequently invalided off Gallipoli and returned to England on 11th November 1915.

Later in the war Percy Reed was transferred to the Cambridgeshire Regiment and was initially given service number 9343. He was then posted to the 2/1st Cambridgeshire Regiment and given service number 330339. On 2nd January 1918 he was posted to the 15th Infantry Base Depot at Etaples and ended up being transferred to the Royal Engineers Transportation Branch on 27th February 1918 as a Pioneer.

Percy Reed served with the Royal Engineers in France and was wounded on 1st June 1918. He recovered from his wounding and was disembodied from the Army on 12th July 1919 under service number 523960.

Rfn. George REEVES, 1786

Rifleman George Reeves enlisted in the Isle of Wight Rifles on 2nd September 1914. He originally came from Buckinghamshire. Rifleman Reeves was wounded and captured by the Turks at Gallipoli and spent the remainder of the war as a Prisoner of War at Psamatice.[620]

---

[620] Research undertaken by Ian Meadows.

Rifleman Reeves was discharged from the Army on 18th March 1919 under service number 330346. His Silver War Badge record states that he was discharged due to his wounding.

Rfn. Charles REID, 1928

Rifleman Charles Reid came from Shide and enlisted in the Isle of Wight Rifles on 4th September 1914. He was invalided off Gallipoli suffering from heat stroke and was taken to a hospital in Cairo.

Rifleman Reid returned to serve in the Hampshire Regiment and was discharged on 15th July 1919 under service number 330521. He was given the Silver War Badge for having been wounded.

Rfn. Leonard Victor RIDDELL, 2463

Rifleman Leonard Riddell was roughly 20 years old when he enlisted in the Isle of Wight Rifles in 1915. He served with the battalion at Gallipoli.

In February 1917 Leonard Riddell began his service in 'C' Company of the 15th (Service) Battalion (2nd Portsmouth) of the Hampshire Regiment on the Western Front. He held the rank of Lance Corporal and was given service number 27788. On 20th April 1917 he fell ill with Pyrexia of unknown origin and was admitted into No. 17 Casualty Clearing Station where he spent 4 days recovering.[621]

The 15th (Service) Battalion (2nd Portsmouth) took part in the Battle of Pilckem Ridge on 31st July 1917. This was the opening phase of the Third Battle of Ypres and the weather quickly deteriorated with heavy rainfall. The ground quickly became waterlogged. Due to these conditions, Lance Corporal fell ill with Trench Fever and on 3rd August 1917 he was admitted into No.

---

[621] www.forces-war-records.co.uk: Military Hospitals Admissions and Discharge Registers WW1 - MH106/167, First World War Representative Medical Records of Servicemen from 139th Field Ambulance

11 Casualty Clearing Station. He spent between the 5th August 1917 and the 19th August 1917 at No. 18 General Hospital in Camieres, France and was then transferred to No. 6 Convalescent Camp.[622]

Lance Corporal Riddell returned to serve with the 15th (Service) Battalion (2nd Portsmouth) and in November 1917 the battalion moved to Italy. At the end of the war Leonard Riddell decided to re-enlist in the Hampshire Regiment and was given service number 01058.

Rfn. Victor ROACH, 1787

Rifleman Victor Roach served with the Isle of Wight Rifles throughout the war and was disembodied from the Army on 8th May 1919 under service number 330437.

Rfn. Edward Morris ROBERTS, 1949

Rifleman Edward Roberts enlisted in the Isle of Wight Rifles on 4th September 1914. He was good friends with Rifleman Coulbert who was also in 'C' Company.

Rifleman Roberts was wounded at Gallipoli and by November 1915, had been admitted into the Military Hospital in Sheffield. An update on Rifleman Roberts' condition was published in the Isle of Wight County Press on 27th November 1915:

> In addition to the wounds in the ear, peck, and the right hand, the injuries have produced paralysis of the arms and one side.[623]

Rifleman Roberts was discharged from the Army on 31st March 1916. His Silver War Badge record states that he was discharged due to sickness.

---

[622] www.forces-war-records.co.uk: Military Hospitals Admissions and Discharge Registers WW1 - MH106/1141 First World War Representative Medical Records of No. 18 General Hospital: 03/08/1917 to 18/08/1917.
[623] Isle of Wight Count Press, 27th November 1915, p5

Rfn. Frank William ROGERS, 2314

Rifleman Frank Rogers was listed in the Isle of Wight County Press on 9th October 1915 as having been wounded at Gallipoli.

After recovering from his wounding, Rifleman Rogers returned to serve with the Isle of Wight Rifles and attained the rank of Lance Corporal. He was disembodied from the Army on 4th April 1919 under service number 330756.

Rfn. Owen ROGERS, 1693

Rifleman Owen Rogers came from Little Marlow in Buckinghamshire and enlisted in the Isle of Wight Rifles at Newport. He was one of the men recruited by Lieutenant Colonel Rhodes.

Rifleman Rogers continued serving with the Isle of Wight Rifles and was killed in action during the Second Battle of Gaza on 19th April 1917. He is commemorated on the Jerusalem Memorial and his service number was 330389.[624]

Rfn. Percy ROLF, 2413

Rifleman Percy Rolf and his brother Rifleman Charles Rolf came from Newport. Both went to Gallipoli with the Isle of Wight Rifles. Rifleman Percy Rolf enlisted in the Isle of Wight Rifles on 5th May 1915, but his brother, Rifleman Charles Rolf had served in the battalion before the outbreak of war.

Rifleman Percy Rolf was reported to have been wounded in the Isle of Wight County Press on 4th September 1915. It is likely that he was wounded during the fighting at Anafarta Ridge. Rifleman Percy Rolf re-joined the Isle of Wight Rifles but was discharged from the Army on 29th July 1916 due to sickness and was given the Silver War Badge. His brother, Rifleman Charles

---

[624] www.ancestry.co.uk: UK, Soldiers Died in the Great War, 1914-1919

Rolf had been killed in action on 12th August 1915 during the advance on Anafarta Ridge.

Rfn. Bernard Thorne ROLFE, 1961

Rifleman Bernard Rolfe came from Shanklin. He was initially reported to have been wounded on 12th August 1915 during the advance on Anafarta Ridge and was later presumed to have been killed on 12th August 1915. Rifleman Rolfe is commemorated on the Helles Memorial.

Rfn. Charles William RUSSELL, 2154

Rifleman Charles Russell served with the Isle of Wight Rifles throughout the war and survived the war. His latter service number was 330664.

Rfn. Arthur Victor SALMON M.M., 2031

Rifleman Arthur Salmon enlisted in the Isle of Wight Rifles on 4th December 1914 at the Drill Hall in Newport. He came from Havenstreet and was 18 years old. His brother, Rifleman Hector Salmon, also served with the Isle of Wight Rifles and both of them survived the war.

Rifleman Arthur Salmon was wounded at Gallipoli in the arm, head and chest by a Turkish bomb on 2nd September 1915 which caused him to have a deterioration in the sight of his right eye. Rifleman Salmon was invalided off Gallipoli and admitted into Hamrun Military Hospital, Malta for further treatment. He re-joined the battalion on 27th December 1915 at Sidi Bishr, Alexandria.[625]

Rifleman Salmon was awarded the Military Medal for his role as a signaller during the Second Battle of Gaza and was also promoted to the rank of Lance Corporal. He was then posted to the Imperial School of Instruction at Zeitoun as a Signalling

---

[625] www.ancestry.co.uk: Cover for Discharge Document

Instructor on 28th August 1917 with the temporary rank of Corporal. On the 13th September 1918, Arthur Salmon was transferred to the 20th Corps Signalling School at Zeitoun under the rank of Lance Corporal and on 5th December 1918 he was posted back to the Isle of Wight Rifles.

Lance Corporal Salmon was discharged from the Army on 5th May 1919 under service number 330587. He was awarded the Silver War Badge and a gratuity of £70 due to the damage to his right eye from the wounding on 2nd September 1915. He was not given an Army Pension because it was deemed that he did not have a permanent disability.

Rfn. Edward SAUNDERS, 2375

Rifleman Edward Saunders came from Ryde. At some point after his deployment to Gallipoli, Rifleman Saunders was posted to the 3/8th Hants, a reserve battalion of the Isle of Wight Rifles and when the Territorial Forces received new service numbers, he was given service number 330797. Edward Saunders was later transferred to the Oxfordshire and Buckinghamshire Light Infantry and served in the 2/1st Buckinghamshire battalion as a Private with service number 285106.[626]

Edward Saunders was killed in action on 22nd August 1917 during the Third Battle of Ypres at the age of 19. He has no known grave and is commemorated at Tyne Cot Memorial.

Rfn. Ernest SAUNDERS, 2368

Rifleman Ernest Saunders joined the Isle of Wight Rifles in March 1915. He fell ill at Gallipoli with diarrhoea and was

---

[626] www.ancestry.co.uk: UK, WWI Service Medal and Award Rolls, 1914-1920 - British War Medal and Victory Medal

admitted on to H.M.A.T Ship Assaye on 3rd October 1915. He was 17 years old at the time.[627]

Rifleman Saunders returned to serve with the Isle of Wight Rifles. He was disembodied from the Army on 21st August 1919 under service number 330792.

Rfn. Frederick SCOTT, 1587

Rifleman Frederick Scott came from Shanklin. He was wounded at Gallipoli during August 1915. In a letter to his father published in the Isle of Wight County Press on the 2nd October 1915 he wrote that *'he was struck on the head with shrapnel, causing severe concussion and was afterwards shot in the leg.'* He received further treatment to his wounds at a hospital in Egypt and during this time he fell ill with Enteric which led to him leaving Mustapha Reception Hospital on 6th November 1915 for England.

Later in the war Rifleman Scott reached the rank of Sergeant with the Machine Gun Corps. He was disembodied from the Army on 19th March 1919 under service number 102779.

Rfn. Reginald George Washington SCRIVENER, 1713

Rifleman Reginald Scrivener served with the Isle of Wight Rifles at Gallipoli and was discharged from the battalion on 14th January 1916.

Reginald Scrivener re-enlisted into the 1st battalion of the Royal Warwickshire Regiment and was given service number 38568. He was later transferred to the 12th Battalion of the Royal Irish Rifles and was given service number 12/52457. Both of these battalions fought on the Western Front.

---

[627] www.forces-war-records.co.uk: Military Hospitals Admissions and Discharge Registers WW1 - MH106/1913, First World War Representative Medical Records of H.M.A.T Ship Assaye: 02/10/1915 - 11/10/1915

Reginald Scrivener survived the war.

Rfn. Harold William SEARLE, 1962

Rifleman Harold Searle came from Shanklin. He was reported to be missing in action in the Isle of Wight County Press on 11th September 1915 and was later presumed to have been killed during the advance on Anafarta Ridge on 12th August 1915. Rifleman Searle was 21 years old and is commemorated on the Helles Memorial.

Rfn. William Augustus SHARPE, 1289

Rifleman William Sharpe came from Shanklin and enlisted in the Isle of Wight Rifles at Sandown. He was 21 years old when he was killed in action on 10th September 1915. Rifleman Sharpe is buried at 7th Field Ambulance Cemetery, Gallipoli.

Rfn. Albert SHEATH, 2034

Rifleman Albert Sheath came from Whitwell and enlisted in the Isle of Wight Rifles on 5th December 1914. At Gallipoli during August 1915, he was wounded in his right eye and was subsequently taken prisoner and held at Constantinople.

Rifleman Sheath was discharged from the Army on 13th June 1919 under service number 330589. He received the Silver War Badge for his wounding.

Rfn. Charles Henry SHEATH, 1695

Rifleman Charles Sheath deployed to Gallipoli with the Isle of Wight Rifles. Later in the war he was transferred to the Labour Corps and was discharged from the Army on 28th November 1917 under service number 190398.

Rfn. William SILSBURY, 1697

Rifleman William Silsbury came from Bradbury. He continued to serve with the Isle of Wight Rifles after Gallipoli and was given service number 330390 when the Territorial Forces received new service numbers.

Rifleman Silsbury took part in the Second Battle of Gaza on 19th April 1917. He was initially reported as wounded and missing and was later found to have been taken prisoner by the Turks during the battle.[628] Rifleman Silsbury was held as a prisoner of war at Bab Toulma Hospital in Damascus. He was disembodied from the Army on 12th March 1919.

Rfn. Frank George SLADE, 1048

Rifleman Frank Slade came from Cowes and enlisted in the Isle of Wight Rifles on 28th February 1911 at the age 17 years and 3 months. He served throughout the Isle of Wight Rifles' deployment to Gallipoli and left with the battalion to Egypt. Rifleman Slade departed Egypt for England on 11th February 1916 and was discharged from the Army on 10th March 1916 for completing his service period.[629]

Rfn. Stanley Arthur SMALL, 2295

Rifleman Stanley Small came from High Wycombe. He had his Army medical at Marlow on 23rd January 1915 and officially enlisted in the Isle of Wight Rifles on 25th January 1915 at Newport. He was 19 years and 5 months old.

On 30th August 1915 *'while at Gallipoli Rifleman Small slipped, extending his right knee.'*[630] He was subsequently invalided off Gallipoli to Egypt. Whilst still with an injured knee, Rifleman Small fell ill with tonsillitis and was admitted to the Red Cross Hospital at Giza on 19th September. On 19th December 1915 Rifleman Small was transferred to a Convalescent Camp at

---

[628] www.forces-war-records.co.uk: First World War Daily Reports (Missing, Wounded & Prisoner of War) - War Office Daily List No.5344, 22/08/1917
[629] www.ancestry.co.uk: British Army WWI Pension Records 1914-1920 – Territorial Force Attestation
[630] www.ancestry.co.uk: British Army WWI Pension Records 1914-1920 – Territorial Force Attestation

Luxor with Synovitis of the Right Knee and on 3rd March 1916 he was admitted to the Hospital at Boulac Palace in Cairo. Following his stay at Boulac Palace, Rifleman Small embarked on Hospital Ship Nevasa on 25th April 1916 to return to England. On returning to England, he was admitted to the London General Hospital at Wandsworth.

Rifleman Small was examined by an Army Medical Board on 24th August 1916 due to having Synovitis of the Right Knee. He had previously spent 12 months *'with a bad limp'* but could now walk. However, he was deemed to be medically unfit for further military service. Rifleman Small was discharged from the Army on 8th September 1916 and given an Army Pension along with the Silver War Badge.[631]

Rfn. Leonard James SOUTHAM, 1699

Rifleman Leonard Southam came from Little Marlow in Buckinghamshire and was one of the men recruited by Lieutenant Colonel Rhodes. Rifleman Southam continued to serve with the Isle of Wight Rifles after Gallipoli and was given service number 330392 when the Territorial Forces received new service numbers. He was killed in action on 19th April 1917 at the age of 27 during the Second Battle of Gaza and is commemorated at the Jerusalem Memorial.[632]

Rfn. Robert James SOTHCOTT, 1446

Rifleman Robert Sothcott came from Sandown and attested in the Isle of Wight Rifles on 18th February 1914 when he was 17 years and 8 months old. His British Army pension record states that he was wounded at Gallipoli on 19th October 1915:

---

[631] www.ancestry.co.uk: British Army WW1 Pension Records 1914-1920 – Territorial Force Attestation
[632] www.forces-war-records.co.uk: Soldiers Died in the Great War 1914-1919

A piece of shrapnel caused a flesh wound over the right patella. It did not penetrate the joint but caused some internal damage.[633]

Whilst Rifleman Sothcott was at hospital with his knee wound, he became ill with enteric and had to be invalided back to England. He arrived in England on 5th April 1916 and was posted to the 4th Reserve Battalion on 10th July 1916.

On 1st January 1917 Rifleman Sothcott was transferred to the 17th Hants. He was still suffering with knee trouble and went before a Medical Board on 19th January 1917 where he was found to be medically unfit:

> The knee joint is slightly swollen and there is some evidence of fluid in the joint. The leg cannot be fully extended. He complains of pain at the back of leg.[634]

Rifleman Sothcott was discharged from the Army on 2nd February 1917 as a result of the damage to his knee and was given the Silver War Badge. At a later Medical Board, it was decided that Rifleman Sothcott was not incapacitated and on 6th November 1917 he was awarded a £15 gratuity.

Rfn. Frederick SPANNER, 1820

Rifleman Frederick Spanner was reported as having been wounded at Gallipoli in the 16th October 1915 edition of the Isle of Wight County Press. Following his recovery, he was transferred to the Suffolk Regiment and given service number 243140. Later on, in the war Frederick Spanner joined the Royal Engineers as a Pioneer and was given service number 527504. On 19th March 1919 he was placed on the Z Reserve list.

---

[633] www.ancestry.co.uk: British Army WW1 Pension Records 1914-1920
[634] www.ancestry.co.uk: British Army WW1 Pension Records 1914-1920

Rfn. Charles SPRAGG, 1431

Rifleman Charles Spragg was serving in the Isle of Wight Rifles at the outbreak of war. He was wounded at Gallipoli, most likely during the advance on Anafarta Ridge on 12th August 1915, but possibly on the 10th or 11th August 1915. On 13th August 1915, Rifleman Spragg sent a field service postcard from hospital stating that he was in hospital wounded.

Rifleman Spragg continued to serve with the Isle of Wight Rifles and was disembodied from the Army on 26th February 1919 under service number 330241.

Rfn. Richard SQUIBB, 2095

Rifleman Richard Squibb served with the Isle of Wight Rifles throughout the war and survived the war. His latter service number was 330628.

Rfn. Percy STAMP, 1642

Rifleman Percy Stamp came from Shanklin and enlisted in the Isle of Wight Rifles at Newport. He continued to serve with the battalion after Gallipoli and was given service number 330350 when the Territorial Forces received new service numbers.

Rifleman Stamp died of wounds on 7th November 1917. He was probably wounded during the Third Battle of Gaza. He is buried at Gaza War Cemetery.

Rfn. William STANTON, 1162

Rifleman William Stanton served with the Isle of Wight Rifles throughout the war. He was disembodied from the Army on 12th August 1919 under service number 330102.

Rfn. Charles STARK, 1720

Rifleman Charles Stark was wounded during the Anafarta Ridge offensive. He was invalided off Gallipoli on a hospital ship destined for Malta but died during the voyage on 14th August 1915. He is commemorated on the Helles Memorial.

Rfn. Joseph STARK, 1721

Rifleman Joseph Stark came from Horsham, Sussex and enlisted in the Isle of Wight Rifles in Newport. He was reported missing after the advance on Anafarta Ridge and a number of months later was presumed to have been killed in action on 12th August 1915. Rifleman Stark is commemorated on the Helles Memorial.

Rfn. William STRANGE, 2208

Rifleman William Strange served with the Isle of Wight Rifles throughout the war. He was disembodied from the Army on 2nd August 1919 under service number 330696.

Rfn. Ernest Hedley SYMES, 1754

Rifleman Ernest Symes came from Chichester and enlisted in the Isle of Wight Rifles at Newport. His brother, Lance Corporal Leonard Symes also served with the Isle of Wight Rifles at Gallipoli.

Rifleman Ernest Symes was initially reported as missing in the Isle of Wight County Press on 25th September but it was later realised that he had been killed in action on 22nd August 1915. Rifleman Symes was 19 years old and is commemorated on the Helles Memorial. His brother was discharged from the Army on 25th October 1916.

Rfn. Reginald William THOMPSON, 2425

Rifleman Reginald Thompson came from West Cowes. He continued to serve with the Isle of Wight Rifles after Gallipoli and was given service number 330827 when the Territorial Forces received new service numbers. Rifleman Thompson was 19 years old when he was killed in action during the Second

Battle of Gaza on 19th April 1917.[635] He has no known grave and is commemorated on the Jerusalem Memorial.

Rfn. Owen TREVETT, 1094

Rifleman Owen Trevett came from Cowes and was serving in the Isle of Wight Rifles when war broke out.

Rifleman Trevett's parents received news of his death by a letter from Chaplain-Captain the Reverend J C L Blamires (NZ Armed Forces). The letter was subsequently published in the Isle of Wight County Press on 25th September 1915. Chaplain-Captain the Reverend J C L Blamires stated that *'Rifleman Trevett was carrying water and a stray bullet shot him through the chest'* about 8.30pm on Friday 3rd September.[636] Chaplain-Captain the Reverend J C L Blamires grabbed his surgical bag and rushed up the hill to attend to Rifleman Trevett. On reaching Rifleman Trevett, a couple of New Zealand soldiers were already with him and two minutes later, Rifleman Trevett passed away.

Rifleman Trevett was buried the next morning with the Burial Service having been led by Chaplain-Captain the Reverend J C L Blamires. However, despite having been buried, Rifleman Trevett has no known grave. He was 20 years old and is commemorated on the Helles Memorial.

Rfn. Raymond TRINDER, 1952

Rifleman Raymond Trinder came from Lake and enlisted in the Isle of Wight Rifles at Sandown. He was reported as missing after the advance on Anafarta Ridge and was later presumed to have been killed on 12th August 1915 during the advance. Official notification of his death was published in the Isle of Wight County Press on 29th July 1916. Rifleman Trinder has no known grave and is commemorated on the Helles Memorial.

---

[635] www.forces-war-records.co.uk: Soldiers Died in the Great War 1914-1919
[636] Isle of Wight County Press, 25th September 1915.

Rfn. William TRUEMAN, 1572

Rifleman William Trueman served at Gallipoli with his brother Rifleman Edmund Trueman. William fell ill and was invalided off Gallipoli during September 1915 and returned to England to be treated at London General Hospital.

Later in the war, Rifleman William Trueman was transferred to the 1/4th Hants. In 1918 the 1/4th Hants were deployed to Persia from the Middle East. Rifleman William Trueman survived the war and was demobilised from the Army on 30th August 1919. His brother, Edmund, was killed on 19th April 1917 during the Second Battle of Gaza.

Rfn. Percy TWITCHEN, 1702

Rifleman Percy Twitchen came from Little Marlow in Buckinghamshire and was one of the men recruited by Lieutenant Colonel Rhodes. Rifleman Twitchen continued serving with the Isle of Wight Rifles after Gallipoli and was given service number 331550. His previous service numbers were 1702 and 8/3536.

Rifleman Twitchen was killed in action during the Second Battle of Gaza on 19th April 1917. He has no known grave and is commemorated on the Jerusalem Memorial.

Rfn. Thomas TWITCHEN, 1788

Rifleman Thomas Twitchen was invalided off Gallipoli on 9th October 1915 and spent between the 15th October and the 20th December 1915 at a hospital in Malta. It is unknown if he was wounded or ill. He returned to serve with the Isle of Wight Rifles on 29th December 1915 and remained with the battalion until the 15th October 1917.

On 16th October 1917, Rifleman Twitchen was posted to the 21st Rifle Brigade who were also part of the Egyptian Expeditionary Force. He was given service number 212095. The 21st Rifle

Brigade were deployed to India and arrived in India on 1st October 1918. Rifleman Twitchen served with this battalion in India until 25th October 1919.[637]

Rfn. Edgar TYZACK, 2278

Rifleman Edgar Tyzack and his brother Rifleman Albert Tyzack came from Wycombe Marsh in Buckinghamshire and were recruited to the Isle of Wight Rifles by Lieutenant Colonel Rhodes. Both were killed in action on 12th August 1915 during the advance on Anafarta Ridge and are commemorated on the Helles Memorial.

Rfn. Charles Reginald WATKINS, 1789

Rifleman Charles Watkins came from Wooburn Green, Buckinghamshire. He was one of Lieutenant Colonel Rhodes' recruits. Rifleman Watkins was wounded during the advance on Anafarta Ridge on 12th August 1915 and subsequently died of his wounds on the same day. He was 19 years old and is commemorated on the Helles Memorial.[638]

Rfn. William Comerford WATSON, 2299

Rifleman William Watson continued to serve with the Isle of Wight Rifles after Gallipoli and was given service number 330746. He was Discharged to Commission on 15th April 1917 and became a Second Lieutenant in the Durham Light Infantry. William Watson then went on to join the RAF and became a Lieutenant. He survived the war.

---

[637] www.ancestry.co.uk: UK, WWI Service Medal and Award Rolls, 1914-1920 - British War Medal and Victory Medal
[638] Commonwealth War Graves Commission: https://www.cwgc.org/

Rfn. Edward James WATTS, 1761

Rifleman Edward James Watts was also known Jim Watts. He came from Cowes and was 44 years old when he enlisted in the Isle of Wight Rifles on 2nd September 1914 at Newport.

Rifleman Watts received a gunshot wound to his right thigh on 12th August 1915 during the attack on Anafarta Ridge. He was invalided off Gallipoli and was admitted to No. 19 General Hospital in Alexandria. Rifleman Watts returned to England on 12th November 1915 and received further treatment at Sutton Coldfield General Hospital.

On recovering from his wounding, Rifleman Watts was posted to the 1/6th Hants and given service number 281821. He spent from the 22nd September 1916 to 26th October 1919 in India and was discharged from the Army on 22nd December 1919. Rifleman Watts was given an Army pension due to the long-term effects of his wounding at Gallipoli.[639]

Rfn. Harold WAVELL, 1545

Rifleman Harold Wavell came from Lake and enlisted in the Isle of Wight Rifles at Newport. He continued to serve with the Isle of Wight Rifles after Gallipoli. He reached the rank of Sergeant and was latterly given service number 330294.

Harold Wavell was killed in action during the Second Battle of Gaza on 19th April 1917. He was 27 years old and is buried at Gaza War Cemetery.

Rfn. Leonard Victor WEEKS, 1912

Rifleman Leonard Weeks continued to serve with the Isle of Wight Rifles after Gallipoli. He was disembodied from the Army on 22nd February 1919 under service number 330511.

---

[639] www.ancestry.co.uk: British Army WWI Pension Records 1914-1920 – Cover for Discharge Documents

Rfn. Eric Harold WHEELER, 1630

Rifleman Eric Wheeler served at Gallipoli and later in the war he was transferred to the Machine Gun Corps where he reached the rank of Corporal.

Corporal Eric Wheeler was admitted to No. 3 Casualty Clearing Station with Pyrexia of unknown origin on 9th October 1918 and on 11th October 1918 he was admitted to No. 20 Ambulance Train. At the time, he was serving with the 21st Battalion of the Machine Gun Corps in France.[640]

Corporal Wheeler was disembodied from the Army on 10th April 1919 under service number 106228.

Rfn. Thomas WHEELER, 1793

Rifleman Thomas Wheeler served with the Isle of Wight Rifles throughout the war and was disembodied from the Army on 4th July 1919 under service number 330440.

Rfn. Archibald Thomas WHITE, 2393

Rifleman Archibald White served with the Isle of Wight Rifles throughout the war and was disembodied from the Army on 7th August 1919 under service number 330810.

Rfn. Edward WHITE, 1790

Rifleman Edward White was transferred to the Machine Gun Corps at some point after his deployment to Gallipoli and reached the rank of Lance Sergeant. He was disembodied from the Army on 4th April 1919 under service number 50255.

---

[640] www.forces-war-records.co.uk: Military Hospitals Admissions and Discharge Registers WW1 - MH106/382, First World War Representative Medical Records of Servicemen from No. 3 Casualty Clearing Station

Rfn. George WHITE, 1821

Rifleman George White served with the Isle of Wight Rifles throughout the war and reached the rank of Corporal. He was disembodied from the Army on 18th April 1919 under service number 330456.

Rfn. George WHITE, 2304

Rifleman George White came from Brading and enlisted in the Isle of Wight Rifles at Sandown on 1st February 1915. He was wounded in his left shoulder by a piece of shrapnel on 4th September 1915 and was invalided off Gallipoli, returning to England on 25th September 1915. Rifleman White was discharged from the Army on 11th August 1916 as he was deemed to be *'no longer fit for military service'* and was given the Silver War Badge.[641]

Rfn. Horace WHITE, 1792

Rifleman Horace White enlisted in the Isle of Wight Rifles on 2nd September 1914. He served at Gallipoli and was discharged from the Army on 8th September 1916 due to 'sickness' and as a result of this was given the Silver War Badge.[642]

Rfn. John William WHITE, 1791

Rifleman John White came from Wooburn in Buckinghamshire and enlisted in the Isle of Wight Rifles at Newport. He was one of the men recruited by Lieutenant Colonel Rhodes. Rifleman White reached the rank of Lance Sergeant and was killed in action during the Second Battle of Gaza. He was 23 years old at the time and his service number was 330439. He is buried at Gaza War Cemetery.[643]

---

[641] www.ancestry.co.uk: British Army WWI Pension Records 1914-1920 – Territorial Force Attestation
[642] www.ancestry.co.uk: UK, Silver War Badge Records, 1914-1920
[643] https://www.cwgc.org/find-war-dead/casualty/651645/white,-john-william/

Rfn. Gilbert WHITTINGTON, 1813

Rifleman Gilbert Whittington came from Arreton. He was listed as missing in the 11th September 1915 edition of the Isle of Wight County Press and official notification of his death was published in the Isle of Wight County Press on 29th July 1916. Rifleman Whittington had been killed in action on 12th August 1915 during the advance on Anafarta Ridge. He has no known grave and as a result of this, he is commemorated on the Helles Memorial.

Rfn. Arthur WHY M.M., 1795

Rifleman Arthur Why was transferred to the Machine Gun Corps at some point after his deployment to Gallipoli. He reached the rank of Lance Corporal and for his actions with the Machine Gun Corps he was awarded the Military Medal. Arthur Why was disembodied from the Army on 6th May 1919.

Rfn. Harry Leonard WILLIAMS, 1624

Rifleman Harry Williams served with the Isle of Wight Rifles throughout the war. He was disembodied from the Army on 5th May 1919 under service number 330340.

Rfn. William Leslie WILLIS, 1394

Rifleman William Willis enlisted in the Isle of Wight Rifles on 7th January 1914. He remained with the battalion after Gallipoli and was given service number 330218 when the Territorial Forces received new service numbers. Rifleman Willis was discharged from the Army on 14th December 1918 at the age of 22 years due to 'wounds' and was given the Silver War Badge.[644]

Rfn. Victor Ralph WINDSOR, 2207

Rifleman Victor Windsor was transferred to the 1/4th Hants at some point after his service at Gallipoli and was given service number 281823. The 1/4th Hants operated in Mesopotamia and

---

[644] www.forces-war-records.co.uk: Silver War Badge List 1914-1918

towards the end of the war in Persia. After the war Victor Windsor continued to serve with the Hampshire Regiment under service number 06003.

Rfn. Frank Harry WOLFE, 2223

Rifleman Frank Wolfe came from Ryde and enlisted in the Isle of Wight Rifles at Newport. He continued to serve with the battalion after Gallipoli, was given service number 330706 and reached the rank of Corporal. Frank Wolfe was killed in action at the age of 27 during the Second Battle of Gaza on 19th April 1917. He is commemorated on the Jerusalem Memorial.[645]

Rfn. Edward WOODLEY, 2353

Rifleman Edward Woodley came from High Wycombe in Buckinghamshire and enlisted in the Isle of Wight Rifles at Newport on 1st March 1915. He was 16 years old at the time and went on to serve with the battalion at Gallipoli. Rifleman Woodley was discharged from the Army on 31st December 1915 for being underage.

Edward Woodley re-enlisted into the Hampshire Regiment at the age of 18 on 6th March 1917 at High Wycombe. On 20th December 1917 he embarked a transport ship at Southampton for France and on 23rd December 1917 he joined 'C' Infantry Base Depot at Rouen. He was transferred to the 7th battalion of the Somerset Light Infantry on Christmas Day and joined the battalion in the field on 27th December 1917.

Edward Woodley was wounded by a bayonet in his right thigh on 10th May 1918. On recovering from this wound he was posted to the 2/4th battalion of the Somerset Light Infantry on 3rd July 1918 and by March 1919 he had been transferred to the 51st battalion of the Hampshire Regiment who were part of the Occupation Forces of the Rhineland.

---

[645] www.ancestry.co.uk: UK, Commonwealth War Graves, 1914-1921 and 1939-1947

On 5th May 1919, Edward Woodley re-enlisted into the Oxfordshire and Buckinghamshire Light Infantry at Suppelback and became a cook with the battalion. He was discharged from the Army on 31st March 1921.[646]

Rfn. Albert Walter WRIGHT, 1576

Rifleman Albert Wright enlisted in the Isle of Wight Rifles on 11th August 1914. He served at Gallipoli and was discharged from the Army on 18th August 1916 due to 'sickness' and as a result was awarded the Silver War Badge.[647]

Rfn. G. WRIGHT, 1794

Rifleman Wright served with the Isle of Wight Rifles at Gallipoli. Later in the war he joined the Royal Flying Corps/Royal Air Force and was given service number 410286. He survived the war.

Rfn. William George YOUNG, 1916

Rifleman William Young came from Nettlestone and enlisted in the Isle of Wight Rifles at Newport. He was killed in action on 8th October 1915 at the age of 26 and is buried at the 7th Field Ambulance Cemetery, Gallipoli.[648]

---

[646] www.ancestry.co.uk: British Army WWI Service Records, 1914-1920 – Record of Service
[647] www.forces-war-records.co.uk: Silver War Badge List 1914-1918
[648] https://www.cwgc.org/find-war-dead/casualty/605740/young,-william-george/

'D' Company

CSM. Frank FIELDER, 653

Company Sergeant Major Frank Fielder came from Winchester and enlisted in the Isle of Wight Rifles at East Cowes. He was reported as missing after the action on 12th August 1915 and was later presumed to have died on 12th August 1915 during the advance on Anafarta Ridge. He was 29 years old and is commemorated on the Helles Memorial.

CQMS. Bertie CLARK D.C.M., 86

Company Quartermaster Sergeant Bertie Clark continued to serve with the Isle of Wight Rifles after Gallipoli and was given service number 330009. He was promoted to the rank of Temporary Sergeant Major on 5th February 1917.[649]

Bertie Clark received a Mention In Despatches which was published in the London Gazette on 15th January 1918:

> The Officer has been brought to the notice of the Secretary of State for War by General Sir Edmund Allenby, G.M.C.G., K.C.B., Commanding in Chief, Egyptian Expeditionary Force, for distinguished service in the connection with military operations under his command.[650]

He was also awarded the Distinguished Conduct Medal. The citation for his award was published in the London Gazette on 9th March 1919:

---

[649] www.forces-war-records.co.uk: UK Army List 1918
[650] www.forces-war-records.co.uk: Gazetted Awards and Mentions in Despatches – London Gazette, 15/01/1918, p933

For continuous good work and devotion to duty. He has frequently shown coolness and ability in action.[651]

Bertie Clark was disembodied from the Army on 1st August 1919.

Sgt. Harry GREEN, 125

Sergeant Harry Green was wounded around 8.30pm on 12th August 1915 by a bullet which had hit his left shoulder, passed through it and exited under his ear. By midnight he had been taken back to the Field Dressing Station where he spent the night lying on a stretcher. He was then taken to the beach to be evacuated and was subjected to Turkish shelling of the beach. Sergeant Green was put on a hospital ship headed for Lemnos. Unfortunately, the ship caught fire so he was transferred to the Franconia which sailed to England. On return to England, he was admitted to Hyde Park Hospital in Plymouth.

Sergeant Green was later transferred to the Labour Corps and remained as a Sergeant under service number 491136. He was disembodied from the Army on 16th April 1919.

Sgt. Reginald GROVES, 758

Sergeant Reginald Groves came from East Cowes and had served with the Isle of Wight Rifles prior to the outbreak of war. It was reported in the Isle of Wight County Press on 29th July 1916 that Sergeant Groves was *'a smart soldier and was much respected.'*[652]

Sergeant Groves was killed in action on 12th August 1915 during the advance on Anafarta Ridge and official notification of his death was published in the Isle of Wight County Press on 29th July 1916. He was 24 years old and he is commemorated on the Helles Memorial.

---

[651] www.forces-war-records.co.uk: Gazetted Awards and Mentions in Despatches – London Gazette, 09/03/1919, p11106
[652] Isle of Wight County Press, 29th July 1916, p4

Sgt. Percy Reginald HOBBS, 1154

Sergeant Percy Hobbs came from Cowes and enlisted in the Isle of Wight Rifles on 11th June 1912. He was part of the machine gun section at Gallipoli. Sergeant Hobbs was wounded in the trenches at Gallipoli on 8th September 1915 by a piece of shrapnel hitting his left thigh and was taken to Floriana Hospital in Malta for further treatment.

Sergeant Hobbs returned to serve with the Isle of Wight Rifles and was discharged from the battalion on 16th April 1919. His Silver War Badge record states that his discharge was due to a wounding.

Sgt. Frederick George JACOBS, 1410

Sergeant Frederick Jacobs enlisted in the Isle of Wight Rifles on 19th January 1914. He served with the Isle of Wight Rifles at Gallipoli and remained with the battalion throughout the war.

Sergeant Jacobs was discharged from the Army on 14th Mary 1919 due to 'sickness.' He was 26 years old and his service number at the time was 330228.[653]

Sgt. Henry William JENNING, 1232

Sergeant Henry Jenning was transferred to the 1st Garrison Battalion of the Devonshire Regiment later in the war. This battalion performed garrison duties in Egypt and then Palestine. Henry Jenning was given service number 51174 and reached the rank of Company Quartermaster Sergeant. After the war he re-joined the Isle of Wight Rifles as a Company Quartermaster Sergeant and his service number was 5488609.

---

[653] www.forces-war-records.co.uk: Silver War Badge List 1914-1918

Sgt. Frederick John LEFTWICH, 747

Sergeant Frederick Leftwich came from Cowes. He was 6 foot 5 inches tall and was the 'champion heavy-weight boxer of the regiment.'[654]

Sergeant Leftwich was killed on 12th August 1915 during the advance on Anafarta Ridge and official notification of his death was published in the Isle of Wight County Press on 29th July 1916. He is commemorated on the Helles Memorial.

Sgt. Maurice MATTHEWS D.C.M., 1683

Sergeant Maurice Matthews continued serving with the Isle of Wight Rifles after Gallipoli and on 11th January 1918 it was published in the London Gazette that Sergeant Matthews had received a Mention in Despatches on 28th June 1917, along with a number of other personnel, *'for gallant or distinguished conduct in the Field of for other valuable services.'*[655] Sergeant Matthews was also later awarded the Distinguished Conduct Medal.[656]

Sergeant Matthews was disembodied from the Army on 3rd April 1919 under service number 330380.

Sgt. David Darcy PALMER, 74

Sergeant David Palmer came from Ryde and enlisted in the Isle of Wight Rifles at Ryde on 6th April 1908. He was 39 years and 9 months old and his full-time employment was as a School Attendance Officer for Isle of Wight County Council.

Sergeant Palmer made it through the Gallipoli campaign without being wounded or becoming seriously ill. He was promoted to

---

[654] Isle of Wight County Press, 29th July 1916, p4
[655] www.forces-war-records.co.uk: Gazetted Awards and Mentions in Despatches - London Gazette Issue 30474, 11/01/1918, p800
[656] www.forces-war-records.co.uk: Gazetted Awards and Mentions in Despatches - London Gazette 18/02/1918

the rank of Temporary Acting Company Quartermaster Sergeant on 26th November 1915 and he set sail with the battalion to Alexandria where he was then promoted to the rank of Company Sergeant Major on 22nd December 1915.

On 5th March 1916, Company Sergeant Major David Palmer joined the 54th Infantry Base Depot and on 25th March 1916 he embarked on H.T. Huntsend for England. Company Sergeant Major Palmer was discharged from the Army on 28th April 1916 due to completing his period of service. He had served with the Isle of Wight Rifles for 8 years and 23 days and on discharge was 48 years old.[657]

Sgt. Frank RUSSELL, 685

Sergeant Frank Russell served with the Isle of Wight Rifles at Gallipoli and was discharged from the Army on 18th February 1916.

L/Sgt. William Charles AUBREY, 132

Lance Sergeant William Aubrey was 21 years old when he enlisted in the Isle of Wight Rifles on 8th April 1908 at East Cowes. He had previously served with the 5th Volunteer Battalion of the Hampshire Regiment, the predecessor of the Isle of Wight Rifles. He worked for Ratsey and Lapthorne as a Sailmaker.

Lance Sergeant Aubrey made it through the Gallipoli campaign without being wounded or becoming seriously ill and went with the battalion to Alexandria. He returned to England on 14th April 1916 and was discharged from the Army on 28th April 1916 for having completed his period of service.[658]

---

[657] www.ancestry.co.uk: British Army WWI Pension Records 1914-1920 - Proceedings on Discharge and Territorial Force Attestation.
[658] www.ancestry.co.uk: British Army WWI Pension Records 1914-1920 – Territorial Force Attestation

L/Sgt. Alfred Gwynne JONES, 748

Lance Sergeant Alfred Jones came from Cowes. By the time of the landings at Gallipoli he was a Sergeant. Sergeant Jones was one of the 50 men from 'D' company who had been tasked with guarding the 54th Division's Head-Quarters from 10th August 1915 until 14th August 1915. He therefore, missed the advance on Anafarta Ridge on 12th August 1915.

Sergeant Jones continued to serve with the Isle of Wight Rifles after their Gallipoli campaign and reached the rank of Company Quartermaster Sergeant. His latter service number was 330040. On 2nd April 1918 he was Discharged to Commission and became a Second Lieutenant in the Egyptian Labour Corps and went on to survive the war.

Cpl. Walter ARNOLD, 504

Corporal Walter Arnold enlisted in the Isle of Wight Rifles on 7th January 1909. After the attack on Anafarta Ridge, he was initially reported as missing. He had however, been wounded by a bullet in his right leg and taken prisoner. He spent his captivity in Tachapa Hospital in Constantinople. At the end of the war, he was released and on returning to England was discharged from the Army on 12th December 1918 under service number 330034. He received the Silver War Badge due to his wounds.

Cpl. Alfred ATTRILL, 250

Corporal Alfred Attrill came from Whitwell. He was reported to be in Queen Mary's Military Hospital, Whalley, along with five other members of the Isle of Wight Rifles in the Isle of Wight County Press on 1st January 1916. However, it is was not reported if had been wounded at Gallipoli or had fallen ill.

Corporal Attrill was killed in action during the Second Battle of Gaza on 19th April 1917. He was 29 years old and is buried at Gaza War Cemetery.

Cpl. Thomas CHIVERTON, 446

Corporal Thomas Chiverton remained with the Isle of Wight Rifles after Gallipoli and was promoted to the rank of Sergeant. He was discharged from the Army on 28th February 1918 at the age of 31 years due to sickness and was given the Silver War Badge. His latter service number was 330028.[659]

Cpl. Robert Bernard Vince JACOBS, 202

Corporal Robert Jacobs enlisted in the Isle of Wight Rifles on 4th June 1908. He became sick at Gallipoli and during October 1915 was admitted to a hospital in Cairo. He was then invalided home to England and spent time at the County of London War Hospital in Epsom.

Corporal Jacobs continued to serve with the Isle of Wight Rifles throughout the rest of the war. He was discharged from the Army on 9th April 1919 under service number 330014 and the rank of Lance-Sergeant. His Silver War Badge record states that he was discharged due to sickness.

Cpl. Thomas George OLIVER, 1375

Corporal Thomas Oliver joined the Isle of Wight Rifles in 1913. He was wounded and *'taken prisoner at Kaba Tépé on August 12th.'*[660] He received treatment at a hospital in Constantinople then spent his time as a prisoner at Bile Medik.

Corporal Oliver was disembodied from the Army on 25th March 1919 under service number 330204.

Cpl. James Gibson SWINTON, 2185

Corporal James Swinton continued to serve with the Isle of Wight Rifles after Gallipoli. He was Discharged to Commission on 28th February 1917 and became a Second Lieutenant in the 4th

---

[659] www.ancestry.co.uk: UK, Silver War Badge Records, 1914-1920
[660] Isle of Wight County Press, 11th September 1915, p8

battalion of the Black Watch (Royal Highlanders). He was killed in action on 25th March 1918 during the German Spring Offensive and is commemorated on the Pozieres Memorial.

Cpl. Douglas Frank SPARKS, 1060

Corporal Douglas Sparks enlisted in the Isle of Wight Rifles at Cowes and had been in the battalion for a number of years prior to deploying to Gallipoli.

Corporal Sparks was initially reported as missing and later presumed to have been killed in action on 12th August 1915. He was 20 years old and is commemorated on the Helles Memorial.

L/Cpl. Percy William BOXALL, 2015

Lance Corporal Percy Boxall came from Newport. He was hit by a piece of shrapnel at Gallipoli on 12th September 1915. He was sent to a hospital in Malta for further treatment and then to a hospital in Portsmouth.

Lance Corporal Boxall returned to serve with the Isle of Wight Rifles and was disembodied from the battalion on 31st July 1919 under service number 330578.

L/Cpl. Ernest Henry CAWS, 777

Lance Corporal Ernest Caws came from East Cowes. He continued to serve with the Isle of Wight Rifles after Gallipoli and reached the rank of Sergeant with service number 330041. He was killed in action at the age of 37 during the Second Battle of Gaza on 19th April 1917 and is buried at Gaza War Cemetery.

L/Cpl. John Thomas COLEMAN, 2315

Lance Corporal John Coleman was reported in the Isle of Wight County Press on 12th February 1916, to have been wounded. It is likely that he was wounded towards the end of the Isle Wight

Rifle's Gallipoli deployment. He was also reported as holding the rank of Sergeant.[661]

John Coleman reached the rank of Company Sergeant Major with the Isle of Wight Rifles and he served with the battalion until 26th July 1918 when he was transferred to the 19th (Western) Rifle Brigade who were in Egypt. By September 1918, Company Sergeant Major Coleman 212260, was back in England, in Falmouth, with the 25th Rifle Brigade.[662] [663] [664]

L/Cpl. John COOK, 468

Lance Corporal John Cook enlisted in the Isle of Wight Rifles at Wroxhall. He was promoted to the rank of Corporal in August 1915. According to the diary of an officer in the Isle of Wight Rifles which was printed in the Isle of Wight County Press on 25th September 1915, Corporal Cook was killed by a sniper whilst in the trenches on the 3rd September 1915. A letter from Captain Marsh to Corporal Cook's wife notifying her of her husband's death was also published in the Isle of Wight County Press on 25th September 1915. In the letter, Captain Marsh described Corporal Cook as one of his 'best NCOs.'

Corporal Cook is buried at 7th Field Ambulance Cemetery, Turkey.

L/Cpl. Harold KINGSWELL, 78

Lance Corporal Harold Kingswell continued serving with the Isle of Wight Rifles after Gallipoli. At the end of the war he held the rank of Acting Sergeant and his service number was 330008.

---

[661] Isle of Wight County Press, 12th February 1916, p5
[662] www.ancestry.co.uk: British War Medal and Victory Medal Records
[663] www.ancestry.co.uk: British Army WWI Medal Rolls Index Cards, 1914-1920
[664] http://www.longlongtrail.co.uk/army/regiments-and-corps/the-british-infantry-regiments-of-1914-1918/the-rifle-brigade-1914-1918/

L/Cpl. Frank LE BRUN, 2092

Lance Corporal Frank Le Brun came from Wimbledon but chose to enlist in the Isle of Wight Rifles at Newport as some of his relatives resided on the Isle of Wight. He enlisted on 15th December 1914 and on 25th January 1915 was promoted to Lance Corporal.[665]

Lance Corporal Le Brun received serious head wounds at Gallipoli and was invalided off the peninsular. He succumbed to his wounds whilst on a hospital ship on 14th August 1915 and was buried at sea.[666] He was 27 years old and is commemorated on the Helles Memorial.

L/Cpl. Augustus Ernest LONG, 1483

Lance Corporal Augustus Long enlisted in the Isle of Wight Rifles at Wroxhall on 4th August 1914. He undertook transport work at Gallipoli and during the latter part of the campaign was *'attached to 4th Co. A.S.C., Anzac.'*[667]

On 14th December 1915, Lance Corporal was admitted into the 21st General Hospital, Alexandria and was reported to be dangerously ill with dysentery and by 1st January 1916 was deemed to be out of danger. He returned to England and was admitted into the 2n Western General Hospital, Manchester on 1st February 1916. The severe illness resulted in Lance Corporal being discharged from the Army on 30th August 1916.[668]

L/Cpl. Charles Leonard MAYBEE, 427

Lance Corporal Charles Maybee served with the Isle of Wight Rifles at Gallipoli with his brother Rifleman William Maybee. Lance Corporal Charles Maybee continued serving with the Isle of Wight Rifles throughout the war and was promoted to the rank

---

[665] http://www.isle-of-wight-memorials.org.uk/people-npt/npt_le_brun_f.htm
[666] www.ancestry.co.uk: UK, Soldiers Died in the Great War, 1914-1919
[667] Isle of Wight County Press, 4th March 1916, p8
[668] www.ancestory.co.uk: British Army WWI Pension Records 1914-1920

of Sergeant. He was demobilised from the Army on 20th August 1919 under service number 330027. His brother, William, was discharged from the Army on 18th August 1916 due to ill health as a result of falling ill with dysentery at Gallipoli.

L/Cpl. Norman Lansdowne RUSSELL, 1459

Lance Corporal Norman Russell came from Gurnard and enlisted in the Isle of Wight Rifles on 26th March 1914. He was one of the battalion's machine gunners at Gallipoli and was wounded on the 3rd September 1915 by a shrapnel bullet which hit his right shoulder, breaking the collar bone and lodging itself in his left breast. Lance Corporal Russell was invalided off Gallipoli and taken to the 19th General Military Hospital in Alexandria, Egypt.

On 29th January 1916, the Isle of Wight County Press reported that Lance Corporal Russell was at a convalescent home in Croydon and that he had recovered his sight and speech following the wounding, but still required assistance with walking.[669]

Lance Corporal Russell was discharged from the Army on 4th October 1916 due to sickness and was given the Silver War Badge.

L/Cpl. Alfred SALMON, 1906

Lance Corporal Alfred Salmon had served with the Isle of Wight Rifles for 8 years before the Gallipoli campaign. He was originally reported as missing after the advance on Anafarta Ridge but it transpired that he had been killed on 12th August 1915 during that fateful attack and official notification of his death was published in the Isle of Wight County Press on 29th July 1916. He was 32 years old. Like so many of his comrades, he is commemorated on the Helles Memorial.

---

[669] Isle of Wight County Press, 29th January 1916, p5

L/Cpl. Arthur Ernest TOSDEVIN, 1979

Lance Corporal Tosdevin was reported as having been wounded and missing after participating in a patrol on 7th November 1915. He was later presumed to have died of his wounds on the 7th November 1915. Lance Corporal Tosdevin's body was not found and so he is commemorated on the Helles Memorial.

Prior to confirmation of Lance Corporal Tosdevin's death, The Isle of Wight County Press reported the following regarding Lance Corporal Tosdevin on 11th December 1915:

> He was first wounded through the shoulder. He was also in hospital with jaundice, but he recovered, and had been back in the trenches about a month, when he was wounded again.[670]

L/Cpl. John WOOLLINGS, 1493

Lance Corporal John Woollings served with the Isle of Wight Rifles at Gallipoli. He was promoted to Corporal and went on to serve with the 2/8th Hants under service number 330268. At some point during 1917/1918, John Woollings was transferred to the 5th battalion of the Royal Berkshire Regiment where he fought on the Western Front. He was disembodied from the Army on 26th February 2019 under the rank of Lance Sergeant and service number 220784.[671]

Bugler Albert Alfred Harding DENNIS, 1085

Bulger Albert Dennis came from Ventnor. He continued serving with the Isle of Wight Rifles after Gallipoli and was given service number 330066. Albert Dennis was killed in action on 19th April

---

[670] Isle of Wight County Press, 11th December 1915, p8
[671] www.ancestry.co.uk: UK, WWI Service Medal and Award Rolls, 1914-1920 - British War Medal and Victory Medal

1917 during the Second Battle of Gaza and is buried at Gaza War Cemetery.[672]

Bugler John Richard HOWELL, 1082

Bugler John Howell served with the Isle of Wight Rifles throughout the war and was disembodied from the Army on 16th August 1919 under service number 330064.

Bugler William Daniel PAYNE, 1059

Bugler William Payne came from Cowes and enlisted in the Isle of Wight Rifles on 24th May 1911 at the age of 16. He made it through the Gallipoli campaign without being wounded or becoming seriously ill and went with the battalion to the Alexandria. William Payne returned to England on 17th May 1916 and was discharged from the Army on 26th May 1916 after having completed his service period.[673]

Bugler Arthur THEARLE, 1989

Bugler Arthur Thearle served with the Isle of Wight Rifles throughout the war and was disembodied from the Army on 3rd April 1919 under service number 330556.

Rfn. William ABBOTT, 219

Rifleman William Abbott came from Gurnard and enlisted in the Isle of Wight Rifles at East Cowes. He was originally recorded as missing after the attack on Anafarta Ridge and later on was presumed to have been killed on 12th August 1915 during the advance. He was 29 years old and is commemorated on the Helles Memorial.

---

[672] https://www.cwgc.org/find-war-dead/casualty/649882/dennis,-albert-alfred-harding/
[673] www.ancestry.co.uk: British Army WWI Pension Records 1914-1920 – Territorial Force Attestation

Rfn. Frederick Cecil ADBY, 2387

Rifleman Frederick Cecil Adby came from West Wycombe and enlisted in the Isle of Wight Rifles on 20th April 1915. He was discharged from the Army under service number 330804 on 3rd August 1919 due to a wounding and was given the Silver War Badge. He was 23 years old at the time of being discharged from the Army.[674]

Rfn. Harold ARNOLD, 1081

Rifleman Harold Arnold came from Ventnor and enlisted in the Isle of Wight Rifles at the age of 18 on 9th November 1911. He fell ill with dysentery on 6th November 1915 and was invalided off Gallipoli to Egypt for treatment at Benha Government Hospital where he was admitted on 9th November 1915. On 26th December 1915, Rifleman Arnold began his journey back to England from Alexandria via Mudros.

Rifleman Arnold was discharged from the Army on 22nd September 1916 due to the lasting effects that dysentery had on his health. He was given the Silver War Badge and an Army Pension.[675]

Rfn. Thomas Frank ARNOLD, 1980

Rifleman Thomas Arnold came from Newport. He was presumed to have been killed on 12th August 1915 during the advance on Anafarta Ridge and official notification of his death was published in the Isle of Wight County Press on 29th July 1916. Rifleman Arnold was 18 years old and he is commemorated on the Helles Memorial. His father, Thomas, was serving in the 2/8th Hants whilst Rifleman Arnold was at Gallipoli.

---

[674] www.ancestry.co.uk: UK, Silver War Badge Records, 1914-1920
[675] www.ancestry.co.uk: British Army WWI Pension Records 1914-1920 - Territorial Force Attestation

Rfn. Harry Edwin BAKER, 1549

Rifleman Harry Baker was wounded in the leg by a piece of shrapnel during August 1915 at Gallipoli.

On returning to fitness, Rifleman Baker re-joined the Isle of Wight Rifles and served with them throughout the rest of the war. He was disembodied from the Army on 16th July 1919 under service number 330295.

Rfn. Frederick BARRETT, 2018

Rifleman Frederick Barrett enlisted in the Isle of Wight Rifles on 2nd December 1914. He fell ill with dysentery at Gallipoli between the middle of September and the beginning of October 1915 and was initially taken to a hospital in Malta. He was then invalided back to England, arriving on the 15th October 1915.

Rifleman Barrett was later transferred to the 2/4th Hants and given service number 205457. He served in India with the 2/4th Hants from the 24th October 1916 until the 27th April 1917 and then went with the 2/4th Hants to fight in the Palestinian campaign which the Isle of Wight Rifles were also involved in. The 2/4th Hants last battle in Palestine was in April 1918 and on 22nd May 1918 the battalion left Egypt for France. However, on the 24th May 1918 Rifleman Barrett was back in the United Kingdom and assigned to the Royal Defence Corps. He was given service number 94954 and the rank of Private.

Frederick Barrett's Silver War Badge record states that he was discharged from the Army on 25th February 1919 due to wounds so he was presumably wounded during the Palestinian campaign and as a result of this was then transferred to the Royal Defence Corps as at the time there was a critical manpower crisis in light of the costly German Spring Offensive.

Rfn. James BARTLETT, 1994

Rifleman James Bartlett came from St. Helens and enlisted in the Isle of Wight Rifles at Sandown. He was reported as having been wounded at Gallipoli in the Isle of Wight County Press' 2nd October 1915 edition.

Rifleman Bartlett returned to serve with the Isle of Wight Rifles and was given service number 330561 when the Territorial Forces received new service numbers. Rifleman Bartlett was killed in action during the Second Battle of Gaza on 19th April 1917 and is commemorated on Jerusalem Memorial.

Rfn. Frank BAX, 1432

Rifleman Frank Bax enlisted in the Isle of Wight Rifles at Cowes. He was in the battalion's machine gun section at Gallipoli and took part in the advance on Anafarta Ridge. Within a few weeks' later, Rifleman Bax had fallen seriously ill with dysentery. He passed away on 29th September 1915 whilst on a hospital ship and was buried at sea. Rifleman Bax is commemorated on the Helles Memorial.

Rfn. William George BEALE, 2245

Rifleman William Beale served with the Isle of Wight Rifles throughout the war and was demobilised from the Army on 7th March 1919 under service number 330718.

Rfn. John William BELL, 1433

Rifleman John Bell came from Cowes and enlisted in the Isle of Wight Rifles on 6th January 1914. He fell ill with dysentery at Gallipoli and was admitted to The General Hospital in Gibraltar on 15th October 1915. Rifleman Bell was then invalided back to England and spent between the 7th November 1915 and 31st December 1915 in The Beaufort War Hospital, Bristol.

Rifleman Bell was transferred to the 22nd Rifle Brigade and posted on to the 2nd Garrison Battalion of the King's Liverpool Regiment with whom he deployed to Salonika on 23rd January 1917. Whilst at Salonika, Rifleman Bell contracted Malaria and as a result spent time at 43rd General Hospital in Salonika. On recovering, he returned to his unit in Salonika and remained in Salonika into 1919. He was disembodied from the Army on 26th April 1919.[676]

Rfn. Walter Ernest BEST, 1581

Rifleman Walter Best was reported in the 16th October 1915 edition of the Isle of Wight County Press as having been wounded at Gallipoli. He returned to serve with the Isle of Wight Rifles and was disembodied from the battalion on 19th July 1919 under service number 330308.

Rfn. Richard John BETTENSON, 2405

Rifleman Richard Bettenson came from Ryde. He was killed in action during the Second Battle of Gaza on 19th April 1917 at the age of 19 and is commemorated on the Jerusalem Memorial. His latter service number was 330818.[677]

Rfn. Robert BILK, 928

Rifleman Robert Bilk came from Cowes and joined the Isle of Wight Rifles in 1910. He was listed as missing after the advance on Anafarta Ridge and later presumed to have been killed during the action on 12th August 1915. He was 23 years old and is commemorated on the Helles Memorial.

---

[676] www.ancestry.co.uk: British Army WWI Service Records, 1914-1920 - Cover for Discharge Documents
[677] www.forces-war-records.co.uk: Soldiers Died in the Great War 1914-1919

Rfn. George BIRD, 2311

Rifleman George Bird was transferred to the Machine Gun Corps (Cavalry) after Gallipoli and was given service number 135125. He survived the war.

Rfn. Malcolm Harry BISHOP, 2404

Rifleman Malcolm Bishop enlisted in the Isle of Wight Rifles on 29th April 1915. He was given service number 330817 when the Territorial Forces received new service numbers and was later transferred to the 2nd Hants. Rifleman Bishop was discharged from the Army on 26th February 1919 at the age of 22 due to 'wounds' and was given the Silver War Badge.[678]

Rfn. E. L. BLAKE, 1464

Rifleman Blake enlisted in the Isle of Wight Rifles on 22nd April 1914. Later in the war he volunteered for the Royal Flying Corps and became a carpenter. His rank was Air Mechanic 3rd Class and his service number was 405887. He survived the war.[679]

Rfn. Woodford BLYTHE, 1998

Rifleman Woodford Blythe was transferred to the Labour Corps later in the war and was given service number 361017. He was disembodied from the Army on 31st August 1919.

Rfn. Alfred Henry BRETT, 1412

Rifleman Alfred Brett served with the Isle of Wight Rifles throughout the war and was disembodied from the Army on 4th August 1919 under service number 330230.

Rfn. Archibald F. BRETT, 1878

Rifleman Archibald Brett enlisted in the Isle of Wight Rifles during September 1914 at the age of 22. He was invalided off

---

[678] www.ancestry.co.uk: UK, Silver War Badge Records, 1914-1920
[679] www.forces-war-records.co.uk: RAF Formations List 1918 - AIR 1/819/204/4/1316

Gallipoli in early November 1915 on Hospital Ship Galeka with *'cellulitis of the thigh'* and was admitted into No. 19 General Hospital in Alexandria on 10th November 1915. He was then sent to the Convalescent Depot at Mustapha on 16th November 1915.[680]

Later in the war, Archibald Brett was transferred to the Machine Gun Corps and given service number 50252. He reached the rank of Sergeant and was disembodied from the Army on 22nd April 1919.

Rfn. William BRINE, 1807

Rifleman William Brine became ill at Gallipoli at the end of the Isle of Wight Rifles' deployment to Gallipoli. He was invalided off Gallipoli on 8th December 1915 after escaping from a hospital that had come under Turkish shell fire and seeking refuge at a neighbouring hospital. Rifleman Brine then spent time at hospital in Abbassia, Cairo.[681]

Rifleman Brine was discharged from the Army on 14th November 1916 due to sickness and was awarded the Silver War Badge.

Rfn. Reginald BROWN, 2442

Rifleman Reginald Brown received a gunshot wound to his arm at Gallipoli during August 1915 and was taken to a hospital in Alexandria, Egypt for treatment. After recovering from the wounding, Rifleman Brown was temporarily attached to the 1st London RAMC based in Egypt. In a letter home to a friend in Cowes, published in the Isle of Wight County Press on 25th December, he wrote:

> My wound has healed, although the doctor now tells me I have the bullet in the bone of my arm. I have left the

---

[680] www.forces-war-records.co.uk: Military Hospitals Admissions and Discharge Registers WW1 - First World War Representative Medical Records of No. 19 General Hospital: 29/10/1915 to 21/11/1915, MH106/1228

[681] Isle of Wight County Press, 12th February 1916, p5

I.W. Rifles, for a time at least, and am at present attached to the R.A.M.C. The section I am with has to do with the different camps around these parts and keep them in sanitary condition. I can assure the work is far more congenial than up in the Peninsula endeavouring to dodge bullets and shells.[682]

Rifleman Brown returned to serve with the Isle of Wight Rifles and reached the rank of Corporal. He was disembodied from the Army on 8th August 1919 under service number 330837.

Rfn. William Eli BRUNSDEN, 2433

Rifleman William Brunsden came from Marlow in Buckinghamshire and was born in 1900. He enlisted in the Isle of Wight Rifles on 17th May 1915 and at the time was either 14 or 15 years old.

Rifleman Brunsden fell ill with diarrhoea at Gallipoli and was admitted to No. 5 Canadian Stationary Hospital at Cairo on 4th October 1915. He re-joined the Isle of Wight Rifles at Alexandria on 30th January 1916.

On 11th August 1916 and 31st August 1916, Rifleman Brunsden's mother wrote to the Territorial Forces Record Office in Exeter requesting that her son be released from the Army as he was underage. She enclosed his birth certificate to prove that he was born in 1900. The Army duly agreed to discharge Rifleman Brunsden for being underage and on 14th October 1916 he boarded HT Caledonia to return to England. Rifleman Brunsden was formally discharged from the Army on 8th November 1916.[683]

---

[682] Isle of Wight County Press, 25th December 1915, p5
[683] www.ancestry.co.uk: British Army WWI Pension Records 1914-1920 - Territorial Force Attestation

Rfn. Ernest Stuart BUCKETT, 2429

Rifleman Ernest Buckett served with the Isle of Wight Rifles at Gallipoli and was discharged from the Army on 7th January 1916. He was awarded the Silver War Badge but records do not state whether it was due to a wounding or sickness.

Ernest Buckett re-joined the Army later in the war and served with the Royal West Kent Regiment as a Private under service numbers G/20954, L/13102 and 6335283. He survived the war and received the India General Service Medal with the North West Frontier Force Clasp.[684]

Rfn. Ernest John BUNDY, 2227

Rifleman Ernest Bundy enlisted in the Isle of Wight Rifles on 11th January 1915. He was invalided off Gallipoli between the middle of August and early September 1915 due to having a fever and was brought back to the 4th General Hospital at Denmark-Hill.

Rifleman Bundy was discharged from the Army on 16th September 1916 owing to sickness and was awarded the Silver War Badge.

Rfn. Henry Evelyn BURTON, 1822

Rifleman Henry Burton came from Newport. He is presumed to have been killed at Gallipoli on 12th August 1915 during the advance on Anafarta Ridge. He was 21 years old and is commemorated on the Helles Memorial.

Rfn. Charles BUTCHERS, 1538

Rifleman Charles Butchers came from Whitwell. He enlisted in the Isle of Wight Rifles on 8th August 1914. In the Isle of Wight County Press on 11th December 1915, Rifleman Butchers was

---

[684] www.ancestry.co.uk: British Army WWI Medal Rolls Index Cards, 1914-1920

reported to be in hospital but it was not clarified if he had been wounded or was sick.

Rifleman Butchers was discharged from the Army on 15th December 1916 due to sickness and was given the Silver War Badge.

Rfn. Harry Trevor CARLEY, 467

Rifleman Harry Carley enlisted in the Isle of Wight Rifles on 18th December 1908 and served with the battalion throughout the war. He was discharged from the Army at the age of 29 on 15th July 1919 under service number 330031. His Silver War Badge record states that he was discharged from the Army due to 'sickness.'[685]

Rfn. Walter Frank CASSELL, 1663

Rifleman Walter Cassell came from Niton and enlisted in the Isle of Wight Rifles at Newport on 31st August 1914 at the age 22. He had previously served with a Territorial Unit of the Royal Field Artillery for 4 years.[686]

Rifleman Cassell did not sail with the Isle of Wight Rifles to Gallipoli on the Aquitania. Instead, he sailed from Devonport on 28th July 1915 aboard HMT Minatou and did not join up with the Isle of Wight Rifles until the 9th December when they were at Mudros. Rifleman Cassell then sailed with the battalion to Alexandria.

On 30th December 1916, Rifleman Cassell was kicked in the right knee by a horse and was admitted into 26th Stationary Hospital in Ismailia. He re-joined the Isle of Wight Rifles at Moascar on 25th January 1917 and then suffered with Shell Shock between late March and the middle of April 1917 and spent time at the 36th

---

[685] www.forces-war-records.co.uk: Silver War Badge List 1914-1918
[686] www.ancestry.co.uk: British Army WWI Service Records, 1914-1920- Territorial Force Attestation

Stationary Hospital at Mohamydia. Rifleman Cassell was *'discharged to duty'* on 13th April 1917.

Rifleman Cassell went before a medical board at Kanatara on 10th June 1917 and was diagnosed with having flat feet. He was subsequently transferred to the 21st Rifle Brigade on 22nd July 1917 and given service number 211760. Walter Cassell was then transferred to the Labour Corps on 27th September 1917 and was given service number 357692.

Walter Cassell fell ill with influenza and on 23rd July 1918 was admitted to the 21st General Hospital in Alexandria where he spent 4 days recovering. He was transferred to the Royal Army Service Corps on 9th October 1918 and was posted to Remount Depot at Kantara. He was discharged from the Army on 4th July 1919 and applied for an Army Pension as he was suffering with his right knee.[687]

Rfn. Bertram CAVE, 1262

Rifleman Bertram Cave continued to serve with the Isle of Wight Rifles after Gallipoli and was given service number 330149 when the Territorial Forces received new service numbers. At some point in 1917/1918, Bertram Cave transferred to the Royal Engineers and worked on the railways for the remainder of the war. He held the rank of Sapper and his service numbers were 521664 followed by WR/194510.

Rfn. George Alfred CAWSTON, 1589

Rifleman George Cawston enlisted in the Isle of Wight Rifles with his brother Herbert Cawston. They both fought at Gallipoli. Their sequential service numbers suggest that they joined the battalion together on the same day.

---

[687] www.ancestry.co.uk: British Army WWI Pension Records 1914-1920 - Cover for Discharge Documents

Rifleman George Cawston had to be invalided back to England due to dysentery. He had recovered by the beginning of December and was posted to Parkhurst Barracks. His brother, Herbert, died of wounds at Gallipoli on 25th November 1915 and is commemorated on the Helles Memorial.

At some point during the war, Rifleman Cawston was transferred to the Labour Corps and given service number 140707 and the rank of Private. He was discharged from the Labour Corps on 4th February 1919.

Rfn. Herbert CAWSTON, 1590

Rifleman Herbert Cawston enlisted in the Isle of Wight Rifles with his brother Herbert Cawston. Their sequential service numbers suggest that they joined the battalion together on the same day. Herbert is recorded as having enlisted at Niton, Isle of Wight.[688]

Both Herbert and George went to Gallipoli with the Isle of Wight Rifles. George was taken ill with dysentery and returned to England. Herbert died of his wounds at Gallipoli on 25th November 1915. At the end of the war his body was not recoverable so Rifleman Herbert Cawston is commemorated on the Helles Memorial. His brother, George, survived the war.

Rfn. Fred CHARLO, 2397

Rifleman Fred Charlo served with the Isle of Wight Rifles throughout the war. He was disembodied from the Army on 5th September 1919 under service number 330813.

Rfn. Andrew Thomas CHEESMAN, 1883

Rifleman Andrew Cheesman came from Newport and enlisted in the Isle of Wight Rifles at Newport. He was reported as missing after the advance on Anafarta Ridge on 12th August 1915 and was

---

[688] www.ancestry.co.uk: UK, Soldiers Died in the Great War, 1914-1919

number 144955. William Corbyn remained with the Labour Corps for the rest of the war and was placed on the reserve list on 27th March 1919.[689]

Rfn. Harry CORNEY, 2093

Rifleman Harry Corney came from Newport and joined the Isle of Wight Rifles shortly after the outbreak of war. Early in the Isle of Wight Rifles' Gallipoli campaign, he was hospitalised due to sunstroke.

Rifleman Corney continued serving with the Isle of Wight Rifles and was latterly given service number 330626. He was killed on 19th April 1917 during the Second Battle of Gaza and is buried at Gaza War Cemetery.

Rfn. Godfrey COTTON, 1591

Rifleman Godfrey Cotton was transferred to the Royal Field Artillery, Territorial Forces, at some point after the Isle of Wight Rifle's deployment to Gallipoli. He became a Gunner and was given service number 851546. Godfrey Cotton survived the war.

Rfn. Frederick Henry COX, 2062

Rifleman Frederick Cox was one of the men from Buckinghamshire recruited by Lieutenant Colonel Rhodes. He was captured by the Turks at Gallipoli and spent his time as a Prisoner of War at Afion.

Rifleman Cox was disembodied from the Army on 11th March 1919 under service number 330607.

Rfn. Thomas CREASY, 2217

Rifleman Thomas Creasy enlisted in the Isle of Wight Rifles on 9th January 1915. He served with the battalion at Gallipoli and

---

[689] www.ancestry.co.uk: British Army WWI Service Records, 1914-1920 – Territorial Force Attestation

later in the war he was transferred to the Labour Corps and given service number 246616. Thomas Creasy was discharged from the Army on 29th March 1919 due to 'sickness' and was given the Silver War Badge.[690]

Rfn. Walter CROUCH, 1263

Rifleman Walter Crouch enlisted in the Isle of Wight Rifles on 1st March 1913 at the age of 33 years and 8 months. He had previously spent one and a half years with the 5th Volunteer Battalion of the Hampshire Regiment.

Rifleman Crouch did not serve overseas with the Isle of Wight Rifles and instead remained with the 2/8th Hants, the reserve battalion of the Isle of Wight Rifles. Rifleman Crouch was discharged from the Army on 23rd May 1916 due to bronchitis and was given the Silver War Badge.[691]

Rfn. Francis Henry James DAMP, 1884

Rifleman Francis Damp came from Newport. He was invalided off Gallipoli suffering from debility and was admitted into a hospital in Cairo in November 1915.

Rifleman Damp returned to serve with the Isle of Wight Rifles and was given service number 330495 when the Territorial Forces received new service numbers. On 21st July 1917, Francis Damp was Discharged to Commission and became a Second Lieutenant in the 4th Hants for the remainder of the war.

Rfn. Sidney Charles DAY, 1519

Rifleman Sidney Day came from Basingstoke and enlisted in the Isle of Wight Rifles at Newport on 6th August 1914. He was 20 years old.

---

[690] www.ancestry.co.uk: Silver War Badge Records, 1914-1920
[691] www.ancestry.co.uk: British Army WWI Pension Records 1914-1920 – Territorial Force Attestation

Rifleman Day was wounded at Gallipoli in his left knee by shrapnel on 1st October 1915 and was invalided off the peninsular. He landed back in England on 9th November 1915 and was discharged from the Army on 26th May 1916 due to the effects of his wounding. He was given the Silver War Badge and an Army pension.[692]

Rfn. Albert George DELLAR, 1967

Rifleman Albert Dellar continued to serve with the Isle of Wight Rifles after Gallipoli. He rose up the ranks to Sergeant and was given service number 330543.

Sergeant Albert Dellar was reported as having been wounded in the War Office Daily List on 28th November 1917. It is likely that he was wounded during the Third Battle of Gaza.[693] On recovering from his wounding, Albert Dellar returned to serve with the Isle of Wight Rifles and was promoted to the rank of Warrant Officer Class II. Towards the end of the war, Albert Dellar was transferred to the King's Royal Rifle Corps holding the same rank and with service number 52686.

Rfn. Edwin DENTON, 1983

Rifleman Edwin Denton remained with the Isle of Wight Rifles after Gallipoli and was given service number 330553. He was wounded, most likely during the Third Battle of Gaza, and this was reported in the War Office Daily List on 28th November 1917.[694]

Rifleman Denton was disembodied from the Army on 30th July 1919.

---

[692] www.ancestry.co.uk: British Army WWI Pension Records 1914-1920 – Territorial Force Attestation
[693] www.forces-war-records.co.uk: First World War Daily Reports (Missing, Wounded & Prisoner of War) - War Office Daily List No.5428, 28/11/1917, NLS 1917_WList18
[694] www.forces-war-records.co.uk: First World War Daily Reports (Missing, Wounded & Prisoner of War) - War Office Daily List No.5428, 28/11/1917, NLS 1917_WList18

Rfn. Walter Thomas DIBBENS, 2038

Rifleman Walter Dibbens enlisted in the Isle of Wight Rifles at Newport. He continued serving with the Isle of Wight Rifles after Gallipoli and was killed in action during the Second Battle of Gaza on 19th April 1917. His service number at the time was 330592. Rifleman Dibbens is buried at Gaza War Cemetery.

Rfn. Albert Victor DIMMER, 1223

Rifleman Albert Dimmer served with Isle of Wight Rifles throughout the war and reached the rank of Sergeant with service number 330133. Albert Dimmer re-enlisted in the Isle of Wight Rifles after the war and remained as a Sergeant. He was given service number 5488440.

Rfn. George Edwin DIMMER, 2301

Rifleman George Dimmer came from Longdown and enlisted in the Isle of Wight Rifles at Newport. He was killed in action at Gallipoli on 20th October 1915 and is buried at the 7th Field Ambulance Cemetery.[695]

Rfn. Reginald DIMMICK, 1966

Rifleman Reginald Dimmick came from Freshwater. He was one of the many members of the Isle of Wight Rifles who became ill with dysentery at Gallipoli and by October 1915 he was at a hospital in Malta recovering and *'expecting to be sent back to the firing line.'*[696]

Rifleman Dimmick returned to serve with the Isle of Wight Rifles throughout the rest of the war and was disembodied from the battalion on 5th August 1919 under service number 330542.

---

[695] www.ancestry.co.uk: UK, Soldiers Died in the Great War, 1914-1919
[696] Isle of Wight County Press, 6th November 1915, p5

Rfn. Charles DOLLERY, 2160

Rifleman Charles Dollery enlisted in the Isle of Wight Rifles on 29th December 1914. Following Gallipoli, he was transferred to the Rifle Brigade under service number 330670 and for the latter part of the war, he served with the Royal Army Medical Corps. Charles Dollery was discharged from the Army on 13th August 1919 and was given the Silver War Badge. He was 26 years old and his service number was 538620.[697]

Rfn. Bert Reginald DOWNER, 2276

Rifleman Bert Downer came from Ryde and joined the Isle of Wight Rifles in January 1915. He took part in the advance on Anafarta Ridge on 12th August 1915 and made it through the Gallipoli campaign *'without a scratch or illness.'*[698]

Rifleman Downer was disembodied from the Isle of Wight Rifles on 4th August 1919 under service number 330733.

Rfn. Reginald DOWNER, 1921

Rifleman Reginald Downer was wounded during the advance at Anafarta Ridge. His brother Sidney Downer, also in the Isle of Wight Rifles, wrote home with the news of the action and his brother's wounding:

> Reg was not quite so lucky, as he was slightly wounded in the back of the head, and has gone to hospital.[699]

After recovering from his wounding, Rifleman Reginald Downer returned to serve with the Isle of Wight Rifles. He was promoted to Lance Corporal and with the change in service numbers for the Territorials, was given the service number 330516. He was killed

---

[697] www.ancestry.co.uk: UK, Silver War Badge Records, 1914-1920
[698] Isle of Wight County Press, 29th January 1916, p5
[699] Isle of Wight County Press, 4th September 1915, p6

in action on 19th April 1917, aged 21, during the Second Battle of Gaza and is listed on the Jerusalem Memorial.

Rfn. William DRAPER, 1119

Rifleman William Draper came from Cowes and enlisted in the Isle of Wight Rifles at Cowes. He continued to serve with the Isle of Wight Rifles after Gallipoli and was given service number 330082. Rifleman Draper was killed in action during the Third Battle of Gaza on 2nd November 1917. He was 23 years old and is buried at Gaza War Cemetery.[700]

Rfn. George DYER, 1593

Rifleman George Dyer enlisted in the Isle of Wight Rifles on 15th August 1914. He was reported as having been wounded at Gallipoli in the 25th September 1915 edition of the Isle of Wight County Press.

Rifleman Dyer was discharged from the Army on 24th August 1916. His Silver War Badge record states that he was discharged due to 'sickness.'[701]

Rfn. Stanley Hilton DYER, 564

Rifleman Stanley Dyer came from East Cowes and enlisted in the Isle of Wight Rifles at East Cowes on 20th January 1909. He was 17 years and 8 months old and was employed as a painter.

Rifleman Dyer served with the Isle of Wight Rifles at Gallipoli and avoided serious illness and wounding. He went to Alexandria with the battalion and landed back at England on 4th April 1916 for his discharge from the Army. Rifleman Dyer had spent over 7 years with the Isle of Wight Rifles and was discharged from the

---

[700] https://www.cwgc.org/find-war-dead/casualty/649925/draper,-/
[701] www.ancestry.co.uk: UK, Silver War Badge Records, 1914-1920

Army on 17th April 1916 on completion of his period of service.[702]

Rfn. Albert John William ELDRIDGE, 1668

Rifleman Albert Eldridge joined the Isle of Wight Rifles between August and September 1914 at the age of 26. He fell ill with dysentery at Gallipoli during August 1915 and was admitted into No. 19 General Hospital, Alexandria on 25th August 1915. He was then invalided back to England on 15th September 1915.[703]

Rifleman Eldridge returned to serve with the Isle of Wight Rifles and remained with the battalion for the rest of the war. He was disembodied from the Army on 15th July 1919 under service number 330368.

Rfn. William Lionel EVANS, 2150

Rifleman William Evans enlisted in the Isle of Wight Rifles on 1st January 1915. He continued to serve with the battalion after Gallipoli and was given service number 330660. Rifleman Evans was discharged from the Army on 5th June 1919 at the age of 24 due to 'sickness' and was given the Silver War Badge.[704]

Rfn. Arthur FLEMING, 1968

Rifleman Arthur Fleming served with the Isle of Wight Rifles throughout the war. He was disembodied from the Army on 31st July 1919 under service number 330544.

Rfn. Harry Bertram John FLOYD, 1194

Rifleman Harry Floyd was living in Bucklands, Hampshire when he enlisted in the Isle of Wight Rifles at Cowes. He was reported

---

[702] www.ancestry.co.uk: British Army WWI Pension Records 1914-1920 – Territorial Force Attestation
[703] www.forces-war-records.co.uk: Military Hospitals Admissions and Discharge Registers WW1 - MH106/1224 No. 19 General Hospital: 06/08/1915 to 15/08/1915
[704] www.forces-war-records.co.uk: Silver War Badge List 1914-1918

as having been wounded at Gallipoli in the Isle of Wight County Press' 2nd October 1915 edition.

Rifleman Floyd returned to serve with the Isle of Wight Rifles and was given service number 330122 when the Territorial Forces received new service numbers. He was killed in action during the Second Battle of Gaza on 19th April 1917 at the age of 22 years old and is commemorated on the Jerusalem Memorial.

Rfn. Percy S. F. FOX, 1113

Rifleman Percy Fox was transferred to the 19th Rifle Brigade after Gallipoli and was given service number 1296 and later 202016. Later in the war, Percy Fox was transferred to the Labour Corps. He ended his Army Service with the Royal Army Ordnance Corps and on 16th July 1919 he was placed on the 'Z' Reserve List under service number 041388.

Rfn. Philip GILBERT, 1709

Rifleman Philip Gilbert was reported as missing after the advance on Anafarta Ridge and was later presumed to have been killed during the advance on 12th August 1915. Official notification of his death was published in the Isle of Wight County Press on 29th July 1916. Rifleman Gilbert was 19 years old and came from Ventnor. He is commemorated on the Helles Memorial.

Rfn. Frederick GODDARD, 2420

Rifleman Frederick Goddard came from East Cowes and enlisted in the Isle of Wight Rifles at Newport. Following Gallipoli, he was transferred to the 6th Battalion of the Somerset Light Infantry and given service number 204757 along with the rank of Private.

Frederick Goddard was killed in action during the Battle of St Quentin on 21st March 1918. He was 19 years old. Frederick Goddard has no known grave and is commemorated on Pozieres Memorial.

Rfn. E GOODCHILD, 1477

Rifleman Goodchild came from Cowes. He was invalided off Gallipoli between October 1915 and November 1915 and taken to a hospital in Malta due to illness.

Rifleman Goodchild went on to join the Royal Flying Corps which later became the Royal Air Force and was given service number 406075. He survived the war.

Rfn. Frank GRAY, 1416

Rifleman Frank Gray was transferred to the Army Ordnance Corps at some point after he served with the Isle of Wight Rifles at Gallipoli. He was given the rank of Private and service number 026445. Frank Gray survived the war and was placed on the reserve list on 23rd February 1919.

Rfn. Frank Hiram GRIFFEN, 2369

Rifleman Frank Griffen enlisted in the Isle of Wight Rifles on 8th April 1915. He continued to serve with the Isle of Wight Rifles after their deployment to Gallipoli and was given service number 330793. He was discharged from the Army on 3rd December 1918 at the age of 24 due to 'wounds' and was given the Silver War Badge.[705]

Rfn. Lancelot Roy HALLIDAY, 1195

Rifleman Lancelot Halliday was residing in Southsea, Portsmouth when he enlisted in the Isle of Wight Rifles at Cowes. He was originally reported as missing in action and then presumed to have been killed in action. The 1914/1915 Star records state that Rifleman Halliday died on or since the 12th August 1915 however, the Commonwealth War Graves Commission records and the UK Soldiers Died in the Great War

---

[705] www.ancestry.co.uk: UK, Silver War Badge Records, 1914-1920

records have Rifleman Halliday's date of death as 22nd August 1915. He is commemorated on the Helles Memorial.

Rfn. Albert HARDING, 2094

Rifleman Albert Harding came from Ventnor. He was wounded at Gallipoli during August 1915. Rifleman Harding continued to serve with the Isle of Wight Rifles throughout the war and sadly died on 16th November 1918 aged 41. He is buried at Beirut War Cemetery.

Rfn. George HARDING, 1596

Rifleman George Harding continued to serve with the Isle of Wight Rifles after Gallipoli. He was disembodied from the Army on 3rd April 1919 under service number 330318.

Rfn. Cecil HARVEY, 1419

Rifleman Cecil Harvey was 16 years old when he served in the Isle of Wight Rifles at Gallipoli with his brother, Rifleman Herbert Harvey, who is presumed to have died on 22nd August 1915. They came from Ventnor.

Rifleman Cecil Harvey was taken ill with dysentery and was admitted to St Patrick's Hospital, Malta in November 1915 and after recovering, continued to serve with the Isle of Wight Rifles. Rifleman Cecil Harvey survived the war and his latter service number was 330233. He decided to re-enlist on 5th January 1920, joining the Royal Engineers as a Pioneer and was given service number 619721.

Rfn. Ernest Walter HATCHER, 1541

Rifleman Ernest Hatcher remained with the Isle of Wight Rifles after Gallipoli until he was disembodied from the Army on 15th July 1919 under service number 330290.

Rfn. Charles HAWES, 2395

Rifleman Charles Hawes came from High Wycombe in Buckinghamshire and enlisted in the Isle of Wight Rifles at Newport. He was killed in action during the Second Battle of Gaza on 19th April 1917 at the age of 18 and is commemorated on the Jerusalem Memorial. His service number at the time of his death was 330811.[706]

Rfn. William H. HAYLES, 2266

Rifleman William Hayles came from Newport. He enlisted in the Isle of Wight Rifles on 18th January 1915 and served at Gallipoli with his brother, Rifleman Edgar Hayles. They both avoided being wounded whilst serving with the Isle of Wight Rifles at Gallipoli and they both survived the war.

In the Isle of Wight County Press on 12th February 1916 it was reported that Rifleman William Hayles had been posted to Parkhurst Barracks after having been *'invalided home some time ago.'*[707]

Rifleman William Hayles returned to serve with the Isle of Wight Rifles and was given service number 330728 when the Territorial Forces were given new service numbers. He was discharged from the Army on 30th April 1919. His Silver War Badge record states that he was discharged due to sickness.

Rfn. William George HAYTER, 1124

Rifleman William Hayter had been in the Isle of Wight Rifles for a number of years before going to Gallipoli. He was wounded in August 1915.

Later in the war, Rifleman Hayter became a Sergeant in the Isle of Wight Rifles. His service number being 330085. He was then transferred to the 3/4th Hants and given the service number

---

[706] www.forces-war-records.co.uk: Soldiers Died in the Great War 1914-1919
[707] Isle of Wight County Press, 12th February 1916, p5

later in the war and as a result was discharged from the Army on 6th April 1918 at the age of 24. He was given the Silver Badge War.[711]

Rfn. Harry HOUSE, 2400

Rifleman Harry House came from Fulham. He enlisted in the Isle of Wight Rifles on 26th April 1915 and served at Gallipoli with the battalion. He was discharged from the Army on 4th October 1916 due to 'sickness' and was given the Silver War Badge.[712]

Rfn. Ernest Alfred HOWELL, 167

Rifleman Ernest Howell served with the 5th Battalion of the Hampshire Regiment from 3rd November 1905 to 6th April 1908. The 5th Battalion went on to become the 8th Battalion of the Hampshire Regiment (Isle of Wight Rifles) and on 7th April 1908, Rifleman Howell was official transferred to the renamed battalion. He was 19 years old and 4 months old at the time.

Rifleman Howell served with the Isle of Wight Rifles throughout their Gallipoli campaign and sailed to Alexandria with the battalion. On 5th March 1916, Rifleman Howell was sent *'to 54th Infantry Base Depot for passage to England'* and on 25th March 1916 he *'embarked for England per H.T. Huntsend'* for discharge as his period of service was coming to an end. Rifleman Howell was formally discharged from the Army on 28th April 1916.[713]

Rfn. William Charles HUNNYBUN, 2409

Rifleman William Hunnybun served with the Isle of Wight Rifles at Gallipoli and for the remainder of the war. He was disembodied from the Army on 8th August 1919 under service number 330820.

---

[711] www.ancestry.co.uk: UK, Silver War Badge Records, 1914-1920
[712] www.forces-war-records.co.uk: Silver War Badge List 1914-1918
[713] www.ancestry.co.uk: British Army WWI Pension Records 1914-1920 – Territorial Force Attestation

Rfn. Horace HUNT, 1230

Rifleman Horace Hunt came from Ventnor and enlisted in the Isle of Wight Rifles on 20th January 1913. He was taken prisoner during the Second Battle of Gaza on 19th April 1917 and was discharged from the Army due to 'wounds' on 18th March 1919. Rifleman Hunt was 22 years old at the time of his discharge and was given the Silver War Badge. His service number was 330135.[714]

Rfn. Norman HUNTER, 1384

Rifleman Norman Hunter served with the Isle of Wight Rifles throughout the war and reached the rank of Sergeant. He fell ill with Pyrexia towards the end of the war and was admitted onto H.M.A.T Ship Assaye on 12th October 1918 at Haifa and on 14th October 1918 he arrived in Alexandria.[715]

Sergeant Hunter was disembodied from the Army on 12th April 1919 under service number 330212.

Rfn. Joseph INCE, 1379

Rifleman Joseph Ince came from West Cowes and enlisted in the Isle of Wight Rifles on 12th November 1913 at the age of 18.

Rifleman Ince received a slight bayonet wound to his right thigh on 13th August 1915 which was recorded as accidental. For this, he was treated by the 32nd Field Ambulance. Rifleman Ince then fell ill with Enteritis and was admitted to a hospital on Malta on 10th September 1915. He was subsequently invalided back to England on Hospital Ship Hunslett on 6th November 1915.[716]

---

[714] www.ancestry.co.uk: UK, Silver War Badge Records, 1914-1920
[715] www.forces-war-records.co.uk: Military Hospitals Admissions and Discharge Registers WW1- Military Hospitals Admissions and Discharge Registers WW1 - MH106/1932, First World War Representative Medical Records of H.M.A.T Ship Assaye: 12/10/1918 - 18/10/1918
[716] www.ancestry.co.uk: British Army WWI Pension Records 1914-1920 - Cover for Discharge Documents

After a period of time back in England, Rifleman Ince embarked a transport ship on 12th January 1917 at Devonport for Alexandria to re-join the Isle of Wight Rifles. He re-joined the battalion at Mazar on 7th February 1917 and was given service number 330208. He fought with the battalion during the Second Battle of Gaza on 19th April 1917 and received gunshot wounds to his right wrist and sacrum.[717]

Rifleman Ince spent ten months in various hospitals around Egypt and on 20th February 1918 he was classified as 'B3' by a medical board and was discharged to duty on 22nd February 1918. He was transferred to the 20th Rifle Brigade on 5th March 1918 and was given the rank of Private along with service number 211956. He spent the rest of the war with this unit and during this time he was occasionally posted to help out the Royal Engineers in Kantara.[718]

Joseph Ince was medically assessed for an Army Pension on 23rd May 1919 at Alexandria. Due to his wounding the medical officer stated that the '*degree of his disablement from the wounding was 30%*' however, his records did not state if he was awarded an Army Pension. Joseph Ince was disembodied from the Army in London on 19th July 1919.[719]

Rfn. Charles Edward JACKMAN, 1068

Rifleman Charles Jackman came from Shanklin. He enlisted in the Isle of Wight Rifles on 18th October 1911. During August 1915, whilst at Gallipoli, he was wounded in the leg.

---

[717] www.ancestry.co.uk: British Army WWI Pension Records 1914-1920 - Cover for Discharge Documents
[718] www.ancestry.co.uk: British Army WWI Pension Records 1914-1920 - Cover for Discharge Documents
[719] www.ancestry.co.uk: British Army WWI Pension Records 1914-1920 - Cover for Discharge Documents

Rifleman Jackman was discharged from the Army on 11th September 1916 due to sickness and received the Silver War Badge.

Rfn. Archibald JEFFERIES, 2407

Rifleman Archibald Jefferies enlisted in the Isle of Wight Rifles on 1st May 1915. Whilst at Gallipoli he began to suffer with rheumatism. He was invalided back to England and by the beginning of November 1915, Rifleman Jefferies was being treated at The Royal Chest Hospital in London. On 3rd December 1915, Rifleman Jefferies was discharged from the Army due to being medically unfit. He was given the Silver War Badge.

Rfn. Charles Frank JENVEY, 2113

Rifleman Charles Jenvey enlisted in the Isle of Wight Rifles on 28th December 1914. He was taken ill at Gallipoli during August 1915 and returned to England to be treated at Netley Hospital. Rifleman Jenvey was discharged from the Army on 30th August 1916 due to sickness and was awarded the Silver War Badge.

Rfn. Harry JONES, 2075

Rifleman Harry Jones came from Newport. He remained with the Isle of Wight Rifles after Gallipoli and was given service number 330614. He was reported as having been wounded in the War Office Daily List on 20th September 1917.[720]

Rifleman Jones survived the war and re-enlisted into the Hampshire Regiment. He was given service number 06111.

---

[720] www.forces-war-records.co.uk: NLS 1917_WList08 – War Office Daily List No. 5369, 20/09/1917

Rfn. Ernest Alfred Charles JORDAN, 1992

Rifleman Ernest Jordan served with the Isle of Wight Rifles throughout the war and was disembodied from the Army on 12th April 1919 under service number 330559.

Rfn. George JOYNER, 2415

Rifleman George Joyner was transferred to the 1/6th Hants at some point after Gallipoli and was given service number 281806. The 1/6th Hants were based in India and deployed to Basra in September 1917. They remained in Mesopotamia to the war's conclusion.

George Joyner was placed on the Class Z list on 2nd October 1919.

Rfn. Charles KING, 1116

Rifleman Charles King fell ill with dysentery at Gallipoli during September 1915 and was invalided back to England. He was treated at the University War Hospital in Southampton.

Rifleman King returned to serve with the Isle of Wight Rifles and with the Territorial Force renumbering in 1917, was given service number 330080. Charles King finished his Army war service in the Royal Engineers holding the rank of Sapper and service number 521700.

Rfn. Ernest Edgar KING, 1534

Rifleman Ernest King served with the Isle of Wight Rifles throughout the war. He was disembodied from the Army on 4th July 1919 under service number 330288.

Rfn. Percy William KING, 1985

Rifleman Percy King was initially reported as missing in action and then later presumed to have been killed in action on 12th August 1915 during the advance on Anafarta Ridge. He was 18 years old. Rifleman King is commemorated on the Helles Memorial.

Rfn. Charles Henry KNIGHT, 2117

Rifleman Charles Knight was on the National Reserve when he joined the Isle of Wight Rifles. He served at Gallipoli with his brothers Percy and John Knight.

During the advance on Anafarta Ridge, John was killed, and on 13th August 1915, Percy was wounded. Rifleman Charles Knight was wounded later on in the Gallipoli campaign. He was wounded in the leg and ankle when a shrapnel shell burst near the cookhouse that he was working in and had to be invalided off Gallipoli. By December 1915, he had been admitted into a hospital in Egypt and afterwards was brought back to England where he spent time at Highfield Hospital. On the 29th January 1916, the Isle of Wight County Press reported that he had returned home and but still had to use crutches.[721]

Rifleman Charles Knight was transferred to the Somerset Light Infantry and given service number 34510 along with the rank of Private. He was disembodied from the Army on 2nd April 1919. His brother, Percy Knight, was discharged from the Army in October 1917 due to a second wounding he received at Gallipoli.

Rfn. Albert LALE, 1083

Rifleman Albert Lale served with the Isle of Wight Rifles throughout the war. He reached the rank of Lance Corporal and was disembodied from the Army on 28th April 1919 under service number 330065.

Rfn. George James LANGDON, 1620

Rifleman George Langdon was one of the battalion's bandsman and stretcher bearers. He was wounded by shrapnel on 3rd

---

[721] Isle of Wight County Press, 29th January 1916, p5

September 1915 along with seven others in the Isle of Wight Rifles. The piece of shrapnel *'was extracted from his knee in the clearing hospital on the beach and Langdon was conveyed in a New Zealand hospital ship to Lemnos and thence to the St. Elmo Hospital, Malta.'*[722]

Rifleman Langdon returned to England and spent time recovering at Northwood House, Red Cross Hospital. He was discharged from Northwood House on Monday 29th November 1915. On returning to full fitness, Rifleman Langdon re-joined the Isle of Wight Rifles and continued to serve with the battalion throughout the rest of the war. He was disembodied from the Army on 19th March 1919 under service number 330338.

Rfn. Rhupert LANGSTON, 2055

Rifleman Rhupert Langston was transferred to the 1/6th Hants at some point after Gallipoli. The 1/6th Hants were originally based in India and they were deployed to Basra in September 1917. The battalion remained in Mesopatamia to the war's conclusion and Rhupert Langston was disembodied from the Army on 7th April 1919 under service number 281809.

Rfn. Frank LEE, 1435

Rifleman Frank Lee came from Cowes and was already serving in the Isle of Wight Rifles when war broke out. He was killed on 12th August 1915 during the advance on Anafarta Ridge at the age of 19. He is commemorated on the Helles Memorial.

Rfn. Frank William LEWIS, 1420

Rifleman Frank Lewis enlisted in the Army in January 1914. He continued serving with the Isle of Wight Rifles after their deployment to Gallipoli and was given service number 330234.

---

[722] Isle of Wight County Press, 30th October 1915, p5.

Rifleman Lewis was transferred to the 2nd Hants at some point between 1917 and May 1919 and he sailed with the 2nd Hants to Northern Russia in May 1919. During this deployment he served with the Headquarters Company of the 2nd Hants and suffered an injury to his knee which resulted in him being admitted into No. 85 General Hospital, Solombala on 14th July 1919.[723]

At the end of his service period, Rifleman Lewis re-enlisted into the Hampshire Regiment and was given service number 05265.

Rfn. Herbert LEWIS, 1471

Rifleman Herbert Lewis served with the Isle of Wight Rifles throughout the war and was disembodied from the Army on 3rd April 1919 under service number 330259.

Rfn. John LOMATH, 1944

Rifleman John Lomath was reported to have been wounded at Gallipoli in the 25th September 1915 edition of the Isle of Wight County Press. He was also reported as holding the rank of Lance Corporal.

Once Lance Corporal Lomath had recovered from his wounding, he returned to serve with the Isle of Wight Rifles and remained with the battalion for the rest of the war. He was disembodied from the Army on 23rd February 1919 under service number 330530.

Rfn. Robert Frank Ernest MACKETT, 1233

Rifleman Robert Mackett was born in Ventnor on 28th July 1897. He served with the Isle of Wight Rifles throughout the war. Robert Mackett was discharged from the Army on 24th July 1919 under service number 330137 and on 28th July 1919 he joined the

---

[723] www.forces-war-records.co.uk: Military Hospitals Admissions and Discharge Registers WW1 - MH106/1385, First World War Representative Medical Records of No. 85 General Hospital: 31/01/1919 to 26/08/1919. No. 85 General Hospital at SOLOMBALA North Russia Expeditionary Force.

Royal Navy and was given service number SS/122878. He served in the Royal Navy until 27th July 1924 and then spent a period of time in the Royal Artillery under service number 759017.[724]

Rfn. Cecil Frank MANNING, 1896

Rifleman Cecil Frank Manning enlisted in the Isle of Wight Rifles on 4th September 1914. On 12th August 1915, during the advance on Anafarta Ridge, he was wounded in both hands and in his shoulder. Rifleman Manning was invalided back to England and was treated at a hospital in Plymouth. Due to his wounding, he was discharged from the Army on 24th April 1916 and given the Silver War Badge.

Rfn. Harold D. MARTIN, 2097

Rifleman Harold Martin continued serving with the Isle of Wight Rifles after Gallipoli and he was later given service number 330630. Either in 1917 or 1918, Harold Martin transferred to the Machine Gun Corps. He was disembodied from the Machine Gun Corps on 22nd March 1919 under service number 114809 and the rank of acting Corporal. He then went on to re-enlist in the Isle of Wight Rifles and became a Colour Sergeant. His latter service number with the battalion was 5489622.

Rfn. William MATTHEWS, 1684

Rifleman William Matthews was taken ill at Gallipoli with dysentery. He was initially treated at St George's Hospital in Malta then on 27th November 1915 he was admitted into Highfield-Lane Hospital in Southampton.

Rifleman Matthews continued to serve with the Isle of Wight Rifles. He was discharged from the battalion on 14th December 1918 under service number 330381.

---

[724] www.ancestry.co.uk: UK, Royal Navy Registers of Seamen's Services, 1848-1939 - The National Archives of the UK; Kew, Surrey, England; Royal Navy Registers of Seamen's Services; Class: ADM 188; Piece: 1128

Rfn. William Henry MAYBEE, 428

Rifleman William Maybee enlisted in the Isle of Wight Rifles at Ventnor on the 24th November 1908. He was 20 years and 3 months old and was over 6 foot tall. He had previously been on a voluntary placement with the 5th Volunteer Battalion of the Hampshire Regiment – the predecessor to the Isle of Wight Rifles. His brother, Lance Corporal Charles Maybee also served with the Isle of Wight Rifles.

Rifleman Maybee became ill with dysentery at Gallipoli on 31st October 1915. He was admitted into the General Military Hospital at Gibraltar on 7th November 1915 and was then invalided back to England where he was admitted into Devonport Military Hospital on 27th November 1915.

On the 4th August 1916, Rifleman Maybee went before a Medical Board. His medical report stated that he had *'been unable to do any marching or carrying a pack on account of being short of breath.'*[725] Rifleman Maybee was classified as medically unfit and was subsequently discharged from the 2/8th Hants on 18th August 1916. He was awarded an Army pension that was reviewed annually and the reports suggests that his condition slowly improved.

Rfn. C C MEAGER, 1097

Rifleman Meager came from Cowes. He became ill with dysentery at Gallipoli and was invalided back to England. He was admitted into Northwood House, Red Cross Hospital on Wednesday 1st December 1915.

Later in the war, Rifleman Meager joined the Royal Flying Corps, which later became the Royal Air Force, and was given service number 406147. He survived the war.

---

[725] www.ancestry.co.uk: British Army WWI Pension Records 1914-1920 - Territorial Force Attestation

Rfn. Arthur MEANING, 1970

Rifleman Arthur Meaning came from Freshwater and enlisted in the Isle of Wight Rifles on 26th November 1914. He was reported as having been wounded at Gallipoli in the Isle of Wight County Press on 18th September 1915.

Rifleman Meaning continued to serve with the Isle of Wight Rifles. He was discharged from the Army on 31st July 1919 under service number 330546. His Silver War Badge record states that he was discharged due to 'wounds.'

Rfn. Arthur MERWOOD, 1597

Rifleman Arthur Merwood enlisted in the Isle of Wight Rifles on 15th August 1914 at the age of 15 years and 8 months. He contracted Tuberculosis during the war and was discharged from the Army on 17th November 1917 due to 'sickness.' For this he was given the Silver War Badge. Rifleman Merwood was 20 years old at the time of his discharge and his service number was 330319.[726] [727]

Rfn. W. MEW, 452

Rifleman Mew continued serving with the Isle of Wight Rifles after Gallipoli and was given service number 330029. He transferred to the Royal Engineers in either 1917 or 1918 and was disembodied from the Army on 15th July 1919 under service number 521695.

Rfn. Frederick Edwin MILLER, 2027

Rifleman Frederick Miller came from Newport. He was reported as missing in the Isle of Wight County Press on 11th September 1915. He was later presumed to have been killed during the advance on Anafarta Ridge on 12th August 1915 and official notification of his death was published in the Isle of Wight

---

[726] www.ancestry.co.uk: UK, Silver War Badge Records, 1914-1920
[727] https://livesofthefirstworldwar.iwm.org.uk/lifestory/3016088

County Press on 29th July 1916. Rifleman Miller was 18 years old and he is commemorated on the Helles Memorial.

Rfn. James MILLIGAN, 1090

Rifleman James Milligan came from Ventnor and enlisted in the Isle of Wight Rifles on 5th December 1911. He was 20 years and 4 months old and was a butcher.

Rifleman Milligan contracted Enteric Fever whilst at Gallipoli and arrived back in England on 9th November 1915 where he continued to receive hospital treatment. Such was the severity of the Enteric Fever and the after effects from the illness, Rifleman Milligan was discharged from the Army on 11th December 1917 and given the Silver War Badge.

In 1920 James Milligan decided to re-enlist in the Isle of Wight Rifles. He was given service number 5488004 and the rank of Rifleman.[728]

Rfn. Reginald Harry MOREY, 1981

Rifleman Reginald Morey joined the Isle of Wight Rifles towards the end of 1914. He was wounded at Gallipoli on 24th September 1915.

Rifleman Reginald Morey returned to serve with the Isle of Wight Rifles and was disembodied from the Army on 31st July 1919 under service number 330551.

Rfn. Sidney Arthur MOREY, 1687

Rifleman Sidney Morey enlisted in the Isle of Wight Rifles on 3rd September 1915 with his brother Edgar Morey. They came from Cowes.

---

[728] www.ancestry.co.uk: British Army WWI Pension Records 1914-1920 – Territorial Force Attestation

On 25th August 1915, Rifleman Sidney Morey suffered a dislocation to his right shoulder and was taken to a hospital in Alexandria for treatment. He later became ill with diarrhoea and was *'admitted to hospital at Cairo on November 13th.'*[729]

Rifleman Sidney Morey returned to serve with the Isle of Wight Rifles and survived the war. He was discharged from the Army on 14th December 1918 under service number 330384. His brother, Edgar, was discharged from the Army on 26th November 1915 due to his wounding.

Rfn. George MORRIS, 1598

Rifleman George Morris served with the Isle of Wight Rifles throughout the war and was disembodied from the battalion on 15th July 1919 under service number 330320.

Rfn. Harold James MUNNS, 1599

Rifleman Harold Munns continued to serve with the Isle of Wight Rifles after Gallipoli. He was disembodied from the battalion on 18th April 1919 under service number 330321.

Rfn. John Frederick NAYLOR, 2428

Rifleman John Naylor was wounded during the latter part of the Isle of Wight Rifles' deployment at Gallipoli.

Rifleman Naylor returned to serve with the Isle of Wight Rifles and reached the rank of Corporal. He was then transferred to the Machine Gun Corps and remained as a Corporal throughout the rest of the war. Corporal Naylor was discharged from the Army on 16th May 1919 under service number 114806.

Rfn. George Thomas NEW, 1395

Rifleman George New enlisted in the Isle of Wight Rifles on 7th January 1914. He served with the battalion throughout the war

---

[729] Isle of Wight County Press, 11th December 1915, p8

and was discharged from the Army on 14th December 1918 under service number 330219 at the age of 23.[730]

Rfn. Evelyn Fred NEWMAN, 2022

Rifleman Evelyn Newman came from Havenstreet. He remained with the Isle of Wight Rifles after Gallipoli and was given service number 330584.

Rifleman Newman was killed in action during the Second Battle of Gaza on 19th April 1917. He was 20 years old and is buried at Gaza War Cemetery.[731]

Rfn. Albert NEWNHAM D.C.M., 1418

Rifleman Albert Newnham came from Ventnor and enlisted in the Isle of Wight Rifles on 21st January 1914 at the age of 17 years and 8months old. He went to Gallipoli with the battalion and on 16th September 1915 he was *'admitted to the 15th Stationary Hospital, Mudros with Myalgia.'*[732] Rifleman Newnham was then admitted to a hospital in Malta on 25th October 1915 and four months later, he re-joined the Isle of Wight Rifles in Cairo.

Rifleman Newnham became ill with Diphtheria whilst he was in Egypt with the Isle of Wight Rifles and he was admitted to the 1st Australian Stationary Hospital at Ismailia on 1st August 1916. On 18th August 1916 he was transferred to the Abbassia Convalescent Depot and on 25th October 1916, Rifleman Newnham boarded a hospital ship at Alexandria which was bound for England.[733]

---

[730] www.ancestry.co.uk: UK, Silver War Badge Records, 1914-1919
[731] https://www.cwgc.org/find-war-dead/casualty/650947/newman,-/
[732] www.ancestry.co.uk: British Army WWI Pension Records 1914-1920 – Cover for Discharge Documents
[733] www.ancestry.co.uk: British Army WWI Pension Records 1914-1920 – Cover for Discharge Documents

After a period of time back in England, Albert Newnham set sail for France from Southampton on 20th May 1917 as a Private soldier. He was posted to the 2nd Hants under service number 330232. He served on the Western Front and was later attached to the 1/4th Battalion of the Leicestershire Regiment. He was wounded by a gunshot wound to his left side on 29th September 1918 and for his actions, presumably on the same day, he was awarded the DCM.[734] The citation for his DCM is below:

> For conspicuous gallantry and devotion to duty. He did twenty-four hours' continuous work in charge of a squad of stretcher-bearers, and carried on with his duties after being knocked down and badly shaken when his aid-post was hit. He dragged his wounded company commander to a place of safety under heavy fire, and though weak after his injuries, went and fetched in a wounded man. His pluck and energy were splendid. (5.12.18)[735]

Albert Newnham was discharged from the Army on 10th March 1919 and given the Silver War Badge along with an Army Pension due to the continuation of him suffering from pains in his joints.[736]

Rfn. Harold Walter NEWNHAM, 1982

Rifleman Harold Newnham came from Newport. He went with the Isle of Wight Rifles to Gallipoli and continued to serve with the battalion later in the war. He was promoted to the rank of Corporal and was given service number 330552 when the Territorial Forces received new service numbers.

---

[734] www.ancestry.co.uk: British Army WWI Pension Records 1914-1920 – Cover for Discharge Documents

[735] www.ancestry.co.uk: UK, Citations of the Distinguished Conduct Medal, 1914-1920 - Original data: Walker, R. W., and Chris Buckland, compilers. Citations of the Distinguished Conduct Medal, 1914–1920. 4 sections. Uckfield, East Sussex, United Kingdom: Naval and Military Press, 2007.

[736] www.ancestry.co.uk: British Army WWI Pension Records 1914-1920 – Cover for Discharge Documents

Corporal Newnham was killed in action on 2nd November 1917 during the Third Battle of Gaza. He was 22 years old and is buried at Gaza War Cemetery.[737]

Rfn. William John NORTON, 2243

Rifleman William Norton came from Marlow in Buckinghamshire. He continued serving with the Isle of Wight Rifles after Gallipoli and was latterly given service number 330716. He was killed in an accident on 14th August 1917 at the age of 27 and is buried at Gaza War Cemetery.

Rfn. Percy PAINE, 1225

Rifleman Percy Paine originally came from Wilton in Wiltshire. He enlisted in the Isle of Wight Rifles at Cowes. After the advance on Anafarta Ridge, Rifleman Paine was reported as missing and was later presumed to have been killed during the advance on 12th August 1915. Rifleman Paine has no known grave and is commemorated on the Helles Memorial.[738]

Rfn. Wilfred PALFREY, 1570

Rifleman Wilfred Palfrey served with the Isle of Wight Rifles throughout the war and reached the rank of Sergeant. He was disembodied from the Army on 23rd April 2019 under service number 330305.

Rfn. Ernest PALMER, 2149

Rifleman Ernest Palmer served with the Isle of Wight Rifles at Gallipoli and later in the war he was transferred to the Labour Corps with whom he was discharged from on 10th March 1919 under service number 279734.

---

[737] https://www.cwgc.org/find-war-dead/casualty/650949/newnham,-/
[738] www.ancestry.co.uk: UK, Soldiers Died in the Great War, 1914-1919

Rfn. Ernest Walter PARSONS MM, 1424

Rifleman Ernest Walter Parsons joined the Isle of Wight Rifles on 21st January 1914. He was 17 years old.

Rifleman Parsons served at Gallipoli and went onto fight in the Second Battle of Gaza with the Isle of Wight Rifles where due to his actions rescuing Lt Butler who was wounded, he was awarded the Military Medal.

Rifleman Parsons was wounded on 6th November 1917 during the latter stages of the Third Battle of Gaza. His attestation papers provide details on his movements and postings after his wounding. Rifleman Parson was sent home on a hospital ship on 21st December 1917 and posted to the Hampshire Regiment's Depot on 2nd January 1918. Following that he was posted to 4th Reserve Battalion on 1st March 1918 and then transferred to the Labour Corps on 13th September 1918 and given the rank of Private and service number 646666.

Rfn. Herbert Frank PAYNE, 1990

Rifleman Herbert Payne served with the Isle of Wight Rifles throughout the war and survived it. His latter service number was 330557.

Rfn. Frederick PEACH, 20

Rifleman Frederick Peach served with the Isle of Wight Rifles throughout their Gallipoli campaign and remained with the battalion until he was transferred to the 21st Rifle Brigade on 19th September 1917. He was given service number 212011. The 21st Rifle Brigade operated in Palestine until they were deployed to India in later September 1918.

After the war, Rifleman Peach re-enlisted in the Isle of Wight Rifles and was given service number 5488026.

Rfn. Alfred John PINK, 1993

Rifleman Alfred Pink served with the Isle of Wight Rifles throughout the war and reached the rank of Acting Corporal. He was disembodied from the Army on 5th May 1919 under service number 330560.

Rfn. Sydney Arthur PORTER, 1971

Rifleman Sydney Porter came from Newport and was a barber and wig maker. He enlisted in the Isle of Wight Rifles on 26th November 1914.

On 12th August 1915, during the advance on Anafarta Ridge, Rifleman Porter was wounded and badly mistreated by the Turks before finally being taken prisoner. It was due to this experience that he became known as "The Man the Turks Could not Kill." He received treatment for his wounds at Hospital De la Marine in Constantinople.

Rifleman Porter was released from Kut Al Amara on 1st November 1918 and during the voyage home, he suffered with sunstroke and contracted malaria. He was discharged from the Army on 18th March 1919 under service number 330547 due to the wounds he had suffered and was given the Silver War Badge.[739] Rifleman Porter was 25 years old. He returned to being a barber.

Rfn. Arthur PRATT, 2061

Rifleman Arthur Pratt was one of the men recruited by Lieutenant Colonel Rhodes. His family came from Upper Bourne End in Buckinghamshire, however, at the time of enlisting, Rifleman Pratt's residence was in Maidenhead, Berkshire.

Rifleman Pratt was reported as having been wounded at Gallipoli in the Isle of Wight County Press' 18th September 1915 edition.

---

[739] www.ancestry.co.uk: Silver War Badge Records, 1914-1919

Rifleman Pratt recovered from his wounding and continued to serve with the Isle of Wight Rifles. He reached the rank of Corporal and was given service number 303606 when the Territorial Forces received new service numbers.

Corporal Pratt took part in the Second Battle of Gaza on 19th April 1917 and was killed in action. He was 30 years old and is commemorated on the Jerusalem Memorial.

Rfn. Ernest George PRIMMER, 1268

Rifleman Ernest Primmer came from Ventnor. He received wounds to his foot in August 1915 at Gallipoli. On recovering from his wounds, Rifleman Primmer returned to serve with the Isle of Wight Rifles at Gallipoli where he then fell ill and in the Isle of Wight County Press on 20th November 1915 he was reported as being in hospital at Alexandria suffering with dysentery.[740]

Rifleman Primmer was killed in action on 19th April 1917 during the Second Battle of Gaza and is commemorated on the Jerusalem Memorial under service number 330151.

Rfn. Frederick READ, 1926

Rifleman Frederick Read came from Newport. He was killed in action on 12th August 1915 and is commemorated on the Helles Memorial.

Rfn. Harry READ, 1903

Rifleman Harry Read served at Gallipoli with his brother James Read who died during the advance on Anafarta Ridge on 12th August 1915.

Rifleman Harry Read was promoted to Lance Corporal following his work on listening patrols at Gallipoli. He came through the Gallipoli campaign unscathed and went with the battalion to

---

[740] Isle of Wight County Press, 20th November 1915, p5

Egypt. Harry Read reached the rank of Sergeant and remained with the Isle of Wight Rifles until being transferred to the 21st Rifle Brigade on 16th October 1917 with a number of other men from the Isle of Wight Rifles, including Rifleman Thomas Twitchen. Sergeant Harry Read 212096 landed in India on 1st October 1918 with the 21st Rifle Brigade and remained in India until 25th October 1919.[741]

Rfn. Harry REED, 1995

Rifleman Harry Reed quickly rose to the rank of Sergeant and for his service with the Isle of Wight Rifles at Gallipoli, he received a Mention in Despatches:

> With reference to the despatch on the 10th April ((London Gazette No. 29541), the following is mentioned for distinguished and gallant services rendered during the period of General Sir Charles Monro's Command of the Mediterranean Expeditionary Force.[742]

Harry Reed remained with the Isle of Wight Rifles after Gallipoli and was disembodied from the Army on 31st July 1919 under service number 330562.

Rfn. George Charles RIDETT, 2179

Rifleman George Ridett served with the Isle of Wight Rifles at Gallipoli and afterwards was transferred to the 5th battalion of the Loyal North Lancashire Regiment. He was given service number 38685 and fought on the Western Front with the 5th battalion. Later in the war he was posted to the 4th battalion of the Loyal North Lancashire Regiment and for his actions with the 4th

---

[741] www.ancestry.co.uk digital records: British War Medal and Victory Medal, Rifle Brigade (Prince Consort´s Own), Piece 1729: Rifle Brigade (Prince Consort's Own).
[742] www.forces-war-records.co.uk: Search Records of Soldiers Awards from the London Gazette - Gazette No 29664, 07/11/1916, p6949

battalion on the Western Front, was awarded the Military Medal.[743]

George Ridett survived the war and at the war's end held the rank of Lance Corporal.

Rfn. Francis ROCKELL, 2332

Rifleman Francis Rockell was transferred to the 1/4th Hants at some point after his service at Gallipoli with the Isle of Wight Rifles. The 1/4th Hants operated in Mesopotamia and towards the end of the war deployed to Persia.

Francis Rockell was demobilised from the Army on 30th August 1919 under service number 281813.

Rfn. Harry ROLFE, 2069

Rifleman Harry Rolfe came from Buckinghamshire. He was reported as having been wounded in the Isle of Wight County Press on 25th December 1915.[744]

Rifleman Rolfe returned to serve with the Isle of Wight Rifles and was discharged from the Army on 13th August 1917 under service number 330611.

Rfn. Frederick Edward ROWETT, 1436

Rifleman Frederick Rowett was born at Stamshaw, Portsmouth on 22nd September 1896.[745]

Rifleman Rowett served with the Isle of Wight Rifles at Gallipoli and later in the war transferred to the Royal Engineers. He was given the rank of Pioneer and service number 208897. At the end of the war, Frederick Rowett re-enlisted into the Royal Engineers

---

[743] www.ancestry.co.uk: UK, British Army Recipients of the Military Medal, 1914-1920
[744] Isle of Wight County Press, 25th December 1915, p5
[745] www.ancestry.co.uk: UK, Royal Air Force Airmen Records, 1918-1940 - The National Archives of the UK, Kew, Surrey, England; Kew, Surrey, England; Air Ministry: Air Member for Personnel and Predecessors: Airmen's Records; Series Number: AIR 79

and was given service number 313868. He then went on to join the RAF on 30th June 1922 under service number 351907.[746]

Rfn. Arthur Albert RUSSELL, 1439

Rifleman Arthur Russell originally came from Chale. His family moved to Cowes and he went on to enlist in the Isle of Wight Rifles at Cowes. After the advance on Anafarta Ridge Rifleman Russell was reported as missing. He was later presumed to have been killed during the advance on 12th August 1915 and is commemorated on the Helles Memorial. Rifleman Russell was 19 years old.

Rfn. Ernest RUSSELL, 1586

Rifleman Ernest Russell survived the war and his latter service number was 330313.

Rfn. Robert RUSSELL, 470

Rifleman Robert Russell survived the war and obtained the rank of Sergeant. His latter service number was 330032.

Rfn. William Henry RUSSELL, 1102

Rifleman William Russell was reported in the 16th October 1915 edition of the Isle of Wight County Press as having been wounded at Gallipoli.

Once Rifleman Russell was fit for active service again, he returned to serve with the Isle of Wight Rifles and when the Territorials received their new service number, he was given service number 330074. In the latter part of the war, Rifleman Russell was transferred to the Worcestershire Regiment and given service number 75093. Rifleman Russell was disembodied from the Army on 12th August 1919.

---

[746] www.forces-war-records.co.uk: Nominal index of all service personnel serving in a theatre of war 1914-1919

Rfn. Arthur William George SALISBURY, 2473

Rifleman Arthur Salisbury came from Cowes. He served with the Isle of Wight Rifles at Gallipoli and later in the war was transferred to the 1st Garrison Battalion of the Notts and Derby (Sherwood Foresters) Regiment where he was given the rank of Private and service number 78010. It was with this battalion, that he was killed in an accident on 2nd January 1918 at the age of 25. Arthur Salisbury is buried at Kantara War Memorial Cemetery in Egypt.[747]

Rfn. Albert Victor SALTER, 1235

Rifleman Albert Salter came from Ventnor and enlisted at Ventnor. He was wounded on 17th September 1915 and passed away on 20th September 1915 at the age of 17. Rifleman Salter is buried at Embarkation Pier Cemetery, Gallipoli.

Rfn. Frederick James SALTER, 2023

Rifleman Frederick Salter came from Arreton and enlisted in the Isle of Wight Rifles on 3rd December 1914. He *'was officially reported to be in 19 General Hospital, Alexandria on December 12th suffering from severe general peritonitis.'*[748]

Rifleman Salter was discharged from the Army on 18th August 1916 due to sickness and was given the Silver War Badge. However, Frederick Salter decided to re-enlist later in the war as a driver in the Royal Field Artillery and was given service number 277550. He survived the war.

Rfn. Albert SARNEY, 2070

Rifleman Albert Sarney was one of the men from Buckinghamshire recruited by Lieutenant Colonel Rhodes. He came from Flackwell Heath in High Wycombe and enlisted in

---

[747] https://www.cwgc.org/find-war-dead/casualty/475386/salisbury,-arthur-william-george/
[748] Isle of Wight County Press, 1st January 1915, p5

the Isle of Wight Rifles at Newport. Rifleman Sarney was killed in action during the advance on Anafarta Ridge on 12th August 1915 at the age of 23 and is commemorated on the Helles Memorial.

Rfn. Percy SAUNDERS, 1472

Rifleman Percy Saunders served with the Isle of Wight Rifles throughout the war. He was disembodied from the Army on 14th May 1919 under service number 330260.

Rfn. Ralph SAWYER, 1905

Rifleman Ralph Sawyer came from Newport and prior to joining the Isle of Wight Rifles, he was an active member of the local community including being a Patrol Leader with the Scouts in Newport.[749]

Rifleman Sawyer was reported as missing and then was later presumed to have been killed on 12th August 1915 during the advance on Anafarta Ridge. Official notification of his death was published in the Isle of Wight County Press on 29th July 1916. Rifleman Sawyer was 21 years old and he is commemorated on the Helles Memorial.

Rfn. Albert F. SCOUSE M.M., 2474

Rifleman Albert Scouse came from High Wycombe and was one of the men recruited by Lieutenant Colonel Rhodes. He served at Gallipoli and for a period of time afterwards, continued to serve with the Isle of Wight Rifles under service number 330855.

In the latter part of the war, Albert Scouse served with the 15th Hants. The 15th Hants fought on the Western Front until being deployed to Italy in November 1917. They returned to France in March 1918. It was with his service in the 15th Hants that Albert

---

[749] Trench Art: the stories behind the talismans, Judy Waugh, Fontaine Press Pty Ltd

Scouse was awarded the Military Medal *'for bravery in the field.'*[750]

Albert Scouse survived the war.

Rfn. G. A. SCOVELL, 2291

There are no records for Rifleman G. A. Scovell 2291. However, there were records for Rifleman George Henry Scovell 1323 and so it is possible that Rifleman George Henry Scovell 1323 is actually the correct person and was inaccurately listed on the 'Roll of Officers, Warrant Officers, Non-Commissioned Officers and Riflemen Proceeding Overseas' which was printed in the Isle of Wight County Press on 24th July 1915. The information on Rifleman George Henry Scovell 1323 is below:

Rfn. George Henry SCOVELL, 1323

Rifleman George Scovell came from Newport and *'joined up in the "Princess Beatrice's" I.W. Rifles early in the war, when he was employed at the boot shop of Mr A.P. Knight, Pyle Street.'*[751]

There is no 1914/15 Star record for Rifleman George Scovell 1323, which suggests that he may have not sailed on the Aquitania to Gallipoli. Occasional medal omissions did occur and so it is possible that Rifleman George Scovell 1323 did serve at some point at Gallipoli.

Rifleman Scovell 1323 was later given service number 330178. He died of wounds on 22nd April 1917 at a hospital in Kantara and probably received his wounds on 19th April 1917 during the Second Battle of Gaza. He was 20 years old and is buried at Kantara War Memorial Cemetery.

---

[750] www.forces-war-records.co.uk: Search Records of Soldiers Awards from the London Gazette - Gazette issue 31405, p7675, 13/06/1919
[751] Isle of Wight County Press, April 1917

Rfn. Archibald Harry SHARPE, 2389

Rifleman Archibald Sharpe came from High Wycombe and formally enlisted in the Isle of Wight Rifles at Newport. He continued to serve with the Isle of Wight Rifles after Gallipoli under service number 330806 and was killed in action on 2nd November 1917 during the Third Battle of Gaza. Archibald Sharpe was 23 years old and is buried at Gaza War Cemetery.[752]

Rfn. Frederick SHAVE, 1951

Rifleman Frederick Shave came from Lake. He was friends with George White and worked with George as a gardener before the war. Frederick Shave even married George White's sister, Alice May White.[753]

By October 1915, Rifleman Shave had fallen ill with dysentery and on recovering returned to serve with the Isle of Wight Rifles. He survived the war and was disembodied from the Army on 6th April 1919 under service number 330533.

Rfn. Walter SHEATH, 1469

Rifleman Walter Sheath came from Whitwell, Ventnor and enlisted in the Isle of Wight Rifles on 7th May 1914 at the age of 21.[754]

Following his deployment to Gallipoli with the Isle of Wight Rifles, Walter Sheath volunteered to join the Royal Flying Corps. He became a rigger and was given service number 408410. With the formation of the Royal Air Force on 1st April 1918, Walter Sheath was transferred to the RAF and went on to reach the rank of Aircraftsman First Class.[755]

---

[752] https://www.cwgc.org/find-war-dead/casualty/651287/sharpe,-archibald-harry/
[753] Isle of Wight Rifles: www.wwwight.co.uk
[754] www.ancestry.co.uk: UK, Royal Air Force Airmen Records, 1918-1940 - The National Archives of the UK, Kew, Surrey, England; Kew, Surrey, England; Air Ministry: Air Member for Personnel and Predecessors; Airmen's Records; Series Number: AIR 79
[755] www.forces-war-records.co.uk: RAF Formations List 1918 - AIR 1/819/204/4/1316

Walter Sheath died on 3rd July 1919 and is buried at Whitwell New Burial Ground on the Isle of Wight.

Rfn. Frederick Roland SHILTON, 1929

Rifleman Frederick Shilton enlisted in the Isle of Wight Rifles on 4th September 1914. He was in the battalion's Transport Section at Gallipoli and was promoted to the rank of Lance Corporal. On the 12th February 1916, the Isle of Wight County Press reported that Lance Corporal Shilton had returned to the Isle of Wight Rifles after a period in hospital at Alexandria due to sickness.[756]

Lance Corporal Shilton was taken prisoner during the Second Battle of Gaza and was held as a prisoner in Nazarth and Damascus.[757] He was discharged from the Army on 12th March 1919 and his Silver War Badge record stated that he was discharged due to having been wounded.

Rfn. William Harold SIMMONS, 2244

Rifleman William Simmons came from Bovingdon Green, Marlow in Buckinghamshire. He was one of the men recruited by Lieutenant Colonel Rhodes and he formally enlisted in the Isle of Wight Rifles at Newport.

Rifleman Simmons continued to serve with the Isle of Wight Rifles after Gallipoli and was given service number 330717. He was killed in action during the Second Battle of Gaza at the age of 22 and is commemorated on the Jerusalem Memorial.[758]

Rfn. Albert SINNICKS, 1069

Rifleman Albert "Tom" Sinnicks came from East Cowes. He was killed in action during the advance on Anarfarta Ridge on 12th August 1915 and official notification of his death was published in the Isle of Wight County Press on 29th July 1916. Rifleman

---

[756] Isle of Wight County Press, 12th February 1916, p5
[757] Research undertaken by Ian Meadows
[758] www.forces-war-records.co.uk: Soldiers Died in the Great War 1914-1919

Sinnicks was 21 years old and he is commemorated on the Helles Memorial.

Rfn. James Edward SMITH, 2126

Rifleman James Smith came from Upper Bourne End in Buckinghamshire and was one of the men recruited by Lieutenant Colonel Rhodes. He formally enlisted in the Isle of Wight Rifles at Newport.

Rifleman Smith continued to serve with the Isle of Wight Rifles after Gallipoli and was given service number 330644. He was killed in action during the Second Battle of Gaza at the age of 22 and is buried at Gaza War Cemetery.[759]

Rfn. Harry Hilton SNOW, 1470

Rifleman Harry Snow came from Whitwell and fought with the Isle of Wight Rifles at Gallipoli, *'through which he came without a scratch.'*[760]

Rifleman Snow continued serving with the Isle of Wight Rifles after Gallipoli and fought in their Palestinian campaign under service number 330258. In November 1918 he fell ill with pneumonia and passed away on 4th November 1918. He was 26 years old and is buried at Kantara War Memorial Cemetery.

Rfn. Frederick L. STAGG, 1257

Rifleman Frederick Stagg served with the Isle of Wight Rifles at Gallipoli and later in the war was transferred to the 1st Garrison Battalion of the Essex Regiment with whom he was given service number 203542. Towards the end of the war, Frederick Stagg was posted back to the Hampshire Regiment and given service number 05357. He went on to re-enlist in the Isle of Wight Rifles

---

[759] https://www.cwgc.org/find-war-dead/casualty/651349/smith,-james-edward/
[760] Isle of Wight County Press, 11th January 1919, p5

after the war and served with the battalion under service number 5486617.

Rfn. Joseph <u>Walter</u> Ernest STALLARD, 1077

Rifleman Walter Stallard came from Cowes and joined the Isle of Wight Rifles in 1911. He was wounded in the back and taken prisoner at Gallipoli during August 1915, mostly likely on the 12th August 1915. The Turks took him to a hospital in Constantinople but he succumbed to his wounds on 25th August 1915. He was 20 years old and is buried at Haidar Pasha Cemetery, Istanbul, Turkey.

Rfn. Harry STANLEY, 2274

Rifleman Harry Stanley served with the Isle of Wight Rifles at Gallipoli. He was transferred to the 21st Rifle Brigade on 7th November 1917, a battalion used for garrison duties in the Egyptian Expeditionary Force, and was given service number 212144. Then on 4th February 1918, Harry Stanley was transferred to the Royal Army Service Corps. He was disembodied from the Royal Army Service Corps on 4th August 1919 under service number T/393638.[761]

Rfn. Albert V. STONE, 2321

Rifleman Albert Stone enlisted in the Isle of Wight Rifles in either January 1915 or February 1915. He became ill at Gallipoli with 'Pyrexia of unknown origin' and was admitted on to HM Hospital Ship Assaye on 4th October 1915. By this time, Rifleman Stone was serving in 'B' Company of the battalion and he was 18 years old.[762]

---

[761] www.ancestry.co.uk: UK, WWI Service Medal and Award Rolls, 1914-1920: 1914-1915 Star - The National Archives of the UK; Kew, Surrey, England; WWI Service Medal and Award Rolls; Class: WO 329; Piece Number: 2901

[762] www.forces-war-records.co.uk: Military Hospitals Admissions and Discharge Registers WW1 - MH106/1913, The National Archives in Kew, First World War Representative Medical Records of H.M.A.T Ship Assaye: 02/10/1915 - 11/10/1915.

After his service at Gallipoli, Albert Stone was transferred to the 2/7th Hants and later in the war he was posted to the Oxfordshire and Buckinghamshire Light Infantry with the rank of Private and service number 50614.

Albert Stone survived the war.

Rfn. Alfred STONE, 2355

Rifleman Alfred Stone was transferred to the 2/4th Hants after serving with the Isle of Wight Rifles at Gallipoli and was given service number 205464. The 2/4th Hants served in India, Mesopotamia and towards the end of the war in Persia.

Alfred Stone was disembodied from the Army on 13th March 1919.

Rfn. Walter Henry STONE, 2392

Rifleman Walter Stone came from High Wycombe in Buckinghamshire and was one of the men recruited by Lieutenant Colonel Rhodes. He was killed in action during the Second Battle of Gaza on 19th April 1917 at the age of 26 years and is commemorated on the Jerusalem Memorial. His service number at the time was 330809.[763]

Rfn. George SWADLING, 2348

Rifleman George Swadling served with the Isle of Wight Rifles at Gallipoli and was discharged from the battalion on 4th February 1916. He then went on to enlist in the Oxfordshire and Buckinghamshire Light Infantry under service number 48415 and survived the war.

British and Colonial Other Ranks. H.M.Hospital Ship ASSAYE Lines of Communication Mediterranean Expeditionary Force.
[763] https://www.cwgc.org/find-war-dead/casualty/1647199/stone,-walter-henry/

Rfn. Alfred Edgar TAYLOR, 2235

Rifleman Alfred Taylor served with the Isle of Wight Rifles throughout the war. He reached the rank of Corporal and his latter service number was 330713. He survived the war.

Rfn. Alfred George THOMAS, 1463

Rifleman Alfred Thomas enlisted in the Isle of Wight Rifles on 21st April 1914. He was wounded and taken prisoner at Gallipoli, most likely during the advance on Anafarta Ridge on 12th August 1915. Rifleman Thomas was taken to a hospital in Constantinople for treatment and had to have his right hand amputated.

Rifleman Thomas was discharged from the Army on 28th August 1918, aged 22 years old and received the Silver Badge for wounds.

Rfn. Alfred TROWBRIDGE, 1561

Rifleman Alfred Trowbridge served with the Isle of Wight Rifles throughout the war. He was disembodied from the Army on 3rd April 1919 under service number 330299.

Rfn. Bertie TUCK, 2036

Rifleman Bertie Tuck continued to serve with the Isle of Wight Rifles after Gallipoli and was given service number 330591. He was taken prisoner during the Second Battle of Gaza on 19th April 1917 and spent his time as a prisoner of war at Nazareth and Tel Helif.

Rifleman Tuck was disembodied from the Isle of Wight Rifles on 3rd April 1919 and went on to join the Royal Field Artillery with whom he was given service number 277312.

Rfn. Albert TYZACK, 2452

Rifleman Albert Tyzack and his brother Rifleman Edgar Tyzack came from Wycombe Marsh in Buckinghamshire and were recruited to the Isle of Wight Rifles by Lieutenant Colonel Rhodes. Both were killed in action on 12th August 1915 during the advance on Anafarta Ridge and are commemorated on the Helles Memorial.

Rfn. Louis James VANASSCHE, 1421

Rifleman Louis Vanassche came from Ventnor and enlisted in the Isle of Wight Rifles on 21st January 1914. He remained with the battalion after Gallipoli and was given service number 330235.

It was reported in the War Office Daily List No.5428 on 28th November 1917 that Rifleman Vanassche had been wounded. The Isle of Wight Rifles took part in the Third Battle of Gaza at the beginning of November 1917 and it is likely that Rifleman Vanassche was wounded at some point during the battle.[764]

Following his wounding and recovery, Louis Vanassche was transferred to the Labour Corps and was given the rank of Private along with service number 548682. He was discharged from the Army on 25th July 1919 due to 'sickness' and was given the Silver War Badge.[765]

Rfn. William VANNER, 1991

Rifleman William Vanner was given service number 330558 when the Isle of Wight Rifles and other Territorial Force units received new service numbers in 1917. Towards the end of the war, he was transferred to the Royal Engineers and given the rank

---

[764] www.forces-war-records.co.uk: British Army daily reports (missing, dead, wounded & POWs) WWI - NLS 1917_WList18, War Office Daily List No. 5428, 28/11/1917

[765] www.ancestry.co.uk: UK, Silver War Badge Records, 1914-1920

of Sapper along with service number 521653. He survived the war.

Rfn. John VERNON, 2073

Rifleman John Vernon came from Wooburn Green in Buckinghamshire and formally enlisted in the Isle of Wight Rifles at Newport. He served at Gallipoli and died back in England on 17th August 1916 at the age of 19 years old. He is buried at Wooburn (St. Paul's) cemetery.[766]

Rfn. Alexander Douglas WALLACE, 1972

Rifleman Alexander Wallace came from Cowes and enlisted in the Isle of Wight Rifles at Newport on 26th November 1914. He fell ill at Gallipoli with Enteritis and was admitted into a hospital at Malta on 27th October 1915. He was then invalided back to England on 28th November 1915 aboard Hospital Ship Brazile and arrived in England on 7th December 1915.

Rifleman Alexander Wallace spent a period of time with the 4th (Reserve) battalion of the Hampshire Regiment under service number 330548 before being transferred to 627 Home Service Employment Company of the Labour Corps based at Sutton Veny, Wiltshire on 30th June 1917. He was later on transferred to the 442nd Agricultural Company of the Labour Corps. With the Labour Corps, Alexander Wallace held the rank of Private with service number 279749.

On 6th November 1918, Alexander Wallace was admitted to hospital with Influenza. This also developed into Pneumonia and on 20th November 1918 he passed away from Influenza and Pneumonia. Alexander Wallace was 21 years old and is buried at Cowes (Northwood) Cemetery.[767]

---

[766] https://www.cwgc.org/find-war-dead/casualty/344202/vernon,-john/
[767] www.ancestry.co.uk: British Army WWI Service Records, 1914-1920 - Territorial Force Attestation

Rfn. George WARING, 1227

Rifleman George Waring was transferred to the Devonshire Regiment after he served with the Isle of Wight Rifles at Gallipoli. He was given service number 50267 and the rank of Private. Following service with the Devonshire Regiment, George Waring was transferred to the Labour Corps and given service number 361714. George Waring's final Army service was with the Royal Engineers as a Sapper. He was disembodied from the Army on 5th May 1919 under service number 521691.

Rfn. Charles Henry WARNE, 1473

Rifleman Charles Warne came from Whitwell. He was reported to be *'seriously ill in hospital'* in the Isle of Wight County Press on 16th October 1915.

Rifleman Warne returned to serve with the Isle of Wight Rifles and in 1917 under the new numbering system for the Territorial forces, was given service number 330261. After the war, Rifleman Warne re-enlisted in the Isle of Wight Rifles and was given service number 05248.

Rfn. Edgar Septimus WARREN, 1501

Rifleman Edgar Warren came from Ventnor and enlisted in the Isle of Wight Rifles at Ventnor. He remained with the Isle of Wight Rifles after Gallipoli and was given service number 330271.

Rifleman Warren was killed in action on 19th April 1917 during the Second Battle of Gaza. He was 33 years old and is buried at Gaza War Cemetery.

Rfn. Frederick Arthur WATKINS, 2282

Rifleman Frederick Watkins served at Gallipoli with the Isle of Wight Rifles was transferred to the 2/4th Hants later in the war.

From April 1917, the 2/4th Hants fought in the Palestinian campaign as part of the Egyptian Expeditionary Force.

Frederick Watkins was disembodied from the Army on 3rd March 1919 under service number 205442.

Rfn. Arthur Jack WATSON, 1805

Rifleman Arthur Watson came from Ryde. He was reported to be missing in the Isle of Wight County Press on 11th September 1915 and was later presumed to have been killed in action on 12th August 1915 during the advance on Anafarta Ridge. Official notification of his death was published in the Isle of Wight County Press on 29th July 1916. Rifleman Watson was 19 years old and is commemorated on the Helles Memorial.

Rfn. Frederick George Henry WEAVING, 1978

Rifleman Weaving came from Merstone and enlisted in the Isle of Wight Rifles at Newport. He died at Gallipoli on 16th November 1915 at the age of 18 as a result of Jaundice. He is buried at Ari Burnu Cemetery, Anzac Cove, Turkey.[768]

Rfn. Wilfred Herbert WEEKS, 1973

Rifleman Wilfred Weeks enlisted in the Isle of Wight Rifles on 26th November 1914. On 12th August 1915, during the Isle of Wight Rifles advance on Anafarta Ridge, he was shot in the shoulder and the side and was invalided back to England where he was admitted into Westminster Hospital on 3rd September 1915 and had the bullet extracted from his shoulder under a local anaesthetic. The wounding had left Rifleman Weeks with *'limited movement of his shoulder.'*[769]

---

[768] www.ancestry.co.uk: UK, Army Registers of Soldiers' Effects, 1901-1929 - National Army Museum; Chelsea, London, England; Soldiers' Effects Records, 1901-60; NAM Accession Number: 1991-02-333; Record Number Ranges: 227501-229000; Reference: 104

[769] www.ancestry.co.uk: British Army WW1 Pension Records 1914-1919

Later on in the war, Rifleman Weeks was transferred to the 25th Reserve Battalion of the Rifle Brigade and given service number 207274. He then joined the 21st Rifle Brigade. Rifleman Weeks was recorded as having served in Egypt from 12th January 1917 until the end of the war, with the latter 3 months of the war spent attached to the Tele. School in Abbasia, Cairo, Egypt.[770]

Rifleman Weeks was disembodied from demobilisation on 8th July 1919 and given an Army Pension due to being classified as permanently disabled, with a severity grading of less than 20%, from his wounding on 12th August 1915.[771]

Rfn. Sydney Gordon WELCH, 979

Rifleman Sydney Welch served with the Isle of Wight Rifles at Gallipoli. On 24th February 1917, he was transferred to the Gloucestershire Regiment and then to the Labour Corps on 30th June 1917. Sydney Welch was discharged from the Army after the war but re-enlisted into the Royal Army Service Corps on 16th February 1920. He was discharged from the Royal Army Service Corps on 13th November 1920.[772]

Rfn. Alfred John WEST, 2121

Rifleman Alfred West enlisted in the Isle of Wight Rifles on 28th December 1914. His wounding at Gallipoli around November 1915 was confirmed in the War Office Casualty List on 2nd January 1916.[773]

---

[770] www.ancestry.co.uk: UK, WWI Service Medal and Award Rolls, 1914-1920, British War Medal and Victory Medal

[771] www.ancestry.co.uk: British Army WW1 Pension Records 1914-1919

[772] www.ancestry.co.uk: UK, WWI Service Medal and Award Rolls, 1914-1920, 1914-1915 Star

[773] www.forces-war-records.co.uk: British Army daily reports (missing, dead, wounded & POWs) WWI - DT03011916

Rifleman West was discharged from the Army on 23rd August 1916 due to 'sickness' and was given the Silver War Badge.[774]

Rfn. Edgar WESTMORE, 1238

Rifleman Edgar Westmore came from Ventnor and enlisted in the Isle of Wight Rifles at Ventnor. He continued to serve with the Isle of Wight Rifles after Gallipoli and was given service number 330139.

Rifleman Westmore was killed in action during the Second Battle of Gaza on 19th April 1917. He was 23 years old. Rifleman Westmore has no known grave and is commemorated on the Jerusalem Memorial.

Rfn. George Charles WHEELER, 2408

Rifleman George Wheeler served with the Isle of Wight Rifles throughout the war and his latter service number was 330819. Rifleman Wheeler died on 21st December 1918 and is buried at Cairo War Memorial War Cemetery.

Rfn. Charles WHITE, 1996

Rifleman Charles White was born in 1894 and lived in Avenue Road in Sandown which is the same road that George and Will Cooper lived in. Charles White enlisted in the Isle of Wight Rifles at Sandown and is possibly one of the Whites that enlisted with Reginald Brooks Butt, George Cooper, Will Cooper and Frank Butcher. Rifleman White fell ill with dysentery at Gallipoli and died of it on 23rd September 1915 whilst on a hospital ship headed for Malta. He is buried at Pieta Military Cemetery.[775]

Rfn. Herbert Frank WHITE, 2173

Rifleman Herbert White came from Oakfield and enlisted in the Isle of Wight Rifles at Newport. He was killed in action on 19th

---

[774] www.ancestry.co.uk: UK, Silver War Badge Records, 1914-1920
[775] Isle of Wight County Press, 9th October 1915, p8

April 1917 during the Second Battle of Gaza and is commemorated on the Jerusalem Memorial. His service number was 330679.[776]

Rfn. Ralph WITNEY, 2351

Rifleman Ralph Witney came from High Wycombe in Buckinghamshire and enlisted in the Isle of Wight Rifles on 1st March 1915 giving his age as 19 years old. He went on to serve at Gallipoli with the battalion.

By 15th September 1915, Army Authorities had been shown Rifleman Whitney's birth certificate – it stated that Rifleman Witney's date of birth was 28th June 1899, making him 16 years old. The Army then set in a motion an endeavour to get Rifleman Whitney brought back home and discharged from the Army. Whilst this was happening, Rifleman Witney became ill with dysentery and was taken to Malta by Hospital Ship Formosa. He was admitted to a hospital at Malta on 15th October 1915.

On 25th October 1915, Rifleman Witney boarded Hospital Ship Brasille which was headed for England. On arriving in England, Rifleman Witney was sent to the 2nd Birmingham War Hospital and was admitted into the hospital on 1st November 1915. He remained there until 4th January 1916 and he was then sent to Newport on the Isle of Wight where he was discharged from the Army on 14th January 1916 for being under 17 years old.[777]

Rfn. Douglas Alfred WILLIAMS, 1425

Rifleman Douglas Williams came from Cowes and enlisted in the Isle of Wight Rifles on 21st January 1914. He was listed as sick in the Isle of Wight County Press on 6th November 1915 and was

---

[776] www.ancestry.co.uk: UK, Soldiers Died in the Great War, 1914-1919
[777] www.ancestry.co.uk: British Army WWI Pension Records 1914-1920 – Territorial Force Attestation

discharged from the Army on 25th August 1916 due to sickness. As a result, Rifleman Williams was given the Silver War Badge.

Rfn. George WILLINGS, 1915

Rifleman George Willings came from Newport. He was reported as missing after the action on the 12th August 1915 in the Isle of Wight County Press on 2nd October 1915. He did however, survive the advance and returned to serve with the battalion for the remainder of the war. He was disembodied from the Army on 14th March 1919.

Rfn. Harry WOLFE, 2344

Rifleman Harry Wolfe served with the Isle of Wight Rifles throughout the war and was disembodied from the Army on 2nd May 1919 under service number 330777.

Rfn. Charles Albert WOODFORD, 2171

Rifleman Charles Woodford served in the Isle of Wight Rifles at Gallipoli with his two brothers; Rifleman George Henry Woodford and Rifleman Harry William Woodford. At the same time, their youngest brother, Frank, was in the reserve battalion (2/8th Hants).

Rifleman Charles Woodford was wounded between the middle of August and early September in his right arm by a piece of shrapnel and was taken to a hospital in Malta for further treatment.

On recovering from his wounding, Rifleman Charles Woodford returned to serve with the Isle of Wight Rifles throughout the rest of the war. He was disembodied from the battalion on 3rd August 1919 under service number 330678.

Both George and William were killed in action during 1917.

Rfn. Ernest Victor WOODFORD, 1600

Rifleman Ernest Woodford served with the Isle of Wight Rifles throughout the war and was disembodied from the Army on 23rd March 1919 under service number 330322.

Rfn. George Henry WOODFORD, 1987

Rifleman George Woodford served in the Isle of Wight Rifles at Gallipoli with his two brothers; Rifleman Charles Albert Woodford and Rifleman Harry William Woodford. At the same time, their youngest brother, Frank, was in the reserve battalion (2/8th Hants).

Rifleman George Woodford became sick at Gallipoli between the middle of August and early September 1915. He was invalided back to Plymouth for further hospital treatment. In January 1916, Rifleman Woodford was posted to Parkhurst Barracks.

Later in the war George Woodford was transferred to the 1st Battalion of the Duke of Cornwall's Light Infantry and given service number 260059. He reached the rank of Lance Corporal and took part in some of the fighting during the Third Battle of Ypres where he lost his life on the 4th October 1917. He is buried at Tyne Cot Cemetery.

Rifleman Charles Albert Woodford survived the war but Rifleman Harry William Woodford was killed on 7th June 1917.

Rfn. Percy WOODFORD, 1601

Rifleman Percy Woodford continued to serve with the Isle of Wight Rifles after their Gallipoli deployment and when the Territorial Forces received their new service numbers, he was given service number 330323. At some point in 1917 or 1918, Percy Woodford transferred to the Royal Engineers and became a Pioneer with service number 521679. He was placed on the Z Reserve List on 3rd July 1919.

Rfn. A. WOODLEY, 2390

Rifleman Woodley served with the Isle of Wight Rifles at Gallipoli and at some point, after the campaign he transferred to the Royal Flying Corps and was given service number 410259. He survived the war.

Rfn. Edwin George WOODNUTT, 1806

Rifleman Edwin Woodnutt's wounding was recorded in the Isle of Wight County Press on 4th September 1915 with him holding the rank of Lance Corporal. He had received a gunshot wound to his left arm and left hip, most likely during the advance on Anafarta Ridge, and was taken to a military hospital in Malta for treatment.

Lance Corporal Woodnutt was discharged from the Army on 14th March 1917 under service number 330448.

Rfn. Donald Arthur WRIGHT, 2085

Rifleman Donald Wright fell ill with dysentery between the middle of August and the middle of September 1915 and was invalided off Gallipoli to a hospital in Malta. His brother, Rifleman Reginald Wright was wounded around the same time and was taken to the same hospital.

Rifleman Donald Wright was later given the service number 330620. He was taken prisoner during the Second Battle of Gaza on 19th April 1917 and died in captivity on the 23rd October 1917. He is buried at Baghdad (North Gate) War Cemetery.

Rfn. Herbert F YAXLEY, 1240

Rifleman Herbert Yaxley was invalided off Gallipoli suffering with debility and septic poisoning. He was admitted into Tigen Hospital in Malta.

Later in the war, Rifleman Yaxley was transferred to the King's Royal Rifle Corps and was given service number 51398. He survived the war and re-enlisted.

Rfn. Albert Victor YOUNG, 1084

Rifleman Albert Young was invalided off Gallipoli on 9th September 1915 but it is unknown if this was due to him being ill or wounded. He was later transferred to the 22nd Rifle Brigade and served in Salonika with the unit from 23rd January 1917 until 11th November 1918. His service number was 207275.

Rfn. Bertie John YOUNG, 883

Rifleman Bertie Young continued to serve with the Isle of Wight Rifles after the Great War and in May 1922 he was awarded the Territorial Efficiency Medal. His latter service number was 330045.

Rfn. Herbert YOUNG, 2138

Rifleman Herbert Young enlisted in the Isle of Wight Rifles on 2nd January 1915 and was initially based at Newport. He fell ill with diarrhoea at Gallipoli and on 27th October 1915 he was admitted into a hospital at Malta. Rifleman Young was invalided back to England aboard Hospital Ship Glencart Castle on 18th November 1915.

Once Rifleman Young was fully fit, he was posted to the 4th Hants, a reserve battalion of the Hampshire Regiment and he stayed with this unit until 12th January 1917 when he boarded a transport ship at Devonport headed for Alexandria. Rifleman Young landed in Alexandria on 27th January 1917 and on 2nd February 1917 he re-joined the Isle of Wight Rifles at Romani and shortly afterwards was given service number 330653.

Rifleman Young received a gunshot wound to his right wrist during the Second Battle of Gaza on 19th April 1917 and on the same day he received treatment at the 2/1st East Anglian Field

Ambulance. The following day he was admitted into the 36th Stationary Hospital at Mohamydia and on 25th April 1917 Rifleman Young was admitted into the 31st General Hospital at Port Said. He then spent time at the 15th General Hospital at Alexandria from 28th May 1917 and at Convalescence Hospital Montazah in Alexandria from 28th June 1917.

The wounding meant that Rifleman Young was classified as Class Biii by the Medical Board at Convalescence Hospital Montazah on 7th August 1917. Rifleman Young was sent to 2 Infantry Base Depot at Alexandria on 9th August 1917 and on 23rd August 1917 he was transferred to the 7th Battalion of the Royal Warwickshire Regiment and given service number 269428. He was then subsequently transferred to the 1st Garrison Battalion of the Royal Warwickshire Regiment at Mustapha on 30th August 1917.

Herbert Young joined a detachment of the 1st Garrison Battalion of the Royal Warwickshire Regiment at Kantara on 29th September 1918 and on 27th February 1919 he embarked on a ship headed for the UK at Port Said. Herbert Young was discharged from the Army on 11th April 1919.[778]

Rfn. Percy George YOUNG, 998

Rifleman Percy Young served with the Isle of Wight Rifles at Gallipoli and afterwards spent a period of time with the 1st Garrison Battalion of the Notts and Derby Regiment before re-joining the Isle of Wight Rifles again. The 1st Garrison Battalion of the Nots and Derby Regiment were based in Malta in October 1915 and later in the war were redeployed to Egypt.

Rifleman Young was disembodied from the Army on 1st August 1919 under service number 330051.

---

[778] www.ancestry.co.uk: British Army WWI Pension Records 1914-1920

Company Unknown

Rfn. Bert BEASLEY, 1763

Rifleman Bert Beasley served with the Isle of Wight Rifles throughout the war and was disembodied from the Army on 26th June 1919 under service number 330418.

Rfn. George Edgar JAGO, 1043

Rifleman George Jago enlisted in the Isle of Wight Rifles at Cowes on 28th February 1911. At Gallipoli, he fell ill with Enteritis and on 13th August 1915 he was treated by the 30th Field Ambulance who were based on the west side of 'A' Beach, Suvla Bay. Rifleman Jago was subsequently sent to the 26th Casualty Clearing Station and he then spent time at hospitals on Mudros and Malta. Rifleman Jago was invalided to England on 3rd November 1915 and was discharged from the Army on 27th February 1916.[779]

Rfn. Charles LOBB, 938

Rifleman Charles Lobb enlisted in the Isle of Wight Rifles at Cowes on 10th February 1910 at the age of 17 years. He came through the Gallipoli campaign unscathed and returned to England on 15th January 1916. Rifleman Lobb was discharged from the Army on 19th February 1916.[780]

Rfn. George Jacob PHARAOH 1047

Rifleman George Pharaoh served with the Isle of Wight Rifles at Gallipoli and was discharged from the Army on 1st March 1916.

---

[779] www.ancestry.co.uk: British Army WWI Pension Records 1914-1920
[780] www.ancestry.co.uk: British Army WWI Pension Records 1914-1920

RAMC Attached

Capt. G RAYMOND

Captain Raymond was a doctor before the war in Newport. He served in the Isle of Wight Rifles before being transferred to the Royal Army Medical Corps. He went on to become the medical officer for the battalion. His brother, Second-Lieutenant Frederick Raymond also served in the Isle of Wight Rifles at Gallipoli.

Captain Raymond was spoken very highly of by the soldiers. In a letter home by Rfn. S Pullen on 19th August 1915, he stated that Captain Raymond had been doing *'glorious work for the wounded.'*[781]

The constant influx of terrible casualties and no time for rest took its toll on Captain Raymond and in a letter dated 19th August 1915, L/Cpl. H Thorn (RAMC) wrote that *'Capt. Raymond is knocked up owing to having no rest.'*[782] On 11th September 1915 news came through in the Isle of Wight County Press that Captain Raymond was *'rapidly recovering in a London hospital from the effects of shell shock and overwork.'*[783] Later in September 1915 he returned to Newport for convalescence suffering with hearing loss in one ear.

Captain Raymond survived the war.

Lce-Sgt. Frank Randolph STEARS, 1270, D Company

Lance-Sergeant Frank Stears served at Gallipoli with his brother, Sergeant Charles Stears. Lance-Sergeant Stears was reported as being sick with dysentery, enteritis and tonsilitis in the Isle of

---

[781] Isle of Wight County Press, 4th September 1915, p4.
[782] Isle of Wight County Press, 4th September 1915, p4.
[783] Isle of Wight County Press, 11th September 1915, p8.

Wight County Press on 30th October 1915 and at the time of publication, was at a hospital in Dartford.

He survived the war and was disembodied from the RAMC on 2nd April 1919.

Lce-Cpl. Charles Harold THORN, 1874, C Company

Lance-Corporal Thorn came from Cowes. At Gallipoli, he wrote a number of letters home which were published in the Isle of Wight County Press. In the 4th December 1915 edition of the Isle of Wight County Press, Lance-Corporal Thorn was reported as being *'indisposed and in hospital in Cairo.'*[784]

Lance-Corporal Thorn survived the war and was disembodied from the Army on 26th March 1919.

Pte. Reginald James BROOKS BUTT, 2137, C Company

Reginald Brooks Butt came from Sandown, Isle of Wight. He was a student at Portsmouth Grammar School when war broke out and was due to go back to study. Reginald was 16 years old and considering a medical career. Reginald first tried to join the 3rd Wessex, RAMC, but was turned down, presumably for being under age. On 4th September 1914 he joined the Isle of Wight Rifles with his cousins; Frank Butcher, George Cooper, Will Cooper, and the two Whites – possibly Lance Corporal George White, 1631 and Rifleman Charles White, 1996.

At some point in the run up to the Gallipoli deployment he and George Cooper were transferred to the Royal Army Medical Corps. Both he and George Cooper had a St John's Ambulance First Aid certificate so this may be why they were transferred to the RAMC. Reginald wanted to serve with his cousins and managed to stay with the Isle of Wight Rifles, albeit attached via the RAMC.

---

[784] Isle of Wight County Press, 4th December 1915, p5.

Reginald landed at Gallipoli on 10th August 1915 with the Isle of Wight Rifles and saw action at Anafarta Ridge. Suffering from enteric fever and frost bite, Reginald was invalided off the peninsula in late November 1915 and returned to England. He was then re-mustered into the RAMC as a stretcher bearer in the 26th (3rd Wessex) Field Ambulance attached to the 8th Division along with his cousin, George Cooper. Both he and George Cooper went out to France in April 1916 and served at the Somme in 1916 and then at Ypres in 1917.

During the opening phase of the Battle of Passchendaele, the 26th Wessex Field Ambulance was based at Remy Sidings with an advanced Aid Post at Birr Cross Roads. They were moved into reserve on the 3rd August but on 4th August a stretcher party, including Reginald, was called to help the 76th Field Ambulance as they were overwhelmed with casualties. On the night of 4th/5th August 1917, whilst bringing a wounded soldier back from 'no man's land,' Reginald was hit by a shell fragment in the leg which severed the artery and shattered the bone. He was taken back to the front line by his fellow stretcher bearers and given a blood transfusion and then taken to the Casualty Clearing Station at Remy Sidings, Lijssenthoek. In May 1918, he was formally discharged from the army and received an honourable discharge certificate. Reginald required a stick to help him walk for the rest of his life.

Despite Reginald's traumatic experience and wounding during the war, he showed great resolve and began a career as a civil servant. At the outbreak of the Second World War he tried to enlist again but due to his damaged leg was turned away. He continued as a civil servant in the Air Ministry at the War Office, London and volunteered to be a Fire Warden. Reginald finished his career as a Director in the Air Ministry. For his work as a civil servant, he received an MBE and the Queen's Coronation Medal to add to his World War One medals; 1914/15 Star, British War Medal and the Victory Medal.

Of the group of cousins he joined up with, only he and Frank Butcher were still alive in 1922. Reginald was very good friends with George Cooper and was devastated when he passed away. For many years, Reginald did not return to the Isle of Wight. It was only once he retired that Reginald started to tell his son about his war time experiences.

Pte. George Henry COOPER, 2138, C Company

George Cooper joined the Isle of Wight Rifles on 4th September 1914 along with his brother Will Cooper and cousins Reginald Brooks Butt, Frank Butcher, and the two Whites. Before deploying to Gallipoli both he and Reginald Brooks Butt had been transferred to the RAMC but remained with the Isle of Wight Rifles. George was invalided off Gallipoli suffering from enteric fever at the same time as Reginald Brooks Butt.

George along with Reginald Brooks Butt were then posted to the 26th Field Ambulance as stretcher bearers. He served with the 26th Field Ambulance during the Somme, Passchendaele, the German Spring offensive and right through to the end of the war. George developed severe pleurisy during the German's final offensive of 1918 but could not be taken out of the line due to the extreme strain the British Army was under. The delay proved fatal and he died in a sanatorium at St. Lawrence on the Isle of Wight on 12th March 1921 at the age of 27. He is buried in Sandown churchyard.

Other Attached Personnel

Arm-Sgt. Alfred J SANDERS, 1743, A Company

Alfred Sanders was attached to the Isle of Wight Rifles from the Royal Army Ordnance Corps. He survived the war and on 10th April 1919 he was placed on the Z Reserve.

Pte. Samuel Stephen KENTFIELD, 27299, B Company

Samuel Kentfield was a regular soldier in the British Army. He was on operations with the 10th Hampshire Regiment from 6th October 1914 under service number 5206. On returning to England, he was reassigned to the 16th Liverpool Regiment under service number 27299. By the 29th July 1915 he was attached to the Isle of Wight Rifles. At the end of the war he was serving with the 4th Cheshire Regiment under service number 63048.

Known Re-Enforcements from the Second Battalion of the Isle of Wight Rifles

Second Lieutenant William Gordon HARKER

Second Lieutenant Gordon Harker was an actor before the war. He joined the Isle of Wight Rifles as an officer and was posted to Gallipoli from the reserve battalion in October 1915 as the battalion were in desperate need of officers after suffering many losses. Second Lieutenant Harker's British Army WW1 Medal Rolls Index Card, 1914-1920 states that he arrived at Gallipoli on 15th October 1915 and the Isle of Wight Rifles' War Diary states that he joined the battalion at Gallipoli on 19th October 1915.

Gordon Harker served with the Isle of Wight Rifles at Palestine, holding the rank of Lieutenant and was wounded in the thigh and shoulder during the Second Battle of Gaza. He survived the war and left the Isle of Wight Rifles with rank of Captain.

After the war, Gordon Harker returned to acting and performed on the stage as well in many films, including four Alfred Hitchcock films.

Second Lieutenant Alfred Olaf HYTTEN

Second Lieutenant Hytten came from Lewisham. He joined the battalion at Gallipoli along with Second Lieutenants Harker, Shelley and Pocock on 19th October 1915.

Second Lieutenant Hytten was promoted to the rank of acting Captain in the Isle of Wight Rifles on 19th April 1917 – the date of the Second Battle of Gaza. He survived the war, holding the rank of Captain.

Second Lieutenant Percy John SHELLEY

Second Lieutenant Shelley joined the battalion at Gallipoli on 19th October 1915. He survived the war, holding the rank of Lieutenant.

Second Lieutenant Charles Arthur POCOCK

Second Lieutenant Pocock joined the Isle of Wight Rifles at Gallipoli on 19th October 1915.

In the UK Army List for 1918, Second Lieutenant Pocock was recorded as holding the rank of Lieutenant and being attached to the 11th (Service) Battalion (Pioneers) on 31st July 1917.[785]

During the first few months of 1918, Lieutenant Pocock was wounded.[786]

Lieutenant Pocock survived the war.

---

[785] www.forces-war-records.co.uk: UK Army List 1918
[786] www.forces-war-records.co.uk: British Army daily reports - missing, dead, wounded & POWs – WWI: War Office Daily List No.5542, 17/04/1918

Other Officers of the Isle of Wight Rifles

Major Arthur Edward MAYES

Major Arthur Mayes was recorded in the UK Army List 1907 as holding the rank of Captain with the 5th Volunteer Battalion, the predecessor to the Isle of Wight Rifles, on the 18th October 1906. By the outbreak of war, he had spent at least 8 years with the battalion and due to his seniority and experience he took the command of the battalion's depot which was set up at Newport Drill Hall on 10th August 1914.

Major Mayes did not go to Gallipoli with the battalion. He presumably remained on the Isle of Wight helping to build the strength of the 2nd Battalion of the Isle of Wight Rifles. By 1st June 1916, Arthur Mayes had been promoted to Lieutenant Colonel and had been posted to the 1st Garrison Battalion of the Hampshire Regiment which had recently moved to St. Omer in France. He remained with this unit and survived the war. The 1st Garrison Battalion later became known as the 19th Garrison Battalion of the Hampshire Regiment.[787] [788]

Captain P V P Stone DSO

Captain P V P Stone was originally an officer with the Norfolk Regiment and went on to become the Isle of Wight Rifles' adjutant. Towards the beginning of the war, he was posted back to the Norfolk Regiment and went on to serve with the Norfolk Regiment in France. He was promoted to Major and in 1917 was acting as a Temporary Brigadier General in a staff officer's role in France.[789]

---

[787] www.forces-war-records.co.uk: UK Army List 1918
[788] https://www.longlongtrail.co.uk/army/regiments-and-corps/the-british-infantry-regiments-of-1914-1918/hampshire-regiment/
[789] www.forces-war-records.co.uk: Search Records of Soldiers Awards from the London Gazette

Captain Stone received a Mention in Despatches and was awarded the Distinguished Service Order. He survived the war.

Lieutenant R. Charles Marvin

Lieutenant Marvin was recorded in the Army List of January 1914 as holding the rank of Lieutenant with the Isle of Wight Rifles on 9th October 1911. He was discharged from the Army on the 7th November 1916 and given the Silver War Badge.

Gallipoli Roll of Honour

One hundred and fifty-two men lost their lives as a result of the Gallipoli campaign. On top of those killed in action, many died of wounds at a later date and several succumbed to illness.

12th August 1915:

    Major Ernest Lewis

    Captain Arthur Holmes Gore

    Captain Graham Loader

    Captain Clayton Ratsey

    Captain Donald Ratsey

    Lieutenant James Alexander Young

    Second Lieutenant Laurence Watson

    Second Lieutenant Frederick Raymond

    Company Sergeant Major Frank Fielder

    Company Sergeant Major Walter Purkis

    Sergeant Reginald Groves

    Sergeant Frederick Leftwich

    Lance Sergeant Harry Leal

    Corporal John Barton

    Corporal Thomas Boyce

    Corporal Douglas Sparks

Corporal William Witham

Lance Corporal Eric Holbrook

Lance Corporal Edward Miles

Lance Corporal Alfred Salmon

Lance Corporal Alfred Whittington

Rifleman William Abbott

Rifleman Thomas Arnold

Rifleman Herbert Baker

Rifleman John Baker

Rifleman Leonard Ball

Rifleman Adolphus Ballard

Rifleman Walter Ballard

Rifleman Robert Bilk

Rifleman Frank Brett

Rifleman William Buckett

Rifleman Henry Burton

Rifleman Andrew Cheesman

Rifleman Henry Cole

Rifleman William Finch

Rifleman Edward Foster

Rifleman Philip Gilbert

Rifleman Frank Green

Rifleman George Guy

Rifleman Arthur Hale

Rifleman Bertram Hamilton

Rifleman Herbert Harvey

Rifleman Lawrence Hatcher

Rifleman George Hills

Rifleman George Holbrook

Rifleman John Hurry

Rifleman Percy King

Rifleman John Knight

Rifleman William Langdon

Rifleman Frank Lee

Rifleman William Mayo

Rifleman George Meecham

Rifleman Frederick Edwin Miller

Rifleman Percy Paine

Rifleman Ernest Parsons

Rifleman Herbert Peach

Rifleman James Pocock

Rifleman James Punch

Rifleman Arthur Rann

Rifleman James Read

Rifleman Charles Rolf

Rifleman Bernard Rolfe

Rifleman Arthur Russell

Rifleman Albert Sarney

Rifleman Albert Saunders

Rifleman Ralph Sawyer

Rifleman Harold Searle

Rifleman Reginald Sibbick

Rifleman Arthur Simmonds

Rifleman Albert Sinnicks

Rifleman Harry Smart

Rifleman Joseph Stark

Rifleman Raymond Trinder

Rifleman Harry Trowbridge

Rifleman Albert Tyzack

Rifleman Edgar Tyzack

Rifleman Edward Urry

Rifleman Frederick Urry

Rifleman William Urry

Rifleman Walter Vincent

Rifleman Alfred Ward

Rifleman Charles Watkins

Rifleman Arthur Watson

Rifleman Gilbert Whittington

Rifleman Francis Yeate

13th August 1915:

    Sergeant George Woodford

    Rifleman Clifford King

    Rifleman Hubert Watson

    Rifleman Bertie Wray

14th August 1915:

    Lance Sergeant William Silvester

    Lance Corporal Frank Le Brun

    Rifleman James Devereux

    Rifleman Thomas Newman

    Rifleman Charles Stark

16th August 1915:

    Rifleman Frederick Cecil Miller

17th August 1915:

    Rifleman Lawrence Searle

18th August 1915:

    Second Lieutenant William Bartlett

    Rifleman William Dunstan

    Rifleman Hubert Haward

    Rifleman Harry Sheppard

20th August 1915:

    Second Lieutenant Percy Latham

Rifleman H Horscroft

22nd August 1915:

    Corporal Sydney Bunce

    Rifleman Isaac Foss

    Rifleman Lancelot Halliday

    Rifleman Ernest Kerley

    Rifleman Ernest Symes

    Rifleman George Toogood

    Rifleman Charles Wapshott

23rd August 1915:

    Rifleman Sidney Downer

    Rifleman Oliver Harding

24th August 1915:

    Rifleman Arthur Coombes

25th August 1915:

    Sergeant Raymond Sibley

    Rifleman Charles Barton

    Rifleman J Stallard

29th August 1915:

    Rifleman H Hayden

3rd September 1915:

    Corporal John Cook

Rifleman Frederick Hollis

4th September 1915:

Rifleman Ronald Weaver

5th September 1915:

Rifleman Philip Chapman

Rifleman Owen Trevett

10th September 1915:

Rifleman William Sharpe

11th September 1915:

Rifleman Alfred Woodford

14th September 1915:

Lieutenant Walter Read

18th September 1915:

Rifleman George Chick

Rifleman Arthur Silsbury

19th September 1915:

Rifleman Arthur Greenham

20th September 1915:

Rifleman Albert Salter

23rd September 1915:

Serjeant Cecil Wales

Rifleman Charlie White

27th September 1915:

    Rifleman Frank Bax

30th September 1915:

    Rifleman William North

2nd October 1915:

    Rifleman George Ash

8th October 1915:

    Rifleman William Young

9th October 1915:

    Rifleman Sidney Ginger

    Rifleman George Walker

16th October 1915:

    Serjeant Percy Ellaway

17th October 1915:

    Lance Corporal Walter Butcher

20th October 1915:

    Rifleman George Edwin Dimmer

29th October 1915:

    Lance Corporal Thomas Alexander

31st October 1915:

    Rifleman Albert Downer

    Rifleman Frederick Smith

2nd November 1915:

    Private Christopher Arnold

7th November 1915:

    Lance Corporal Arthur Tosdevin

16th November 1915:

    Rifleman George Weaving

22nd November 1915:

    Private Alfred Ball

25th November 1915:

    Rifleman Herbert Cawston

29th November 1915:

    Rifleman Albert Coward

    Rifleman George Dunn

11th December 1915:

    Rifleman Francis Foot

9th January 1916:

    Rifleman Charles Vincent

The Men from Buckinghamshire

Name	Company	From
Rfn W Crump	A	High Wycombe
Rfn J Devereaux	A	High Wycombe
Rfn T Hawes	A	High Wycombe
Rfn F Swadling	B	Marlow
Rfn L Ball	B	Wooburn Green
Rfn G Reeves	C	N/K
Rfn T Bowdrey	C	Bourne End
Rfn W Lunnon	C	Bourne End
Rfn W Mayo	C	Flackwell Heath
Rfn A Pepper	C	High Wycombe
Rfn E Pope	C	High Wycombe
Rfn S Small	C	High Wycombe
Rfn E Woodley	C	High Wycombe
Rfn O Rogers	C	Little Marlow
Rfn L Southam	C	Little Marlow
Rfn P Twitchen	C	Little Marlow
Rfn J Brooks	C	Marlow
Rfn W East	C	Marlow
Rfn W North	C	Marlow
Rfn J Patmore	C	Wooburn
Rfn W Patmore	C	Wooburn
Rfn J White	C	Wooburn
Rfn C Watkins	C	Wooburn Green
Rfn E Tyzack	C	Wycombe Marsh
Rfn F Cox	D	N/K
Rfn H Rolfe	D	N/K
Rfn W Simmons	D	Bovingdon Green
Rfn A Sarney	D	Marlow
Rfn C Hawes	D	Flackwell Heath
Rfn A Scouse	D	High Wycombe
Rfn A H Sharpe	D	High Wycombe
Rfn W H Stone	D	High Wycombe
Rfn R Witney	D	High Wycombe
Rfn W Brunsden	D	Marlow

Rfn W Norton	D	Marlow
Rfn A Pratt	D	Upper Bourne End
Rfn J Smith	D	Upper Bourne End
Rfn F Adby	D	West Wycombe
Rfn J Vernan	D	Wooburn Green
Rfn A Tyzack	D	Wycombe Marsh

Photos

CQMS William Charles Cooper

Pte Reginald James Brooks Butt (RAMC attached)

Rifleman Sid Porter, 1915

Corporal Albert Sangar and Amy

Acknowledgements

My interest in the Isle of Wight Rifles came from my late father James Brookes-Butt passing down the stories told to him by his father Reginald James Brooks Butt. Sadly, my father passed away in September 2022 but prior to his passing he was able to help me with my research which I am very grateful for and he also provided me with the photos of his father and CQMS William Cooper.

The Isle of Wight County Press kindly gave me permission to use their archives for the research which has provided me with a wealth of information on the Isle of Wight Rifles' Gallipoli campaign.

I would like to thank Michael Wills, the grandson of Cpl Albert Sanger who gave me a photo of his grandfather along with information on his grandfather and Lt. Brannon.

Finally, I would like to thank Ian Meadows, the nephew of Rifleman Sid Porter. He has provided photos and information on his uncle, the list of Prisoners of War and has helped me to piece together information on some of the soldiers that were difficult to identify in army records.

References

Books

- The Gallipoli Experience Reconsidered, Peter Liddle, Pen & Sword
- The Fall of the Ottomans: The Great War in the Middle East 1914-1920, Eugene Rogan, Lane
- The Isle of Wight Rifles, D J Quigley, Saunders
- Battle Story – Gallipoli 1915, Peter Doyle, The History Press
- The First World War in the Middle East, Kristian Coates Ulrichsen, Hurst
- Trench Art: the stories behind the talismans, Judy Waugh, Fontaine Press Pty Ltd
- Isle of Wight in the Great War, M. J. Trow, Pen & Sword Military
- Guests of the Unspeakable, Sir Thomas White
- Gallipoli – The Dardanelles Disaster in Soldiers' Words and Photographs, Richard Van Emden and Stephen Chambers, Bloomsbury
- British Regiments at Gallipoli, Ray Westlake, Pen & Sword
- Gallipoli Then and Now, Steve Newman, After the Battle
- At The Trail, Isle of Wight Rifles 1908-1920, Gareth Sprack, Cross Publishing

Newspaper Archives

- Archives from the Isle of Wight County Press
- Watford Observer
- Portsmouth Evening News

Official Records

The following records were obtained via Ancestry.co.uk:

- War Diaries:
    - Isle of Wight Rifles
    - 9th Corps General Staff
    - 54th Division
    - 54th Division ADMS
    - 53rd (Welsh) Division
    - 163rd Brigade
    - 4th Norfolks
    - 5th Norfolks
    - 5th Suffolks
    - 3rd Welsh Field Ambulance
    - 1/5th Essex
- Service Records (also known as attestation papers)
- Pension Records: Proceedings on Discharge and Territorial Force Attestation
- UK, Soldiers Died in the Great War, 1914-1919
- UK, Army Registers of Soldiers' Effects, 1901-1929 - National Army Museum; Chelsea, London, England; *Soldiers' Effects Records, 1901-60*; NAM Accession Number: *1991-02-333*; Record Number Ranges: *227501-229000*; Reference: *104*
- UK, WWI Service Medal and Award Rolls, 1914-1920: 1914-1915 Star - The National Archives of the UK; Kew, Surrey, England; *WWI Service Medal and Award Rolls*; Class: *WO 329*; Piece Number: *2901*
- British War and Victory Medal
- Silver War Badge Records

- UK, Royal Air Force Airmen Records, 1918-1940 - The National Archives of the UK, Kew, Surrey, England; Kew, Surrey, England; Air Ministry: Air Member for Personnel and Predecessors: Airmen's Records; Series Number: AIR 79
- Census Records; 1891, 1901, 1911
- UK, Commonwealth War Graves, 1914-1921 and 1939-1947
- UK, Royal Navy Registers of Seamen's Services, 1848-1939 - The National Archives of the UK; Kew, Surrey, England; Royal Navy Registers of Seamen's Services; Class: ADM 188; Piece: 1128
- UK, Citations of the Distinguished Conduct Medal, 1914-1920: Original data: Walker, R. W., and Chris Buckland, compilers. Citations of the Distinguished Conduct Medal, 1914–1920. 4 sections. Uckfield, East Sussex, United Kingdom: Naval and Military Press, 2007.
- UK, British Army Recipients of the Military Medal, 1914-1920
- UK, Royal Air Force Airmen Records, 1918-1940 - The National Archives of the UK, Kew, Surrey, England; Kew, Surrey, England; Air Ministry: Air Member for Personnel and Predecessors: Airmen's Records; Series Number: AIR 79

The following records were obtained from Fold3.com

- UK, WW1 Pension Ledgers and Index Cards 1914-1923

The following records were obtained via Forces War Records:

- British Red Cross and Order of St John Enquiry List 1917 (Wounded and Missing)
- British Army Court Martials 1914-1950 (WO86/69)
- Embarkation Records of Servicemen WWI
- First World War Daily Reports (Missing, Wounded & Prisoner of War):
  - NLS 1918_WList29
  - War Office Daily List No.5327, NLS 1917_WList01
  - War Office Daily List No.5428, 28/11/1917, NLS 1917_WList18
  - War Office Daily List No. 5488, NLS 1918_WList28
  - DT03011916
  - War Office Daily List No.5638, 08/08/1918, NLS 1918_WList54
  - War Office Daily List No.5344, 22/08/1917
  - War Office Daily List No. 5425, 24/11/1917, NLS 1917_Wlist17
  - NLS 1917_WList08 – War Office Daily List No. 5369, 20/09/1917
  - War Office Daily List No.5542, 17/04/1918
- Gazetted Awards and Mentions in Despatches
  - Gazette Issue 30746, 11/06/1918, p7053
  - Gazette Issue 30312, 25/09/1917, p10025
  - Gazette issue 30340, 16/10/1917, p10715

- o Gazette Issue 30474, 11/01/1918, p800
- o London Gazette No. 29541, 10/04/1916 *and* London Gazette, 07/11/1916, p6949
- o London Gazette, 21/06/1916, p6144
- o Gazette 15/02/1917, p1611
- o Gazette 26/01/1918
- o London Gazette, 15/01/1918, p933
- o London Gazette, 09/03/1919, p11106
- o London Gazette Issue 30474, 11/01/1918, p800
- o London Gazette 18/02/1918
- Military Hospitals Admissions and Discharge Registers WW1:
  - o MH106/1224 No. 19 General Hospital: 06/08/1915 to 15/08/1915
  - o MH106/1225 No. 19 General Hospital: 01/09/1915 to 27/09/1915
  - o MH106/226 No. 19 General Hospital Alexandria 27/09/1915 to 11/10/1915
  - o MH106/1228 No. 19 General Hospital: 29/10/1915 to 21/11/1915
  - o MH106/1814 Medical Records of Catterick Camp Military Hospital: 12/08/1919-04/11/1919
  - o MH106/1913 Records of H.M.A.T Ship Assaye: 02/10/1915 - 11/10/1915
  - o MH106/1915
  - o MH106/167, First World War Representative Medical Records of Servicemen from 139th Field Ambulance
  - o MH106/1141 First World War Representative Medical Records of No.

18 General Hospital: 03/08/1917 to 18/08/1917
  - MH106/382, First World War Representative Medical Records of Servicemen from No. 3 Casualty Clearing Station
  - MH106/1932, First World War Representative Medical Records of H.M.A.T Ship Assaye: 12/10/1918 - 18/10/1918
  - MH106/1385, First World War Representative Medical Records of No. 85 General Hospital: 31/01/1919 to 26/08/1919. No. 85 General Hospital at SOLOMBALA North Russia Expeditionary Force.
  - MH106/1913, The National Archives in Kew, First World War Representative Medical Records of H.M.A.T Ship Assaye: 02/10/1915 - 11/10/1915. British and Colonial Other Ranks. H.M.Hospital Ship ASSAYE Lines of Communication Mediterranean Expeditionary Force.
- Nominal index of all service personnel serving in a theatre of war 1914-1919
- Search Records of Soldiers Awards from the London Gazette - Gazette No 29664, 07/11/1916, p6949
- Silver War Badge List 1914-1918
- Soldiers Died in the Great War 1914-1919
- UK Army Lists 1907, 1914, 1916, 1918, 1933
- WW1 & WW2 Nurses Records

- RAF Formations List 1918
  - AIR 1/819/204/4/1316

Prisoner of War records were obtained from the International Committee of the Red Cross: https://grandeguerre.icrc.org

Websites

- Isle of Wight Rifles: www.wwwight.co.uk
- https://aegeanairwar.com/articles/came-down-suvla
- http://www.wightatwar.org.uk/island-stories/captain-clement-villar
- https://www.sites.google.com/site/iowrifles/sgt-bishop-diary
- http://www.royalhampshireregiment.org/about-the-museum/timeline
- http://www.longlongtrail.co.uk/army/regiments-and-corps/the-british-infantry-regiments-of-1914-1918/hampshire-regiment/
- https://www.forces-war-records.co.uk
- https://the.hitchcock.zone/wiki/Gordon_Harker
- https://www.sites.google.com/site/iowrifles/home
- http://www.iowtodunkirk.com/the-bee-goes-to-war/the-crew-of-the-bee/engineer-fred-reynard/
- http://www.royalhampshireregiment.org/about-the-museum/timeline/palestine-1917/
- https://www.forces-war-records.co.uk/maps/units/674/hampshire-regiment/18th-isle-of-wight-rifles-princess-beatrices-battalion/

- http://www.longlongtrail.co.uk/army/order-of-battle-of-divisions/54th-east-anglian-division/
- https://stevesmith1944.wordpress.com/2015/07/12/part-3-the-15th-norfolk-regiment-at-gallipoli/
- https://www.historic-uk.com/HistoryUK/HistoryofBritain/5th-Battalion-Norfolk-Regiment-The-True-Story/
- http://bedfordregiment.org.uk/5thbn/5thbtn1915diary.html
- http://bedfordregiment.org.uk/5thbn/5thbtnkiretchbattle1915.html
- http://www.ramc-ww1.com/profile.php?cPath=274_280_12&profile_id=4964
- http://www.isle-of-wight-memorials.org.uk/
- http://fightingthroughpodcast.co.uk/16-gallipoli-ww1-memoir/4593981882
- https://friendsofim.com/category/Gallipoli-Blog/page/4/
- https://www.iwm.org.uk/collections/item/object/80012762
- http://www.isle-of-wight-memorials.org.uk/wargraves/npt/newport_quantrill_wc.htm
- http://www.gallipoli-association.org
- http://www.jacksontree.co.uk/RememberThemFrame1.htm?
- http://www.isle-of-wight-memorials.org.uk/people-npt/npt_le_brun_f.htm
- http://www.stedmundsburychronicle.co.uk/galleryww1/galleryww1page_04a.htm
- http://www.eadt.co.uk/news/remembering-bury-st-edmunds-first-zeppelin-raid-100-years-on-1-4054830

- https://www.suffolkarchives.co.uk/places/a-z-of-suffolk/z-is-for-zeppelin/
- https://www.longlongtrail.co.uk/army/regiments-and-corps/the-british-infantry-regiments-of-1914-1918/hampshire-regiment/
- https://salonikacampaignsociety.org.uk/researching/northamptonshire-regiment/
- https://www.longlongtrail.co.uk/army/regiments-and-corps/the-british-infantry-regiments-of-1914-1918/devonshire-regiment/
- https://www.longlongtrail.co.uk/army/regiments-and-corps/the-british-infantry-regiments-of-1914-1918/the-rifle-brigade-1914-1918/
- https://www.cwgc.org/find-war-dead/casualty/402759/bailey,-george/
- https://www.cwgc.org/find-war-dead/casualty/110999/janes,-sydney-harold/
- https://www.cwgc.org/find-war-dead/casualty/1647199/stone,-walter-henry/
- https://www.cwgc.org/find-war-dead/casualty/344202/vernon,-john/
- https://sites.google.com/site/iowrifles/rifleman-mills-diary/the-diary-transcript
- http://www.isle-of-wight-fhs.co.uk/Northwoodmemorials/chessell_ajr.pdf
- https://livesofthefirstworldwar.iwm.org.uk/story/83453
- http://www.marlowsociety.org.uk/MRWW1/userfiles/file/Rifleman-John-Brooks.pdf
- https://billiongraves.com/grave/John-Patrick-Murphy/22685573
- http://www.iancastlezeppelin.co.uk/29th30th-april/4585768340

- http://www.stedmundsburychronicle.com/Chronicle/C20pics/zepp1915.jpg
- http://www.hertfordshire-genealogy.co.uk/data/occupations/military/military-hampshire-reg.htm
- https://bearalley.blogspot.com/2010/12/edward-r-home-gall.html
- https://www.stpaulsbarton.co.uk/content/pages/documents/1542300370.pdf
- IWM Collections: https://www.iwm.org.uk/collections/item/object/80012762 & https://www.iwm.org.uk/collections/item/object/80031371
- https://www.naval-history.net/WW1NavyBritishBVLSMN1507.htm
- Fred Rayner's memoirs: http://fightingthroughpodcast.co.uk/16-gallipoli-ww1-memoir/4593981882
- www.firstworldwar.com/battles/scimitarhill.html
- https://www.royal-irish.com/events/battle-of-scimitar-hill-suvla
- Isle of Wight Fire Brigades Federation http://www.iwfbf.co.uk/439511031
- Roads to the Great War: 100 Years Ago Today: Kitchener Arrives at Gallipoli (roadstothegreatwar-ww1.blogspot.com)

Other

- Carisbrooke Castle

www.ingramcontent.com/pod-product-compliance
Lightning Source LLC
Chambersburg PA
CBHW050018130526
44590CB00042B/643